JUSTIFYING INJUSTICE

Postwar legal scholars commonly consider the Third Reich's judicial system to be the paradigm of "evil law." By examining how crucial parts of this distorted normative order evolved and were justified by regime-loyal legal theorists, we can appreciate how law can bend to a political ideology and fail to keep state power from transgressing elementary standards of humanity and the rule of law. From 1933 to 1939, a flood of publications reflected on the question of how to adapt law to the political ends of National Socialism, debating both the normative and constitutional foundations of the National Socialist state and the proper form and content of criminal and police law in this new political framework. These debates, the main threads of which are central to this book, reveal the normative ideas driving the Führer state and the legal subtext to the Nazi regime's escalating atrocities.

HERLINDE PAUER-STUDER is Professor of Ethics and Political Philosophy at the University of Vienna, Austria. From 1997 to 1998 she was Fellow at the E. J. Safra Center for Ethics, Harvard University, and in 2006 Fulbright Scholar, New York University. In 2016 she held the Austrian Chair at Stanford University. Her publications include *Konrad Morgen: The Conscience of a Nazi Judge* (co-authored with J. David Velleman, 2015).

JUSTIFYING INJUSTICE

Legal Theory in Nazi Germany

HERLINDE PAUER-STUDER
University of Vienna

CAMBRIDGE
UNIVERSITY PRESS

CAMBRIDGE
UNIVERSITY PRESS

University Printing House, Cambridge CB2 8BS, United Kingdom

One Liberty Plaza, 20th Floor, New York, NY 10006, USA

477 Williamstown Road, Port Melbourne, VIC 3207, Australia

314–321, 3rd Floor, Plot 3, Splendor Forum, Jasola District Centre, New Delhi – 110025, India

79 Anson Road, #06–04/06, Singapore 079906

Cambridge University Press is part of the University of Cambridge.

It furthers the University's mission by disseminating knowledge in the pursuit of education, learning, and research at the highest international levels of excellence.

www.cambridge.org
Information on this title: www.cambridge.org/9781107159303
DOI: 10.1017/9781316671412

First published 2020

A catalogue record for this publication is available from the British Library.

ISBN 978-1-107-15930-3 Hardback

To Flora

CONTENTS

ACKNOWLEDGMENTS

In writing this book I was helped by many people. My greatest thanks are to J. David Velleman. In conversations we had during a term I spent as a Fulbright Scholar at New York University, he convinced me that writing about National Socialism was also a responsibility for analytic philosophers and should be taken more seriously by them. The joint work we did on the topic, particularly on the case of SS Judge Konrad Morgen, taught me so much about the complex distortions of Nazi ideology and why it was crucial to confront the issue of Nazi legal theory. David also generously commented on several chapters of the current book.

For his wonderful editorial work, which greatly helped to improve the text, I am indebted to Paul Miller. I also thank Grace Doris Paterson for written comments.

Materials related to this book have been presented at the University of Basel, the University of Flensburg, the J.W.G.-University Frankfurt am Main, the Fritz-Bauer-Institute Frankfurt am Main, the University of Glasgow, the University of Hamburg, the University of Iowa, the University of Kentucky, Lund University, McDaniel College (Maryland), the Queen Mary College of the University of London, the L.M. University Munich, the Norwegian University Center in Paris, the University of São Paulo, the University of South Carolina, and the Wissenschaftskolleg in Berlin. I thank the organizers of the workshops and talks at these institutions and all the participants for their comments and responses. I also would like to thank the students who attended seminars I held on materials of the book.

The book has benefited from discussions with many colleagues. For feedback and comments I owe thanks to: Franz Altner, Monika Betzler, Stephan Bird-Pollan, Olle Blomberg, Johann Chapoutot, David Dyzenhaus, Bijan Fateh-Moghadam, Rainer Forst, Miguel Garcia, Olav Gjelsvik, Stefan Gosepath, Christoph Grabenwarter, Hans Petter Graver, Raphael Gross, Niels de Haan, Christoph Hanisch, Marion Heinz, Ulrike

Heuer, Gunnar Hindrichs, Veronika Hofer, Katarina Hruskovicova, Clemens Jabloner, Nadja Kayali, Felix Koch, Werner Konitzer, Martin Kusch, Konrad Paul Liessmann, Christian List, Kirk Ludwig, Rachael Mellin, Leonhard Menges, Reinhard Merkel, Paul Miller, Edgar Morscher, Julian Nida-Rümelin, Carlos Núñez, George Pavlakos, Grace Doris Paterson, Nada Ina Pauer, Fabienne Peter, Lucas Petroni, Hugh Pryce, Wlodek Rabinowicz, Matthew Rachar, Oliver Rathkolb, Ilse Reiter-Zatloukal, Arthur Ripstein, Toni Rønnow-Rasmussen, Joachim Rückert, Michael Schefczyk, Hans Bernhard Schmid, Thomas Schramme, Werner Schubert, David Schweikard, Anna Maria Sigmund, Karl Sigmund, Alexander Somek, Sybille Steinbacher, Johannes Steizinger, Michael Stöltzner, Michael Stolleis, Christopher Theel, and Miloš Vec.

Thanks also to Florian Kolowrat for help with the bibliography and for assistance in bringing the manuscript into final form. And thanks to Finola O'Sullivan from Cambridge University Press for taking the book into the program and Marianne Nield for support in the submission and production process.

I am deeply grateful to my family. It is not easy to hear about Germany's and Austria's darkest period time and again over several years. A special thanks goes to our younger daughter Flora who traveled with me to Lublin, searching for material on the SS Judge Konrad Morgen. This book is dedicated to her.

I am also indebted to institutions. Most of the manuscript was written in the Ludwig-Wittgenstein-Reading Room of the Austrian National Library in Vienna. I thank the librarians for patiently providing me with material from the National Library's large collection of literature from the Nazi period. The research resources from the Library of Congress in Washington, D.C. also proved invaluable. Particular thanks are due to Dr. Grant G. Harris from the European Division and to the Law Library for support and assistance in finding relevant literature.

NOTE ON TRANSLATIONS AND REFERENCE POLICY

All translations from the German original texts by Nazi jurists are my own. I have left the titles of the works (books, articles) in the original German.

When books and articles originally published in German have appeared in English translation, I have (for the most part) used the available English translation. Corrections of translations by me are noted in brackets.

1

Introduction

How was National Socialism (NS) possible? How could a democratic system like the Weimar Republic give way to a totalitarian state order? How did racial ideology get pushed to such extremes that it ended in historically unprecedented horrors, crimes, the Holocaust? This book aims to shed light on these questions through an investigation of Nazi law and legal thinking.

Postwar legal scholars commonly consider the Third Reich's judicial system to be the paradigm of "evil law," so wicked and perverted that it does not deserve to be called law in the first place. But many aspects of this legal order, which terrified and terrorized so many, still merit closer scholarly scrutiny.[1] By examining how crucial parts of this distorted normative order evolved and how it was justified by regime-loyal legal theorists, we can better understand how law can bend to a political ideology such that it completely fails to keep a state power from transgressing all common moral and legal standards.

Especially in the period 1933 to 1939, a virtual flood of publications appeared on how to adapt law to the political ends of National Socialism. Legal scholars who sided with the Nazi regime debated both the normative and constitutional foundations of the National Socialist (NS) state, as well as the proper form and content of criminal and police law in this new political framework. Particularly appalling is the inordinate attention given to incorporating Nazi racial doctrine into law.

These debates, the main threads of which this book will discuss, reveal the normative ideas driving the Führer state and the legal subtext to the regime's escalating inhumanity and violence. The numerous quotations from the Nazi jurists' original texts seek to give readers an immediate impression of how these lawyers thought and argued, the extent to which

[1] See also Steinweis, Alan E., Rachlin, Robert D., "Introduction," in Steinweis and Rachlin (eds.), *The Law in Nazi Germany. Ideology, Opportunism, and the Perversion of Justice* (New York and Oxford: Berghahn, 2013), pp. 1–13.

they shared the regime's ideology, theoretically undergirded its policies, and, ultimately, attempted to give normative form to a political power that tended toward normative unboundedness.

The regime-loyal jurists examined here were mostly university professors and high-ranking officials in the Third Reich's ministerial bureaucracy. While many of them endorsed Nazism out of deep conviction, others did so for career reasons. Indeed, some high-ranking jurists had deep reservations about the infiltration of National Socialism into the law and even surreptitiously endeavored to thwart it (as, for instance, Franz Gürtner, the Reich's Minister of Justice from 1933 to 1941). But in the end they all succumbed to the Nazis' political power.[2]

Among the leading jurists of the Third Reich were not only Nazi Party members, but even SS men – for example Reinhard Höhn and Wilhelm Stuckart, State Secretary in the Interior Ministry. Foremost among the more fanatic NS ideologues were Hans Frank (President of the Academy for German Law) and Roland Freisler (State Secretary in the Justice Ministry and, from 1942, President of the People's Court, or *Volksgerichtshof*). Frank, who in 1939 became Governor General of those areas of occupied Poland not incorporated into the Reich (the so-called *Generalgouvernement*), was so deeply implicated in NS crimes that he received the death sentence at the Nuremberg Trial against the Major War Criminals (1946). And Freisler, notorious for his excessive punishments and death sentences, is emblematic of the gruesome nature of the NS court system.

Considering the differences in the NS jurists' professional positions and political involvement, it is not surprising to see variance in the tone and style of their texts – programmatic phraseology regularly alternates with fairly sober argument.[3] Nevertheless, these legal thinkers and officials shared something important: all were skeptical about democracy, often to the extent of expressing outright contempt for the Weimar Republic. They thus welcomed Weimar's demise and Hitler's nomination to Reich Chancellor. Many of them (particularly those in academia) completely misread the political situation, seeing in the rise of National Socialism a mere opportunity for establishing a strong authoritarian state that would overcome the conflicts and party fissures shattering Weimar democracy, while ignoring how much the Nazi

[2] See Gruchmann, Lothar, *Justiz im Dritten Reich 1933–1940. Anpassung und Unterwerfung in der Ära Gürtner* (München: Oldenbourg, 1988).

[3] A list with short biographical notes at the end of the book informs readers about the NS jurists' positions and their affiliations with the Nazi state.

movement itself contributed to these political crises. Seeing themselves as the designers of the new state order, many legal scholars (especially early into Nazi rule) underestimated Hitler's uncompromising will to power and reluctance to accept any normative restrictions on his authority. They also failed to recognize the true strength and influence of the Nazi Party and its associated organizations, above all the SS.

1.1 National Socialist Law. Guidelines and Institutions

National Socialist legal theory rejected formalism and positivism in favor of a material conception of law, characterized by such substantive values as "communal unity," "honor," "racial homogeneity," and "racial equality." Individual rights were dismissed as remnants of an antagonistic relationship between sovereign and subjects, which no longer correlated with the tight, trust-based relationship between the Führer and the *völkisch* community.

Germanness and German law were central to NS legal theory. Accordingly, the author of preliminary remarks to a 1935 *National Socialist Handbook of Law and Legislation* reminded readers that point 19 of the 1920 Nazi Party program had already proposed to replace Roman law, which "served a materialistic world-order," with German communal law (*Gemeinrecht*), which aligned with the moral feelings and sense of justice of those national comrades (*Volksgenossen*) whose lives it regulated.[4] This way, the author claimed, the opposition between law and morality would be abandoned. Instead of protecting individual interests, the law ought to foster the community, according to the principle "public interest precedes individual benefit (*Gemeinnutz geht vor Eigennutz*)."[5]

The ideological mastermind of these guidelines was the Handbook's editor, Hans Frank, who had joined the Nazi Party in 1923 and was eager to establish an organizational framework for implementing a National Socialist form of law. With the Nazi seizure of power in 1933, the Association of German Jurists, which Frank had founded on October 28, 1928, became the most important jurist organization in Germany and parent to the organizations of German judges, lawyers, auditors, university teachers and notaries. Together with these subunits, the Association had 80,000 members by May 1933, among whom were

[4] Coblitz, Wilhelm, "Vorbemerkungen," in Frank, Hans (ed.), *Nationalsozialistisches Handbuch für Recht und Gesetzgebung* (München: Zentralverlag der NSDAP, Franz Eher Nachf., 1935), pp. VII–XI, here: p. VII.

[5] Ibid.

10,173 Party members.[6] Frank also headed the Nazi Party's Legal Office (NSDAP *Reichsrechtsamt*), which he established on Hitler's order in October 1930. Besides legal support for Nazi Party members, it offered courses in legal politics and racial doctrine and developed directives for law reform.[7]

In March 1933, Frank became Minister of Justice in Bavaria, and in April 1933 "Reich Commissar for the Coordination (*Gleichschaltung*) of the Judiciary in the German states and for the Renewal of the Legal Order." In 1934, when the coordination was largely completed, Frank was nominated Reich Minister (without portfolio). On June 26, 1933, Frank founded the Academy for German Law and acted as its President until August 20, 1942, when Hitler, angered by Frank's speeches criticizing the disempowerment of the judiciary, replaced him with Otto Georg Thierack.[8]

In the prewar years, Frank turned the Academy for German Law into a central institution for the promotion and distribution of NS legal thinking and ideology. The Academy's journal, which appeared from 1934 until 1944, became an essential forum for debate among NS jurists.[9] Frank's goal was to secure Nazi Party influence on law reform and legislation. He thus created special working committees (*Arbeitsausschüsse*) within the Academy, tasked with developing new legal policies and regulations. The protocols of these committees' meetings are an invaluable source for understanding the legal-political discussions and ensuing legal changes in the Nazi era.[10] Yet, Frank's ambitious program to ideologically

[6] See "Der Bund Nationalsozialistischer Deutscher Juristen und die Deutsche Rechtsfront," in Frank (ed.), *Nationalsozialistisches Handbuch für Recht und Gesetzgebung*, pp. 1566–1571, here: p. 1568.

[7] See "Das Reichsrechtsamt der NSDAP," in Frank (ed.), *Nationalsozialistisches Handbuch für Recht und Gesetzgebung*, pp. 1555–1565. For a discussion of the guidelines for a National Socialist criminal law, issued by the NSDAP Reichsrechtsamt, see Chapter 4.2 of this book.

[8] On October 2, 1933, the establishment of the Academy for German Law was proclaimed at the German Jurists' conference, taking place at the University of Leipzig. The Academy was officially recognized as a corporation of public law.

[9] See *Zeitschrift der Akademie für Deutsches Recht* 1934–1944, ed. by Frank, Hans (until 1942; from then by Otto Georg Thierack), 11 vols. (München, Berlin: C.H. Beck, 1934–1944).

[10] See *Akademie für Deutsches Recht 1933–1945. Protokolle der Ausschüsse*, ed. by Schubert, Werner (Frankfurt am Main: Peter Lang, 1986–2019), vol. I–XXIII. Although these committees could, as the editor Werner Schubert notes, not directly influence legislation, they were highly important, and their discussions and results were (while not necessarily approved) taken into account by the ministerial bureaucracy. See Schubert, Werner "Vorbemerkungen zur Gesamtedition," in *Akademie für Deutsches Recht 1933–1945. Protokolle der Ausschüsse*, vol. 1 (1986), pp. VIII–XIX, here: pp. XVII–XVIII.

transform the entire juridical landscape ultimately failed, not least because of the ministerial bureaucracy's skepticism and reluctance.

Franz Gürtner, the Reich's Justice Minister, sought to counterbalance Frank's power and curb the influence of the Academy. On November 3, 1933, he announced the establishment of an official commission (approved by Hitler) for criminal law reform under his chairmanship at the Ministry of Justice.[11] From 1934 to 1939, this commission drafted a new penal code for the German Reich, though it was not signed by Hitler and thus did not come into force. Still, the committee's efforts resulted in some striking legal amendments (for example, the admission of analogy in criminal law in 1935), which had a tremendous impact on judicial thinking and decisions.[12]

All the efforts of regime-loyal lawyers to align the legal order with National Socialist doctrine could not dispel Hitler's notorious distrust of jurists and discomfort with rules and normative restrictions. The war only intensified his aversion toward the judiciary. In a Reichstag speech on April 26, 1942, Hitler announced that he would intervene in "wrongly decided" judicial cases and remove judges from office "who evidently did not recognize the need of the hour" that Germany's survival was more important than "formal law (*Recht*)."[13] The speech was immediately followed by an official warrant from the obedient Greater German Reichstag making Hitler the Reich's Supreme Justiciar (*oberster Gerichtsherr)* who could – "without hindrance from existing legal provisions" – dismiss judges "who had violated their duties" and caused great

[11] The protocols of the meetings of the Official Commission for Criminal Law Reform (*Amtliche Strafrechtskommission*) are published. See *Quellen zur Reform des Straf- und Strafprozeßrechts 1933–1939. Protokolle der Strafrechtskommission des Reichsjustizministeriums*, ed. by Schubert, Werner; Regge, Jürgen; Rieß, Peter; Schmid, Werner (Berlin, New York: Walter de Gruyter, 1988–1994), 4 vols. Gürtner nominated Frank as his deputy, but otherwise tried to neutralize Frank's influence on the commission's consultations. Frank left the Official Criminal Law Commission in 1935, not without reminding Gürtner that the final approval of a new penal code would depend on the Nazi Party. See "Einleitung," *Protokolle der Strafrechtskommission des Reichsjustizministeriums*, 1. Teil (1988), pp. XIII–LVIII, here: pp. XV–XVI. (Note that the different volumes are best to identify by the year of publication, 1988, 1989, 1990, 1994; in 1990 there appeared a further volume with various drafts of the revised German Penal Code on which the commission worked.)

[12] See also Chapter 4.5 of this book.

[13] See "Hitler's Reichstag speech from April 26, 1942," in Domarus, Max, *Hitler. Reden und Proklamationen 1932–1945. Kommentiert von einem Zeitgenossen*, vol. II Untergang, Zweiter Halbband 1941–1945 (München: Süddeutscher Verlag, 1965), pp. 1865–1876, here: pp. 1874–1875.

inquietude among jurists.[14] Even Frank protested this move, a step resulting in the loss of all his juridical positions in the Reich.

Hitler's proactive stance against wayward judges encouraged Gürtner's successor as Justice Minister, Otto Georg Thierack, to send the so-called "Letters to Judges" to the Reich's state prosecutors and judges.[15] These pamphlets, first distributed in October 1942, discussed how cases deemed unacceptable to the NS leadership should have been decided according to National Socialist principles. Ironically, the "Letters" point up the regime's limits in controlling the judiciary. Even the Justice Minister (a committed National Socialist) did not dare to question openly, let alone abolish, the principle of judicial independence.[16]

Yet the political pressure on state prosecutors and judges in the Third Reich was pervasive – the judiciary increasingly lost its competencies to the police; the courts often acted under Gestapo surveillance; and defendants (particularly political opponents) acquitted in a trial were repeatedly taken into political police custody. In the Eastern occupied

[14] Ibid., pp. 1876–1877. The meeting of the Greater German Reichstag on April 26, 1942 was the last one. The elections to this Greater German Reichstag had taken place on April 11, 1938 (together with a plebiscite about the Anschluss of Austria) with only one list of candidates (nearly all of them National Socialists). In a Reichstag meeting on July 13, 1934, in which Hitler justified the Röhm purge (the murder of the SA leader Ernst Röhm and more than 100 SA men by the SS), he already claimed to have acted as the highest Justiciar of the German *Volk*. On April 26, 1942 he requested the official confirmation of holding that power. Hitler's striking presumption of July 13, 1934, as well as the murderous action against the SA, were justified by Carl Schmitt in his article "Der Führer schützt das Recht. Zur Reichstagsrede Adolf Hitlers vom 13. Juli 1934," in *Deutsche Juristen-Zeitung* 39, 15, 1934; reprinted in Schmitt, Carl, *Positionen und Begriffe im Kampf mit Weimar-Genf-Versailes 1923–1939* (Hamburg: Hanseatische Verlagsanstalt, 1940), pp. 199–203; for an English translation see Schmitt, "The Führer Protects the Law. On Adolf Hitler's Reichstag Address 13 July 1934," in Rabinbach, Anson and Gilman, Sander L. (eds.), *The Third Reich Sourcebook* (Berkeley, Los Angeles, London: University of California Press, 2013), pp. 63–67.

[15] See Boberach, Heinz (ed.), *Richterbriefe. Dokumente zur Beeinflussung der deutschen Rechtsprechung 1942–1944* (Boppard am Rhein: Harald Boldt, 1975). Gürtner died on January 29, 1941. On August 20, 1942 Hitler nominated Otto Georg Thierack as Justice Minister (after an interim period in which State Secretary Franz Schlegelberger acted as interim Justice Minister).

[16] In a circular decree from September 7, 1942, sent to the President of the Reich's Court of Justice, to the President of the People's Court and to several state prosecutors, Thierack declared that the "Letters to Judges" were not directives (*Weisungen*) to judges, but were meant as illustrations of "how the judicial leadership thought of National Socialist law application." See "Runderlaß des Reichsministers der Justiz vom 7. September 1942," in *Richterbriefe*, pp. 1–3, here: p. 2. On the complex attitude of the regime toward judges see Graver, Hans Petter, "Why Adolf Hitler Spared the Judges. Judicial Opposition Against the Nazi State," in *German Law Journal* 19, 4 (2018), pp. 845–877.

territories, the Gestapo's drumhead trials (*Standgerichtsbarkeit*) replaced ordinary court proceedings.

Some legal theorists who in the 1930s had emphatically embraced National Socialism in their writings and served willingly in law reform committees were dismayed by these developments and the regime's radicalization in wartime.[17] Yet their change of mind came late, too late. In a time of "total mobilization," skeptical concerns and objections voiced by a professional group for which the Führer never had much respect were to no avail.

1.2 Theoretical Foundations

Although virtually obsessed with the idea of "renewing German law in congruence with the National Socialist worldview," the President of the German Law Academy nonetheless struggled to specify the meaning of such a form of law, as the Academy's Panel for Legal Philosophy records show.[18] Following the Panel's pompous founding session on May, 3, 1934, in Weimar's Nietzsche Archive (with speeches by Frank and Alfred Rosenberg), the committee's members were asked in a letter (dated May 8, 1934) by the committee's vice chair Carl-August Emge to respond in writing with suggestions for interpreting "German" in relation to the law.[19] The answers were disappointing (even to Emge) in that

[17] One legal theorist who in 1944 openly criticized the consequences of NS criminal law was Georg Dahm (see Chapter 4.8 of this book).

[18] See "Ausschuss für Rechtsphilosophie der Akademie für Deutsches Recht," Nietzsche-Archive (Goethe-and-Schiller-Archive) in Weimar, Nr. 72/1588. The complete file is reprinted in *Akademie für Deutsches Recht 1933–1945. Protokolle der Ausschüsse*, vol. XXIII: *Weitere Nachträge* (1934–1939), ed. with an introduction by Schubert, Werner (Frankfurt am Main: Peter Lang, 2019), pp. 45–78 (references are to this reprint). Members of the Panel for Legal Philosophy were (among others): Hans Frank (chairman), Carl-August Emge (vice-chairman), Alfred Rosenberg, Martin Heidegger, Carl Schmitt, Julius Binder, Erich Jung, Erich Rothacker, Rudolf Stammler, Hans Freyer, Jakob von Uexküll. As Werner Schubert notes, it is uncertain whether after June 1934 any meetings of this committee took place because no further protocols could be found in the archives. Schubert considers it unlikely that the Panel for Legal Philosophy met secretly, as recently some scholars have suggested. See Schubert, "Einleitung," in *Akademie für Deutsches Recht 1933–1945. Protokolle der Ausschüsse*, vol. XXIII, pp. 9–44, here: pp. 13–18.

[19] The founding session was hosted by Friedrich Nietzsche's sister, Elisabeth Förster-Nietzsche. In his opening speech, Frank invoked Nietzsche for the purposes of National Socialism. Apart from the programmatic speeches given by Frank, Rosenberg, and Emge, the Weimar file contains written responses by several members (Binder, von Uexküll, Rothacker, Jung, Stammler) on how to define the committee's tasks in light of Frank's and Rosenberg's talks.

they merely repeated the well-worn phrases that German law in the National Socialist sense was not grounded in "abstract universalism" and "cosmopolitan thinking," but derived from the German people's community, which would, wrote one member, "determine the essence of German volition and thinking."[20]

That Frank's lofty plans did not materialize as hoped was due largely to the elusive character of Nazi ideology.[21] The major source of that world-view was the Führer. Translating Hitler's ideas – laid out in lengthy tirades in *Mein Kampf* and numerous speeches – into normative language and arguments proved daunting indeed.

Nevertheless, NS legal theorists worked hard to provide the necessary normative framework. Drawing upon classical political philosophy, jurists argued that the Führer's comprehensive authority lay in his personal embodiment of the collective will, thus echoing Rousseau's grounding of sovereign power (the general will) in the *Social Contract*.[22] Of course,

20 See "Antwort von Prof. D. J. Binder vom 9.5.1934," in "Ausschuss für Rechtsphilosophie," in *Akademie für Deutsches Recht 1933–1945. Protokolle der Ausschüsse*, vol. XXIII, pp. 58–61, here: p. 60. Besides Binder, also von Uexküll, Jung, Stammler, and Rothacker responded in written form. Rothacker recommended the establishment of a special department (possibly as part of the Kaiser-Wilhelm-Gesellschaft) with jurists, historians, sociologists, philosophers, and racial doctrine experts for investigating the exact meaning of *Volk* and Germanness. See "Antwort von Prof. Dr. Erich Rothacker vom 20.5. 1934," in "Ausschuss für Rechtsphilosophie," pp. 65–67, here: pp. 65–66. The Weimar file contains no written answers by Heidegger or Schmitt to Emge's request. On Rothacker's attitude toward National Socialism see Steizinger, Johannes, "From *Völkerpsychologie* to Cultural Anthropology. Erich Rothacker's Philosophy of Culture," in *Hopos* 10, 1 (2020), pp. 308–328.

21 In his magisterial study *Behemoth* (1942), Franz Neumann wrote that "National Socialist ideology is constantly shifting. It has certain magical beliefs –leadership adoration, the supremacy of the master race –but its ideology is not laid down in a series of categorical and dogmatic pronouncements." Neumann, Franz, *Behemoth, The Structure and Practice of National Socialism 1933–1944*, with an introduction by Hayes, Peter (Chicago: Ivan R. Dee, 2009), p. 39.

22 See Rousseau, Jean-Jacques, "Of the Social Contract," in Rosseau, *The Social Contract and other later political writings*, ed. and transl. by Gourevitch, Victor (Cambridge: Cambridge University Press, 1997), pp. 39–152, see particularly Book I, ch. 6 ("Of the Social Pact"), pp. 49–51. Rousseau's problem was how to find a form of political association that would allow each person to secure her freedom; his solution was a social agreement that everyone, equal to all others, would freely consent to accept a sovereign power, that is, "(E)ach of us puts *his person and his full power in common under the supreme direction of the general will.*" Ibid., p. 50 (italics in the original). There has been discussion among political theorists whether Rousseau's characterization of the political body arising from this agreement was potentially totalitarian since it eliminated the independence of the individual. Particularly controversial was Rousseau's claim that "this act of association produces a moral and collective body made up of as many

these legal thinkers knew that Rousseau intended to justify a republican, if not a democratic form of government. They thus criticized Rosseau's notion of the general will (*volonté générale*) for being "too individualistic" and sought a normatively richer interpretation of the concept. As "bearer ... of the objective will of the *Volk*," argued the constitutional lawyer Ernst Rudolf Huber, the Führer would "form in himself (*in sich*) the *völkisch* collective will, thus embodying the political unity and entirety of the people vis-à-vis all particular wishes."[23]

For Huber, this substantive form of collective will was not fictitious like the "general will" of democracy, but had a real basis in the order of being (*Seinsordnung*),[24] by which he obviously meant to say that the sovereign power in the Führer state need not be vindicated by a hypothetical thought experiment, asking whether everyone had reason to consent to this power.[25] Rousseau's "*volonté générale*," Huber argued, was merely "a compromise between various conflicting social interests."[26]

Karl Larenz similarly criticized Rousseau's justification of sovereignty and authority. The collective will in Rousseau, that is, the *volonté générale*, he objected, would merely embody "the generalized particular

members as the assembly has voices, and which receives by this same act its unity, its common *self*, its life and its will." Rousseau, "Of the Social Contract," p. 50 (italics in the original). For a critique of Rousseau as a forerunner of totalitarianism see Nisbet, Robert A., "Rousseau and Totalitarianism," in *The Journal of Politics* 5, 2 (1943), pp. 93–114. While there is no room here for a detailed examination of such a reading of Rousseau (let me say that I consider it implausible), note that NS legal theorists obviously did not, as our discussion shows, consider Rousseau helpful for outlining the normative foundations of the NS state.

23 Huber, Ernst Rudolf, *Verfassungsrecht des Großdeutschen Reiches*, 2nd ed. (Hamburg: Hanseatische Verlagsanstalt, 1939), pp. 195–196.

24 Ibid., p. 196.

25 Ibid., p. 196.

26 Ibid., p. 195. Huber adds that Hegel had already (in *Grundlinien der Philosophie des Rechts*, § 258) aptly refuted Rousseau's doctrine of the general will. Although Huber does not quote Hegel directly, he obviously had the following passage of Hegel's text in mind: "But Rousseau considered the will only in the determinate form of the *individual* [einzelnen] will (as Fichte subsequently also did) and regarded the universal will not as the will's rationality in and for itself, but only as the *common element* arising out of this individual [einzelnen] will as a *conscious will*. The union of individuals [der Einzelnen] within the state thus becomes a *contract*, which is accordingly based on their arbitrary will and opinions, and on their express consent given at their own discretion; and the further consequences which follow from this, and which relate merely to the understanding, destroy the divine [element] which has being in and for itself and its absolute authority and majesty." Hegel, G. W. F., *Elements of the Philosophy of Right*, ed. by Wood, Allen W., transl. by Nisbet, H.B. (Cambridge University Press, 1991), § 258, p. 277.

interests of the individuals, brought down to a common denominator."[27] Thus Larenz ignored Rousseau's crucial distinction between the *volonté de tous* (the sum of individual wills denoting particular interests) and the *volonté générale*, which was more than the mere intersection of individual interests. After all, Rousseau's overall aim was to secure citizens' *freedom* by way of their common acceptance of a sovereign power from an impartial practical standpoint (taking the interests of all equally into account).

The distorted interpretations of Rousseau outlined above were due to NS ideology, which merged the single individual into the people's community. The Führer state did not consist of autonomous agents with political rights, but was a *völkisch* community of members with exclusively communal obligations.

According to Larenz, Hegel's philosophy came closer to National Socialism's understanding of law than that of Rousseau. For Hegel, he wrote, "law is 'something sacred' because it is the general will's givenness – that is, law is the form and expression of the objective ethics *(objektive Sittlichkeit)* alive in a *Volk*."[28] Following Hegel, Larenz associated law's ethical value with the objective spirit inherent in the life order and the ethical order (*Sittenordnung*). "The roots [of law] are most closely connected with ethics . . .," he wrote, "in fact not with an individualistic one, but with ethics as the community's way of life, in Hegel' s words 'the true spirit of a family and a *Volk*'."[29]

The Third Reich quickly developed into a state with unmistakable totalitarian features. In addition to restricting basic civil rights and liberties, it directly intervened into spheres of social life that in the democratic Weimar era were exempt from state's control, including how to spend leisure time, whom to choose as spouse, and whether to have children.[30] Particularly disturbing was the impact of racial ideology, which brutally excluded Jewish citizens and disrupted social and intimate bonds between Jewish and non-Jewish Germans.

27 Larenz, Karl, *Deutsche Rechtserneuerung und Rechtsphilosophie* (Tübingen: J.C.B. Mohr [Paul Siebeck], 1934), p. 7.

28 Ibid., p. 6.

29 Ibid. Larenz emphasizes that in contrast to Kant, for whom the state and public law existed for preserving and securing private law, Hegel would subordinate private law to the state. Ibid., p. 9. The predominance of public law over private law was a principle of NS legal doctrine.

30 See Koonz, Claudia, *The Nazi Conscience* (Cambridge, MA and London: Harvard University Press, 2003), pp. 69–102.

These intrusions into the realm of personal freedom aimed to align citizens politically. The official NS justification was more mundane – namely that national unity required citizens to lead their lives in the same way, based on a uniform worldview and shared ethical convictions.

That National Socialism sought to regulate the lives of all of its citizens conflicted with the basic principles of enlightenment philosophy. This explains the striking fact that the NS legal thinkers did not refer to Kant's political and legal philosophy. After all, Kant's separation of law and ethics was incompatible with the NS state's expansion of legal authority to the ethical attitudes of citizens. Nazi ambitions clearly clashed with Kant's limitation of state power to securing the equal freedom of citizens in the outer sphere of freedom, that is, their interactions in public space. For Kant, the state must not control individuals' convictions (inner freedom). His conception of freedom, spelled out in the formula that "no one can coerce me to be happy in his way (as he thinks of the welfare of other human beings)" contrasts sharply with Nazi ideology. The famous passage in the *Gemeinspruch* – that a paternalistic government "in which the subjects ... are constrained to behave only passively, so as to wait only upon the judgment of the head of state as to how they *should be* happy ... is the greatest *despotism* thinkable (a constitution that abrogates all the freedom of the subjects, who in that case have no rights at all)" – reads like a damning judgment about the Führer state.[31] Hitler's alleged commitment to enhance the *Volk's* well-being was no more than a handy rationale for his accumulation of comprehensive power.

Although NS jurists could not rely on Kant's political philosophy, they famously instrumentalized his reflections on ethics by taking certain Kantian concepts – the good will, unconditional obligation, and the categorical imperative, for example – out of context. Kant's claim that ethical duties are valid independently of serving such purposes as maximizing happiness or utility, was thus misinterpreted. NS rhetoric simply transformed the Kantian idea that ethical obligations hold for their own sake (*um ihrer selbst willen*) into the requirement that duties must be obeyed "unconditionally" – that is, with no consideration for their content and justification. While "unconditional" in Kant's system means that ethical duties are not dependent (conditional)

[31] Kant, Immanuel, "On the common saying: That may be correct in theory, but it is of no use in practice," in Kant, *Practical Philosophy*, ed. and transl. by Gregor, Mary (Cambridge: Cambridge University Press, 1996), pp. 273–309, here: p. 291 (Academy edition of Kant's writings TP AA 08:291).

on instrumental considerations, the Nazis interpreted "unconditional" in the sense of blind obedience to authoritarian orders that could not be called into question.

In this way, NS ideologues ignored that Kant developed procedures (in form of the categorical imperative tests) to assess whether certain ways of acting are permissible or forbidden, that is, if there is an obligation not to act in a certain way. Kant's tests, roughly stated, require us to either ask whether our subjective principles of acting (our maxims) can be universalized or whether they are compatible with respect for others as human beings.[32]

Precisely such standards of critical ethical deliberation which take others and their dignity as human beings into consideration, irrespective of ethnicity, are foreign to the Nazis' mindset and racial politics. Any appeal to universally valid ethical principles clashed with the NS state's aggressive partiality toward the so-called "Aryan" ethnic community.[33]

32 Kant suggests several formulations of the categorical imperative. The two formulas of the categorical imperative that involve testing procedures are the Formula of Universal Law (FUL) ("Act only in accordance with that maxim through which you can at the same will that it become a universal law"), and the Formula of Humanity (FH) ("So act that you treat humanity, whether in your own person or in the person of any other, always at the same time as an end, never merely as a means"). The FUL test requires us to examine whether our maxims can be universalized without a contradiction (incoherence) in thinking or in willing. The test associated with FH requests us to check whether our maxim of acting amounts to instrumentalizing another person for our purposes (that is, treating her as a mere means). See Kant, "Groundwork of The Metaphysics of Morals (1785)," in Kant, *Practical Philosophy*, pp. 37–108, here: pp. 73–82 (Academy edition GM AA 4:421–4:432). For a detailed discussion of Kant's testing procedures, see Korsgaard, Christine M., *Creating the Kingdom of Ends* (Cambridge: Cambridge University Press, 1996), pp. 77–132.

33 Even Adolf Eichmann had to concede that Kant's universalism conflicted with the strict particularity of National Socialism. When one of the judges at the trial in Jerusalem asked Eichmann about his reference to Kant in the police interrogations, Eichmann quoted Kant's categorical imperative, giving a reformulation which took the idea of universal law-making into consideration. However Eichmann – becoming aware that he had made his own argument somewhat macabre – added that in the course of the "Final Solution" he had not been able to stick to Kant's principle any more. See Arendt, Hannah, *Eichmann in Jerusalem. A Report on the Banality of Evil* (New York: Penguin Books, 2006), pp. 135–136. The judge's question referred to a passage in Eichmann's interrogation records, where the interrogating officer, Avner Less, had confronted Eichmann with the argument in an article of the *Stern* magazine from July 9, 1960, that Eichmann (at the time of his imprisonment in Israel) was merely clutching at the straw of "having only done his duty" in justifying his actions. In the interrogation Eichmann responded with anger, claiming that duty for him was an inner commitment and that he had always lived according to the "Kantian norm." Police D'Israel, *Vernehmungsprotokoll Adolf Eichmann*, Tape transcription, vol. 55, pp. 36–37, Simon Wiesenthal-Archive Vienna.

Accordingly, the NS jurists polemicized against the principle of universal equality. The guiding principle of National Socialism was equality among the members of a specific race rather than equality of all humankind.

NS legal theorists strove to dispel the impression that the Third Reich was headed toward totalitarianism. They were well aware that any association of the NS state with an all-powerful "Leviathan" would spoil the image of the Führer as a trustworthy ruler, deeply caring for the *Volk*'s well-being.[34] Furthermore, a state form that denied personal freedom conflicted, as these thinkers realized, with the regime's moralizing image of society as a close-knit community in which everyone voluntarily strove for moral self-perfection. Even Roland Freisler, a ferocious defender of Nazi dictatorship, emphasized that National Socialism had to leave room for some decisional freedom. Community members were thus not submissive objects without a will of their own, but rather subjects who actively encountered life's challenges with an "I should, I will, I can!"[35] Of course, the freedom of the will conjured by Freisler was not true personal autonomy, entailing a claim to rights. Rather his performative formula expressed an enthusiastic identification with National Socialism, one which mirrored the regime's grip on the ethical motivations of the *Volksgenossen*.

1.3 Overview of the Book

The Nazis' seizure of power was a radical break with the preceding political order, setting up an abrupt end for Germany's first democracy.

[34] This explains why there are hardly any references to Thomas Hobbes in the NS theorists' texts. The notable exception is Carl Schmitt's study *Der Leviathan in der Staatslehre des Thomas Hobbes. Sinn und Fehlschlag eines politischen Symbols* (Hamburg: Hanseatische Verlagsanstalt, 1938). But Schmitt reads Hobbes as a liberal, far from defending a totalitarian concept of the state. For Schmitt, such an erroneous interpretation of Hobbes (relating him to totalitarianism) was the result of a one-sided concentration on the mythological components of the notion of "Leviathan." Hobbes' theory, as Schmitt remarked critically, "would indeed amount to a strange philosophy of the state if its entire idea was directed at nothing more than driving poor human individuals from the total fear experienced in the natural state into the similarly total fear of a Moloch or Golem rule." See Schmitt, *Der Leviathan in der Staatslehre des Thomas Hobbes. Sinn und Fehlschlag eines politischen Symbols*, p. 112. On Schmitt's reading of Hobbes see also Dyzenhaus, David, "'Now the Machine Runs Itself'. Carl Schmitt on Hobbes and Kelsen," in *Cardozo Law Review* 16, 1 (1994), pp. 1–19.

[35] Freisler, Roland, "Willensstrafrecht. Versuch und Vollendung," in *Das kommende deutsche Strafrecht. Bericht über die Arbeit der amtlichen Strafrechtskommission. Allgemeiner Teil* (1935), pp. 11–48, here: p. 15. Without the assumption of free will, the idea of NS criminal law theorists that punishment involved the perpetrator's atonement would not have worked.

However, the Nazis could rely upon authoritarian practices of governance that characterized the final period of Weimar, foremost the shift to a presidential dictatorship. Chapter 2 explores the normative background for the Weimar Republic's demise, paying particular attention to the shortcomings in the Weimar Constitution (the possibility of governing by presidential emergency decrees and the absence of a constitutional court with clear competencies for judicial review, for example) that abetted democracy's collapse. The chapter closely examines the controversy in fall 1932 over whether the president, as the "guardian of the constitution," was ex officio beyond judicial control, or if such a viewpoint contradicted the spirit of the Weimar Constitution. Chapter 3 examines how legal thinkers justified Hitler's accumulation of power, as when he, as Reich Chancellor, assumed the office of Reich President after Hindenburg's death in August 1934. As we will see, the nimbus enjoyed by Hindenburg as a former military general was co-opted by the Führer to bolster his image as a guardian of the state. The chapter also examines how legal theorists tried to conceal the state's transformation into a dictatorship by interpreting the Third Reich as either an authoritarian rule-of-law state or a particular kind of a unitary state, a so-called total state.

The remarkable normative shifts after the National Socialists assumed power also affected criminal law. Chapter 4 outlines how NS criminal law theorists increasingly focused on the perpetrator's evil will rather than on the criminal act itself. This led them to suggest a so-called will-based criminal law, which would make penal law particularly vulnerable to the racial and social prejudices of Nazi ideology. Since racism was a constituent feature of the NS state, Chapter 5 explores the theoretical background of its antisemitic racial ideology, which culminated in the destruction of European Jewry. Of special concern here is to show how parts of the ministerial bureaucracy were not only well-informed about the regime's increasingly radical plans, but that they interacted with the SS in the transition to mass murder, belying the tired argument that the ministerial bureaucracy tried to hamper the Final Solution.

A particularly terrifying aspect of life in Nazi Germany was the omnipresent Secret State Police (Gestapo). Chapter 6 outlines how the police, controlled by Heinrich Himmler from June 1936, was transformed from an executive power into an instrument of "inner warfare" that undermined the judiciary. The SS was a state within the state, the heart of terror, persecution, and murder. While a thorough analysis of this complex apparatus is beyond the scope of this book, from a legal viewpoint it is significant that, from October 1939 (soon after the outbreak of World War II), the SS had its own military jurisdiction (for Waffen SS members and special SS and police units). Chapter 7 thus explores the normative framework of this jurisdiction, which was formally based on the Military Penal Code though highly susceptible to SS ideology and Himmler's perverted code of "decency and manly uprightness." Especially challenging for the SS jurisdiction were capital crimes committed by SS officers in the occupied parts of Poland, as well as the increasingly evident fact that orders for mass murder came directly from the highest SS court instances, Himmler and Hitler himself. The chapter examines the reflections of SS Judge Norbert Pohl on the foundations of the SS jurisdiction, and how SS Judge Konrad Morgen tried to cope with his knowledge about the planned annihilation of Jews and the murder of concentration camp inmates generally.

The final chapter considers the philosophical consequences of NS law for legal philosophy. According to a prominent postwar response, Nazi law posed a special problem for legal positivism, particularly because of the positivist separation of law and morality. As a general verdict on positivism this assessment is, I argue, hardly justified given the efforts to unify law and morality in Nazi legal theory. I end by suggesting that a normative justification for the separation of law and morality, which largely derives from understanding the function of law as securing autonomous agency and nonviolent coordination with others, brings us to an understanding of law beyond the old debates between legal positivism and natural law.

2

From the Weimar Republic to the Third Reich

2.1 "A State Without Substance." The NS Thinker's Disdain for Weimar Democracy

In his 1933 book *The Total State*, Ernst Forsthoff rendered the following verdict on the Weimar Republic:

> The Weimar Constitution, the democracy without a people, the liberal order with multiple antiquated freedoms, signified the bid for a state without substance. ... With the loss of the monarchy, authoritarian statehood was gone and the state fell prey to the schemes of various societal forces. In this way, the state lapsed into a degeneration (*Entartung*) which most clearly expressed itself through the empty running (*Leerlauf*) of a purely formal legal system. ... As political decision-making was handed over to societal forces, the state transformed into a mere apparatus, a functionalism without any essential content and thus a structure capable of serving all conceivable purposes. The state as mere apparatus became a tool in the hands of the strongest among the various social-political powers to appear in every possible disguise. The state was subject to a total social-political power struggle.[1]

[1] Forsthoff, Ernst, *Der totale Staat* (Hamburg: Hanseatische Verlagsanstalt, 1933), pp. 20, 26–27. In 1934, Forsthoff published a second, revised edition of this text. However, all page numbers and quotations from Forsthoff's book refer to the first edition of 1933. On the differences between the first and the second edition of Forsthoff's book see Meinel, Florian, *Der Jurist in der industriellen Gesellschaft. Ernst Forsthoff und seine Zeit* (Berlin: Akademie Verlag, 2011), pp. 89–92, which offers a detailed analysis of Forsthoff's work and career. According to Meinel, Forsthoff reacted in the second edition to the changed political conditions in 1934 (including the proclamation of the unity of Party and State, the imminent integration of the offices of Reich Chancellor and Reich President, the dismissal of Jews from public service) with an increased adjustment to the NS regime. Forsthoff's work was strongly influenced by Carl Schmitt.

The passage typifies the denigration of democracy and the distorted image of political developments that frequently appear in texts written by legal theorists who fell for the Nazi regime. In his damning rhetoric, Forsthoff passes over National Socialism's aggressive role in producing the impasse faced by the Weimar Republic in the last months of 1932 – a political stalemate that precipitated the collapse of the democratic system itself.

In deploring the demise of the imperial order, Forsthoff drew upon a common thread in the writings of NS legal theorists. The military and political breakdown after World War I had a deep impact on German public life. The conditions of the Versailles Peace Treaty fueled national resentments that hampered the new democracy from the start. Inflation and the currency crisis in the early 1920s intensified feelings of loss and political disorientation. Large parts of the population experienced not only economic insecurity but an outright existential threat. Their longing for stability was exploited by right wing circles. In particular, the National Socialist German Worker's Party (NSDAP) emerged as a political factor from 1925 onwards.

For NS jurists, the turn toward National Socialism was closely related to the German soldiers' "front experience" (*Fronterlebnis*), which generated an intense and novel feeling of community and togetherness. The collective "we" experienced in the trenches, they claimed, gave rise to a new political order: the NS state. Otto Koellreutter depicted this transition thus:

> As a result of the World War, which led to the political collapse of the bourgeois world, there emerged in National Socialism a different political understanding of the national idea. "National Socialism" means conveying the front experience to political life and enforcing it against the ruling "bourgeois spirit." This new national idea consciously builds upon a healthy *völkisch* and thus social foundation.[2]

For Koellreutter, the fact that the NS movement could become a counter-principle to liberal democracy was owed to the "spirit of the front-line fighters" – that is, to those soldiers who "not only speak of community, but have experienced it and the *Führertum* that arose from it."[3] Reinhard Höhn agreed that the front experience created "the community of the

[2] Koellreutter, Otto, *Grundriß der Allgemeinen Staatslehre* (Tübingen: J. C. B. Mohr [Paul Siebeck], 1933), p. 25.

[3] Koellreutter, Otto, *Deutsches Verfassungsrecht. Ein Grundriss* (Berlin: Junker & Dünnhaupt, 1938), p. 21 (italics in the original).

front soldier," which found continuity in "the National Socialist movement and its formations."[4] The Führer epitomized for him the "strongest community personality," which, moreover, was a source of his normative authority.[5]

What is presented here as the necessary course of history is in fact a carefully constructed ideological narrative. It is no coincidence that NS legal theoreticians appealed to the community spirit of the front fighters. The NSDAP claimed not to be a traditional political party but a movement prepared to continue the fight for a completely new socio-political order. By emphasizing the vital importance of the social and communal bonds created by the "fighters' experience," the NS jurists concealed the thuggish aspects of National Socialism, above all the brute terror and violence the SA Stormtroopers already exercised in the final months of the Weimar Republic.

The difficult political and economic conditions in the Weimar Republic further enabled National Socialist legal theorists to depict the transition to the Führer state as somehow inevitable. They saw no value in democracy, reducing it to a mere conflictual power struggle by strategically minded party politicians. Their disdain of Weimar democracy was expressed in a series of stereotypical reproaches: lack of political authority, reduction to mere formal legalism, lack of material substance and of substantial values, no inner connectedness with the German people.

The NS legal thinkers viewed Weimar as a doomed attempt to transfer elements of an outmoded conception of the state into the twentieth century, with its radically different social-political challenges. For them, institutions like parliament only made sense in the framework of nineteenth-century monarchy, where it counterbalanced royal power by emphasizing citizens' rights. Such oppositional mechanisms were dispensable in a polity determined to overcome any and all political contrast between the "sovereign" and the "people," thus aspiring to total state unity. In other words, in the National Socialist state there was no political antagonism between the Führer and the people's community (*Volksgemeinschaft*), and hence no need for a representational body to control the leader's legal decisions and measures.

NS-leaning jurists denounced parliamentary democracy as "empty legal formalism" and blamed value pluralism and liberal tolerance for

[4] Höhn, Reinhard, "Volk, Staat und Recht," in Höhn, Reinhard; Maunz, Theodor; Swoboda, Ernst (eds.), *Grundfragen der Rechtsauffassung* (München: Duncker & Humblot, 1938), pp. 1–43, here: p. 8.

[5] Ibid.

"ethical disorientation." Ernst Forsthoff encapsulated this reasoning by insisting that liberal democracy necessarily ended in the "agnostically disqualified state," a state allegedly unable to communicate "right" and "wrong" to its citizens.[6] For Forsthoff, a political attitude that "does not know any true community conscience and lacks a relation to people and nationhood, to honor, dignity and tradition," can only conceive of the state as an instrumentally rational bureaucratic entity.[7]

In terms of legal theory, NS jurists chiefly faulted Weimar democracy for its close connection to legal positivism. The main target of their aggressive criticism was Hans Kelsen's theory of law and state, particularly his legal constructivism and procedural conception of legality. Otto Koellreutter thus summarized these objections:

> In Germany, the 1918 November revolution ushered in a superficial victory of formal democracy and legal positivism. Yet, from their experience of world war, the German people, and above all the post-war German youth, increasingly saw through the fragility of this legal constructivism, which found its utmost logical consequent in Kelsen's "pure" theory of law and state. For Kelsen, the state became the endpoint of a mere construction that identified the state with the legal system.[8]

The writings of legal theorists who endorsed the National Socialist takeover in 1933 display a deep-seated contempt for the first democratic period in Germany, an attitude that unfortunately was broadly shared. The polemical and aggressive rhetoric by legal theoreticians, many of whom taught at universities and thus influenced the intellectual development of future jurists, paved the way for the acceptance of an authoritarian and eventually totalitarian state.

In the remainder of this chapter, I will examine crucial events and political decisions that accelerated Germany's turn from republic to dictatorship – crossroads offering important lessons for both legal theory and political philosophy.

2.2 The Weimar Constitution. A Document of Political Compromise?

Events moved quickly toward the end of the German Empire. In early November 1918, the crews of naval ships in Kiel, ordered to fight against

[6] Forsthoff, *Der totale Staat*, p. 10.
[7] Ibid., p. 11.
[8] Koellreutter, *Deutsches Verfassungsrecht*, p. 21.

British sea forces in what seemed like a forlorn military operation, refused to follow orders. The mutiny, which widened and triggered a general strike by workers, showed that the government could no longer control the people's frustration about the war. Protests in other parts of the Reich, particularly Bavaria, followed. On November 9, Emperor Wilhelm II abdicated and went into exile. That same day, the Republic was proclaimed.

As the strongest political party, the Social Democrats were obliged to lead the government. On November 10, interim Chancellor Max von Baden handed over the chancellorship to Friedrich Ebert, the leading representative of the Social Democratic Party (SPD). Ebert formed a provisional coalition government to tide the republic over the difficult period until nationwide elections could be held.[9] The political situation was indeed tumultuous. On the radical left, the communist Spartacists called for revolution and a soviet-type government; on the radical right, demobilized soldiers and irregular militia groups, the so-called volunteer corps (*Freikorps*), endangered domestic peace and security.

Ebert, feeling the unruly pressure of the Spartacists in Berlin, made a difficult decision: He called on the support of the military to maintain public order. The intervention, backed by *Freikorps* fighters, quickly ended a communist revolt that arose from January 4 to 15, 1919. Not only were many communists killed; the Spartacist leaders Rosa Luxemburg and Karl Liebknecht were murdered outright. In late April 1919, the revolutionary Central Council in Munich, which had set up a Bavarian Council Republic (*Räterepublik*), was also crushed by military and *Freikorps* units.[10]

The effect of this pact between Ebert and the military was long-lasting. First, it allowed the militarists, discredited as they were by their defeat in the world war, to reassert themselves. Especially in Bavaria, the *Freikorps* remained a political force despite their open hostility to the republic. Second, the communists now mistrusted the Social Democrats so deeply that cooperation between the two parties remained impossible throughout the Weimar period – a fact that contributed to the weakness of the opposition against the rising NSDAP.

[9] Ebert, leader of the Majority Socialists (MSPD), first built a coalition with the Independent Socialists (USPD). See Snyder, Louis L., *The Weimar Republic. A History of Germany from Ebert to Hitler* (Princeton, N. J.: D. Van Nostrand Company, 1966), pp. 22–27; Eyck, Erich, *A History of the Weimar Republic*, vol. 1, transl. by Hanson, Harlan P. and Waite, Robert G. L. (Cambridge, MA: Harvard University Press, 1962), pp. 49–51.

[10] See Mommsen, Hans, *The Rise and Fall of Weimar Democracy*, transl. by Forster, Elborg and Jones, Larry Eugene (Chapel Hill & London: North Carolina University Press, 1996), pp. 36–50.

The challenges for Ebert's interim government were enormous in the deeply divided political landscape of postwar Germany. Nevertheless, the Social Democrats' plan to hold general elections to a National Assembly (*Nationalversammlung*) found broad approval. Held on January 19, 1919, the elections clearly confirmed the position of the three parties supporting a transition to parliamentary democracy: The Social Democrats, Centrists, and German Democratic Party won a solid majority of 331 of the total 423 seats in the National Assembly, with 165, 91, and 75 seats respectively. A coalition cabinet was formed, and the National Assembly elected Ebert the first President of the Weimar Republic.[11]

The government had two major priorities: to settle the peace treaty with the Allies and devise a constitution for the republic. Already on November 11, 1918, the Allies had required the Germans to sign an unconditional armistice. The government had hoped for lenient terms in accord with President Woodrow Wilson's Fourteen Points peace plan. The harsh conditions of the Versailles Treaty, however, proved otherwise.[12] With the Allies threatening further military action and enforcing a food embargo, the Weimar politicians had no alternative to accepting the treaty. On June 23, 1919, a majority of the National Assembly voted in its favor, and on June 28, 1919 the German delegation signed the "*Friedensdiktat*" in a humiliating ceremony in Versailles Palace.

The signing sent shockwaves across Germany. Ominously, the onus of responsibility for the "national humiliation" fell to the political representatives of the Weimar Republic, foremost to the coalition cabinet and the Social Democratic President, rather than to the militarists who had planned and executed the disastrous war. Conservative and militarist circles who had already promulgated the "stab-in-the-back-theory" – that is, that Germany had not been defeated by the foreign armies but rather by leftists and Jews – saw the treaty as further confirmation that the government could not be trusted to act in the interest of the German people. It was not long before resentment over Versailles turned against the republic and the democratic political system as such.

[11] The so-called Weimar Coalition of SPD, DDP, and Centrists managed to be in power until 1920. After 1920, the formation of a government backed by a strong majority in the Reichstag was only possible by also including the German People's Party (DVP), a party that initially had been against the acceptance of the Weimar Constitution. This "Great Coalition" of four parties was difficult to handle.

[12] The cabinet under Chancellor Philipp Scheidemann, divided over the Versailles peace agreement, resigned (six ministers supported the acceptance of the peace treaty; eight ministers were against it). A new cabinet was formed under Chancellor Gustav Bauer who signed the Versailles peace treaty.

On November 15, 1918, Ebert entrusted constitutional law professor Hugo Preuss, a leading figure in the German Democratic Party, with drafting a constitution for the newly proclaimed republic.[13] Preuss set up an advisory committee and appointed its members based upon the proportional strength of their parties in the National Assembly. To the advisory circle, he also invited the famous sociologist Max Weber. On July 31, 1919, the final draft of the constitution was accepted by a majority of the National Assembly. The Weimar Constitution was proclaimed on August 11, 1919.

For Preuss, the guiding ideas for the constitution were "the organization of the law, political freedom, and social law."[14] He took care to combine the commitment to democracy and the rule of law with a social and plebiscitary component, that is, consideration of the will of the people.[15] Thus, the preamble of the constitution stated that it reflected

[13] Preuss became Interior Minister in Ebert's coalition government that was formed after the elections in January 1919. He resigned as Minister of the Interior in protest to the conditions of the Versailles Treaty on June 28, 1919, yet continued to work out the constitution.

[14] Preuss, Hugo, "Rede über die neue Reichsverfassung (1919)," in Preuss, *Gesammelte Schriften, Vierter Band: Politik und Verfassung in der Weimarer Republik*, ed. with an introduction by Lehnert, Detlef (Tübingen: Mohr Siebeck, 2008), pp. 589–590, here: p. 590. Gerhard Anschütz, a renowned constitutional lawyer, signified statehood of the Reich, unitarianism, and democracy as the main ideas of the Weimar Constitution. The principle of "statehood of the Reich" reflected for Anschütz that the Reich was not merely an association of the *Länder*, but a unity of the people held together by a supreme power; "unitarianism" indicated that the Reich, and not the *Länder*, was responsible for large parts of legislation. Though the states (*Länder*) enjoyed some autonomy and independence, the Reich was, in Anschütz's view, not a purely federal state. The principle of "democracy" was for him met since the Weimar Constitution was an act of self-legislation of the German people; moreover, the constitution granted the participation of the people by stating that the Reich President and the members of the Reichstag had to be elected by way of public general elections. See Anschütz, Gerhard, *Drei Leitgedanken der Weimarer Reichsverfassung* (Tübingen: J.C.B. Mohr [Paul Siebeck], 1923), pp. 12–32.

[15] Ernst Fraenkel described the distinction between a representative and a plebiscitary system of governance thus: the representative one is aiming to represent the majority opinion, in so far as this is compatible with general well-being; the plebiscitary system presupposes a unitary will of the people, assuming that this will of the people reflects the general interest. The plebiscitary component was associated with the Reich President's strong position (i.e., granting unity) and also with his election by popular vote. See Fraenkel, Ernst, "Die repräsentative und die plebiszitäre Komponente im demokratischen Verfassungsstaat," in Fraenkel, Ernst, *Deutschland und die westlichen Demokratien*, 9th ed., ed. with an introduction by Brünneck, Alexander von (Baden-Baden: Nomos, 2011), pp. 165–207, esp. pp. 199–205. Fraenkel criticized sharply Preuss's emphasis of the plebiscitary component, noting: "In its hour of birth, the Weimar Republic had committed itself to a plebiscitarian type of democracy; in its hour of death it payed the price [for that decision]." Ibid., p. 202. Fraenkel's critique addressed the extensive powers given to the Reich President by Article 48 and the general mistrust of the parliament.

the will of the German people to restore and solidify "its Reich in freedom and justice."[16]

Article 1 of the constitution designated the German Reich as a republic. The first part of the constitution regulated relations between the Reich and the states (*Länder*), set the terms for the Reichstag and Reichsrat (a bicameral legislative body), and defined the rights and duties of the Reich President and government. Reichstag members were to be elected in a secret public vote. The Reich President would be elected directly by the people for a seven-year term, with the possibility of reelection.

The second main part of the constitution addressed the basic rights and duties of all Germans, granting the usual civil rights and liberties: equality before the law, freedom of speech, religious freedom, freedom of conscience, and freedom from arbitrary state interventions. Altogether, writes the historian Louis L. Snyder, the Weimar Constitution was "a letter-perfect document embodying the best features of the British Bill of Rights, the French Declaration of the Rights of Man and the Citizen, and the first Ten amendments of the American constitution."[17] Yet, Snyder soberly adds, from a political perspective the constitution was "a compromise document which accepted the outer forms of democracy, but breathed no democratic life into the structure that had been created."[18]

From the beginning, the Weimar Constitution was not received with broad approval, let alone enthusiasm. In a 1919 speech, Preuss emphasized that:

[16] An English translation of the Weimar Constitution is available in an Appendix to Schmitt, Carl, *Constitutional Theory*, ed. and transl. by Seitzer, Jeffrey (Durham and London: Duke University Press, 2008), pp. 409–440; the original German text of the constitution is reprinted in Anschütz, Gerhard, *Die Verfassung des Deutschen Reichs vom 11. August 1919*, Vierte Bearbeitung, 14th ed. (Berlin: Georg Stilke, 1933), pp. XII–XXXXVIII. In the preface to this edition which appeared in February 1933, Anschütz remarked that his revised commentary on the Weimar Constitution appeared in a time of "gravest inner political fights and commotions – commotions which endangered the Weimar Constitution in its foundations and normative power." Ibid., p. VI. Note that Anschütz, opposing National Socialism, voluntarily retired from his professorship in Heidelberg on March 31, 1933, living in "inner emigration" during the NS period. He died in 1948.

[17] Snyder, Louis L., *The Weimar Republic* (Princeton: van Nordstrand, 1966), p. 40.

[18] Ibid., p. 43. Snyder emphasizes that the Weimar Constitution, though seeking to satisfy all parties, "gratified none. The Majority Socialists had not been able to achieve even their minimum program. The Independent Socialists regarded the constitution simply as a betrayal of the people. The Democrats considered its language far too proletarian and charged that it had loopholes which would lead to radical experimentation. The Centrists denounced it for its attention to secular ideas. The Nationalists damned it as an inexcusable break with Germany's traditional past." Ibid.

> The German Constitution came about in the shadow of a terrible defeat. It did not come easily to the people, but entered history in arduous negotiations. ... The constitution rests on an alliance of Democrats, Social Democrats, and Centrists. And these very different parties will have to continue to work together. This will not be possible *without compromise. ... Everything depends upon finding a middle ground for the three democratic parties to move forward.*[19]

This passage reveals the fragility of the constitutional basis of the new republic. In addition to acknowledging the difficulties in bringing about a constitution, Preuss tied its efficacy to the cooperation of the political parties forming the coalition government in 1919. However, a constitution's normative authority should hold independently of the political powers involved in its emergence and be above party politics generally. Preuss's statement is significant for the fate of the Weimar Constitution: It never became a normative stronghold for governing and guiding political life in Germany between 1919 and 1932.

Why did the spirit of the Weimar Constitution not come to life? Critical observers cite the lack of positive engagement on behalf of the political parties and Reichstag representatives, the opposition included. They simply had no sense of their responsibility for a lively and constructive political culture, according to these critics.

During the imperial period, the role and influence of the political parties had been severely restricted. Otto von Bismarck had sidelined all parties that challenged the traditional system of strong state authority – Liberals, Social Democrats, and Communists above all. After Bismarck's resignation in 1890, Wilhelm II continued this strategy of preventing the parties from taking part in political decisions. Consequently, most representatives could not acquire policy-making or governing experience. Fully aware of their limited influence and marginalized status, politicians in the German Empire had little desire to accept responsibility or seek power. Instead, they adopted an attitude of defiance.[20] As Max Weber critically remarked in 1918: "For the last forty years, all parties were accustomed to thinking that the Reichstag's only task was to engage in

[19] Preuss, "Rede über die neue Reichsverfassung (1919)," p. 589 (italics in the original).

[20] The historian Franklin C. West notes the following on the attitude of deputies to the Reichstag in the Weimar era: "They prided themselves on their 'experience,' but overlooked the fact that most of that experience had been gained under an authoritarian, bureaucratic system which excluded representatives of the political parties from nearly all significant political and administrative decisions." See West, Franklin C., *A Crisis of the Weimar Republic. A Study of the German Referendum of June 20, 1926* (Philadelphia: The American Philosophical Society, 1985), p. 18.

'negative politics.' Bismarck's legacy became shockingly evident in this 'will to powerlessness' to which he had condemned the parliamentary parties."[21]

Preuss affirmed that the collapse of the German monarchic-hierarchical system revealed to a "horrendous extent the fateful consequences of the absence of a politically experienced opposition, prepared for assuming governmental responsibilities." For Preuss, the old order led to "the politically fruitless fragmentation of our purely dogmatic party system that, out of entrenched habit, is attuned to *irresponsible critique of any government* and does not fathom at all the political mission of an opposition able to assume governmental power."[22] Only in Germany, he complained, have "the gentry and the bourgeoisie completely missed the political profession, namely to prepare the preliminary and transitory stages to parliamentary democracy by building up an aristocratic or plutocratic parliamentarism." As a result, Germany must "transition in a single step from a hierarchical state (*Obrigkeitsstaat*) to democratic parliamentarism."[23]

The lack of a constructive engagement by political representatives that Weber and Preuss deplored amplified the troubles of Weimar democracy. The deeply divided party landscape and penchant for political scheming, power conflicts, and sheer intrigue estranged many citizens from the parliamentary political system and aggravated the tenuous context in which the republic emerged. But there was also an article in the constitution itself that played a key role in Weimar's demise.

2.3 Article 48

Article 48, the so-called "Dictatorship Article" (*Diktatur-Artikel*), allowed the Reich President to intervene in the political process via

[21] Weber, Max, *Parlament und Regierung im nachgeordneten Deutschland. Zur politischen Kritik des Beamtentums und Parteiwesens* (München und Leipzig: Duncker & Humblot, 1918), p. 69.

[22] Preuss, "Um die Reichsverfassung von Weimar (1924)," in Preuss, *Gesammelte Schriften, Vierter Band: Politik und Verfassung in der Weimarer Republik*, pp. 367–438, here: p. 389 (italics in the original).

[23] Preuss, "Zur Verabschiedung der neuen Reichsverfassung (1919)," in Preuss, *Gesammelte Schriften, Vierter Band: Politik und Verfassung in der Weimarer Republik*, pp. 85–87, here: p. 86.

Willibalt Apelt also criticizes that the ruling political and social powers far too long were clinging to the old, rigid traditions. See Apelt, Willibalt, *Geschichte der Weimarer Verfassung*, 2nd ed. (München and Berlin: C. H. Beck, 1964), pp. 37–38.

emergency decree.[24] Section 1 of the article specified that the President may, if necessary, deploy the army to force a state (*Land*) to fulfill its constitutionally or legally imposed duties toward the Reich. Article 48, section 2 defined the measures the Reich President might take to restore public order and security should they be disturbed or endangered. In addition to the right to call upon the assistance of the armed forces, the President could abrogate articles of the constitution that guaranteed the protection of basic civil rights and liberties. These included Article 114 (individual freedom), Article 115 (freedom of residence), Article 117 (privacy of the postal service and of communication by telegraph and telephone), Article 118 (freedom of expression), Article 123 (freedom of assembly), Article 124 (freedom of organization), and Article 153 (the protection and guarantee of personal property). Article 48, section 3 obligated the Reich President to inform without delay the Reichstag about the measures taken on the basis of sections 1 and 2.[25]

[24] Article 48 reads:

> "48.1: If a Land does not fulfill its duties according to the Reich Constitution or Reich statutes, the President of the Reich can compel it to do so with the aid of the armed forces.
>
> 48.2: If in the German Reich the public security and order are significantly disturbed or endangered, the Reich President may take the necessary measures for their restoration, if necessary with the aid of the armed forces. For this purpose, he may provisionally suspend, in whole or in part, the basic rights established in Articles 114, 115, 117, 118, 123, 124 and 153.
>
> 48.3: The Reich President must inform the Reichstag without delay of all the measures instituted according to paragraph 1 or 2 of this Article. The measures must be set aside at the request of the Reichstag.
>
> 48.4: In the case of immediate danger, a Land government may institute for its own territory the type of measures designated in paragraph 2 on an interim basis. The measures are to be set aside at the demand of the Reich President or the Reichstag.
>
> 48.5: A Reich statute determines the details of these provisions." Cited according to "The Weimar Constitution," Appendix to Schmitt, Carl, *Constitutional Theory*, pp. 409–440, here: p. 417 (transl. slightly changed, H.P.-St.). For a German version see Anschütz, Gerhard, *Die Verfassung des Deutschen Reichs vom 11. August 1919*, p. XXII.
>
> Article 48 regulated two different subjects: Section 1 of the Article regulated the Reich execution against a German state (*Land*) that had not fulfilled its obligations toward the Reich; only sections 2–4 referred to the prerogatives of the President to restore public order and security. See Preuss, "Die Bedeutung des Artikel 48 der Reichsverfassung (1925)," in Preuss, *Gesammelte Schriften, Vierter Band: Politik und Verfassung in der Weimarer Republik*, pp. 571–575.

[25] Initially, the drafters of the constitution had intended that section 3 of Article 48 should require the Reichstag's authorization of presidential emergency measures. However, this

How did an article granting the President such extensive executive powers find its way into the constitution of a parliamentary democracy?[26] First, given the politically unstable situation, the constitution's drafters aimed to protect the republic against the potentially destructive forces of the extreme right and radical left. Second, some constitutional committee members were concerned that the Reichstag might maintain a defiant position vis-à-vis the government and block necessary reforms. Max Weber in particular pleaded for establishing the Reich President as a counterweight to the parliament.[27]

condition was weakened to a mere duty on behalf of the Reich President to inform the parliament about his making use of emergency decrees – a regulation with fateful later consequences. See Kurz, Achim, *Demokratische Diktatur? Auslegung und Handhabung des Artikels 48 der Weimarer Verfassung 1919–25* (Berlin: Duncker & Humblot, 1992), p. 37. Hans Mommsen notes that if the initial suggestion of the German Democratic Party (DDP) that the Reich President might use his emergency powers without any countersign had been accepted, "the consequence might very well have been the creation of a head of state with virtually unlimited power." See Mommsen, *The Rise and Fall of Weimar Democracy*, p. 57.

[26] The powers of the Reich President were regulated in Article 41–51 of the Weimar Constitution, those of the Reich Chancellor and the government in Article 52–58. The Reich Chancellor was head of the government (consisting of the Chancellor and the ministers) and responsible to the Reichstag. The President nominated the Chancellor and the ministers, whom the Chancellor suggested, on the condition that they enjoyed the confidence of the Reichstag.

[27] For Max Weber's discussion contributions in the consultations on the new constitution, see "Beiträge zur Verfassungsfrage anläßlich der Verhandlungen im Reichsamt des Innern vom 9.-12. Dezember 1918," in Weber, Max, *Zur Neuordnung Deutschlands. Schriften und Reden 1918–20*, ed. by Mommsen, Wolfgang J. in cooperation with Schwentker, Wolfgang (Tübingen: J.C.B. Mohr [Paul Siebeck], 1988), pp. 49–90, here: p. 85 (= *M. Weber Gesamtausgabe*, vol. XVI). In those consultations, Weber argued that "Germany's socialization will be impossible without any occasional personal intervention by the Reich's sovereign (*Reichs-Oberhaupt*)." Ibid, p. 82. In his introduction to this volume with Max Weber's writings in the period from 1918 to 1920, Wolfgang Mommsen notes that Weber, although committed to democratic liberalism, wanted to make room for "the possibility of a truly plebiscitary leader-sovereignty (*Führerherrschaft*)." See Mommsen, Wolfgang J., "Einleitung," in Weber, Max, *Zur Neuordnung Deutschlands*, pp. 1–45, here: p. 11. That Weber held such a view is confirmed by a newspaper article Weber published in February 1919, in which he argued that only "the election of the President of the Reich by the people will provide an opportunity and occasion to *select leaders* [*Führerauslese*] and hence also to reorganise the parties along lines which will supersede the completely antiquated system of management by notables [*Honoratiorenwirtschaft*] that existed up till now." Weber, "The President of the Reich," transl. by Speirs, Ronald in Weber, *Political Writings*, ed. by Lassmann, Peter and Speirs, Ronald (Cambridge University Press, 1994), pp. 304–308, here: p. 306. (For the German version see Weber, *Zur Neuordnung Deutschlands*, pp. 220–224, here: p. 221). Mommsen also mentions that Weber's suggestions for a plebiscitary Reich leadership exceeded the views and position of the German Democratic Party (DDP) and, except for the direct election of the Reich President, did not find approval. See Mommsen, "Einleitung," in Weber, Max, *Zur Neuordnung Deutschlands*, pp. 1–45, here: p. 11. See also

Preuss was initially skeptical of Weber's desire for strengthening the position of the President, but he gave in on the basis of two constitutional provisions: that the Reich President be popularly elected; and that only in an emergency situation the Reich President could take action independently of a potentially recalcitrant, politically scheming and factious Reichstag.[28] As Preuss explained his position in a speech on the new constitution in 1919: "The constitution is unwilling to create parliamentary absolutism. This danger has been eliminated by having the President elected by immediate popular vote. Such a juxtaposition of both powers [that is, parliament and President] excludes any arbitrariness."[29]

Apart from seeking a balance of power between the President and parliament, considerations of legitimacy figured into this rationale. The underlying logic: If the Reich President was directly elected by the people, then he was confirmed and backed by the "public will." By contrast, the government could never have such a strong claim to legitimacy since it was the outcome of strategic political bargaining on behalf of the parties. While the government rested on political compromise, the Reich President enjoyed the approval of the constituency. The office of the Reich President thus symbolized unity and stability, whereas the government inherited and reflected the conflictual parliamentary power play.

This understanding of the normative foundations of the Weimar Republic's two major political institutions was prominent in conservative and right wing circles. Combined with the still widespread endorsement of a hierarchical state (*Obrigkeitsstaat*) in Germany, the constitution's guarantee of extensive presidential powers lent itself to the rise of authoritarianism.

Mommsen, Wolfgang J., *Max Weber and German Politics 1890–1920*, transl. by Steinberg, Michael S. (Chicago and London: The University of Chicago Press, 1984), pp. 332–389; Bollmeyer, Heiko, *Der steinige Weg zur Demokratie. Die Weimarer Nationalversammlung zwischen Kaiserreich und Republik* (Frankfurt am Main: Campus, 2007), pp. 222–228.

28 In his history of the Weimar Constitution, Willibalt Apelt writes that in the consultations concerning the future structure of the Reich "some suggestions by the well-known sociologist Max Weber received particular attention," for example, "that the Reich President should, just as in the United States, be elected directly by the people so that he would have special authority toward the parliament." Apelt, *Geschichte der Weimarer Verfassung*, p. 57. Apelt adds that Weber managed to win Preuss's support for this proposal, although Preuss had initially tended to leave the President's election, as in France, to the representatives of the people. For a concise discussion of the debate between Weber and Preuss see also Kennedy, Ellen, "Introduction: Carl Schmitt's *Parlamentarismus* in Its Historical Context," in Schmitt, Carl, *The Crisis of Parliamentary Democracy*, transl. by Kennedy, Ellen (Cambridge, MA: The MIT Press, 1988), pp. xiii–xlix.

29 Preuss, "Rede über die neue Reichsverfassung (1919)," p. 590.

What is thus so striking about political developments during the Weimar Republic is that some crucial measures that were vital to the National Socialists' seizure of power (for example, the use of emergency powers in accordance with Article 48) relied upon legitimate constitutional norms. The difference just lies in intention and aim: the endeavor to save democracy versus the determination to destroy it.

In the three months between April and June 1919, Reich President Ebert declared a state of emergency no less than seven times in order to fend off communist coup attempts in Saxony and Northern Germany.[30] In addition to making extensive use of Article 48, Ebert sought to stabilize the government and economy by Enabling Acts (*Ermächtigungsgesetze*) that transferred legislative power from the parliament to the cabinet. Altogether, eight Enabling Acts were passed between 1919 and 1925.[31]

In the beginning, Article 48, section 2 served as a legal basis for the suppression of political unrest and upheaval. But during the severe inflation crisis in 1923, presidential lawmaking in the form of "legislative dictatorship" replaced parliamentary legislation to such a degree that the balance of power between the Reich President and the Reichstag tilted toward the former.[32]

As long as Ebert was President, this accumulation of presidential power did not seriously threaten democracy. Nevertheless, some politicians and constitutional experts eyed the developments warily. Preuss himself remarked in 1925 that the emergency decrees enacted regularly since 1919 could easily be abused, and that they had ultimately done more harm than good.[33] What worried Preuss most was that section 2 of Article 48, which enabled the President to suspend foundational rights temporarily or altogether, would free other state agencies from the usual inhibitions and restrictions imposed by civil rights.

30 See Kurz, *Demokratische Diktatur?*, p. 25. The legal basis for Ebert's declaration of a state of emergency in the period April to June 1919 was the Transitory Law (*Übergangsgesetz*) of March 4, 1919 which transferred all authorities of the former emperor to the Reich President (including the power to declare a state of emergency).

31 Already on March 1, 1919, the National Assembly passed three Enabling Acts in order to empower the government to enact regulations with the force of law. On five occasions the Reichstag transferred its legislative power to the government for the purpose of stabilizing the still fragile economy of the Weimar Republic. See Kurz, *Demokratische Diktatur?*, p. 146.

32 Ibid., p. 153.

33 Preuss, "Die Bedeutung des Artikel 48 der Reichsverfassung (1925)," in Preuss, *Gesammelte Schriften, Vierter Band: Politik und Verfassung in der Weimarer Republik*, pp. 571–575, here: p. 572.

The year 1925 marked the end of the first period of the Weimar Republic. Ebert died that February, and in subsequent presidential elections the conservative Field Marshall Paul von Hindenburg defeated the Social Democratic candidate. The legendary World War I general who had led German forces to an early victory against Russia in the battle of Tannenberg in 1914, stood for German militarism and the old imperial order. He was also known for his anti-republican sentiments. Yet during his first years of office, which were marked by tangible political and economic progress, Hindenburg kept strictly to the terms of the Reich presidency.[34]

Germany's period of relative economic recovery came to a screeching halt after the stock market crash in October 1929. The postwar German economy had relied heavily on American loans. When Black Friday hit Wall Street, American investors quickly withdrew this financing and bankruptcies ensued, unemployment spiked, and large parts of the German population became impoverished almost overnight.

The political consequences were no less striking. Due to the Social Democrats' considerable gains in the 1928 parliamentary elections, party leader Hermann Müller acted as Reich Chancellor from June 21, 1928 until March 27, 1930.[35] Müller governed first by coalition with the German People's Party (DVP), and from spring 1929 through a "great coalition" that also included the German Democratic Party (DDP) and the Bavarian People's Party (BVP). In March 1930, when Müller resigned, unemployment had reached staggering heights and the issue of reparation payments was still unresolved.[36] What ultimately brought down Müller's government was a conflict between the SPD and the conservative DVP over shortening workers' unemployment payments, which was unacceptable for the pro-worker Social Democrats. Müller had hoped that Reich President Hindenburg would intervene by using his emergency powers, but Hindenburg instead nominated as Chancellor the

[34] See Brecht, Arnold, *Prelude to Silence. The End of the German Republic* (New York: Howard Fertig, 1968), pp. 20–22.

[35] Müller had already been Chancellor for a short period from March 27, 1920 until June 20, 1920.

[36] Unemployment rose from two million in 1929 to three million in 1930; in 1932 5.6 million Germans, nearly 37 percent of the labor force, were unemployed. Only in the summer of 1932, months after Brüning's resignation as Chancellor, the reparation payments were, in light of Germany's dreadful economic situation, reduced to a remainder of three billion Goldmarks. This leftover was eventually not paid by the German Reich.

national-conservative Heinrich Brüning, leader of the German Centre Party (DZP).

Brüning's minority government relied more on Hindenburg's emergency decrees than on legislation by the Reichstag. Alarmed at the Nazis' increase of votes in the September 1930 parliamentary elections, the Social Democrats went along with Brüning's "presidential government."[37] Yet the economic crisis deepened. Having lost the support of Hindenburg, who preferred a right wing government independent of Social Democratic approval, Brüning resigned on May 30, 1932.[38] Two days later, Hindenburg nominated the staunch conservative Franz von Papen as Chancellor, thus hastening the end of the Weimar Republic.

2.4 Prussia versus the Reich. The Judgment of the *Staatsgerichtshof* and the Controversy between Carl Schmitt and Hans Kelsen

The last months of the Weimar Republic began with an unprecedented attack on the Prussian state government. On July 20, 1932, Reich Chancellor Franz von Papen dismissed the Prussian cabinet under Chancellor Otto Braun and placed Prussia under the authority of a Federal commissioner. The legal basis for Papen's spectacular step was an emergency decree signed by Reich President Hindenburg. Prussia was accused of having violated the first two sections of Article 48 – that is, that Prussia had not fulfilled its duties toward the Reich (Article 48.1) and had failed to maintain public security and order (Article 48.2) during violent clashes between Nazis, communists, and the police in Altona, Berlin, and other Prussian cities. Ironically, this unrest was spurred on by a measure passed by Papen's own government. Eager to make concessions to the rising Nazi Party, Papen had revoked the prohibition on the Nazi Storm troopers (the SA, or *Sturmabteilung*) in June 1932.[39]

The motives for Papen's political actions against Prussia were purely strategic: To do away with an opposing government in the Reich's largest

37 See Hiden, John W., *The Weimar Republic* (London: Longman, 1974), pp. 65, 117.

38 For a detailed discussion of Brüning's fall see Patch Jr., William L., *Heinrich Brüning and the Dissolution of the Weimar Republic* (Cambridge: Cambridge University Press, 1998), pp. 220–271.

39 Due to a request by the states of Prussia and Bavaria, the Minister of Interior and Defense, Wilhelm Groener, banned the SA on April 13, 1932 – a measure that was approved by Hindenburg.

federal state, where Prussian Chancellor Otto Braun was a Social Democrat, and to win control over its police forces. In July 1932, the Social Democratic Prussian government, having lost its majority in the Prussian parliament that April, was already politically weakened and ripe for a takeover.[40]

The Prussian government answered Papen's measure by following the rule of law and bringing the issue to the State Court (*Staatsgerichtshof*) in Leipzig, which typically handled disputes between the Reich and the *Länder*.[41] The State Court was not a constitutional court with full judicial review competencies.[42] Since the dispute between Prussia and the Reich also involved general constitutional matters, the case challenged the State court by inviting it to overstep its boundaries.

On October 25, 1932, the State Court decided in "Prussia versus the Reich" that the Prussian government had not violated its duties toward the Reich yet had failed to guarantee public security and order (that is, no violation of Article 48.1; but a violation of Article 48.2). The judgment implied that neither the transfer of Prussian government competencies to the Reich nor Papen's dismissal of the Prussian Chancellor and ministers was legally valid. Yet, the court also ruled that the measure to take control of the Prussian police was covered by Article 48.2. Hence, while the Federal commissioner installed by the Papen government should have authority over the police, all other government competencies were to remain with Prussia.

The court perceived this divided judgment as a chance for viable compromise. Yet this was illusory in light of the political circumstances.

40 On April 24, 1932 the Prussian coalition government under the Social Democratic Chancellor Otto Braun lost the elections in Prussia; the NSDAP won and became the strongest party. However, the NSDAP did not have enough votes in the Prussian parliament (*Landtag*) for electing a new government for which, due to a change enacted by the old parliamentary majority on April 12, 1932, an absolute majority instead of a relative majority was necessary. Hence, the coalition government under Braun remained in office, yet it was considered to be in a mere caretaker role. See Vinx, Lars, "Introduction," in *The Guardian of the Constitution: Hans Kelsen and Carl Schmitt on the Limits of Constitutional Law*, ed. with an introduction by Vinx, Lars (Cambridge University Press, 2015), pp. 1–21, here: p. 3.

41 See ibid., p. 4. Vinx uses the term "Court of Justice in matters of State" for referring to the *Staatsgerichtshof*.

42 There was, however, a debate among legal scholars whether the *Staatsgerichtshof* should not be turned into a constitutional court. See Schmitt, Carl, *Der Hüter der Verfassung*, 4th ed. (Berlin: Duncker & Humblot, 1996), pp. 3–7; von Hippel, Ernst, "Das richterliche Prüfungsrecht," in Anschütz, Gerhard and Thoma, Richard, (eds.), *Handbuch des deutschen Staatsrechts*, Band 2 (Tübingen: J.C.B. Mohr [Paul Siebeck], 1932), pp. 546–563.

The court's ruling had created a serious imbalance of power by stripping the Prussian government of authority over its police forces. Why would a power-hungry federal government seek to reconcile itself with an opposing state government that had just been deprived of one of its major executive powers?

Politics played out accordingly: The Reich Government failed to follow the court's order, which required dismissing the Federal Commissioner and transferring back to the Prussian government its executive powers.[43] The whole episode was a defeat of democratic forces. They lost out not only to authoritarian conservativism, but also to National Socialism, which profited from Papen's remarkable step.

The decision of the *Staatsgerichtshof* gave rise to a controversy between the two leading legal theorists at the time – Carl Schmitt and Hans Kelsen. Acting as the Reich's counsel in the Leipzig court proceedings, Schmitt defended the Reich's action against Prussia.[44] Kelsen, at the time professor at the University of Cologne, extensively critiqued the court's judgment and Schmitt's defense of it in an article published in the November 1932 issue of *Die Justiz*.[45] Their contrasting positions give insight into sharply diverging understandings of the state, the relationship between law and politics, and the proper form of constitutional justice. In Schmitt *contra* Kelsen, the deep legal-political disagreements

[43] This structure was still in place when the Nazis took power: They installed Hermann Göring as Federal Commissioner for Prussia. At least, the State Court's judgment, although not politically implemented, stated clearly that the federal structure, set up by the German Constitution, could not be dissolved. (The Papen step had also alarmed other German states besides Prussia, so the case at the *Staatsgerichtshof* was also supported by Bavaria and Saxony.) It remained to the Nazis to destroy this federal structure of the Reich with their program of *Gleichschaltung*. The possibility of the Reich Government facing opposing state governments should be excluded altogether.

[44] Schmitt, Carl, "Schlußrede vor dem Staatsgerichtshof in Leipzig in dem Prozeß Preußen contra Reich (1932)," in Schmitt, *Positionen und Begriffe im Kampf mit Weimar–Genf–Versailles 1923–1939* (Hamburg: Hanseatische Verlagsanstalt, 1940), pp. 180–184.

[45] Kelsen, Hans, "Das Urteil des Staatsgerichtshofs vom 25. Oktober 1932," in *Die Justiz*, 8 (1932), pp. 65–91. Both texts (Schmitt's "Schlußrede" and Kelsen's critique) have been translated into English by Lars Vinx. See Schmitt, "Prussia contra *Reich*: Schmitt's closing statement in Leipzig," in *The Guardian of the Constitution*, ch. 5, pp. 222–227, and Kelsen, Hans, "Kelsen on the Judgment of the *Staatsgerichtshof* of October 25, 1932," in *The Guardian of the Constitution*, pp. 228–253. All quotations from the texts by Schmitt and Kelsen on the *Staatsgerichtshof* proceedings use the translation by Vinx (changes to Vinx's transl. are noted). Note that Vinx's translation of Schmitt's closing statement in Leipzig refers to the 3rd ed. of Schmitt's *Positionen und Begriffe im Kampf mit Weimar–Genf–Versailles 1929–1939* (Berlin: Duncker & Humblot, 1994), pp. 205–210. Since the 1994 reprint is identical in content with the 1940 article, the translation matches with the content of Schmitt's original article.

about the destiny of the Weimar Republic come to light: whether to accept and defend it as a democracy, or rather to transform it into an authoritarian presidential system, if not a presidential dictatorship.[46]

Foremost, Schmitt sought to undermine the position of the dismissed Prussian government by arguing that, by the summer of 1932, it was a mere caretaker government whose very existence depended upon a "notorious and devious trick" – namely, changing the Prussian parliamentary rules of procedure.[47] While the dismissed Prussian government insisted that the presidential decree had violated its state autonomy, Schmitt countered that the very notion of state autonomy, independent of the question of representation, was senseless. He further maintained that nothing followed from the Leipzig Court hearing the case with respect to the dismissed Prussian government's standing and its right to represent the *Land* of Prussia. According to Schmitt, the Reich President had solved the representation issue simply by implementing Article 48. Once he had appointed a commissarial *Land* government and suspended the former *Land* government, the President had, in effect, already decided who had the right to represent the state. Given the presidential decree of July 20, 1932, the ministers of Prussia could, so Schmitt reasoned, only appear before the court "on the basis of a fictitious right to represent that is *ad hoc* and for this case only."[48] Schmitt

46 In an excellent article on the dispute "Prussia against the Reich," David Dyzenhaus claims that Herman Heller's arguments in the court proceedings in Leipzig (Heller was defense counsel for the Social Democratic representatives in the Prussian parliament) amount to a more convincing defense of democracy than Kelsen's critique of the *Staatsgerichtshof's* judgment. See Dyzenhaus, David, "Legal Theory in the Collapse of Weimar: Contemporary Lessons?" *in The American Political Science Review* 91, 1 (1997), pp. 121–134. Although Dyzenhaus's point that Kelsen's commitment to a value-free legal positivism limited his understanding of democracy is important, the issue discussed in the above chapter is merely whether the Reich President should be considered as the guardian of the constitution and hence should be beyond judicial review, as Schmitt claimed, or whether, as Kelsen argued, the true guardian of the constitution should be a constitutional court with the competence of judicial review over all state offices, including that of the Reich President. For a detailed discussion of Heller's legal theory in comparison with Kelsen's and Schmitt's theoretical positions see Dyzenhaus, *Legality and Legitimacy. Carl Schmitt, Hans Kelsen, and Hermann Heller in Weimar* (Oxford: Oxford University Press, 1997).

47 Schmitt, "Prussia contra *Reich*: Schmitt's closing statement in Leipzig," p. 223. As already mentioned (see footnote 40), the Prussian parliament had changed the rules for electing a government on April 12, 1932 (instead of a relative majority, an absolute majority of votes in the Prussian parliament was declared to be necessary). The reason for the change was obviously to prevent the National Socialists from forming a government.

48 Schmitt, "Prussia contra *Reich*: Schmitt's closing statement in Leipzig," p. 223.

conceded that a "commissarial government appointed by the *Reich*, of course, is not a normal government," yet he added polemically that "neither is an acting government a normal government, or even an acting government like the Prussian government that was deposed from its office, tainted as it is by the odium of 12 April."[49]

For Schmitt, the central issue at stake in Leipzig was whether or not "the commissarial government of the state [was] appointed constitutionally by the President, on the basis of Article 48 of the *Reich* constitution."[50] The answer for him seemed obvious: The Reich President had rightfully used his constitutional competencies.

Schmitt's remarks amount to a recitation of the facts rather than an explanation for why the Reich President's emergency decree deposing of the Prussian government was justified. The gist of his reasoning is that the constitution grants the President the right to enact emergency decrees, and in this case the President simply applied his constitutional power. Yet lurking in the background is the question whether the political circumstances actually legitimized the President's decision. In other words, was Hindenburg's use of Article 48 in this case in line with the constitution's definition of the circumstances under which Article 48 could be invoked? Schmitt tried to foreclose this query by arguing that the President not only had the constitutional competencies for emergency measures, but also functioned as the guardian of the constitution and, as such, he sometimes had to make an "essentially political decision which is left to his political discretion, within certain boundaries."[51]

49 Ibid., p. 226. Schmitt refers here again to the changed procedures for forming a government in Prussia. As Vinx points out, Schmitt argued that the dependence of the Prussian caretaker government on being tolerated by the communists in the Prussian parliament already "constituted a threat to public order that permitted the President to temporarily assign all the competences of the Prussian government to a federal commissioner." See Vinx, "Introduction," p. 16.

50 Schmitt, "Prussia contra *Reich*: Schmitt's closing statement in Leipzig," p. 223. Schmitt repeats the question on p. 224: "(I)s it constitutionally permissible for the *Reich* to provide a *Land* with a commissarial state government?"

51 Ibid., p. 226. By "certain boundaries," Schmitt means that the President may not misuse his political discretion. However, since Schmitt attributes to the Reich President the status of a "guardian of the constitution," and, moreover, holds that the Reich President's measures to protect the constitution were not subject to judicial review, it is hard to see how to define and assess a potential misuse of political discretion by the Reich President. Schmitt's view of the President as the guardian of the constitution reach back to his work in the early Weimar period (*Die Diktatur* 1921; *Political Theology*, 1922). For an illuminating discussion of how Schmitt came to mythologize the concept of the guardian of the constitution and his ensuing turn to a non-democratic political conception see

Schmitt put the *Staatsgerichtshof* in its place, asserting that its sole task was "the judicial and legal protection of the constitution."[52] However, the constitution, Schmitt argued, was not merely a legal document or construct, but essentially a political entity. Hence it needed to be protected politically and the logical candidate for this task was the highest political instance of the state – the Reich President. As Schmitt claimed:

> Since a constitution is a political entity, it also needs essentially political decisions, and in this respect, I believe, the President of the *Reich* is the guardian of the constitution; and his very competencies under Article 48 have the purpose of constituting a truly political guardian of the constitution, for the parts that deal with federalism as well as for all other parts.[53]

Schmitt concluded that in appointing a commissarial *Land* government, the President acted as the guardian of the constitution. Implicitly, Schmitt relied here on his conception of the "political," namely that the state must be a kind of political unity that is granted by presidential authority.

This stratagem of appointing the President as guardian of the constitution was available to Schmitt because of the absence of proper constitutional review in the Weimar Constitution. In other words, there was no legal body that could assess whether state institutions were legislating in conformity with the constitution or not. Since the Leipzig court was not a constitutional court, it did not have the competencies to fully address and legally decide the main issue of whether Hindenburg was complying with the constitution. Obviously, this ought to have been decided in light of the guiding normative principles underlying the Weimar Constitution. Yet Schmitt's answer presupposed the political-juridical framework of a presidential system and interpreted the constitution accordingly.

The upshot is this: When Schmitt took the stand as the Reich's advocate at the court in Leipzig in the fall of 1932, he had already abandoned the Weimar Republic as a parliamentary democracy. For Schmitt, the notion of the Weimar Constitution as a *democratic* constitutional foundation was dead in both letter and spirit.

Some authors have argued that Schmitt had no intention to undermine, let alone to destroy, the Weimar Republic. Instead, he went to

McCormick, John P., *Carl Schmitt's Critique of Liberalism. Against Politics as Technology* (Cambridge: Cambridge University Press, 1997), pp. 121–156.

52 Schmitt, "Prussia contra Reich: Schmitt's closing statement in Leipzig," p. 226.

53 Ibid. (transl. slightly changed, H. P.-St.).

Leipzig in order to save the republic against the National Socialists' impending seizure of power.[54] Schmitt, these interpreters hold, affirmed the strong and decisive position of the President as the only means by which to prevent a Nazi government.

Yet even if Schmitt sought to prevent the collapse of the Weimar Republic, he did not intend to safeguard it as a liberal-democratic state. Hostility toward liberal democracy and value pluralism infused his writings in the 1920s and found clear expression in his Leipzig statement. The normative structure he attributed to Weimar is not the one that the drafters of its constitution had in mind, but rather that which resulted from the destructive blows Weimar's enemies dealt to Germany's first democracy. If Schmitt had the republic's defense in mind, it was in the political form it had taken by the summer of 1932 – a presidential dictatorship, with governmental power residing in the use of emergency decrees by the Reich President.[55] In accepting such a conception of the state, Schmitt sanctioned the continuation of the old hierarchical order,

[54] See, for example, Seiberth, Gustav, *Anwalt des Reiches. Carl Schmitt und der Prozeß "Preußen contra Reich" vor dem Staatsgerichtshof* (Berlin: Duncker & Humblot, 2001). As support of his thesis, Seiberth cites a passage from Schmitt's diary in which Schmitt noted on January 25, 1933, shortly before Hitler's nomination to Reich Chancellor on January 30, 1933: " . . ., sad, depressed. The July 20 is gone (*ist dahin*)." Ernst Rudolf Huber, who had close contacts with Schmitt, confirmed that end of January 1933, Schmitt emphatically claimed "The July 20 is gone!" See Huber, Ernst Rudolf, "Carl Schmitt in der Reichskrise der Weimarer Endzeit," in *Complexio Oppositorum. Über Carl Schmitt, Vorträge und Diskussionsbeiträge des 28. Sonderseminars 1986 der Hochschule für Verwaltungswissenschaften Speyer*, ed. by Quaritsch, Helmut (Berlin: Duncker & Humblot, 1988), pp. 33–50, here: p. 38. Interestingly, Huber thought that Schmitt was actively engaged in the planning of the "Preußenschlag" (Papen's dismissal of the Prussian government based upon an emergency decree by Hindenburg). It was, Huber pointed out, against this background that the Reich Government nominated Schmitt as its legal counsel in the court proceedings in Leipzig. Ibid. Huber's statement that Schmitt was involved in the planning of Papen's action against Prussia stands in contrast to Seiberth's thesis that Schmitt was a supporter of Schleicher, not Papen. According to Seiberth, Schmitt saw in Schleicher's connection to the military a chance of winning the support of the military against the National Socialists. See Seiberth, *Anwalt des Reiches*, pp. 78–96. On Schmitt's role in the Leipzig court proceedings and his political standpoint in the summer and fall of 1932 see also Bendersky, Joseph W., *Carl Schmitt. Theorist for the Reich* (Princeton: Princeton University Press, 1983), pp. 157–192.

[55] Schmitt had already outlined this conception of a republic in his 1931 book *Der Hüter der Verfassung*. Parts of this book are translated into English by Vinx; see "The guardian of the constitution: Schmitt's argument against constitutional review," in *The Guardian of the Constitution*, pp. 79–124; "The guardian of the constitution: Schmitt on pluralism and the President as the guardian of the constitution," in *The Guardian of the Constitution*, pp. 125–173.

with the Reich President replacing the emperor while retaining his symbolic aura as representative of the old imperial-military order.[56]

In rejecting Schmitt's argument, Kelsen considered the issue of Reich versus Prussia from the standpoint of the democratic Weimar Constitution. For Kelsen, the President must act within the bounds of the constitution, which entailed respecting its foundational normative principles. He thus did not share Schmitt's assumption that the Reich President enjoyed special status as guardian of the constitution. Rather, Kelsen felt that the decisive criterion for assessing Hindenburg's decree was whether the constitutionally mandated conditions for invoking Article 48 were satisfied.

Kelsen's critique made three main points: The decree of the Reich President was unconstitutional; the Judgment of the State Court in Leipzig was incoherent; and the deficiencies of the State Court's judgment were, to a considerable extent, due to an institutional failure – the absence of a constitutional court in the Weimar state.

According to Kelsen, Hindenburg's July 1932 decree transferred the whole executive competence of a *Land* to the Reich on the basis of Article 48, paragraphs 1 and 2. This amounted in his view to the suspension of two fundamental principles of the Weimar Constitution – federalism and democracy.[57] Kelsen denied that Papen's political actions resulting from Hindenburg's decree had any claim to legitimacy just because the decree was issued by a publicly elected President:

> The fact that the Chancellor of the *Reich*, who has been charged with the exercise of governmental authority in Prussia, is appointed by the President of the *Reich*, and hence by an organ that is elected by the whole of the German people and therefore has a democratic character, is irrelevant, since what is at issue here is the realization of the principle of democracy in a federal state's member state [that is, Prussia].[58]

Here Kelsen rejected Schmitt's justification of the President's use of his considerable powers on the grounds that he represented the "unitary will" of the German people. For Kelsen, democracy depended no more on a "unitary will" than it precluded questioning the particular use a President made of his extensive powers. Kelsen's objection addressed

[56] See also Vinx, "Introduction," p. 13.

[57] See Kelsen, "Kelsen on the Judgment of the *Staatsgerichtshof* of October 25, 1932," p. 230.

[58] Ibid., pp. 230–231 (transl. slightly changed, H. P.-St.). Kelsen makes clear that the political actions were not legitimate just because the decree was issued by a democratically elected President.

an unjustified transfer of legitimacy: The fact that the Reich President was elected by a popular majority did not render his political and legal authority unlimited. Instead, he was obligated to act within the constitutional bounds.

Kelsen criticized the *Staatsgerichtshof* for being inconsistent: On the one hand, by appealing to Article 48, section 1, the court had pronounced the federal execution against Prussia, dismissing the Prussian government and installing a federal commissioner, to be unconstitutional; on the other hand, the court ruled that the same actions were *not* unconstitutional according to Article 48, paragraph 2.[59] Kelsen held that Article 48 could not be divided into two parts, each open to differing legal evaluations. For him, Article 48 constituted a unity.

As Kelsen saw it, a major problem with the *Staatsgerichtshof's* decision of the case (the judgment) was that it did not clearly declare Hindenburg's

[59] Kelsen, "Kelsen on the Judgment of the *Staatsgerichtshof* of October 25, 1932," pp. 246–249. Kelsen noted critically that the *Staatsgerichtshof* "takes it to be possible, in agreement with the decree of 20 July, that one and the same act can be a federal execution under Article 48 paragraph 1 as well as a measure for the restoration of public security and order under Article 48 paragraph 2." Ibid., p. 232. Kelsen also pointed out other incoherencies. For example, the court claimed that it did not want to assess whether the preconditions for the application of Article 48 were fulfilled, but nevertheless the court's judgment, as Kelsen argued, held that there was "a time of severe disturbance and endangerment of public security and order," thus stating that the preconditions for 48.2 were given. Ibid., p. 232. Ernst Rudolf Huber, who did his dissertation with Carl Schmitt and, later on, one of Nazi Germany's eminent constitutional lawyers, also criticized the divided character of the court's judgment, i.e., that the court rejected the measure of the President to install a federal commissar (*Reichskommissar*) in so far as it relied on 48.1, but, by relying on 48.2, accepted the measure of the Reich President that the executive force should be in the hands of the *Reichskommissar* and thus the Reich. Huber's critique, however, rested on different considerations than Kelsen's. The court's division of Article 48 amounted for Huber to an illegitimate separation of Reich execution from dictatorship. The Reich President's dictatorship was, according to Huber, justified in two respects: first, the Weimar Constitution granted the President these extensive powers, and, second, the President's authority guaranteed the political unity of the Reich, thereby preventing that it deteriorated into a disunited party federal state (*Parteienbundesstaat*). For Huber, the President and his measures could not be subject of judicial control for the following reason: A precondition of all judicial control was, as Huber pointed out, a law, that is, a general norm, from which the decision of a particular case could be derived. But the exceptional powers, trusted to the President for the Reich execution and dictatorship, were directed at measures reacting to particular instances of disorder and endangerments. Such situation-bound measures which required an assessment of particular facts could not be judged as right or wrong by appealing to a general norm. Hence, for conceptual reasons, measures by the Reich President were beyond judicial control. See Huber, Ernst Rudolf, *Reichsgewalt und Staatsgerichtshof* (Oldenburg i. O.: Gerhard Stalling, 1932), pp. 32, 64.

decree to be in part unconstitutional, but merely expressed its divided legal view (no violation of Article 48.1, but of 48.2) in its opinion, that is, justification, to its judgment. Yet according to Kelsen, only a court judgment, not a court's opinion, could be executed. The result was for Kelsen that "the President of the *Reich* is under no obligation, in the present case, to discontinue the federal execution that the *Staatsgerichtshof* has qualified as unconstitutional in its opinion, but not in its judgment."[60] Consequently, although the court declared the President's decree to be unconstitutional in so far as it was based on Article 48.1, the Reich President was not required to rescind this part of the decree. Furthermore, Kelsen pointed out, it was unclear whether the court or the President himself was in a position to rescind the presidential decree – a problem that again arose from Weimar's lack of a federal constitutional court.

Kelsen was a strong defender of constitutional jurisdiction.[61] He considered a constitutional court as indispensable for a well-functioning democratic state with a clear separation of powers. Kelsen specified two main functions of constitutional jurisdiction: to reign in the government by checking the constitutionality of its laws, and to protect minorities. For Kelsen, the constitutional court, not the Reich President, was the true guardian of the constitution.

Already in a 1931 article, Kelsen had sharply criticized Schmitt's plea for conceiving of the Reich President as guardian of the constitution.[62] He argued that Schmitt's rejection of constitutional adjudication was connected to his conception of a total state. For Kelsen, Schmitt's interpretation of the office of the Reich President corresponded to a non-democratic conception of the state as "'a closed and homogenous

[60] Kelsen, "Kelsen on the Judgment of the *Staatsgerichtshof* of October 25, 1932," p. 246.

[61] The Austrian constitution of 1920, which Kelsen had mainly drafted, set up the institution of a constitutional court. Ironically, one reason why Kelsen left Austria in 1930 were political controversies affecting the constitutional court. Kelsen took up a position at the University of Cologne which he lost when the National Socialists, based on the Law for the Restoration of Professional Civil Service (*Gesetz zur Wiederherstellung des Berufsbeamtentums*) of April 7, 1933, dismissed Jewish university professors from office. Kelsen eventually emigrated to the United States.

[62] See Kelsen, Hans, "Wer soll der Hüter der Verfassung sein?" in *Die Justiz* 6 (1931), pp. 576–628; reprinted in Kelsen, Hans, *Wer soll der Hüter der Verfassung sein? Abhandlungen zur Theorie der Verfassungsgerichtsbarkeit in der pluralistischen, parlamentarischen Demokratie*, 2nd ed., ed. by van Ooyen, Robert C. (Tübingen: J.C.B. Mohr [Paul Siebeck], 2019), pp. 58–105; transl. by Vinx under the title "Who ought to be the guardian of the constitution? Kelsen's reply to Schmitt" in *The Guardian of the Constitution*, pp. 174–221.

unity.'"[63] He pointed out that Schmitt did not interpret the constitution as a legal source for regulating legislation by norms and defining the status and competencies of the highest executive organs. Instead, the constitution for Schmitt corresponded to "the condition of the 'unity' of the German people."[64] Since Schmitt regarded this unity as material rather than merely formal, Kelsen asserted that it could then only be understood as "some social condition that is judged to be desirable from a certain political viewpoint." Thus, he noted, a "natural law ideal of 'unity' based on wishful thinking replaces the constitution as a piece of positive law."[65]

Schmitt was by no means alone in his dismissal of the institution of a constitutional court. During the Weimar period, many conservative legal and political theorists opposed constitutional jurisdiction. How deeply this resistance was anchored in an authoritarian political outlook came to light at a conference of constitutional law experts (*Staatsrechtslehrertagung*) in Vienna (April 23–24, 1928),[66] where the Berlin professor Heinrich Triepel was particularly vehement in rejecting Kelsen's defense of constitutional jurisdiction. In both its essence and meaning, Triepel argued, the constitution was not subject to formal jurisdiction. The subject of a possible constitutional jurisdiction could, he objected, only be the constitution in its material rather than formal sense. However, in its material dimension the constitution was a political, not juridical, phenomenon – one which only concerned itself "with those processes wherein the spiritual experience of the state's community in its totality prepares, fulfills, and renews itself."[67]

Although Triepel emphasized that he was skeptical of Carl Schmitt's conception of the political (in particular, Schmitt's attempt to infer the

63 Kelsen, "Who ought to be the guardian of the constitution? Kelsen's reply to Schmitt," p. 206. Kelsen quotes here Schmitt directly.

64 Ibid., p. 218.

65 Ibid., pp. 218–219. For a discussion of Kelsen's reply to Schmitt on the guardian of the constitution see also van Ooyen, "Die Funktion der Verfassungsgerichtsbarkeit in der pluralistischen Demokratie und die Kontroverse um den 'Hüter der Verfassung'," in Kelsen, Hans, *Wer soll der Hüter der Verfassung sein? Abhandlungen zur Theorie der Verfassungsgerichtsbarkeit in der pluralistischen, parlamentarischen Demokratie*, pp. VII–XXIII. Van Ooyen notes that Kelsen showed that Schmitt's views were an expression of a totalitarian conception of the sovereignty of the people (*Volkssouveränität*).

66 See *Wesen und Entwicklung der Staatsgerichtsbarkeit. Überprüfung von Verwaltungsakten durch die ordentlichen Gerichte, Verhandlungen der Tagung der Deutschen Staatsrechtslehrer zu Wien am 23. und 24. April 1928*, Berichte von Triepel, Heinrich; Kelsen, Hans; Layer, Max; von Hippel, Ernst (Berlin und Leipzig: Walter de Gruyter & Co., 1929).

67 See "Bericht vom Geheimen Justizrat Professor Dr. Heinrich Triepel in Berlin," in *Wesen und Entwicklung der Staatsgerichtsbarkeit*, pp. 2–28, here: p. 6.

essence of the state from the political), the above passage incorporates concepts – community, totality, unity – that are significant to Schmitt's political thinking and paradigmatic for an anti-democratic outlook. For an analytical thinker like Hans Kelsen, who was determined to keep the sphere of law and legal theorizing free from political ideology, passages such as these must have been difficult to stomach.[68] Even more challenging must have been Triepel's disdain of liberal democracy and his outright approval of an authoritarian state.

Triepel openly disdained the parliamentary system, the *Parteienstaat*. In a speech he gave as Rector of Berlin University on August 3, 1927, he highlighted the shortcomings of political parties, stating that "in Europe, prevalent opinion considers the gulf that has emerged between law and reality, just as reality itself, as the symptom of a disease and, furthermore, perceives party dominance and the party state as a degeneration (*Entartung*) of statehood."[69] At the end of his lecture, Triepel argued that a turn away from the party state was only possible through the development of mass democracy, adding that it "might be conceivable . . . that an ennoblement (*Veredelung*) of 'egalitarian' democracy is taking place through its transformation into a leadership oligarchy (*Führeroligarchie*) such that autonomous and hence responsible state leaders will replace irresponsible party organizations and the manifold anonymous powers hiding behind them."[70] A secure barrier against the encroachment of the party state will only be erected, Triepel concluded, once "the atomistic-individualist conception of the state out of which [the party state] is born gives way to an organic conception of the state."[71]

Triepel's speech is not only a striking document of authoritarian tendencies in academic political and legal theory in the late Weimar period; it also shows how close conservative thinkers were to conceptions of the state and leadership that entered into NS ideology.[72]

[68] Accordingly, Kelsen's Vienna colleague Adolf Merkel, who was present at the Vienna conference, stated in the discussion that Triepel not only expressed a striking skepticism toward the institution of constitutional jurisdiction, but that parts of his talk amounted to open polemics against the institution of a constitutional court. See "Aussprache über die Berichte zum ersten Beratungsgegenstand," in *Wesen und Entwicklung der Staatsgerichtsbarkeit*, p. 98.

[69] Triepel, Heinrich, *Die Staatsverfassung und die politischen Parteien* (Berlin: Otto Liebmann, 1928), p. 34.

[70] Ibid., p. 36.

[71] Ibid.

[72] Note that Heinrich Triepel did not endorse National Socialism and remained an opponent after the National Socialist takeover of power.

Let us return to the judgment of the *Staatsgerichtshof*. On the political level, the court's judgment had no effect. Although the court voiced in part a critique of the Reich President, the president's decree was not rescinded, and the Prussian government was not reestablished in its powers.

For Kelsen, this result was a logical consequence of institutional failures: The powers of the President could only be restricted by procedures defined in the constitution rather than through legal interpretation in the absence of clear guidelines for constitutional review. Kelsen found the President's decree, while radically centralistic, at least understandable from a legal-political standpoint. By contrast, in trying to reconcile two incompatible legal interpretations, the court's judgment only managed to create confusion. The Weimar Constitution, Kelsen concluded, "has not been saved by the *Staatsgerichtshof's* taking the path of the golden middle in its judgment."[73]

By the fall of 1932, Kelsen was clearheaded about the dangerous potential of Article 48:

> As long as the constitution itself does not prevent it, it is the constitution that creates the possibility of transforming the *Reich* from a federal into a unitary state through the application of Article 48, paragraph 2. It would be a form of self-deception to close one's eyes to this possibility and to put one's trust in an "intentional" interpretation of a constitutional article whose wording provides the opportunity to annul the most important organizational determination of other articles.[74]

2.5 Concluding Remarks

The final weeks of the Weimar Republic were characterized by agony and political intrigue. On July 31, 1932, the NSDAP increased its share of the vote in the elections and extended its political influence. It's true that in the November 6, 1932 elections the NSDAP lost 4.2 percent of its votes and there were signs of a recovery among the bourgeois parties.[75] But the political situation had deteriorated relentlessly due to the intrigues between Papen and Kurt von Schleicher, a conservative who had the support of the army. On December 2, 1932, President Hindenburg

[73] Kelsen, "Kelsen on the Judgment of the *Staatsgerichtshof* of October 25, 1932," p. 253 (transl. slightly changed, H.P.-St.).

[74] Ibid. (transl. slightly changed, H.P.-St.).

[75] See Hiden, *The Weimar Republic*, pp. 71–72.

nominated Schleicher as Chancellor. Schleicher's attempt to gain support from the National Socialists failed.

In his efforts to weaken Schleicher, Papen largely ignored the dangers presented by Hitler and the NSDAP. To undermine his imminent opponent Schleicher, Papen was even willing to form a coalition with Hitler and the NSDAP. But Hitler's claim to the chancellorship (the NSDAP was still the largest party) could only be rejected as long as there was a fairly strong political opposition to the National Socialists' taking power. Given the deep fragmentation of the opposing political forces and Papen's determinedness on bringing down the Schleicher government, the basis for such a resistance to Hitler's ambitions was gone. On January 30, 1933 Hindenburg nominated Hitler as Chancellor and Papen as Vice Chancellor.

The conservatives backing Hitler's rise to power assumed that Hitler might be a useful safeguard against bolshevism, and that he and the NSDAP could be controlled. What fateful error this was should have been evident, particularly since at this point it should have been clear what dangers Article 48 of the Weimar Constitution harbored, and, thus, what extensive powers the Weimar Constitution granted to a power-seeking government that was able to convince the Reich President of the necessity of restoring public order and security.

3

The Führer State

3.1 The Path to Dictatorship

Hitler's appointment to Reich Chancellor on January 30, 1933 brought about radical political and legal changes in Germany. The National Socialists saw the chancellorship as the opportunity for achieving comprehensive power. From the beginning, they aimed to neutralize the Reichstag, ban other political parties, and eliminate political opponents.

Hitler's first government was a coalition of the NSDAP and the German National People's Party under Alfred Hugenberg. Besides Hitler, only two other National Socialists belonged to the 1933 cabinet – Minister of Interior Wilhelm Frick, and Hermann Göring as the Federal Commissioner for Prussia. Neither Vice Chancellor Franz von Papen nor Justice Minister Franz Gürtner were Nazi Party members. Yet being part of a coalition government did not curb the Nazis' appetite for absolute power.

By the time Hitler assumed office, the National Socialists knew perfectly well what a powerful tool the emergency decrees provided for replacing parliamentary democracy with authoritarian rule. And they were determined to use Article 48 to build a state that concentrated all authority in the Führer's hands.[1]

But first the Nazis needed a pretext for implementing the emergency ordinance. This was achieved by fomenting public unrest through hate speech and ferocious verbal attacks on parliamentarism and the republican political system. The violent street actions of the

[1] The ground for such a political strategy was already prepared: From 1930 on Weimar parliamentary democracy transformed into a presidential system, not to say presidential dictatorship.

SA and SS against Social Democrats and communists also aimed to create political instability.

Events played into the Nazis' hands as well. On February 27, the former Dutch communist Marinus van der Lubbe set parts of the Reichstag building on fire.[2] The government responded quickly and forcefully, imprisoning communist party leaders and Reichstag deputies, and passing the Decree of the Reich President for the Protection of *Volk* and State on February 28.[3] This so-called Reichstag Fire Decree suspended such basic civil liberties of the Weimar Constitution as freedom of expression and the right to assembly. It also allowed the state to intervene extensively into the private sphere,[4] and empowered Hitler and his subordinate executive authorities to take all necessary measures for restoring public order and security.[5]

The second legal measure paving the way for dictatorship was the Law to Remedy the State of Emergency of *Volk* and Reich (March 24,

[2] Meanwhile historians assume that Marinus van der Lubbe (he was arrested on the spot) had acted alone. The Nazi propaganda depicted the burning of the Reichstag as a collectively organized action of communists.

[3] Ernst Thälmann, the leader of the Communist Party, was imprisoned on March 3, 1933. Göring also reacted with a ban of the Social Democratic press.

[4] The Reichstag Fire Decree of February 28, 1933 starts as follows:

> "Pursuant to Article 48, Section 2, of the Reich Constitution, the following is decreed as a defensive measure against Communist acts of violence endangering the state:
>
> § 1 Articles 114, 115, 117, 118, 123, 124, and 153 of the Constitution of the German Reich are suspended until further notice. Thus, restrictions to personal liberty, on the right of free expression of opinion, including freedom of the press, on the right of assembly and the right of association, and violations of the privacy of postal, telegraphic, and telephonic communications, and warrants for house searches, orders for confiscations as well as restrictions on property, are also permissible beyond the legal limits otherwise prescribed." See "Decree of the Reich President for the Protection of *Volk* and State," in Rabinbach, Anson and Gilman, Sander L. (eds.), *The Third Reich Sourcebook* (Berkeley, Los Angeles, London: University of California Press, 2013), p. 47. For the German text, see "Verordnung des Reichspräsidenten zum Schutz von Volk und Staat vom 28. Februar 1933," in *Recht, Verwaltung und Justiz im Nationalsozialismus*, ed. by Hirsch, Martin; Majer, Diemut; Meinck, Jürgen (Köln: Bund, 1984), p. 89.
>
> Further provisions of the Reichstag Fire Decree obliged federal states and municipalities to implement and obey these regulations; § 5 provided for the imposition of the death penalty for high treason, poisoning, arson, explosion, and damage to railway facilities.

[5] See Gruchmann, Lothar, "Rechtssystem und nationalsozialistische Justizpolitik," in Broszat, Martin and Möller, Horst (eds.), *Das Dritte Reich. Herrschaftsstruktur und Geschichte* (München: C. H. Beck, 1983), pp. 86–87.

1933), better known as the Enabling Act. It authorized the government to enact laws and amend the constitution without parliamentary oversight.[6]

The Enabling Act served as a basis for a number of so-called coordination measures (*Gleichschaltungsmaßnahmen*) for establishing a centrally governed state. The former sovereign federal states became mere administrative units of the Reich. The governors of the federal states were replaced by Reich Governors (*Reichsstatthalter*), that is, federal deputies tasked with exerting control over the states by enforcing Hitler's political orders.[7] The Reich Governors, loyal National Socialists, had the authority to nominate the chairmen of state governments and to call for elections in the states. Most of them were also *Gauleiter*, thus holding office in both the state and the Nazi Party.[8]

The National Socialists' radical reconstruction of the state was accompanied by the systematic obstruction of other political parties. When Nazi leaders claimed that it was impossible for them to form a coalition with the Centrist Party and requested new federal elections, President Hindenburg acceded to their demand – on February 1, 1933, just two days after appointing Hitler as Chancellor, he dissolved the Reichstag. The March 5 elections – the last multiparty elections of the Weimar era – featured sustained Nazi attacks on political opponents and the suspension of the freedoms of expression, association, and

[6] These powers are given primarily in Arts 1 and 2 of the Enabling Act, which read:

> "Article 1. Laws for the Reich can be enacted by the Reich Government not only in compliance with, but also outside the procedures established by the Reich Constitution. . . .
>
> Article 2. Laws for the Reich enacted by the Reich Government may deviate from the Reich Constitution so long as they do not directly affect the institution of the Reichstag and the Reichsrat as such. The executive powers of the Reich President shall remain intact." See "Law to Remedy the State of Emergency of *Volk* and Reich," in *The Third Reich Sourcebook*, p. 52. For the German original text, "Gesetz zur Behebung der Not von Volk und Reich," see *Recht, Verwaltung und Justiz im Nationalsozialismus*, p. 92.

[7] The legal basis was the Second Law for the Coordination of the Federal States and the Reich of April 7, 1933 (*Zweites Gesetz zur Gleichschaltung der Länder mit dem Reich vom 7. April 1933*). The Temporary Law on the Coordination of the Federal States and the Reich of March 31, 1933 (*Vorläufiges Gesetz zur Gleichschaltung der Länder mit dem Reich vom 31. März 1933*) had determined the parliaments of the federal states to be dissolved and newly formed on the basis of the votes of the federal elections from March 5, 1933. Both of these measures were acknowledged by President Hindenburg.

[8] The infiltration of state institutions by the Nazi Party was a main strategy for assuming total power.

assembly.[9] Nonetheless, the NSDAP did not gain an absolute majority and was forced to align itself in the Reichstag with the German Nationalist People Party (DNVP).

The declared goal of the National Socialists was one-party rule. On March 8, 1933, the votes for the communists were annulled. On June 22, 1933, the Social Democratic Party was outlawed on the pretext of treason. DNVP leader Alfred Hugenberg, who thus far had supported Hitler, resigned on June 27, 1933 and his party dissolved itself. By July 1933, all political parties except for the NSDAP had vanished either by ban or self-dissolution. The Law Against the Founding of New Parties (July 14, 1933) sealed this outcome. On November 12, 1933, new federal elections were held, though with only a single list of candidates (mainly Nazi Party members).[10]

The Nazis took a further step toward absolute state control on December 1, 1933, when the Law to Safeguard the Unity of Party and State came into force. Declaring the NSDAP and the state to be "insolubly connected," the law designated the Nazi Party as bearer of the "German idea of the state." In Article 2, the law determined the Deputy (*Stellvertreter*) of the Führer and the leader of the Stormtroopers (SA) to be members of the Reich Government.

The Law for the Reconstruction of the Reich of January 30, 1934 overturned Germany's federal structure by suspending the parliaments of the states (*Länder*) and transferring their sovereignty rights to the Reich. The law also confirmed the government's power to change the constitution. On February 14, 1934, the Reichstag was officially abolished, thus nullifying the states' participation in lawmaking. This measure was crucial for transforming the Reich into a unitary state (*Einheitsstaat*).

On August 2, 1934, President Hindenburg died. The previous day, the National Socialists had passed legislation to unite the offices of Reich President and Chancellor upon his death. Hitler, fully aware of Hindenburg's symbolic aura as military hero, declared that the "greatness of the deceased" had bestowed "unique meaning" upon the title of Reich

[9] See Loewenstein, Karl, "Dictatorship and the German Constitution: 1933–1937," in *The Chicago Law Review* 4 (1937), pp. 537–574, here: pp. 539–541; Fischer, Klaus P., *Nazi Germany. A New History* (New York: Continuum, 1995), pp. 272–273.

[10] Some candidates of the conservative parties were nominated under the label "non-party candidates." The elections were coupled with a plebiscite about Germany's decision to leave the League of Nations (*Völkerbund*).

President, and that he would therefore remain satisfied with calling himself "Führer and Reich Chancellor."[11]

By holding the Reich's highest offices, Hitler validated his status as supreme authority and power. A plebiscite on the fusion of the offices of President and Chancellor held on August 19, 1934 confirmed Hitler as Reich President by almost 90 percent of the votes (with a turnout of 95 percent of eligible voters!). That the Nazis sought to legitimize Hitler's political posturing by a national referendum held nearly three weeks after the fact fits well with their strategy of cloaking political arbitrariness in formal legal correctness.

Germany had thus transformed itself into a full-blown dictatorship in a process whose logic Ernst Fraenkel described in his famous study of National Socialism, *The Dual State*:

> Endowed with all the powers required by a state of siege, the National-Socialists were able to transform the constitutional and temporary dictatorship (intended to restore public order) into an unconstitutional and permanent dictatorship, and to provide the framework of the National-Socialist state with unlimited powers. The National-Socialist *coup d'état* resulted from the arbitrary application of the Emergency Decree of February 28, 1933, which made a mandatory dictatorship absolute.[12]

The National Socialists had used constitutional norms as the means for exerting the kind of power that was illegal by those very same constitutional standards. Manipulation and propaganda did the rest by masking the brutality of such measures as establishing concentration camps and removing Jewish citizens from public service positions.[13]

[11] See "Decree to enforce the Law on the Head of the German Reich of August 1, 1934," (*Erlaß des Reichspräsidenten zum Vollzug des Gesetzes über das Staatsoberhaupt des Deutschen Reiches vom 1. August 1934 vom 2. August 1934*), German version in *Recht, Verwaltung und Justiz im Nationalsozialismus*, pp. 142–143. Hitler's praise of Hindenburg's "greatness" was of course thwarted by the disrespectful act of legally regulating Hindenburg's succession the day before his death. According to historians, Hitler had formed the plan to assume the President's powers already in September 1933. Moreover, a few days before the plebiscite on the merging of the offices on August 19, 1934, the Nazis falsely claimed that in his last will, Hindenburg had expressed the wish that Hitler be his successor. See Mühleisen, Horst, "Das Testament Hindenburgs vom 11. Mai 1934," in *Vierteljahreshefte für Zeitgeschichte* 44, 3 (1996), pp. 355–371, here: p. 365.

[12] Fraenkel, Ernst, *The Dual State. A Contribution to the Theory of Dictatorship*, with an introduction by Meierhenrich, Jens (Oxford: Oxford University Press, 2017), p. 5. The translation of Fraenkel's book is based on the 1974 German edition.

[13] On March 20, 1933, the concentration camp Dachau was erected (inmates were first mainly political adversaries of the regime). The Law for the Restoration of the Professional Civil Service (*Gesetz zur Wiederherstellung des Berufsbeamtentums*) from

The NS regime's penchant for political violence and murder extended to internal conflicts as well. On June 30, 1934, Himmler's SS murdered the leader of the Nazi Stormtroopers (SA), Ernst Röhm, along with more than 100 of his men, on the pretext that they were planning a revolt against Hitler. While such a plot has never been confirmed, what is clear is that Hitler feared the SA's growing power and independence.[14] Yet the Röhm purge (or "Night of the Long Knives") not only diminished the SA, it elevated the militant SS within the power structure of the Third Reich and in the eyes of its Führer.

How could such a regime gain the support of academically schooled jurists? How could experts in legal history and political philosophy lay the normative groundwork for such a murderous form of rule? Moreover, how did they justify it?

In the remainder of this chapter, I outline the efforts of NS legal theorists to define the foundations of the National Socialist state and legitimize the new order. The primary text citations provide a direct impression of the rhetoric, concepts, and ideas used by Nazi jurists to fashion a normative, albeit distorted, political framework for the German Reich.

3.2 The Special Character of the National Socialist Revolution

The process by which the National Socialist takeover unfolded necessitated a dual justification: Politically, it was important to depict the transition from the Weimar Republic to the Third Reich as a radical, revolutionary break. From a normative perspective, however, it was crucial to defend the legality of the process.

Emphasizing the revolutionary nature of the transition from democracy to one-party rule was certainly in the interest of the National Socialist

April 7, 1933 issued Jewish officials to be removed from office. On Hindenburg's request, this law included an exemption for those Jewish officials who had actively served in the German army during World War I; later, this clause was dropped. Since university professors were, for the most part, officials of the state, this legal regulation had a tremendous effect on academic life: Regime-loyal academics took the position of dismissed Jewish professors. A classical study of the law is Mommsen, Hans, *Beamtentum im Dritten Reich. Mit ausgewählten Quellen zur nationalsozialistischen Beamtenpolitik* (Stuttgart: Deutsche Verlags-Anstalt, 1966).

14 Although a certain dissatisfaction with Hitler's course of seeking the support of the industry and the establishment existed among SA members who saw the SA as a revolutionary force, there was no planned revolt by Röhm. The murder of Röhm and leading SA members was a strategy to establish Himmler's SS and the Security Service under Heydrich as forceful powers.

movement, and above all its ideologically motivated Stormtroopers (the SA). However, Hitler knew that the regime also depended upon the acquiescence of such conservative forces as industrialists, who had a strong interest in representing the state's reorganization as legal rather than radical, and took appropriate measures to this end. Thus, in a speech to the Reich Governors and SA leaders on July 6, 1933, Hitler declared the German revolution to be complete.[15] In this sense, the brutal silencing of the SA in late June 1934 was a corollary to the regime's dictatorial achievement, since Hitler viewed the SA as a force whose revolutionary energies were not yet spent.

NS legal theorists sought to reconcile the tension between revolutionary momentum and legal conformity by characterizing Hitler's political coup as a "legal revolution."[16] They insisted on the legality of his power grab by pointing to its continuity with governing by emergency decrees in the Weimar Republic. According to this argument, Hitler's measures were no different from how late-Weimar era governments relied on Hindenburg's invocation of Article 48. What the legal theorists ignored, however, were the strikingly different political ends to which appeals to Article 48 in the Weimar and Nazi eras strived, namely saving a democratic system versus destroying it. As the conservative legal theorist Heinrich Triepel noted in a stunning passage: "[T]he peculiar thing about the revolution of 1933 is that the main part of it – necessarily disregarding illegal single acts or those of dubious legality – was absolutely carried out within the limits of valid constitutional law. *It is a legal revolution.*"[17]

Similarly, Carl Schmitt commented on the fall of the Weimar Republic thus:

> It was of great practical significance that this transition took place legally. For, as ... is also worth mentioning, legality is a functional mode of the state's apparatus of public officials and authorities and thus of political and legal significance. It is also not worthless for a system to relinquish itself formally and, according to its own legality, sign its own death warrant.[18]

[15] See Domarus, Max, *Hitler. Reden und Proklamationen 1932–1945. Kommentiert von einem Zeitgenossen*, vol. I (Triumph) Erster Halbband 1932–1934 (München: Süddeutscher Verlag, 1965), pp. 286–287.

[16] Scheuner, Ulrich, "Die nationale Revolution. Eine staatsrechtliche Untersuchung," Part I, in *Archiv des öffentlichen Rechts* NF 24 (1934), pp. 166–220, here: p. 167.

[17] Triepel, Heinrich, "Die nationale Revolution und die deutsche Verfassung," in *Deutsche Allgemeine Zeitung* 72, 157 (1933); quoted after the reprint in *Recht, Verwaltung und Justiz im Nationalsozialismus*, pp. 116–119, here: p. 117 (italics in the original).

[18] Schmitt, Carl, *Staat, Bewegung, Volk. Die Dreigliederung der politischen Einheit* (Hamburg: Hanseatische Verlagsanstalt, 1933), p. 8.

Conversely, the legal theoreticians were aware that Hitler's assumption of the chancellorship established a regime determined to revamp all state institutions.[19] Although the NS regime did not formally abrogate the Weimar Constitution or even remove the Reich President from office, it was obvious that the Enabling Act established completely new forms of creating law and securing power. Carl Schmitt conceded that neither "the foundations, nor the limits, nor any essential aspect of interpretation which might bind today's state, can be derived from the old, abdicated age."[20]

To navigate this tension between constitutional norms and the usurpation of power, NS jurists coined the phrase "legal revolution." For Ulrich Scheuner, a legal revolution (he sometimes spoke of a "revolution in the constitutional law sense") encompassed three elements: a movement of the people (*Volksbewegung*); a break with the traditional legal order; and a new political principle that shaped the radical rebuilding of state structures.[21] The Nazi takeover fulfilled all those conditions since, Scheuner argued, it was a "genuine revolution," a people's movement marked by "the breakthrough of a new idea of the state" and the creation of "a new form of political life."[22]

Unlike the French revolution or the revolutions of 1848, which aimed at implementing democratic ideals, the goal of the National Socialist revolution, NS thinkers repeatedly emphasized, was to erect a state that was powerful enough to overcome all sources of social opposition. This rightward revolution turned, in Scheuner's words, "decisively against the weakening of the state and the dissolution of all social bonds" and toward the formation of "a strong state standing above all societal forces."[23] The revolutionary impulse was not to preserve the individual's independence from the state, but rather to assure his/her "incorporation into the great connectedness of the nation."[24] As Otto Koellreutter noted, Hitler's revolution had restored German life and the natural conditions of "space and people" (*Raum und Volk*) by radically eliminating the individualist state, with its total detachment from "blood and soil."[25]

[19] According to Ernst Rudolf Huber, the given state system "was not only overcome in its spirit, but also overturned in its institutions and forms." See Huber, *Verfassungsrecht des Großdeutschen Reiches*, 2nd ed. (Hamburg: Hanseatische Verlagsanstalt, 1939), p. 44.

[20] Schmitt, *Staat, Bewegung, Volk*, p. 8.

[21] Scheuner, "Die nationale Revolution," p. 170.

[22] Ibid., p. 167.

[23] Ibid., p. 172.

[24] Ibid., p. 171.

[25] Koellreutter, Otto, *Vom Sinn und Wesen der nationalen Revolution* (Tübingen: J. C. P. Mohr [Paul Siebeck], 1933), p. 28.

Although revolutions invariably break the law, the National Socialist one was different, Scheuner argued, in its careful planning, tight political organization, and the fact that it did not unleash unruly forces. Rather, he stressed, the Nazi revolution found its justification and legitimacy in the post factum recognition and consent of the people's community.[26]

For Koellreutter, the combination of revolutionary change and legality marked the Third Reich as the national manifestation of a rule-of-law state, one in which "the elements of power and order find expression, since it meets the requirements of justice as well as the national-political necessities of life."[27]

Koellreutter and Scheuner also stressed the socialist component of the National Socialist revolution. According to Koellreutter, the National Socialist German Workers Party (NSDAP) placed "the figure of the worker" at the center of political action.[28] For Scheuner, the Third Reich was a socialist state willing to overcome class antagonisms in the "inner unity of the working German people."[29] Of course, for Jewish Germans this unity meant brutal exclusion. The organic connection of state and people, on which the new order was based, had a racial subtext.

3.3 State Order and the Community of People

A central element of NS ideology was the people's community, or *Volksgemeinschaft*. The message was simple: Members of the *Volk* would only attain their appropriate social position and ethical life purpose within a communal order.

Instead of protecting individual rights, the National Socialist legal order focused, wrote Scheuner, on securing "the nation's vital goods, its honor, national health, national customs, and tradition."[30] Obligations to the community, not the rights of the individual against the state, were paramount.[31] Besides the so-called Führer principle (*Führerprinzip*), the

[26] Scheuner, "Die nationale Revolution," p. 175.

[27] Koellreutter, *Vom Sinn und Wesen der nationalen Revolution*, p. 11. That the National Socialist state was respecting the rule of law was a familiar claim among legal theorists. However, they changed the meaning of the term, reducing it to the ability of the state to guarantee its citizens security.

[28] Ibid., p. 35.

[29] Scheuner, "Die nationale Revolution," p. 181.

[30] Scheuner, Ulrich, "Die Rechtstellung der Persönlichkeit in der Gemeinschaft," in Frank, Hans (ed.), *Deutsches Verwaltungsrecht* (München: Zentralverlag der NSDAP, Franz Eher Nachf., 1937), pp. 82–98, here: p. 92.

[31] Ibid., pp. 89–93.

people's community principle (*Volksgemeinschaftsprinzip*) amounted to a source of law (*Rechtsquelle*). As the chief ideologist of NS jurisprudence, the President of the Academy for German Law, Hans Frank, explained it:

> The followership idea and the Führer principle are the fundamental starting points for defining the legal position of the community personality (*Gemeinschaftspersönlichkeit*) within the community. Thereby, the state-oriented subjective public right, [which was] an essential element of liberal juridical doctrine in a bygone world of political ideas, and the juridical state person in administrative law, are overcome. The question is no longer that of the individual and the state or the individual against the state, but that of [being] a community member within the national community. The sum of individuals has been replaced by the people's community, bound by blood and fate. This is the living organism; its political unit is the Reich. And this Reich stands before us as the result of its political creation by National Socialism in its new constitutional form – a unitary state.[32]

The NS thinkers claimed that individual entitlements against the state only made sense as part of bourgeois emancipation movements, foremost those directed against political absolutism and, later, against the nineteenth-century monarchical state. Hence, the development of public law in the nineteenth century produced an individualist legal system harboring basic rights and subjective public rights.[33] The problem, according to NS jurists, was that individual entitlements against the state befit a political system in which sovereign and citizen opposed one another. Only as long as "the King as a sovereign outside society (*außergesellschaftlicher Souverän)* was

[32] Frank, Hans, "Einführung: Nationalsozialismus und Verwaltungsrecht," in Frank (ed.), *Deutsches Verwaltungsrecht*, pp. XI–XXIII, here: p. XII.

[33] Höhn, Reinhard, "Volk, Staat und Recht," in Höhn, Reinhard; Maunz, Theodor; Swoboda, Ernst (eds.), *Grundfragen der Rechtsauffassung* (München: Duncker & Humblot, 1938), pp. 1–27, p. 3. Subjective public rights were defined as rights an individual had against the state, that is, claims against the state that deserved protection by the courts. The concept of subjective public rights evolved in nineteenth-century German law theory; the idea was to extend the notion of a subjective right (that is, the legally protected claim of an individual to demand something from others) to the public sphere, that is the state and its administration. According to Michael Stolleis, subjective public rights were only fully granted by the Weimar Republic in 1925 and from then existed along with the basic rights of the Weimar Constitution that were negative rights, granting an individual protection against inappropriate interventions by the state. In terms of negative and positive rights, one might say that subjective public rights were positive rights against the state or state institutions, particularly claims to services by the administration. See Stolleis, Michael, *A History of Public Law in Germany 1914–1945*, transl. by Dunlap, Thomas (Oxford: Oxford University Press, 2004), pp. 211–212.

in power," Forsthoff wrote, "a true opponent existed against whom it was reasonable to claim individual rights and liberties."[34]

Accordingly, state and citizen formed separate and divergent legal subjects. But the unitary Führer state, which united political leadership with the people's community, would make both basic rights and subjective public rights superfluous. Thus, it was "obvious," declared Koellreutter, that

> liberal basic rights, that is "true" basic rights in this sense, can no longer exist in the German Führer state. For liberal basic rights and the overemphasis on "properly acquired" rights and "subjective public rights" that attend them stand in contradiction to the community as the basic political value of National Socialism. As the result of an individualist idea of state and law, basic rights are damaging to the creation of a *völkisch* community life.[35]

When Koellreutter penned those sentences, the NS state already had suspended basic liberal rights. But NS legal theorists argued that the community's precedence over so-called subjective rights (that is, individual rights to demand something from others) should also hold for administrative laws regulating the activities of government agencies and the bureaucracy. In other words, subjective public rights were to be dispensed with altogether.

In an essay on administrative law in the NS state, Theodor Maunz offered further insight into this sweeping assertion on the abolishment of subjective rights. The implementation of the Führer idea in administrative law, he argued, already had shifted the orientation of administrative

[34] Forsthoff, Ernst, *Der totale Staat* (Hamburg: Hanseatische Verlagsanstalt, 1933), p. 22. Reinhard Höhn points out that the constitutional development in the nineteenth century "in the field of public law" created "the individualist legal system by introducing basic rights, subjective public rights, and, most of all, the state as a legal person that replaces the personality of the sovereign prince." See Höhn, "Volk, Staat und Recht," p. 3. Entitlements toward the monarch were, as Höhn conceded, an essential element in the development of the liberal constitutional state in the course of bourgeois attempts at emancipation.

[35] Koellreutter, Otto, *Deutsches Verfassungsrecht. Ein Grundriss*, 3rd ed. (Berlin: Junker & Dünnhaupt, 1938), p. 89f. Koellreutter echoed here Hans Frank who declared: "In the National Socialist state, the separation of powers in its liberal form, its concept of freedom, its idea of the essence of the state as well as the liberal relation between state and subject, and thus also the doctrine of basic rights and subjective public rights have lost any significance . . ." See Frank, "Einführung: Nationalsozialismus und Verwaltungsrecht," p. XII. See also Maunz, Theodor, "Das Verwaltungsrecht des nationalsozialistischen Staates," in Frank (ed.), *Deutsches Verwaltungsrecht*, pp. 27–48, esp. pp. 35–37; Scheuner, "Die Rechtstellung der Persönlichkeit in der Gemeinschaft," pp. 83–85.

bodies toward recognizing their role in serving the *Volk* rather than dominating it.[36] Yet members of the people's community would only enjoy legal status and protection insofar as they respected the communal order. "All cases of forfeiting [one's individual claims]," Maunz maintained, "are based on the legal idea that one only has legal status as long as one does not sever one's bonds to the community."[37] The consequences of this shift from subjective to communal law were apparent to Maunz in the regulation of property ownership: Should the owner fail to fulfil his ownership duties, the state had the right to confiscate and expropriate the property.

Maunz further insisted that these transformations of administrative law in the NS system affected the understanding and interpretation of corporations. His argument boiled down to this: While the individualist legal standpoint conceived of organizations as a kind of juridical person with its own rights and duties, National Socialist legislation only relied on such an interpretation to the extent that it helped assess organizational liability. For National Socialism, the central unit of state order was the community rather than some fictional person (in the form of corporations) standing beyond the *Volk* and separated from the communal relations of the members of the people (*Volksgenossen*).[38]

The Nazis' degradation of subjective public rights was part of a larger normative shift toward the elimination of private law. As NS police law expert Walter Hamel put it, rejecting subjective public rights essentially annulled "the rational contradiction between public and private law."[39] By prioritizing public over private law, NS jurists justified the regime's intrusions into the private sphere and its increasingly brutal violations of personal freedom.

[36] As examples of legal regulations picking up on this directive, Maunz mentions The German Communal Ordinance of January 30, 1935 (*Deutsche Gemeindeordnung*) and the Law for the Organization of National Labor (*Gesetz zur Ordnung der nationalen Arbeit*). See Maunz, "Das Verwaltungsrecht des nationalsozialistischen Staates," pp. 31–32. On administrative law in the NS state see also Stolleis, Michael, *The Law under the Swastika. Studies on Legal History in Nazi Germany*, transl. by Dunlap, Thomas (Chicago and London: The University of Chicago Press, 1998), pp. 105–111 and pp. 115–126.

[37] Maunz, "Das Verwaltungsrecht des nationalsozialistischen Staates," p. 37.

[38] Ibid., pp. 33–35. As an example of organizations that count as actual and concrete communities, Maunz mentioned the organizations affiliated with the National Socialist Party.

[39] Hamel, Walter, "Wesen und Rechtsgrundlagen der Polizei im nationalsozialistischen Staate," in Frank (ed.) *Deutsches Verwaltungsrecht*, pp. 381–398, here: p. 390.

In reality, the NS jurists' programmatic dismissal of subjective public rights had clear limits. Maunz complained openly that acting courts, instead of following the new guidelines, still relied on the old categories of acquired rights and claims against the state. Resignedly, he concluded that it would take years, if not decades, to eliminate all traces of liberal subjective law and fully erase the distinction between public and private law.[40]

The translation of ideology into legal doctrine produced little more than striking formulas and wordy, repetitive appeals to the *Volk*'s internal order. Maunz himself maintained that the new orientation of administrative law required no less than transforming a jurisprudence of interests (focused on the claims of conflicting parties) to one which anchored law in the homogeneous people's community.[41]

But what does that mean exactly? How would this play out in concrete judicial sentencing? Maunz suggested that other than the jurisprudence of interests, which defined the relation between interests and purposes in a merely formal way, the concrete order thinking would generate a substantial interpretation of the legislation's purpose. In elucidating this claim, however, Maunz merely noted that "the correct substance and source of correct purposes are derived from the order of the *Volk*."[42]

This proposal thus circles back to ideology. As long as the concept of the people's community remained vague, it was a useful foil for projecting all kinds of ideological content onto it.[43] The racial doctrine of National Socialism represented the darkest ideological manifestation of the mythic community.

40 Maunz, "Das Verwaltungsrecht des nationalsozialistischen Staates," pp. 38–41.

41 Maunz referred to Carl Schmitt's doctrine of concrete order thinking, as developed by Schmitt in *Über die drei Arten des rechtswissenschaftlichen Denkens* (Hamburg: Hanseatische Verlagsanstalt, 1934; 2nd ed. Berlin: Duncker & Humblot, 1993). According to Maunz, concrete order thinking would strengthen the position of the person in society by focusing not on an abstract or a fictitious will, but on the person's honor, economic needs and concrete will. See Maunz, Theodor, "Das Ende des subjektiven öffentlichen Rechts," in *Zeitschrift für die gesamte Staatswissenschaft* 96, 1 (1936), pp. 71–111, here: p. 95.

42 Maunz, "Das Verwaltungsrecht des nationalsozialistischen Staates," p. 45.

43 According to Peter Caldwell, the juridical appeals to the people's community did not get beyond "an antiformalist affirmation of activism," centered around the notion of the *Volk* as a kind of "organic, immediately and naturally given entity." Caldwell, "National Socialism and Constitutional Law: Carl Schmitt, Otto Koellreutter, and the Debate over the Nature of the Nazi State, 1933–1937," in *Cardozo Law Review* 16 (1994), pp. 399–427, here: p. 405.

3.4 Authoritarian or Total State?

The extraordinary powers granted by the Enabling Act and the restriction of basic rights and liberties in the Reichstag Fire Decree revealed that the Third Reich was becoming a totalitarian state, with complete control over social life.[44]

The original texts indicate just how hard NS-loyal jurists worked together to dispel this totalitarian image. Nevertheless, these same legal theorists disagreed over whether the new order embodied a total state or an authoritarian state. This debate, which mainly pitted Carl Schmitt, Ernst Forsthoff, and Ernst Rudolf Huber against Otto Koellreutter, offers insight into the legal theorists' attempts to attribute a normative structure to the NS state. Furthermore, the controversy illustrates how these thinkers aimed to outdo each other in their ideological efforts to serve the new rulers.[45]

In his 1932 essay *The Concept of the Political*, Carl Schmitt coined the term "total state."[46] The total state, he argued, would encompass all

[44] According to Hannah Arendt, a totalitarian state is characterized by the leadership's claim to absolute power, the use of propaganda, lies, and most of all, brute terror and violence. Also, she notes, "the leadership constantly shifts the actual center of power, often to other organizations, but without dissolving or even publicly exposing the groups that have been deprived of their power." Arendt, Hannah, *The Origins of Totalitarianism*, with an introduction by Powers, Samantha (New York: Schocken Books, 2004), p. 520.

[45] Besides theoretical disagreements, there was a deep personal rivalry between Carl Schmitt and Otto Koellreutter. Koellreutter, professor at the University of Munich, was one of the first public law professors in 1933 to endorse strongly the NS regime. Koellreutter obviously felt set back by Schmitt's rapid career as the Nazis' most eminent jurist and Schmitt's nomination to "Preußischer Staatsrat" by Hermann Göring, particularly so since Koellreutter considered Schmitt's engagement for National Socialism not to be based on inner commitment but on political opportunism. Already in June 1934, Koellreutter tried to discredit Schmitt in a letter to Hans Lammers, the Chief of the *Reichskanzlei*. In 1936, when Schmitt came under scrutiny and attack by the SS, the SS tried to gain incriminating information on Schmitt from Koellreutter. See Blasius, Dirk, *Carl Schmitt. Preußischer Staatsrat in Hitlers Reich* (Göttingen: Vandenhoeck and Ruprecht, 2001), pp. 155–156. At that point, it became clear to both NS jurists how politically dangerous their controversies and rivalries were. On the rivalry between Koellreutter and Schmitt see also Stolleis, Michael, *A History of Public Law in Germany 1914–1945* (Oxford: Oxford University Press, 2004), pp. 340–341, p. 347. Schmitt resigned from all Party positions in 1936 but remained professor at the Friedrich-Wilhelms University in Berlin and also kept the title of Preußischer Staatsrat. See also Schmidt, Jörg, *Otto Koellreutter 1883–1972. Sein Leben, sein Werk, seine Zeit* (Frankfurt/New York: Peter Lang, 1994), pp. 174–180.

[46] Schmitt, Carl, *The Concept of the Political*, expanded ed. with an introduction and transl. by Schwab, Georg (Chicago and London: University of Chicago Press, 2007), pp. 22–24. Actually the term already came up in Schmitt, "Die Wendung zum totalen Staat (1931),"

societal domains in its effort to overcome the "neutral state" of nineteenth-century liberalism.[47] Accordingly, the total state eliminated the liberal principle of neutrality that exempted certain spheres (besides the economy, Schmitt mentions religion, culture, and education) from statewide regulation.

Above all, a satisfactory conception of the state was premised on the political. For Schmitt, the essence of the political – that is, the source of all political action – lay in the distinction between friend and enemy. Just as morality relied on the concepts of "good and evil" and the economy was grounded in the categories of "useful and harmful," "friend" and "enemy" were constitutive for the political sphere.[48] Schmitt believed that these basic concepts should be interpreted in their "concrete existentialist sense," which is to say that they expressed the inner dynamic of political life without relativizing the state's overall unity. In his view, "enemy" was not tied to hostile psychological feelings toward a private adversary, but rather was directed at the "public enemy." The concept thus referred, Schmitt wrote, to the very real possibility "of one *fighting* collectivity (*Gesamtheit*) of people confronting a similar collectivity."[49]

In order to fend off the belligerent connotations of his notion of the political, Schmitt emphasized that the friend/enemy distinction did not imply that all political life consisted in military action and "bloody war." Yet, the right to go to war (*jus belli*) – that is, the free decision to fight an enemy – was an essential prerogative of the total state.[50]

The total state formula found its way into legal discourse in the early years of Nazi rule. Ernst Forsthoff, a student of Schmitt, devoted an entire

in Schmitt, *Positionen und Begriffe im Kampf mit Weimar-Genf-Versailles 1923–1939* (Hamburg: Hanseatische Verlagsanstalt, 1940), pp. 146–157. For a detailed discussion of Schmitt's understanding of the total state see Scheuerman, William E., *Carl Schmitt. The End of Law* (Lanham, Boulder, New York, Oxford: Rowman & Littlefield, 1999), pp. 85–112. As Jens Meierhenrich notes, Schmitt used the term "total state" in "direct opposition" to Otto Koellreutter's theory of a "national rule-of-law state." See Meierhenrich, Jens, "Fearing the Disorder of Things," in Meierhenrich, Jens and Simons, Oliver (eds.), *The Oxford Handbook of Carl Schmitt* (Oxford: Oxford University Press, 2016), pp. 171–216, here: p. 194.

47 Schmitt, *The Concept of the Political*, pp. 22–23.

48 Ibid., p. 26.

49 Ibid., p. 28 (italics in the original, transl. slightly changed, H.P.-St.). For a critique of the "plasticity" of Schmitt's notion of the enemy see Pendas, Devin, "Criminals, Enemies, and the Politics of Transitional Justice," in Sarat, Austin; Douglas, Lawrence; Umphrey Martha Merrill (eds.), *Criminals and Enemies* (Amherst and Boston: University of Massachusetts Press, 2019), pp. 22–43.

50 Schmitt, *The Concept of the Political*, p. 45. This remark on the free decision to go to war has to be seen in the context of Schmitt's criticism of the League of Nations.

essay to explaining why and how the NS state represented a total state. Following his mentor, Forsthoff associated the political sphere with struggle: In contrast to a purely formal system of legality, true political life would consist in "the encounter of friend and enemy, of power and resistance."[51] Politics, he asserted, must not be a dull tool for mechanical imposition and blunt force, but "a missionary for awakening a new, metaphysically grounded attitude toward the state."[52]

The total state had to be based on a uniformly binding worldview.[53] Moreover, it required power over crucial institutions of public life and could not tolerate the public expression of liberal views. Accordingly, Forsthoff approved the NS regime's restrictions on the press and suppression of opposing political views. He also endorsed the Nazis' reorganization of the civil service,[54] stipulating that all authority relations in the total state be "organized hierarchically, imperatively, in the form of personal rule."[55] In this way, Forsthoff legitimized lawmaking through the will of the Führer.

Nevertheless, Forsthoff denied the total state the right to control all aspects of human life. In order to hold members of the people's community responsible for their actions, even the total state had to grant some individual leeway. Forsthoff qualified this concession by insisting that he did not mean the freedom associated with the "the spirit of 1789," but instead an obligation-generating form of personal decision-making.[56]

The political movement was crucial for the total state. According to Forsthoff, the revolutionary energy of National Socialism created new constitutional orders – the *order of rule* and the *order of the people*. This

[51] Forsthoff, *Der totale Staat*, p. 7.

[52] Ibid., p. 32. Passages like these show the influence of Forsthoff's teacher Carl Schmitt and of the latter's "theology of the political." On Schmitt's political theology see Meier, Heinrich, *The Lesson of Carl Schmitt. Four Chapters on the Distinction between Political Theology and Political Philosophy*, expanded ed., transl. by Brainard, Marcus (New essays in this ed. transl. by Berman, Robert) (Chicago and London: The University of Chicago Press, 2011). On Schmitt's influence on Forsthoff's views see also Caldwell, Peter C., "Ernst Forsthoff in Frankfurt. Political Mobilization and the Abandonment of Scholarly Responsibility," in Epple, Moritz; Fried, Johannes; Gross, Raphael; Gudian, Janus (eds.), *"Politisierung der Wissenschaft." Jüdische Wissenschaftler und ihre Gegner an der Universität Frankfurt am Main vor und nach 1933* (Göttingen: Wallstein, 2013), pp. 249–283.

[53] Forsthoff, *Der totale Staat*, p. 31f. See also Fauser, Manfred, "Das Gesetz im Führerstaat," in *Archiv des öffentlichen Rechts*, N. F. 26 (1935), pp. 129–154, here p. 133.

[54] Forsthoff, *Der totale Staat*, p. 33.

[55] Ibid., p. 38.

[56] Ibid., p. 41.

two-pronged approach was necessary since the total Führer state could not accept the democratic doctrine of the identity of rulers and subjects. Instead, a distinction had to be made between the Führer and his subjects, a difference that for Forsthoff was "only metaphysically realizable."[57] Since, in his view, the claim to power could not merely be based on the Führer's will and personal qualities, the state also had to be bound to the *Volk*.

Thus, the people's community (*Volksgemeinschaft*) formed the second pillar of the total state. Moreover, the National Socialists' understanding of "the communal will" conflicted with the democratic conceptualization of this term, which traced its roots to the eighteenth-century Enlightenment. As Forsthoff explained:

> The *Volk* is today the starting point of all political consideration, the subject of every political effort. *Volk* in this sense is not the *volonté générale* [general will], not the majority, not a mass, but a structured community. Democracy, wanting to lead the people as a *volonté générale* and mass to power, actually disempowered the people. For the power of the people does not reside in the binding force of an egalitarian common will, but in the strength arising from the structured life relations of the *Volk*. By overcoming Rousseau's kind of democracy, the German people must be liberated from powerlessness and given a structure appropriate to its social life relations.[58]

The total state, Forsthoff claimed, was not guided by particular interests and interest conflicts. It rather amounted to an organic unity with "a rank-based order of the people" (*ständische Volksordnung*). The members of the people's community had to have a deep awareness of their belonging to the *Volk* and a total commitment to the people's community.[59]

Forsthoff's explanations closely followed those of Carl Schmitt in his essay *Staat, Bewegung, Volk*. Published in spring 1933, shortly after the Nazis came to power, this text characterized the new state's unity "as a tripartite synthesis of state, movement, and people."[60] Those three

[57] Ibid., p. 31. With this rather obscure appeal to the "metaphysical," Forsthoff presumably tried to overcome the problem that his theses were not in line with Nazi Party doctrine which, after all, upheld the unity of Führer and people.

[58] Forsthoff, *Der totale Staat*, p. 41.

[59] Ibid., p. 45. Forsthoff speaks out in favor of labor service (*Arbeitsdienst*) as a community service.

[60] Schmitt, *Staat, Bewegung, Volk*, p. 11. Koellreutter objects that Schmitt's three-partite characterization of the state's unity "is not an expression of the *völkisch* structure of the state." See Koellreutter, Otto, *Volk und Staat in der Weltanschauung des Nationalsozialismus* (Berlin: Pan Verlagsgesellschaft, 1935), p. 19. Koellreutter also

pillars (Schmitt meanwhile identified the total state with the NS state) corresponded to three principles of order: The hierarchical administration of the state (including the civil service and the army); the tightly organized National Socialist Worker Party (drawing members from all social classes); and, finally, the public-juridical sphere of the self-administration of the people (including the economic and social order). Overall, Schmitt positioned the political movement as the basis of the state, Party, and people.

Schmitt held that this tripartite conception of political unity (that is, state, movement, and people) replaced the liberal concept of a rule-of-law state (*Rechtsstaat*). And since the liberal opposition between the state and private individual had lost its sense, there was no longer any need to protect "the help- and defenseless, poor, isolated individual against the powerful 'Leviathan' state."[61] In other words, the combination of the terms "law" and "state" as *Rechtsstaat* reflected the precise dualism of state and society that the NS state sought to overcome.[62] Schmitt thus insisted that the central purpose of the rule of law was to establish legal certainty (*Rechtssicherheit*), something for which the authoritarian Führer state was well-suited.[63]

Schmitt's rival, the legal theorist Otto Koellreutter, rejected the formula of the total state. For him, the fluid boundaries between the total and the totalitarian state were such that also the total state would extend its power to all spheres of life. Koellreutter preferred to conceive of the National Socialist political system as a form of authoritarian state. In contrast to the total or totalitarian state's claim to comprehensive control, the authoritarian state would restrict political influence.

criticizes that Schmitt locates the state, the movement and the people on the same level of order, while for him the essential political and constitutional problem of the National Socialist state is the relation between the Nazi Party and the state. See Koellreutter, Otto, *Grundfragen unserer Volks- und Staatsgestaltung* (Berlin: Junker & Dünnhaupt, 1936), p. 19–20.

[61] Schmitt, *Staat, Bewegung, Volk*, p. 24.

[62] See Schmitt, "Was bedeutet der Streit um den Rechtsstaat?," in *Zeitschrift für die gesamte Staatswissenschaft/Journal of Institutional and Theoretical Economics* 95, 2 (1935), pp. 189–201, here: p. 201. Schmitt criticized that the liberal conception of the *Rechtsstaat* had turned the state into a mere statutory state (*Gesetzesstaat*) by removing all material content of justice. Schmitt claimed that while the liberal conception of the *Rechtsstaat* at least had a "worldview" and was capable of political fighting, the positivistic conception of the *Rechtsstaat* was reduced to relativism, agnosticism and nihilism. Ibid., p. 196.

[63] See Schmitt, Carl, "Der Rechtsstaat," in Frank, Hans (ed.), *Nationalsozialistisches Handbuch für Recht und Gesetzgebung* (München: Zentralverlag der NSDAP, Franz Eher Nachf., 1935), pp. 3–10.

Power could only be exercised in accordance with the people's "nature and kind."[64]

Koellreutter's authoritarian state was anchored in a "communal ethics" that did not allow individual members of the people's community to prioritize their interests and freedom. Conversely, it did not authorize the government to exercise absolute power for its own sake (that is, without taking the needs of the people into account). For Koellreutter, the National Socialist state met these criteria: The Führer's power transcended mere dominance and despotism since political force served the good of the people's community. In contrast to the total state, he wrote, "the essence of the authoritarian state lies in the presence of a state authority borne by the trust of the people."[65] He added that "the mark of any true leadership is that the will of the Führer becomes a natural expression of the people's will."[66]

According to Koellreutter, the constitutive principles for the authoritarian National Socialist state consisted of the following: protection of the people's national order of life;[67] protection of the *Volksgenossen*; firm political leadership and the "normative shaping" of the *völkisch* order;[68] and a shift from private to public law such "that any legal regulation, including the private law one, must ultimately be a communal regulation (*Gemeinschaftsregelung*)."[69]

For Koellreutter, it was critical to conceive of the National Socialist state as a form of authoritarian rule-of-law state, or, more specifically, a national rule-of-law state.[70] An essential feature of a rule-of-law state was that those in power recognized the "value of law" (*Rechtswert*) and sought a proper balance between the law and political authority. A rule-of-law state could not remain in a state of permanent revolution.[71]

64 Koellreutter, Otto, *Grundriß der Allgemeinen Staatslehre* (Tübingen: J.C.B. Mohr [Paul Siebeck], 1933), p. 65 f.

65 Ibid., p. 64. Koellreutter (absurdly) associates a sheer power-oriented state with the liberal state.

66 Ibid., p. 66.

67 Ibid., p. 11.

68 Koellreutter, *Deutsches Verfassungsrecht*, pp. 12–13.

69 Ibid., pp. 15–16.

70 Already in a 1932 publication, Koellreutter had coined the term "national rule-of-law state." See Koellreutter, Otto, *Der nationale Rechtsstaat. Zum Wandel der Deutschen Staatsidee* (Tübingen: J.C.B. Mohr [Paul Siebeck], 1932). In his publications during the early years of the Nazi regime, he continued to use this term, but later he also used the formulation "National Socialist rule-of-law state."

71 Koellreutter, *Grundriß der Allgemeinen Staatslehre*, p. 108. While Koellreutter refers here critically to the Bolshevist state, his rejection of the concept of permanent revolution also

Koellreutter's emphasis on the value of the law could be interpreted as his attempt to place some restrictions on the exercise of power in the NS state. He believed, for example, that the legal position of the individual must be safeguarded within a national conception of law and legal security. The protection of the individual and his/her personal property was necessary for the maintenance of *völkisch* values and life order.[72]

Carl Schmitt's doctoral student, Ernst Rudolf Huber, also contributed to the debate over whether the Führer state should be understood as a total or as an authoritarian state.[73] Although he argued for the former, Huber cautioned that the NS state's "political totality" had to be correctly interpreted, since "total state" might otherwise sound like an endorsement of "brute violence and tyranny" and "organized pure power."[74]

For Huber, the National Socialist state relied upon a particular notion of totality – namely, the "totality of the *völkisch* idea."[75] This denoted a kind of (historical) natural law that determined the order of the state, and which Huber further clarified through Hegelian concepts:

> [T]his political idea is an objective historical law of life, an unchangeable historical mission. In order to be more than just ideology and utopia, but living reality, it still must include the individual. Beyond that, however, it has supra-individual substance. In Hegel's words, it is objective and not merely subjective spirit; it is the people's spirit (*Volksgeist*) and the people's will (*Volkswille*) in the sense of German idealism and romanticism.[76]

Huber also stressed the role of the political movement, arguing that the term "total state" paralleled Ernst Jünger's phrase "total mobilization."[77]

involves a critique of the identification of National Socialism with a revolutionary political movement, an idea foremost cultivated within the SA.

72 Ibid., pp. 105–108.

73 See Huber, Ernst Rudolf, "Die Totalität des völkischen Staates," in *Die Tat* 26, 1 (1934), pp. 30–42. Huber wrote his dissertation with Schmitt (he got his doctoral degree in 1926), but was never Schmitt's assistant, as he himself notes. See Huber, Ernst Rudolf, "Carl Schmitt in der Reichskrise der Weimarer Endzeit," in *Complexio Oppositorum. Über Carl Schmitt. Vorträge und Diskussionsbeiträge des 28. Sonderseminars 1986 der Hochschule für Verwaltungswissenschaften Speyer*, ed. by Quaritsch, Helmut (Berlin: Duncker & Humblot, pp. 33–50, here: p. 35.

74 Ibid., p. 30.

75 Ibid., p. 35.

76 Ibid.

77 Huber pointed out that the idea of the total state had been inspired by Ernst Jünger's "phrase of total mobilization" (he referred to Jünger's book *Krieg und Krieger* from 1930). See Huber, "Die Totalität des völkischen Staates," p. 30. Huber followed here Carl Schmitt who wrote in his 1931 essay "Die Wendung zum totalen Staat" that Ernst Jünger had introduced a "very concise formula", namely "total mobilization", for describing the

Movement for him was a creative force, opposed to the stasis of bureaucratic state organization.[78] The mobilization of all resources of *völkisch* life would produce a state with a homogenous power structure (no separation of powers, no basic rights, no liberal rule of law).

By definition, Huber emphasized, the total state "unite[d] all power in the hands of the Führer" rather than fragmenting it into executive, legislative, and judicial branches.[79] Thus the judiciary, administration, press, broadcasting, and even film, fell under state control. Judges and courts were likewise obliged to make their decisions according to the will of the leadership rather than their subjective discretion.[80] In general, the administration was to align itself with the political goals and will of the state's leaders.

Huber declared that the Führer state should awaken the people's "readiness for service, for the performance of duties, [and] for sacrifice" and impart to them "a common political worldview."[81] He defined this *völkisch* worldview as a frame of mind with awareness of "the objective basic realities of *völkisch* existence (*Dasein*)."[82] "Worldview," Huber elaborated, "is nothing that one could arbitrarily construct and put together; it is found, not built. It is, in its unchangeable core, contained in the essence and mission of the people. The eternal laws and imperishable mission of the people form the essential content of the worldview."[83]

Again, referring to Hegel, Huber wrote:

> "The state is the actuality of the *völkisch* idea" – this is how we might today modify the spirit of Hegel's famous words ["The state is the actuality of the ethical Idea"]. The state is the full form of *völkisch* spirit and *völkisch* being. The totality of the state secures the total idea and the total people. The total *völkisch* state is the lived reality of a political people, characterized by an all-encompassing and all-permeating idea and carried by a leadership core.[84]

emergence of a state encompassing all spheres. See Schmitt, "Die Wendung zum totalen Staat (1931)," in Schmitt, *Positionen und Begriffe im Kampf mit Weimar-Genf-Versailles 1923–1939*, p. 152.

78 Huber, *Verfassungsrecht des Großdeutschen Reiches*, p. 296.

79 Huber, "Die Totalität des völkischen Staates," p. 40.

80 Ibid., p. 41.

81 Huber, *Verfassungsrecht des Großdeutschen Reiches*, p. 294.

82 Ibid.

83 Ibid.

84 Huber, "Die Totalität des völkischen Staates," p. 42. Hegel's famous words to which Huber referred, mark the beginning of the following passage in Hegel's *Philosophy of Right*: "The state is the actuality of the ethical Idea – the ethical spirit as substantial will, *manifest* and clear to itself, which thinks and knows itself and implements what it knows in so far as it knows it." Hegel, G. W. F., *Elements of the Philosophy of Right*, ed. by Wood, Allen W.; transl. by Nisbet, H. B. (Cambridge: Cambridge University Press, 1991),

Huber distinguished between two meanings of the term "people" (*Volk*): people in the sense of an association of human beings shaped by individual interests and selfishness, and people in the sense of a political unity of human beings that arose from common blood and soil and a shared historical mission. As a consequence, the political people in the total state comprised only "humans of the same kind (*artgleiche Menschen*)," which meant persons of the same race.[85]

The connection of the total state to racial homogeneity was emphasized by other defenders of the total state as well. Helmut Nicolai argued that the transition to the total state was marked by the reintroduction of the concept of race into the new German legal system. "In executing the idea of the 'total' state," he wrote, "we are just removing the liberal as well as the Roman idea of law, [and] replacing them again by German legal thought that never included a sphere of freedom in which one was allowed to do whatever one had in mind, but rather conceived all forms of entitlement from the perspective of duty."[86] In everything he did, the individual member of the *Volk* had to ask himself "whether his actions . . . will not violate the task assigned to him as a German."[87]

Forsthoff also considered racial sameness (*artmäßige Gleichartigkeit*) to be integral to the people's community. Although he shared Schmitt's view that the dichotomy of friend and enemy was constitutive for political life, he emphasized that racial differences (*Artverschiedenheiten*) alone would not create political antagonism. Human beings of different races would only become enemies if, "in their otherness, [they] infringe upon the territorial living space (*Lebensraum*) or . . . the spiritual living space of another people."[88]

The NS theoreticians sought to shield the Führer state from any association with excessive coercion or oppression. Their metaphysically

§ 257, p. 275. Huber's reformulation shows how National Socialism merged ethics with *völkisch* ideology. In the total state, the formation of the political will was, Huber argued, independent of voting; it was an expression of the entirety of the people (*Volksganzen*). He remarked critically that since the French Revolution the problem of the *völkisch* will formation had been rationalistically distorted by reducing the formation of the will to an outer rational process. See Huber, *Verfassungsrecht des Großdeutschen Reiches*, p. 295.

85 Ibid., p. 37. Carl Schmitt maintained that the idea of race and racial sameness (*Artgleichheit*) were indispensable for the National Socialist state and its legal system. See Schmitt, *Staat, Bewegung, Volk*, p. 42.

86 See Nicolai, Helmut, *Rasse und Recht. Vortrag gehalten auf dem Deutschen Juristentag des Bundes nationalsozialistischer deutscher Juristen am 2. Oktober 1933 in Leipzig* (Berlin: Reimar Hobbing, 1933), p. 49.

87 Ibid., p. 50.

88 Forsthoff, *Der totale Staat*, p. 39.

elevated notion of the political, tied to a higher order of "law and justice," served to obscure the Nazi leadership's craving for absolute power. Likewise, construing "totality" as an all-encompassing and unifying worldview masked the regime's aggressive struggle for comprehensive control over all members of society. In sum, by accentuating such concepts as the uniform political movement, the unified worldview, and the racially homogeneous community, and by conflating the order of the *Volk* with the Führer order, NS legal thinkers helped to validate the emerging totalitarian form of rule.

Racial ideology was an integral part of legal thought in the Third Reich. In their texts, the legal thinkers not only missed the opportunity to set normative limits to the NS regime's obsession with "racial purity," but they actively prepared the ground for the brutal and murderous persecution of Jewish members of German society.

3.5 The Constitutional Principles of the National Socialist State

Explaining the constitutional foundations of the Third Reich posed a challenge. While never formally repealed, the Weimar Constitution was subverted by such measures as the Reichstag Fire Decree and the Enabling Act.[89] In the first few weeks of Hitler's chancellorship, the democratic constitution had already lost its normative force. But what replaced it?

In his 1939 study of constitutional law in the Third Reich, Ernst Rudolf Huber wrote that "when Reich President v. Hindenburg placed the leadership of the Reich's government into the hands of Adolf Hitler, and when the people affirmed this decision by a majority, the Weimar Constitution was dead."[90] For Huber, the NS state rested on new constitutional foundations, foremost the Law to Remedy the Distress of People and Reich of March 24, 1933 (the Enabling Act) and the Law

[89] For Karl Loewenstein, the Weimar Constitution "though not formally repealed, has been materially abrogated." See Loewenstein, "Dictatorship and the German Constitution," p. 547. According to Ernst Fraenkel, "(t)he constitutional charter of the Third Reich is the Emergency Decree of February 28, 1933." See Fraenkel, *The Dual State*, p. 3.

[90] Huber, *Verfassungsrecht des Großdeutschen Reiches*, p. 52. Already in his 1933 study *Staat, Bewegung, Volk*, Schmitt had declared: "The Weimar Constitution is no longer valid. All principles and regulations that with respect to worldview and organization were essential for this constitution are, together with all their presuppositions, eliminated." Schmitt, *Staat, Bewegung, Volk*, p. 5.

Concerning the Reconstruction of the Reich of January 30, 1934, which eliminated the authority of the federal states.[91]

The problem with this definition of the NS constitution, however, was that both the Enabling Act and the Law for the Reconstruction of the Reich only became law through the application of Article 76 of the Weimar Constitution.[92] Huber was thus obliged to accept that both measures derived from the very constitution he himself had declared dead by the time those laws came into force.

How did Huber cope with this obvious inconsistency? From an external viewpoint, as he put it, the articles of the Weimar Constitution and the basic constitutional laws of the NS state seemed to be directly linked. But Huber then downgraded the normative value of this legal continuity by arguing that, in this special case, "legality" simply amounted to "a superficial bridging of the gap which in truth separated two essentially different orders."[93] The apparent connection between the Weimar Constitution and that of the Nazi state only underscored "the external propriety" of creating the NS legal system.[94] Moreover, Huber asserted, "the real reasons" for the foundational legality of the new state were evident in "the technical functioning of the judiciary and administrative apparatuses."[95]

For Huber, the decisive factor for the normative validity of legal principles was not their formal legality, but their legitimacy, by which

[91] Huber, *Verfassungsrecht des Großdeutschen Reiches*, p. 47. The Law on the Reconstruction of the Reich dissolved the federal parliaments and transferred the sovereign rights of the federal states, that is, its law-making authority, administrative authority, and judicial authority to the Reich. This law increased the political power of the Reich; the federal states ceased to be independent states. For Huber, the Reich was not an alliance of individual states but an expression of "the political unity of the entire, inseparable German people." Ibid., p. 326.

[92] Ibid., p. 47. The way the Enabling Act had come into force was by political manipulation. Article 76 of the Weimar Constitution stated that the constitution could be changed by legislation, however only if two thirds of the deputies to the Reichstag were present when the issue to change the constitution was discussed in the Reichstag, and if, moreover, two thirds of those deputies who were present voted for changing the constitution. De facto, however, the Nazis had excluded the communist members of the Reichstag from the Reichstag session by having outlawed the Communist Party, and only 94 of the 120 Social Democratic deputies to the Reichstag were permitted to attend the meeting. See Loewenstein, "Dictatorship and the German Constitution," pp. 543–544; see also Fischer, *Nazi Germany. A New History*, pp. 276–278.

[93] Huber, *Verfassungsrecht des Großdeutschen Reiches*, p. 49.

[94] Ibid., p. 49.

[95] Ibid.

he meant their congruence with the principles of the NS movement and worldview. "From mere legality," Huber wrote,

> we must distinguish legitimacy [as] the innermost justification of a political or constitutional act. The legitimacy of the laws of March 24, 1933, and January 30, 1934, does not derive from the Weimar Constitution, but from the National Socialist revolution. Those who conclude . . . that the Weimar Constitution is still valid remain wed to the framework of a failed legal formalism, of constitutional positivism and normativism.[96]

In terms of legitimacy, Huber argued that the laws of March 24, 1933 and January 30, 1934 were normatively independent from the former constitution.[97] The legitimacy of the new constitution derived for Huber from the National Socialist *coup d'état*.

A main problem for NS constitutional theorists was that the National Socialist state had no written constitution or even constitutional document.[98] The NS jurists sought to overcome this by simply identifying the constitution with the basic state laws enacted by the regime from 1933 to 1937. In the third edition of his treaty on *German Constitutional Law* (1938), Otto Koellreutter listed the following "constitutional laws of the German Führer state:"

1. The Law to Remedy the Distress of People and Reich of March 24, 1933 (including the law on its extension, January 30, 1937).
2. The Law on the Popular Referendum of July 14, 1933.
3. The Law to Secure the Unity of Party and State of December 1, 1933.
4. The Law for the Reconstruction of the Reich of January 30, 1934.
5. The Law on the Head of the German Reich of August 1, 1934.
6. The Law on Reich Governors of January 30, 1935.
7. The German Communal Ordinance of January 30, 1935.
8. The Law for the Construction of the Wehrmacht of March 16, 1935.
9. The Nuremberg Laws of September 15, 1935: The Reich Flag Law; The Reich Citizenship Law; The Law for the Protection of German Blood and German Honor.
10. The German Public Officials Law of January 26, 1937.[99]

96 Ibid.

97 According to Huber, these laws should not be interpreted as a kind of exceptions from the Weimar Constitution.

98 Repeatedly, the NS theoreticians belittled this fact by pointing out that also Great Britain did not have any written constitution.

99 Koellreutter, *Deutsches Verfassungsrecht*, p. 19. In his 1939 book on the constitutional law of the German Reich, Huber presented a list of constitutional laws that was mainly identical with Koellreutter's list, except that Huber added the Law on the Reunification

According to Koellreutter, the Führer state did not need a written constitution; rather it required "the political and constitutional formation of a body politic by the *volks*-oriented leadership."[100] The above laws would demonstrate how, through the will of the leadership, "the constitution emerges organically from the necessities of the lives of the people and the state, tearing down and eliminating the old state structure."[101]

Koellreutter felt that defining the constitution through the basic laws of the Reich leadership would render all the usual theoretical disputes of liberal constitutional theory meaningless.[102] Hitler's emergency decrees simply had constitutional status. Likewise, Koellreutter insisted that such measures as the deactivation of the Reichstag, prohibition of competing political parties, and the restriction of basic rights had constitutional validity.

A remarkable feature of Koellreutter's list is the constitutional status of the Nuremberg Laws. Koellreutter had no inhibitions in laying bare the racial commitments of the NS state: Maintaining the purity of the race – "both in its positive support of hereditarily healthy families and in its necessary exclusion of the racially inferior from reproduction" – amounted for him to "one of the most important tasks of National Socialist legislation."[103] He openly embraced the aggressive policies toward Jews, including the denial of their basic personal and civic rights and their increasingly violent social exclusion.

The NS theoreticians had a clear understanding of the liberal constitutional state. Consequently, they undertook an ideological redefinition of normative concepts common to liberal-democratic discourse, including freedom, equality, and legitimacy. As Koellreutter argued:

> Precisely because political content and not legal form is decisive, legal concepts and constructions that have become common in the modern world of states may also be used in National Socialist legal thought as long as one completely understands the change in political meaning. . . . It is

with Austria, the Law with the German Sudeten regions and the Memel region as well as the Decree on the Establishment of the Protectorate of Bohemia and Moravia. See Huber, *Verfassungsrecht des Großdeutschen Reiches*, pp. 55–56.

100 Koellreutter, *Deutsches Verfassungsrecht*, p. 20.

101 Ibid., p. 19.

102 Ibid.

103 Ibid., p. 72. Huber confirmed that the Nuremberg racial laws were anchored in the constitution of the NS state. Racial homogeneity was "the natural foundation of the people," and by means of "the Reich Citizenship Law as well as the Law for the Protection of German Blood and German Honor, the natural way of the German people will be secured for all times." Huber, *Verfassungsrecht des Großdeutschen Reiches*, pp. 153–154.

> the duty of responsible National Socialist jurisprudence to give [the legal terms and constructions] the correct *völkisch* content.[104]

Huber's appeal to the concept of legitimacy, as outlined above, offers a vivid example of such a reinterpretation. Assessing the legitimacy of laws requires both a formal and a moral justification of legal regulations: formally they must fulfill the established procedures of law creation, morally they have to comply with fundamental moral values and principles. In democratic legal systems, legitimacy is thus tied to respect for the principles of human dignity, freedom, and equality.

Outwardly, Huber's application of the concept of legitimacy was consistent with the requisite reference to a value system. He used the principle of legitimacy for a substantial approval of NS constitutional laws, but tied this "inner justification of a political or constitutional act" to National Socialist ideology.[105] The break with the Weimar Constitution therefore happened also at the level of value commitments. In the NS state, Huber wrote, democratic basic rights were not only temporarily suspended, "but have been finally eliminated as elements of the constitution because they are not compatible with the principles of the *völkisch* worldview."[106]

In *Behemoth*, his famous 1942 study of National Socialism's structure and practice, Franz Neumann wrote that "a constitution is more than its legal text; it is also a myth demanding loyalty to an externally valid value system."[107] The NS theoreticians invented their own narrative and myth. Their strategy consisted precisely in ingraining the new system into public consciousness by emphasizing the connection between the constitutional laws and the values of the people's community, which were in

[104] Koellreutter, *Deutsches Verfassungsrecht*, p. 23. See also Höhn, Reinhard, *Die Wandlung im staatsrechtlichen Denken* (Hamburg: Hanseatische Verlagsanstalt, 1934); Höhn, Reinhard, *Rechtsgemeinschaft und Volksgemeinschaft* (Hamburg: Hanseatische Verlagsanstalt, 1935).

[105] Huber, *Verfassungsrecht des Großdeutschen Reiches*, p. 56.

[106] Ibid., p. 361. In the National Socialist state also the concept of ownership changed. As Huber wrote: "The owner is obliged toward people and Reich to administer his property in a responsible way. His legal status is only justified if he complies with this responsibility toward the community. … According to its nature and content, property is a warrant connected to the community." Ibid., p. 373. With respect to confiscation, Huber remarked that in the NS state "new, unwritten principles" would hold for so-called confiscation, principles that necessarily derived from the fact that property was tied to obligation. Ibid., p. 376.

[107] Neumann, Franz, *Behemoth. The Structure and Practice of National Socialism 1933–1944*, with an introduction by Peter Hayes (Chicago: Ivan R. Dee, 2009), p. 8.

turn defined in accordance with the political-ideological ends of National Socialism.[108]

3.6 The Normative Status of the Führer

The Weimar Republic's shift toward a presidential system in the period from September 14, 1930 to January 30, 1933, proved normatively fateful. Hitler's first measures as Chancellor simply continued the practice of ruling through presidential emergency decrees, thus creating the impression of political and legal continuity. In fact, he used those decrees under Article 48 to secure dictatorial power.

When Hitler assumed the powers of Reich President after Hindenburg's death on August 2, 1934, the process of institutional coordination (*Gleichschaltung*) was nearly complete. The Führer, moreover, took great pains to link himself to the symbolic aura, or "myth," that had surrounded Hindenburg since his World War I heroism.[109] Hitler further profited from the normative status jurists had already ascribed to the Reich President in the late Weimar period.

In his book *The Guardian of the Constitution* (1931), Carl Schmitt had argued that the President was the guardian of the state's constitution. By virtue of embodying the offices of both the Chancellor and President after Hindenburg's death, Hitler assumed this role.[110] His position, in short, was beyond judicial review. Schmitt openly attributed to Hitler the normative function of a guardian of law and justice.[111] This power was accentuated by the fact that the Führer was appointed for life and could

[108] As Koellreutter noted: "The difference of the nature of National Socialist constitutional law lies in the change of its political foundations and in the *völkisch* understanding of the essence of the political." Koellreutter, *Deutsches Verfassungsrecht*, p. 22.

[109] See von der Goltz, Anna, *Hindenburg. Power, Myth, and the Rise of the Nazis* (Oxford: Oxford University Press, 2009).

[110] See Schmitt, Carl, *Der Hüter der Verfassung* (1931), 4th ed. (Berlin: Duncker & Humblot, 1996); parts of this text (pp. 73–91 and 149–159) are translated into English by Lars Vinx; see "The guardian of the constitution: Schmitt on pluralism and the President as the guardian of the constitution," in Vinx, Lars (ed.), *The Guardian of the Constitution. Hans Kelsen and Carl Schmitt on the Limits of Constitutional Law* (Cambridge: Cambridge University Press, 2015), pp. 125–173.

[111] The extent to which Schmitt was willing to endorse the Führer's power after the Nazi takeover was drastically shown by his notorious text "The Führer Protects the Law," where Schmitt declared the murders ordered by Hitler in the course of the Röhm purge on June 30th, 1934 to be legitimate and necessary for maintaining the state's order and security. See Schmitt, "The Führer Protects the Law. On Adolf Hitler's Reichstag Address 13 July 1934," in *The Third Reich Sourcebook*, pp. 63–67. For the German original text see Schmitt, "Der Führer schützt das Recht. Zur Reichstagsrede von Adolf Hitler vom 13.

not be removed from office. He had legislative authority and was the highest court instance.

The NS jurists justified this accumulation of power by the ostensible political unity and stability it could grant. In their view, the Führer state compensated for the "power vacuum" of the former parliamentary system through the dualism of a President who stood above party politics and a head of government who conducted business.[112] Nothing should impede the unity of the Führer's office. Huber himself claimed that the classical separation of powers into "law-making state, judicial state, [and] executive state" no longer made sense.[113] Rather, it was "crucial that supreme political leadership lies completely in the hands of one man: one *Volk*, one *Reich*, one *Führer*!"[114]

Obviously, this rhetorical conjuration of a unitary state was belied by the polycentric structure of the Third Reich, in which the Führer's roles as President, Chancellor, and NS Party leader had counterparts in the Presidential Chancellery, Reich Chancellery, and Führer Chancellery.[115] Huber dismissed this compartmentalization as a mere "organizational-technical separation of areas of activity, which does not call into question the essential unity of the office."[116] The Führer's power, he insisted, was total. It thus obliged all members of society to loyalty and obedience and demanded a "political-charismatic" understanding of the Führer's position and standing.[117] Like Hindenburg, claimed NS jurist Manfred Fauser, the Führer saw himself "as a tool of a higher power and as trustee" of his people.[118]

This interpretation of the state had important implications for parliament. Under no circumstances, NS theorists argued, should the Führer's

Juli 1934," in *Deutsche Juristen-Zeitung*, 39, 15, 1934; reprinted in Schmitt, *Positionen und Begriffe im Kampf mit Weimar-Genf-Versailles 1923–1939*, pp. 199–203.

112 Huber, *Verfassungsrecht des Großdeutschen Reiches*, pp. 30–37.

113 Ibid., p. 236.

114 Ibid., p. 216.

115 The Presidential Chancellery was managed by Otto Meißner, the Reich Chancellery was led by Hans Heinrich Lammers, and the Chancellery of the Führer was managed by Philipp Bouhler. Besides these three institutions, there existed from 1941 on also the Chancellery of the Nazi Party, led by Martin Bormann. The Chancellery of the Führer was (besides handling mercy appeals by members of the Nazi Party and granting exceptions to the marriage regulations imposed by the Nuremberg Laws) responsible for enforced sterilizations, based on the Law for the Prevention of Hereditarily Diseased Offspring of 14, 1933 (*Gesetz zur Verhütung erbkranken Nachwuchses*). The Chancellery of the Führer was then involved in the euthanasia program and the murder of handicapped persons (action T4).

116 Huber, *Verfassungsrecht des Großdeutschen Reiches*, p. 230.

117 Ibid., p. 213.

118 Fauser, "Das Gesetz im Führerstaat," p. 134.

authority be restricted by the decisions of parliamentary majorities, which could never represent the people as a whole.[119] The parliamentary model of legislation, so their critique stated, had only led to constant tension, party struggles, and the "tyranny of the majority."

A "political concept of law" would replace constitutionally defined procedural forms of lawmaking.[120] In Koellreutter's words, law in the National Socialist state was "the leadership's political will arrayed in the form of law-making."[121] Or as Huber summarized it:

> Law has ceased to be an act of an autonomous, independent bourgeois parliament; it has turned into a constructive instrument of the political leadership. All legislative power in the new Reich reverts to the Führer's decision, regardless of whether it concerns government laws, Reichstag laws, or laws passed by the people. The bearer of legislative power is thus always the Führer himself.[122]

NS jurists further claimed that the Führer state demanded leadership that transcended formal legality and recognized an idea of justice above the law. The Führer's will should be tied to justice in a *völkisch* sense.[123] Karl Larenz explained this principle thus:

> There is no need for any guarantee that he [the Führer] will maintain justice, since by virtue of his being the Führer he is the "*guardian of the constitution*," which in this case means the guardian of *the unwritten, concrete idea of law (Rechtsidee) of his people*. Thus, a law or legal statute emanating from his will cannot be subject to judicial review.[124]

119 See Nicolai, Helmut, *Grundlagen der kommenden Verfassung. Über den staatsrechtlichen Aufbau des Dritten Reiches* (Berlin: Reimar Hobbing GmbH, 1933), p. 73. As already mentioned in Chapter 2.4 of this book, the Weimar system did not include a constitutional court. The NS state evidently had even less reason for establishing such an institution.

120 Huber, *Verfassungsrecht des Großdeutschen Reiches*, p. 239.

121 Koellreutter, *Deutsches Verfassungsrecht*, p. 57. According to Fauser, law in the NS state had changed from a "compromise-based decision by a coincidental parliamentary majority" to an "act of the will of the political leadership." The "distinction between law-making and executive or ruling power" had lost its significance. Fauser, "Das Gesetz im Führerstaat," p. 136.

122 Huber, *Verfassungsrecht des Großdeutschen Reiches*, p. 237.

123 Ibid., p. 244. "(T)he Führer's will as it is manifest in the law" could be, as Huber emphasized, "nothing other than the conscious and forged form of *völkisch* justice." Ibid. Nicolai justified the transfer of legislative power to the Führer with the assertion that he "has greater knowledge and more expansive experience" than the parliament. Nicolai, *Grundlagen der kommenden Verfassung*, p. 87.

124 Larenz, Karl, *Rechtserneuerung und Rechtsphilosophie* (Tübingen: J.C.B. Mohr [Paul Siebeck], 1934), p. 34 (italics in the original).

Rather, legal statutes were now to be interpreted according to National Socialist principles and the Führer's legislative will, both of which were informed by Nazi racial ideology. Fauser thus maintained that the precondition for any correct interpretation "of the values brought to expression by the law" was "that law-maker and law-user are of the same racial kind (*Artgleichheit*)."[125]

Three kinds of laws were authoritative in the NS state: laws passed by the Reichstag, governmental laws, and laws passed by the people.[126] The NS legal thinkers, however, argued that the Führer's legislative competence also included manifests, decrees, and measures. Fauser even held that "general statements by the political leadership," such as Führer speeches, might create law.[127]

Yet Fauser was not willing to give *carte blanche* to the Führer's arbitrariness. He qualified his position on the unitary state by arguing that not any expression of the leadership's will could be legally binding since that would just lead to undesirable confusion in public life. Fauser further stressed that explanation, justification, and publicity were important for legislative action.[128] Likewise, Koellreutter held that not every expression of the leadership's political will would constitute a legal norm or statute – only those enacted in the form of publicized legislation could qualify.[129]

Their deep ideological commitments notwithstanding, several NS theoreticians tried to set some minimal limits on the impending despotism. Even a devoted Nazi like Helmut Nicolai could demand that legislation had to rely upon stable procedures to distinguish it from "purely private expressions of will."[130] Yet given the Führer's tight grip on legislative power, such demands were no more than wishful thinking. In the end, Nicolai had to satisfy himself with a call for "steadiness and calm in legislation and legal life," and with the knowledge that the Führer may diverge "at will" from any laws presented to him by the Reichstag.[131]

125 Fauser, "Das Gesetz im Führerstaat," p. 142.

126 Publication in the *Reichsgesetzblatt* was still required. The difference between legal and administrative regulations was also kept. Also, a decree was considered a legal source in the National Socialist state.

127 Fauser, "Das Gesetz im Führerstaat," p. 137. As an example, Fauser mentioned the Führer's speeches.

128 Ibid., p. 139. Similarly, Huber noted that the "*völkisch* Reich cannot do without a constant appeal to the people." Huber, *Verfassungsrecht des Großdeutschen Reiches*, p. 239.

129 Koellreutter, *Deutsches Verfassungsrecht*, p. 57.

130 Nicolai, *Grundlagen der kommenden Verfassung*, p. 86.

131 Ibid., p. 89.

One way in which the regime gave lip service to legal norms and popular opinion was through referenda. From 1933 to 1938, referenda were held on Germany leaving the League of Nations (November 12, 1933), fusing the offices of Reich Chancellor and President (August 19, 1934), and on annexing Austria to the Reich (March 1938). Each of these referenda were farcical given that the issue in question had already been settled and freedom of expression was all but eliminated.

Nevertheless, the NS jurists' depiction and defense of those referenda is illuminating. For Huber, their purpose was "to call up and engage the entire living people for a political goal set by the Führer."[132] By holding a referendum, he argued, the Führer did not forfeit his power of political decision-making so much as gain "unity and agreement . . . between the objective will of the people embodied by the Führer and the subjective conviction of the people as it resided in individual members."[133] The August 19, 1934 referendum, in reality a rubber stamp for Hitler's seizure of the functions of Reich Chancellor and President, was for Huber no less than an active affirmation of the "trust that has become the essential foundation of German constitutional life."[134] In a similar manner, Huber defended elections to the Reichstag (which were held until 1938) on the basis of a single NSDAP list by openly avowing that rejecting the NSDAP equated to "self-exclusion from political life."[135]

After the Führer principle, the people's community principle (*Volksgemeinschaftsprinzip*) was the second source of law. When faced with the delicate question of whether the Führer principle preceded or was equal to the community principle, the NS jurists sidestepped the problem by claiming that the Führer had the epistemic competence of knowing exactly what was best for the people and how German continuity and prosperity were best secured. The Führer thus was a direct expression of the will of the people, more so, he was identical with it.[136]

Although comprehensive power was conferred upon the Führer, NS jurists insisted that his personal qualities would guard against his abuse of that power. The Führer's authority was, so the rhetoric, neither autocratic nor arbitrary. Rather, Huber claimed, "it comes from the people – i.e., it has been entrusted to the Führer by the people, it exists for the sake of the

132 Huber, *Verfassungsrecht des Großdeutschen Reiches*, p. 200.
133 Ibid.
134 Ibid., p. 217.
135 Ibid., p. 203.
136 See Majer, Diemut, *Grundlagen des nationalsozialistischen Rechtssystems. Führerprinzip, Sonderrecht, Einheitspartei* (Stuttgart, Berlin, Köln, Mainz: Kohlhammer, 1987), p. 118.

people, its justification stems from the people. It is free of all outward ties because in its inner essence it is most strongly tied to the fate, welfare, task, and honor of the people."[137]

This way of defending the Führer's absolute authority was a direct consequence of the missing control mechanisms in the NS state. A political leadership that allegedly had full insight into the *völkisch* order came to dictate what it considered to be good and right. The Führer's decrees and orders amounted to legal statutes that had to be obeyed out of a deep sense of loyalty and ethical commitment. NS ideology blended legal and ethical duties. Ethics, law, and politics coincided in this distorted normative world.[138]

3.7 Concluding Remarks

The legal thinkers in line with the NS regime portrayed the Third Reich as a state that was beyond political arbitrariness, violence, and terror. They used the aura and authority of the juridical discipline for a professional normalization of what de facto represented a new form of political and legal transgression. Formulas such as "total state," the "unified national people's state," or the "national rule-of-law state" upheld the Third Reich as a particular kind of unified state. The NS jurists borrowed concepts from classical political theory such as "common will," "collective will," and "popular sovereignty" to legitimate the NS state politically, knowing full well that neither its structure nor constitution complied with common state conceptions. Furthermore, they acquiesced in the regime's violations of established normative standards, which were apparent as early as February/March 1933. Overall, the jurists provided the theoretical foundations for a state apparatus based upon the principles of National Socialism, including its notorious racial ideology and the quasi mythical status of the Führer.

Despite their deference to the Nazi regime, some NS jurists still strove in the 1930s to promulgate legislation that minimally satisfied such

[137] Huber, *Verfassungsrecht des Großdeutschen Reiches*, p. 230. If the state, as Theodor Maunz argued, "does not serve the people's community," then it will become "a dead mechanism when the political situation is unhealthy." Maunz, Theodor, "Die Staatsaufsicht," in Höhn, Maunz, Swoboda (eds.), *Grundfragen der Rechtsauffassung*, pp. 45–85, here p. 60.

[138] This internal commitment to an "NS ethos," symbolically reinforced by the oath to the Führer (for example, in the Wehrmacht), allowed for rigorous implementation of Führer orders and explains (at least in part) why orders were still obeyed in the war though the NS regime's horrendous crimes became obvious.

criteria as publicity, predictability, and feasibility. The jurists seriously underestimated the regime's potential to defy all rules and norms. Moreover, Hitler's idiosyncratic leadership style undermined attempts to establish stable normative structures, including clear regulations of permissions, restrictions, and prohibitions.[139] The conditions of war only accelerated these normative transgressions. Even by the standards of ideologically loyal jurists, many of Hitler's wartime orders no longer deserved the name "law." The conditions of publicity and predictability had been too gravely violated.

At the same time, the legal theoreticians contributed significantly to these developments by deliberately binding the foundations of the state to the ideological and political ideas of the Nazi movement. In accepting the principle of the unity of Party and state, they elevated Party law into that of the state.[140] They also justified the conferral of extensive powers to the Führer as part of a new political order that allegedly surpassed the old system in strength, unity, and justice. The NS jurists willingly entrusted all state competencies to one individual.

This endorsement of totalitarian power was motivated by the jurists' deep antipathy toward democracy - an attitude akin to a normative reversal, if not perversion, of Aristotle's thesis that it is better to be ruled by the best laws than by the best man.[141]

[139] See Kershaw, Ian, *The Nazi Dictatorship. Problems and Perspectives of Interpretation*, 4th ed. (London: Arnold, 2000), pp. 69–92.

[140] See Koellreutter, *Deutsches Verfassungsrecht*, p. 59.

[141] Fauser saw the NS state free from this Aristotelian maxim. See Fauser, "Das Gesetz im Führerstaat," p. 129.

4

National Socialist Criminal Law

4.1 First Impulses for Criminal Law Reform

Criminal law is a state's main instrument to regulate the actions of society members. How criminal law is defined and understood thus determines whether and to what extent a state respects or denigrates the legal status and claims of its citizens. The state's response to violations of the law may not constitute an arbitrary exercise of power, but it must conform with the rule of law. Questions of liability and guilt have to be established in accordance with due process – that is, citizens are aware of the charges against them and entitled to fair and impartial court procedures that assess the facts. Finally, sentencing should produce proportionate punishments.

All these normative conditions were violated by the Nazi regime, which transformed criminal law into a blunt political instrument to control, even terrorize, its subjects. Rather than constituting a state's judicial means to protect citizens, criminal law under the Nazis targeted those "criminals" perceived to threaten the purity of the people's community (*Volksgemeinschaft*) and the inviolability of the regime's authority. These effects became particularly pronounced in wartime, when the judiciary increasingly forfeited its competencies to the police, foremost the Secret State Police, the Gestapo.

Criminal law theory prepared the ground for these developments. Immediately after the Nazis' rise to power in 1933, intense discussion arose among NS legal thinkers (including prominent university professors and high-ranking officials in the Ministry of Justice) about how to replace the liberal criminal law of the Weimar Republic with a system that met the political and ideological ends of the Nationalist Socialist state. In other words, they sought ways to transform criminal law so that not only violations of legal statutes would be targeted and punished, but also infringements of duties of loyalty (crimes of omission) toward the people's community.[1]

From the mid-1930s, the view prevailed among jurists that a will-based criminal law would best match the National Socialist worldview.[2] For such a law, the perpetrator's criminal will, rather than the actual result of his or her offense, is decisive for assessing accountability and guilt. The future criminal law should thus focus not just on deeds, but on a perpetrator's convictions and attitudes.

The following writings were programmatically crucial for the ideology-driven reform of criminal law in the NS state.

(a) The 1933 memorandum by the Prussian Minister of Justice, Hanns Kerrl, titled *National Socialist Criminal Law* (a second edition appeared in 1934);[3]
(b) the 1934 *Memorandum of the Central Committee of the Criminal Law Department of the Academy of German Law on the Basic Features of a General German Criminal Law*, published as part of a series by the Academy of German Law (series editor: Hans Frank);[4]
(c) the two-volume edition *The Coming German Criminal Law. Report on the work of the Official Criminal Law Commission*, edited by the Minister of Justice, Franz Gürtner;[5] and

[1] The Introduction to the "Draft of the German Penal Code 1936" described this new direction in the following way: "For National Socialism, the German *Volk* is content and sense of all state measures. . . . National Socialism replaces the former protection of the single person and his economic well-being with the protection of this fate-bound *völkisch* community (*Schicksalsgemeinschaft*), i.e., in its existence, honor, living power, and its external life order." See "Begründung zum Entwurf eines Deutschen Strafgesetzbuchs von 1936," in *Quellen zur Reform des Straf- und Strafprozeßrechts*, vol. 1.2, *Entwürfe eines Strafgesetzbuchs*, ed. by Regge, Jürgen and Schubert, Werner (Berlin, New York: Walter de Gruyter, 1990), p. 1. See also Günther, Klaus, "Von der Rechts- zur Pflichtverletzung," in *Vom unmöglichen Zustand des Strafrechts*, ed. by Institut für Kriminalwissenschaften (Frankfurt am Main: Peter Lang, 1995), pp. 445–460, esp. pp. 452–456.

[2] This is not to say that no disagreements existed among NS legal theoreticians. The vicissitude of the Nazi regime's ideology generated permanent discussions about how to define and articulate the new course and structure of criminal law.

[3] *Nationalsozialistisches Strafrecht. Denkschrift des Preußischen Justizministers*, ed. by Kerrl, Hanns (Berlin: R. v. Decker, G. Schenck, 1934).

[4] Freisler/ Oetker/ Dürr/ Schwarz/ Schoetensack/ Thierack/ Noack/ Mayer/Strauß, *Grundzüge eines Allgemeinen Deutschen Strafrechts. Denkschrift des Zentralausschusses der Strafrechtsabteilung der Akademie für Deutsches Recht über die Grundzüge eines Allgemeinen Deutschen Strafrechts* (Berlin: R. v. Decker, G. Schenck, 1934).

[5] *Das kommende deutsche Strafrecht. Allgemeiner Teil. Bericht über die Arbeit der amtlichen Strafrechtskommission*, ed. by Gürtner, Franz, 2nd revised ed. (Berlin: Franz Vahlen;

(d) the two volumes of *National Socialist Guidelines for a New German Criminal Law*, edited by the NSDAP's Legal Office.[6] These instructions by the Nazi Party's law department set the ideological tone and political direction for the criminal law reform (a point I address in section 4.2 of this chapter).

The memorandum edited by Hanns Kerrl provided the first clues of the new direction that criminal law was to take. In particular, the protection of the people's community and its ethical values was emphasized. There was also a prominent shift from the offense itself to the offender's intentions. The Kerrl memorandum did not clearly distinguish between a threat-focused criminal law (*Gefährdungsstrafrecht*) and a perpetrator-focused criminal law. The difficulty of taking a mere threat as a criterion of criminal punishment inspired the Nazi legal theorists' turn toward a will-based criminal law in combination with a perpetrator-typology.

The most important theoretical impetus for the criminal law reform came from the two-volume *Das kommende deutsche Strafrecht*, published by Minister of Justice Franz Gürtner in his role as head of the Official Commission of Criminal Law Reform (*Amtliche Kommission für die Strafrechtsreform*). Established upon Hitler's orders in late 1933,[7] the commission eventually favored a will-based criminal law that assumed a direct connection between the dangerous criminal intention and the committed offense.[8] In 1935, the commission accomplished a further

1935); *Das kommende deutsche Strafrecht. Besonderer Teil. Bericht über die Arbeit der amtlichen Strafrechtskommission*, ed. by Gürtner, Franz, 2nd revised ed. (Berlin: Franz Vahlen, 1936).

6 *Nationalsozialistische Leitsätze für ein neues deutsches Strafrecht. 1.Teil*, 4th ed., ed. by Frank, Hans, Reichsleiter/Reichsrechtsamt der NSDAP (Berlin: Deutsche Rechts- und Wirtschaftswissenschaft Verlags-Ges., 1935); *Nationalsozialistische Leitsätze für ein neues deutsches Strafrecht. 2. (Besonderer) Teil*, ed. by Frank, Hans, Reichsleiter/ Reichsrechtsamt der NSDAP (Berlin: Deutsche Deutsche Rechts- und Wirtschaftswissenschaft Verlags-Ges., 1936).

7 Members of the commission were: Justice Minister Gürtner, the President of the *Volksgerichtshof* Thierack, the State Secretaries Schlegelberger and Freisler, the ministry officials Dürr, Grau, E. Schäfer, L. Schäfer, K. Schäfer, Leimer, Lorenz, Niethammer, Rietzsch, also the criminal law scholars Dahm, Dohnanyi, Gleispach, Henkel, Kohlrausch, Mezger, Nagler, and Schaffstein. The commissions met 107 times between November 1933 and October 1936, and presented two draft versions of the new criminal law in the period 1934–1935. See Hartl, Benedikt, *Das nationalsozialistische Willensstrafrecht* (Berlin: Weißensee, 2000), pp. 71–75.

8 This is underlined by two extensive contributions by Roland Freisler to the *Allgemeiner Teil* and the *Besonderer Teil* of the criminal law, where Freisler sketched the basic lines of a will-based criminal law. See Freisler, Roland, "Willensstrafrecht; Versuch und Vollendung," in *Das kommende deutsche Strafrecht. Allgemeiner Teil* (1935), pp. 5–48,

major change in criminal jurisdiction by officially allowing analogy in criminal law.

While leading legal theorists actively contributed to the National Socialist reform of criminal law, there were naturally differences of opinion concerning how to align the penal code with National Socialist principles.[9] Quite often, criminal law theoreticians and jurists were torn between their professional juridical expertise and the ideological prerogative of National Socialism, not to mention the requirement to meet the Führer's own expectations. Yet in the end politics prevailed over professional reservations.

The regime, however, did not reward jurists' political servility. Their six-year work on an extensive criminal law overhaul was dismissed by Hitler in mid-December 1939, when he refused to sign the Justice Ministry's newly drafted criminal law code.[10] Hitler's foot-dragging over legal regulations is legendary, and the outbreak of war in September 1939 only increased his reluctance to accept any kind of normative restrictions on his exercise of power. Acknowledging a clearly articulated canon of legal norms and statutes would have limited the regime's grip on criminal law jurisdiction.[11]

Despite the jurists' failure to get their revised criminal law officially approved, the intense theoretical debate over how to adapt criminal law to National Socialism's political ends had a remarkable impact on

here: p. 11–48; see also Freisler, Roland, "Aufbau und Aufgabe des Besonderen Teils. Gestaltung seiner Tatbestände. Einbau des Schutzes der Bewegung in das Gesetz," in *Das kommende deutsche Strafrecht. Besonderer Teil* (1936), pp. 13–77. Freisler, a fanatic National Socialist, was one of the most passionate supporters of a will-based criminal law, and certainly had a strong influence on the Gürtner commission.

9 The deliberations of the Official Commission of Criminal Law Reform under Gürtner were paramount; the discussions of the Academy of German Law's Committee of Criminal Law were also important. See the protocols of this latter committee in *Akademie für Deutsches Recht 1933–1945. Protokolle der Ausschüsse*, ed. by Schubert, Werner, vol. VII, Ausschüsse für Strafprozeßrecht und Strafrechtsangleichung 1934–1941 (Frankfurt am Main: Peter Lang, 1998) and vol. VIII, Ausschüsse für Strafrecht, Strafvollstreckungsrecht, Wehrstrafrecht, Strafgerichtsbarkeit der SS und des Reichsarbeitsdienstes, Polizeirecht sowie für Wohlfahrts- und Fürsorgerecht (Bewahrungsrecht) (Frankfurt am Main: Peter Lang, 1999).

10 See Gruchmann, Lothar, *Justiz im Dritten Reich 1933–1940. Anpassung und Unterwerfung in der Ära Gürtner* (München: R. Oldenbourg, 1988), p. 821. See also Hartl, *Das nationalsozialistische Willensstrafrecht*, p. 277.

11 Hitler often expressed contempt for the jurists. His strategy was to use the work of jurists if appeal to juridical language and arguments was useful for covering the brutality of the regime's actions by a deceptive veil of legality, but to dismiss legal regulations if they amounted to unwelcome restrictions on his political plans.

jurisdiction in the Third Reich. The legal theorists' widely shared endorsement of a will-based criminal law led to an interest in criminal character and to the development of a perpetrator typology. The basic idea was that specific types of criminal offenders (the murderer, the habitual criminal, the traitor) possessed an inner propensity for criminality. The state's task was thus to recognize those predispositions and to prevent their realization in criminal acts. Consequently, legal theorists promoted tightened criminal law measures.

The moralization of criminal law and the ensuing elimination of the distinction between ethical and legal norms broadened the coercive power of the NS state. Ethical duties whose regulation the liberal-democratic state had entrusted to the subject's own conscience now became legal obligations, and violations of ethical obligations toward the people's community counted as violations of the law. This merger of ethical and legal duties not only blurred the lines between ethical decency and integrity on the one hand, and criminality on the other, but even "right" and "wrong" were now determined by NS ideology, with tragic consequences for countless people.

4.2 Ideological Guidelines for Criminal Law in the Third Reich

The Nazi Party's Legal Office openly supported an ethos-based criminal law. This ideological directive was most forcefully expressed in its published *National Socialist Guidelines for a New German Criminal Law*:

> In criminal law, the dominating idea of the people's community (*Volksgemeinschaft*), of loyalty, duty, honor, and just atonement, as well as the equilibrium with the legal and ethical sentiments of the people's community, should find its expression in obligations of the highest regard.[12]
>
> National Socialist criminal law must be based on the duty of loyalty to the people's community. Within National Socialist and German thinking, loyalty to the people's community amounts to the highest *völkisch* duty and, thus, to the highest ethical duty. In German thinking there is harmony between ethical valuation, the sentiment of obligation, and the sense of legality and justice.[13]

The basic principle of the new criminal law was the duty of loyalty toward Führer, state, and people. Otto Georg Thierack, a fanatic National Socialist

[12] "Leitsätze zum nationalsozialistischen Strafrecht," in *Nationalsozialistische Leitsätze für ein neues deutsches Strafrecht. 1.Teil*, p. 12.

[13] Ibid.

and the Reich's Justice Minister from 1942 to 1945, expressed this idea emphatically at the conference of the NS Jurists' Association in 1936:

> Loyalty (*Treue*) is the noblest German hereditary good. It is a pillar of our state edifice and ensures the tight solidarity of the *Volk* against the internal and external enemy. Only the loyalty of followers guarantees the Führer the success of his work and gives him the indispensable joy that comes with his responsibility. Therefore, the violation and breach of loyalty amounts to a betrayal of the entire people's community, which in serious cases can only be atoned by the honorless death of the traitor.[14]

The fight against criminality was a fight against the betrayal of the people's community. Accordingly, punishment constituted atonement for breaching loyalty toward the *Volk*. Its goal was to sanction the "unfaithful and traitorous member of the *Volk*."[15] Punitive measures thus included ostracism (*Ächtung*) from the people's community and the loss of honor (*Ehrverlust*).

In this regard, it was crucial to suspend the separation of law and morality. Since National Socialist morality was based on the community's values, any deviation from the communal value order could, in principle, be interpreted as a violation of law, indeed as a criminal offense. In particular, notions of "honor" and "loyalty" served to bolster the state's hold on citizens' inner attitudes and conscience. The declared end of the *NS Guidelines* was to strengthen and enforce individual commitment to the NS worldview.

This remarkable moralization of criminal law is also apparent in the description of particular crimes and appropriate sentencing in the second volume of the *National Socialist Guidelines for a New German Criminal Law*. According to Article 6, "the determination of legal sentences must start from the disloyal attitude and mindset (*Gesinnung*) of the perpetrator and his realization in action. The protection of abstract legal goods (*abstrakte Rechtsgüter*) as a basic principle [of criminal law] must be rejected."[16]

The Nazi Party thus promoted a conviction-based criminal law (*Gesinnungsstrafrecht*) in which the inner attitude of the perpetrator was paramount. This represented a noticeable shift away from fact-based criminal law.

[14] Thierack, Otto Georg, "Sinn und Bedeutung der Richtlinien für die Strafrechtsreform," in *Deutscher Juristentag 1936, 5. Reichstagung des Bundes National-Sozialistischer Deutscher Juristen*, ed. by National-Sozialistischer Rechtswahrer-Bund (Berlin: Deutscher Rechts-Verlag, 1936), pp. 25–30, here: p. 27.

[15] Ibid.

[16] *Nationalsozialistische Leitsätze für ein neues deutsches Strafrecht. 2. (Besonderer) Teil*, p. 129.

As attitude-based offenses gained in importance, the protection of legal goods like life, liberty, and property – so cherished by liberal criminal law – became less viable in the eyes of the Nazi Party's Legal Office. Several NS legal theorists supported this. Roland Freisler, State Secretary in the Justice Ministry and from 1942 to 1945 notorious President of the People's Court, dismissed the notion of a legal good by arguing that the basic values of *völkisch* life were not external goods possessed by individuals, but rather "essential life necessities."[17] He spoke of "basic legal values" (*Grundwerte des Rechts*), namely race, honor, labour, soil, and state.[18]

The Nazi Party put particular emphasis on "crimes against the substance of the *Volk*," which comprised treason against the people, treason against the Party, crimes against the people's race and strength (*Volkskraft*), and crimes against honor and the National Socialist worldview.[19] By specifying treason against the Party, the Nazis effectively criminalized their political adversaries. This is confirmed in the National Socialist Criminal Law Guidelines: "Attacks on the [NS] movement that are based not on a treacherous attitude toward the *Volk*, but on political antagonism, must also be punished as grave violations of loyalty."[20]

The connection between criminal law and racial ideology broadened the range of criminality. Crimes against the race and strength of the people, for example, included "assaults on substantive biological values" such as genetic makeup (*Erbgut*), procreation, and the people's health, as well as "breaches of sexual morality."[21] The "combination of racial genetic makeup and species-alien hereditary makeup," and the

[17] Freisler, "Aufbau und Aufgabe des Besonderen Teils, Gestaltung seiner Tatbestände. Einbau des Schutzes der Bewegung in das Gesetz," in *Das kommende deutsche Strafrecht. Besonderer Teil* (1936), p. 16. Freisler's radical critique of the concept "legal good" (*Rechtsgut*) which was also shared by the jurists at Kiel University (the so-called *Kieler Schule*), particularly by Schaffstein, did not find general consensus among NS legal scholars. The Official Commission for the Reform of Criminal Law (*Amtliche Strafrechtskommission*) continued to use the concept of a legal good. See Lüken, Erhard-Josef, *Der Nationalsozialismus und das materielle Strafrecht. Ein Beitrag zur Strafrechtsgeschichte* (Dissertation, Universität Göttingen, 1988), pp. 40–41.

[18] Freisler, Roland, *Nationalsozialistisches Recht und Rechtsdenken* (Berlin: Spaeth & Linde, 1938) p. 57.

[19] *Nationalsozialistische Leitsätze für ein neues deutsches Strafrecht. 2. (Besonderer) Teil*, p. 131. Treason (*Volksverrat*) was defined as attack against the "political unity, freedom and power of the German *Volk*." Ibid. And the section "Honor and Worldview" (*Ehre und Weltanschauung*) stated: "Honor and worldview of the German people are its innermost, ethical, and racial centers of power from which it builds its Reich and forms its life." Ibid., p. 134.

[20] *Nationalsozialistische Leitsätze für ein neues deutsches Strafrecht. 2. (Besonderer) Teil*, p. 132.

[21] Ibid., p. 133.

procreation of "unhealthy genetic material," also constituted criminal offenses.[22]

The third category of "crimes against the substance of the *Volk*" concerned "crimes against honor and worldview." These included betrayals of honor (*Ehrverrat*), attacks on the Nazi worldview, and attacks on the "religious sentiments of the German people" (despite the fact that the Party rejected the protection of religious communities and their institutions by way of criminal law sanctions).[23] Why NS law addressed the protection of religious sentiments at all can be explained by the state's readiness to mobilize all possible resources in support of its moralizing pathos, especially if they helped neutralize politically adverse religious movements. In this way, the National Socialist Criminal Law Guidelines noticeably restricted the violation of religious feelings, stating that the "need of atonement comprises all attacks on religious communities insofar as their convictions do not contradict the ethical and moral feelings of the German race."[24]

Interestingly, the ideological stipulations of the Nazi Party's Law Office seemed even too ambitious for legal theorists who otherwise fully embraced National Socialism. The fanatic Nazi jurist Freisler feared that the Party's legal guidelines would put future criminal law on "an extraordinarily narrow foundation." And he objected to basing the "*völkisch* ethical order on a single ethical value" (namely, loyalty and fidelity),[25] since not all criminal wrongdoing would entail a breach of loyalty justifying a loss of honor. Specifically, offenses due to negligence would not fit that categorization.[26]

22 Ibid. The relation between racial doctrine and criminal law was not only endorsed by the *Reichsrechtsamt* of the NSDAP, but also by the Academy of German Law. Saxon's Minister of Justice, Otto Georg Thierack (from 1942 on the Reich's Minister of Justice), wrote in an article in the 1934 Denkschrift of the Academy for German Law: "Blood which is alien to the species must be kept apart; genetically sick (e.g., hereditary mental retardedness), degenerate (e.g. habitual criminality) or contaminated blood (e.g. venereal diseases) must be extinguished and annihilated . . . Racial honor therefore may no longer be denied protection by the criminal law." Thierack, "Sinn und Bedeutung der Richtlinien für die Strafrechtsreform", in *Deutscher Juristentag 1936, 5. Reichstagung des Bundes National-Sozialistischer Deutscher Juristen*, pp. 25–30, here: p. 26.

23 *Nationalsozialistische Leitsätze für ein neues deutsches Strafrecht. 2. (Besonderer) Teil*, p. 134.

24 Ibid., p. 135.

25 Freisler, "Willensstrafrecht; Versuch und Vollendung," p. 45.

26 Ibid., pp. 45–48. According to Freisler, such a grave sanction (loss of honor) would be "an unjust judgment of the many community members who, once in their life, had committed a criminal offense." Ibid., p. 47.

Nevertheless, legal theorists complied with the ideological precepts to a remarkable extent. In so doing, they helped engender the following transformations of criminal law in the Nazi state:

- Deterrence and retaliation (*Vergeltung*) became crucial ends of criminal law;
- The moralization of criminal law and approval of honor-punishment;
- The replacement of the liberal principle *nullum crimen, nulla poena sine lege* by that of *nullum crimen sine poena*;[27]
- The admission of analogy in criminal law;
- The development of a so-called "will-based criminal law."

4.3 Deterrence and Retaliation

The declared juridical goal of the Nazi regime was to replace Weimar's liberal criminal law – which had, among other things, renounced the death penalty – with an authoritarian criminal jurisdiction.[28] This implied a strong focus on deterrence and retaliation.

From a liberal standpoint, criminal law should make citizens aware of the negative consequences of particular *actions*. Punishment is the response to actions that the law clearly defined as wrong. Although punishment is bad, it should, so the liberal line, not be confounded with retaliation, let alone revenge. Since retaliation and revenge are tied to feelings of hatred and wrath, they hardly represent reliable and stable guidelines for criminal jurisdiction. To avoid such atavistic reactions to violations of law, modern legal theories distance themselves from the idea that courts should act as aggrieved authorities seeking vengeance for committed wrongs.

According to NS legal theorists, however, retaliation was central to criminal law. As Edmund Mezger, one of the leading criminal law theorists of the Nazi state, noted: "Punishment must never cease to be just retaliation, otherwise it betrays its own meaning and essence and becomes inept for fulfilling its special tasks."[29]

[27] *Nullum crimen, nulla poena sine lege*: no crime, no penalty without a law; *nullum crimen sine poena*: no crime without punishment.

[28] An informative text is Dahm, Georg and Schaffstein, Friedrich, *Liberales oder autoritäres Strafrecht?* (Hamburg: Hanseatische Verlagsanstalt, 1933).

[29] Mezger, Edmund, *Deutsches Strafrecht. Ein Grundriss* (Berlin: Junker & Dünnhaupt, 1938), p. 136. In the following cited as Mezger, *Deutsches Strafrecht (1938)*.

Mezger distinguished between the essence and purpose of punishment. He defined the former as the reaction of just retaliation, whereas the purpose of punishment was to protect and safeguard the people's community. Mezger claimed that retaliation also had a preventive effect:

> National Socialist law considers the reality of the people's community (*Volksgemeinschaft*), which is based on race, destiny, and fate, to be the highest legal value; the sole justification of punishment consists in its being an indispensable means to sustain the people's community . . . The retaliation of committed crimes is thus an indispensable means for the prevention of future crime: *punitur, ne peccetur.*[30]

Liberal criminal law associates punishment with crime prevention, distinguishing between general prevention and special prevention. General prevention concerns how society can be deterred from committing crimes. It communicates to all members of society that crime does not pay. Often general prevention also tries to enforce the ethical internalization of legal norms. This is problematic when it involves forceful educational interventions by the state. Special prevention focuses on the perpetrator – that is, how individual lawbreakers can be compelled to abstain from future crime. In this context, measures of resocialization become relevant.

Mezger held that retaliatory punishment displayed both general and special preventive effects. Retaliation would contribute to the improvement of the sentenced individual and have an educational impact on society as a whole.[31]

Other Nazi legal theorists were skeptical of the value of special prevention, particularly when the punishment strove for individual resocialization. Hellmuth Mayer argued that only general prevention by way of a harsh sentencing regimen would make sense: "General prevention works via a retaliatory criminal law, which, as a powerful demonstration of an ethical pathos inherent to the state, imposes a taboo on crime."[32] Mayer further justified his dismissal of special prevention thus:

> None of the special preventive measures appeals directly to the ethical self-responsibility, none renders a clear damning verdict on the evil action. Each special preventive justification of punishment gets stuck in

[30] Mezger, Edmund, *Deutsches Strafrecht (1938)*, p. 135. *Punitur ne peccetur:* Punishment is to be inflicted so that no crime will be committed.

[31] Mezger, *Deutsches Strafrecht (1938)*, pp. 135–136.

[32] Mayer, Hellmuth, *Das Strafrecht des Deutschen Volkes* (Stuttgart: Ferdinand Enke, 1936), p. 34.

> real life with mere considerations of utility. Thus, thinking in terms of special prevention deprives criminal law of its strength. Insofar as we notice a softening of criminal law during the Weimar period, the causes lie here. Certain evil forms of degeneration could only develop because we stopped opposing inferior human beings (*Untermenschentum*) in the name of an ethically better law.[33]

According to Mayer, general preventive effects of punishment were most forceful when accompanied by "the proper measure of just vengeance."[34] For him, retaliation and vengeance had ethical power.

These calls for deterrence were met by the extensive use of capital punishment in the Nazi legal system, which in turn provoked a reactive public climate. But rather than easing up on the death penalty, the NS state's criminal law policy sought to reinforce those feelings of hatred and revenge in the people's community as a whole.

4.4 Honor-Punishment

A remarkable normative fact is that law and ethics were unified in National Socialist legal theory. Consequently, legal requirements were equated with ethical obligations. As Freisler declared: "There can be no gap between a legal imperative and an ethical imperative. This is so since imperatives of law are imperatives of decency; however, what is decent is determined by the conscience of the *Volk* and the conscience of the individual member of the *Volk*."[35] This blurring of the lines between ethics and the law also affected criminal law. The prominent legal theorist Wilhelm Sauer vividly illustrated this when he insisted that an ethical understanding of criminal law required that the goal of punishment be "deepened, internalized and moralized," thus prioritizing "the social-ethical retaliation of crime, especially the atonement of guilt."[36] Punishment was an "ethical reaction … demanded by the conscience of the *Volk*," he argued, and thus ought to be directed at the criminal and condemnable will.[37] Similarly, Friedrich Oetker explained in a programmatic handbook that, given how central

[33] Ibid., p. 36.

[34] Ibid.

[35] Freisler, *Nationalsozialistisches Recht und Rechtsdenken*, p. 56.

[36] Sauer, Wilhelm, "Die Ethisierung des Strafrechts. Über die Prinzipien der Strafrechtserneuerung und ihre praktische Auswirkung," in Freisler, Roland (ed.), *Deutsches Strafrecht. Strafrecht, Strafrechtspolitik, Strafprozeß*, Zeitschrift der Akademie für Deutsches Recht, Neue Folge, vol. 1 (Berlin: R. v. Decker, G. Schenck, 1934), pp. 177–190, here: p. 189.

[37] Sauer, "Die Ethisierung des Strafrechts," p. 189.

the "concordance of law and morality (*Sittlichkeit*)" was in "the National Socialist world of ideas," criminal law should attend to the motive [of a criminal deed] – that is, its degree of badness and/or its guilt-reducing effect.[38]

The unification of law and morality in Nazi legal theory removed the distinction between violations of law and violations of ethical norms. Since the bad will took center stage in the preferred ethics-based criminal law, criminal sentencing focused on assessing this mental attitude. Again, Sauer clearly depicts this shift:

> The actual ethical and criminal element is that volition which determines the essence and value of a personality, also because it has been created by [the personality]. Just as in Kantian and Fichtean ethics nothing is good but the good will, so the core of crime lies in the evil will . . . But at all times, the criminal has been marked by the morally reprehensible will which, after all, constitutes the material essence of guilt. This connection between crime and moral viciousness was only obscured when an exaggerated liberal conception drew a sharp line between law and morality, as well as between the will and external behaviour.[39]

For the most part, the development of an ethical criminal law did not get beyond vague appeals to incorporate the ethical values of the people's community. Sauer tried to be more precise in arguing that the "original German (gothic) virtues," which were part of the "German ethical and cultural history," comprised *völkisch* ethics, virtues such as truthfulness, reliability (*Zuverlässigkeit*), goal-directedness, and self-control. The opposite of those virtues were the "typical criminal vices," which also counted as the strongest violations of the "community ethos": obliqueness, betrayal, ravenousness, license, and intemperance.[40]

The moralization of criminal law affected how criminal law judges defined their role. By stressing ethical norms, normative guidelines encouraged judges to follow their consciences and

[38] Oetker, Friedrich, "Grundprobleme der nationalsozialistischen Strafrechtsreform," in Frank (ed.), *Nationalsozialistisches Handbuch für Recht und Gesetzgebung* (München: Franz Eher Nachf., Zentralverlag der NSDAP, 1935), pp. 1317–1361, p. 1320. Oetker also was a member of the Criminal Law Reform Committee of the Academy for German Law. According to Werner Schubert, Oetker, one of the leading criminal theorists of the Wilhelminean Empire and the Weimar Republic, primarily saw in National Socialism a means for the realization of his conservative-authoritarian worldview. See Schubert, Werner, "Introduction," in *Akademie für Deutsches Recht 1933–1945. Protokolle der Ausschüsse*, vol. VII, pp. IX–XXVIII, esp. pp. XI–XIV.

[39] Sauer, "Die Ethisierung des Strafrechts," p. 188.

[40] Ibid.

exercise "duty-bound discretion."[41] These guidelines further entailed respecting the basic "law of the people's well-being" and adjudicating to avenge the material wrong occasioned by the offense and crime.[42] In this way, adjudication was not only meant to take into account the violation of legal statutes, but also the infringement of a higher trans-legal ethical order. Finally, criminal law was obliged to acknowledge and endorse the separation of legal statute and law, *Gesetz* and *Recht*. Freisler expressed this necessity thus:

> [W]e believe that a material understanding of law and of legal wrongdoing must be decisive in criminal law since we do not identify law with legal statute, but develop law out of the ethical order of the *Volk*. In our view, one should therefore not derive criminal law solely from the legal statute; we rather should also recognize an extra-legal source of the law.[43]

The material conception of legal right and wrong should first and foremost be ensured by the judge's thoughtful sentencing. This means that, in addition to the facts of an offense, the judge ought to consider the normative elements of a value-based adjudication. Freisler defined the "genuine normative elements" as: well-being of the Reich; well-being of the *Volk*; good mores (*Sitten*), including decency and the healthy sentiments of the people.[44] Freisler maintained that these normative notions were decisive for a material conception of legal right and wrong that functioned, alongside positive legal statutes, as a second source of legal knowledge.[45]

Sauer emphasized that criminal law should focus on the "redemption of ethical damnability and safeguarding social perilousness."[46] Thus, several Nazi criminal law theorists supported a two-pronged system of criminal legal sanctions:[47] In addition to the usual forms of punishment

[41] Ibid., p. 184.
[42] Ibid.
[43] Freisler, "Aufbau und Aufgabe des Besonderen Teils, Gestaltung seiner Tatbestände. Einbau des Schutzes der Bewegung in das Gesetz," in *Das kommende deutsche Strafrecht. Besonderer Teil* (1936), p. 57.
[44] Ibid., p. 60.
[45] Ibid., p. 61.
[46] Sauer, "Die Ethisierung des Strafrechts," p. 189.
[47] A two-pronged system of criminal law sanctions was not a National Socialist invention; it was a principle of liberal criminal law (an idea going back to Franz von Liszt, a German criminal law expert, professor at the University of Berlin from 1898 until 1917). However, the Nazis understood and used those measures in a particularly harsh way; moreover, they introduced measures (for example, castration) which were alien to a liberal criminal law.

like imprisonment, specific measures to be taken included detention in a mental institution,[48] detention in an asylum (for alcoholics),[49] detention in a workhouse,[50] security detention (*Sicherungsverwahrung*),[51]

[48] A perpetrator's placement in a sanatorium or mental hospital (*Heil- or Pflegeanstalt*) should be ordered if his criminal deed was committed in a state of mental incapacity (*Zustand der Zurechnungsunfähigkeit*) or diminished sanity (*Zustand der verminderten Zurechnungsfähigkeit*). Placement should be as long as the purpose of punhishment required it (possibly even a life sentence); however, an assessment was ordered for every three years.

[49] Placement in a drinker's hospital (*Trinkerheilanstalt*) or a detoxification institution (*Entziehungsanstalt*) was a rehabilitation measure (*Besserungsmaßnahme*), limited to two years.

[50] Placement in a workhouse (*Arbeitshaus*) was a particular measure with respect to tramps (*Landstreicher*), beggars, and prostitutes; it was first limited to two years, in case of recurrence it came without a time limit.

[51] Preventive detention (*Sicherungsverwahrung*) was an additional measure besides punishment for so-called habitual criminals (*Gewohnheitsverbrecher*). In case of similar previous deeds, habitual criminals could be punished with a prison sentence of up to five years; if the new deed amounted to a serious crime, they could be punished by a prison sentence of up to fifteen years. In case the defendant was a "dangerous habitual criminal," the law gave the judge the possibility to enact preventive detention for a non-limited period of time. See Werle, *Justiz-Strafrecht und polizeiliche Verbrechensbekämpfung im Dritten Reich*, p. 95. The basis of this legal regulation was the Law against Dangerous Habitual Criminals of November 24, 1933 (*Gesetz über gefährliche Gewohnheitsverbrecher*). Also preventive detention could be unlimited in time; it could even involve lifelong imprisonment. The idea was to protect the people's community against crimes, even beyond the point of a perpetrator's served prison sentence. An assessment of detention after three years was common. As Mezger noted: "Preventive detention, if necessary lifelong detention, is one of the most important means of the new state's fight against habitual and professional criminals." Mezger, *Deutsches Strafrecht* (1938), p. 150. According to Mezger, from 1933 until 1936, 6160 persons were put in preventive detention; on January 1, 1937, 3258 prisoners (3127 men, 137 women) were in preventive detention. Mezger, *Deutsches Strafrecht* (1938), p. 152.

There is an important distinction between preventive detention (*Sicherungsverwahrung*) and protective custody (*Schutzhaft*). Preventive detention was part of criminal law measures and, as such, a measure of the jurisdiction. Protective custody meant detention in a concentration camp and was a police measure to defend the people's community against so-called enemies of the state; it was in the authority of the Secret State Police (*Gestapo*). Protective custody was defined in § 1, Gestapo Law as "enforced measure" (*Zwangsmaßnahme*) against all persons who, by their behavior, were a danger to the security of the *Volk* and the state. See Werle, *Justizstrafrecht und polizeiliche Verbrechensbekämpfung im Dritten* Reich, p. 547. Protective custody was only ordered on the basis of a protective arrest warrant of the Gestapo. The whole procedure of protective custody was outside the judiciary. See Werle, *Justizstrafrecht und polizeiliche Verbrechensbekämpfung im Dritten Reich,* p. 504. See also Hoefer, Frederick, *The Nazi Penal System I*, in *Journal of Criminal Law and Criminology* 35, 6 (1945), pp. 385–393, esp. pp. 389–390.

prohibition of professional practice,[52] and the castration of dangerous sexual offenders.[53]

The moralization of criminal law not only spurred an increase of social control and surveillance, but also a remarkable intensification of legal sanctions. In addition to the mere formal unlawfulness (that is, the violation of legal statutes), the material unlawfulness became relevant for adjudication. This material dimension of wrongdoing depended on the degree to which "a perpetrator qualified as an enemy of the *Volk* (*Volksschädling*)."[54] By declaring a "trans-legal emergency condition," the regime could justify all kinds of draconian criminal legal measures.[55]

The moralization of law also meant that traits like fidelity, loyalty, and honor found their way into criminal law. Accordingly, several Nazi legal theorists supported the reintroduction of honor-punishment (*Ehrenstrafe*).[56] Georg Dahm, a criminal law professor at the University of Kiel, argued that this punishment helped distinguish between a conception of criminal law that sees it as "a rational technique to fight crime," and one which "ascribes to law a transpersonal dignity and integrates criminal law into the whole context of *völkisch* life."[57]

Dahm claimed that the well-known liberal reservations against honor-punishment had lost their force in the NS legal system. In the liberal state, honor-punishment was forbidden on the basis of the separation of external and internal freedoms. According to liberal doctrine, Dahm wrote, "(l)aw can merely regulate the external coexistence of citizens and is thus only interested in the external legal behaviour, but not in the convictions (*Gesinnungen*) of the perpetrator. The state can take away

52 Prohibition of professional practice (*Untersagung der Berufsausübung*) was a consequence of grave violations of professional duties. Juvenile criminal law included special educational measures such as special custody and care (*Schutzaufsicht and Fürsorgeerziehung*).

53 Castration (*Entmannung*) of dangerous sex offenders (*Sittlichkeitsverbrecher*) meant the removal of gonads (*Keimdrüsen*); this measure was up to a judge's discretion and could be ordered against perpetrators (older than twenty-one years) in the case of sexual abuse of children, exhibitionism, and particularly in the case of sexually motivated manslaughter or murder. According to Mezger, there were 1227 castrations between 1934 and 1936. See Mezger, *Deutsches Strafrecht* (1938), p. 152.

54 Sauer, "Die Ethisierung des Strafrechts," p. 187.

55 Ibid.

56 Dahm, Georg, "Die Erneuerung der Ehrenstrafe," in *Deutsche Juristen-Zeitung* 13, 39 (1934), pp. 822–832; Schaffstein, Friedrich, "Ehrenstrafe und Freiheitsstrafe in ihrer Bedeutung für das neue Strafrecht," in Freisler (ed.), *Deutsches Strafrecht. Strafrecht, Strafrechtspolitik, Strafprozeß*, pp. 273–282.

57 Dahm, Georg, "Die Erneuerung der Ehrenstrafe," p. 822.

rights, but the state cannot take away honor and must not judge internal convictions."[58]

However, in a legal system in which "law and ethics, criminal law and the perception of the *Volk* (*Volksanschauung*) grow together," one could not do away with honor-punishment since each real community would need the loyalty and honor of its members.[59] Accordingly, in his sentences the criminal law judge would also be expressing a value judgment about whether the perpetrator "still belongs or does not belong to the community, and, more generally, who at all belongs to it and where the legal limits lie so that the community does not completely split up with the offender of law."[60]

Similarly, Friedrich Schaffstein argued that the NS state could no longer dismiss honor-punishment. The liberal state's constitutive value relativism had undermined the status and importance of honor-punishment such that what counted as "honorless mindset" varied between social groups and societies generally.[61] However, National Socialism, instead of giving in to cultural and ethical relativism, devised a concise objective notion of "honor." As Schaffstein noted, this definition derived from "the National Socialist unity of legal and moral judgment" – that is, the "totality claim of National Socialist ideology."[62]

What, exactly, did these theorists mean by "honor"? Dahm insisted that it should not be reduced to esteem among "legal comrades" (*Rechtsgenossen*). Honor, he argued, was an evaluative "expression of that which is essential to each community."[63] In this sense, honor amounted to a pathetic formula that demanded unconditional commitment to state goals.

Consequently, honor-punishment was a "political form of punishment" with symbolic meaning for educating the *Volk*.[64] The sanctions that accompanied honor-punishment comprised ostracism, imprisonment, detainment, and monetary fines (*Vermögensstrafen*).[65] While

58 Ibid.

59 Ibid., p. 826.

60 Ibid.

61 See Schaffstein, Friedrich, "Ehrenstrafe und Freiheitsstrafe in ihrer Bedeutung für das neue Strafrecht," in Freisler (ed.), *Deutsches Strafrecht. Strafrecht, Strafrechtspolitik, Strafprozeß*, pp. 273–282; here: p. 279.

62 Ibid.

63 Dahm, "Die Erneuerung der Ehrenstrafe," pp. 826–827.

64 Ibid. Schaffstein argued that honor punishment should have a similar function as imprisonment.

65 Gleispach, Wenzel von "Willensstrafrecht," in *Handwörterbuch der Kriminologie und der anderen strafrechtlichen Hilfswissenschaften*, vol. 2, ed. by Elster, Alexander and

Dahm and Schaffstein rejected corporal punishment and public display of the perpetrator at the pillory, they approved of such measures as publicly announcing a sentence and disclosing the condemned's identity via radio, published photographs, etc.[66] In punishing treason against the *Volk*, ostracism theoretically entailed the loss of Reich citizenship and, even, the death penalty. In Wenzel von Gleispach's words, "Whoever by action or conviction expels himself forever from the people's community must be eliminated."[67]

4.5 *Nullum crimen sine poena* and the Admission of Analogy in Criminal Law

The main goal of criminal law in the Nazi state was to protect the people's community rather than the individual's negative liberties. The state could not, as legal theorist Karl Schäfer claimed, "allow the individual person to misuse his strengths and capacities to harm the *Volk* in its entirety without punishment."[68]

Nazi legal theorists thus rejected a central principle of liberal criminal law: that an action could only be punished if it was legally declared as punishable at the time the offense occurred.[69] This principle of *nullum crimen, nulla poena sine lege*, which was designed to protect citizens against judicial arbitrariness, was condemned by Nazi jurists as the "Magna Carta of the criminal"[70] since it allegedly enabled a perpetrator

Lingemann, Heinrich (Berlin und Leipzig: Walter de Gruyter & Co., 1936), pp. 1067–1079, here: p. 1075.

66 Dahm, "Die Erneuerung der Ehrenstrafe," p. 832. Dahm argued that corporeal punishment, and also public display at the pillory would "neither correspond to the sound perception of the *Volk* nor to a modern conception of the practical tasks of criminal law." Ibid.

67 Gleispach, "Willensstrafrecht," p. 1075.

68 Schäfer, Karl, "Nullum crimen sine poena. (Das Recht als Grundlage der Bestrafung. Zeitliche Geltung der Strafgesetze)," in *Das kommende deutsche Strafrecht. Allgemeiner Teil* (1935), pp. 200–217, here: p. 203.

69 This principle was part of the German Penal Code of 1871 which was still valid in the Nazi state. See "Einleitende Bestimmungen," § 2 in *Das Strafgesetzbuch für das Deutsche Reich*, 7th ed., ed. by Oppenhoff, Th. F. (Berlin: G. Reimer, 1879), p. 21.

For a discussion of the effects of the abondonement of the *nulla poena sine lege* principle see Kirchheimer, Otto, "Criminal Law in National Socialist Germany," in Scheuerman, William E. (ed.), *The Rule of Law under Siege. Selected Essays of Franz L. Neumann and Otto Kirchheimer* (Berkeley, Los Angeles, London: University of California Press, 1996), pp. 172–191.

70 See Dahm, "Das Ermessen des Richters im nationalsozialistischen Strafrecht," in Freisler (ed.), *Deutsches Strafrecht. Strafrecht, Strafrechtspolitik, Strafprozeß*, pp. 87–96, here:

to avoid punishment solely on the basis of a gap in statutory law or the insufficient drafting of a legal statute.[71]

Jurist Karl Schäfer argued that the liberal maxim of protecting individual liberty by only punishing offenses defined as crimes in written legal statute would constrain the judge's free discretion, demoting him to a mere "subsumption machine (*Subsumtionsmaschine*)."[72] Nazi jurists thus mandated replacing *nullum crimen, nulla poena sine lege* by the formula *nullum crimen sine poena* (no crime without punishment).[73] In this way, each crime, regardless of whether it constituted a legally defined offense, would be subject to punishment and atonement.

Accordingly, the jurists sought to extend the authority and discretion of the judge. Although not formally qualified to act as a lawmaker, the judge should have significant power to create law in the interest of the people's community. Schäfer claimed that such an extension of the judge's authority was crucial in the NS criminal law system because this system would use general clauses (*Generalklauseln*) for assessing right and wrong, as well as appeal to a value-based perspective on factual matters – "grounded in the sound sentiments of the *Volk* and similar standards of value" – rather than "a mere description of matters of fact."[74]

In order to broaden the judges' authority and discretion, NS-jurists supported lifting the analogy ban in criminal law. This prohibition

p. 92. See also Gleispach, "Willensstrafrecht," p. 1070. The expression "Magna Carta of the Criminal" was, as Klaus Günther pointed out to me, first introduced by Franz von Liszt, referring to the fact that the principle *nulla poena sine lege* granted a defendant a certain legal certainty. The National Socialist legal thinkers, however, used the expression in a different sense, that is, that a liberal criminal law would allow a perpetrator to escape legal prosecution. According to Mezger, the historical source of the expression "Magna Carta of the Criminal" was Article 39 of the English Magna Carta of 1215. See Mezger, *Deutsches Strafrecht* (1938), p. 29.

[71] Schäfer, "Nullum crimen sine poena," p. 202.

[72] Ibid., p. 204. Similarly, Freisler claimed that the *nullla poena sine lege* principle would turn the judge into a "sentencing automaton" (*Urteilsautomaten*). See Freisler, *Schutz des Volkes oder des Rechtsbrechers? Fesselung des Verbrechers oder des Richters? Einiges über das zweckmäßige Maß der Bindung des Richters an gesetzliche Straftatbestände* (Berlin: R. v. Decker, G. Schenck, 1935), p. 2.

[73] For Werle, *the nullum crimen sine poena*-formula amounted to "the 'trophy' in the victory over a rule-of-law based liberal criminal law." Werle, *Justiz-Strafrecht und polizeiliche Verbrechensbekämpfung im Dritten Reich*, p. 143.

[74] Schäfer, *Nullum crimen sine poena*, p. 204. Gleispach wrote that the judge should be the "original source of the law, but he is not bound to the ideas which have found their admittedly incomplete expression in the various corpus delicti." Gleispach, "Willensstrafrecht," p. 1070.

forbade judges from applying a legal statute to an offense when said offense was not explicitly covered in the statute's wording. By allowing analogy, NS jurists argued, judges would be free to treat like cases alike, thus extending their competency. In this way, judgments would not be restricted to sentencing only those offenses that could be subsumed under a given statute.[75]

The Nazi legal theorists' efforts to expand judicial competencies were successful. When the National Socialist commission for reforming criminal law, under the direction of Justice Minister Gürtner, recommended in 1935 the admission of analogy, it was overruling § 2 of the German Criminal Code (*STGB, Strafgesetzbuch*) whereby an action could only be punished if said punishment was specified in a pre-existing legal statute. The commission suggested the following reformulation of § 2: "If an act [*Tat*] is not explicitly declared punishable by law, but if a statute declares a similar act punishable, then that statute should be applied if its underlying idea of law (*Rechtsgedanke*) and the sound perception of the *Volk* (*gesunde Volksanschauung*) demand punishment."[76] In this way, the commission dismissed a fundamental presupposition of rule-of-law based criminal law. The prohibition of analogy, insofar as it would create new categories of offenses or expand existing ones, was (and still is) a crucial element of liberal criminal law.[77]

But it was precisely the freedom to introduce new categories of offenses, or at least to reinterpret existing ones, that fit the Nazi jurists' ends. Criminal law, in line with the maxim *nullum crimen sine poena*, was to serve as a seamless instrument of deterrence.

NS legal theorists argued that the application of analogy must meet the following conditions: similarity between the act declared punishable by legal statute and that which was not yet legally regulated; applicability of the idea of law (*Rechtsgedanke*), which found expression in a statute, to the similar but not yet legally regulated act; and accordance between the punishment and "the sound perception of the *Volk*."[78]

What, exactly, did NS jurists mean by "the sound perception of the *Volk*"? The reform commission's attempts to specify this notion – that is, by appealing to the "ethical imperative of the community order" – were

75 Krug, Karl, "Drei Grundprobleme des kommenden Strafrechts," in *Zeitschrift der Akademie für Deutsches Recht*, 2 (1935), pp. 98–102, here: p. 99.

76 Cited according to Schäfer, "Nullum crimen sine poena," p. 204.

77 In liberal criminal law analogy is permissible if applied to a perpetrator's grounds of excuses or grounds which exclude punishment (for example, acts of self-defense).

78 Schäfer, "Nullum crimen sine poena," p. 205.

not very successful. The commission considered the "idea of law expressed in a criminal statute" to be crucial.[79] The principle of analogy, which became part of Article 1 of the "Law Amending Criminal Law" (*Strafrechtsänderungsgesetz*) on June 28, 1935, read:

> Whoever commits an act that is declared punishable by law, or which deserves to be punished according to the fundamental idea of a penal statute and the sound perception of the *Volk*, will be punished.
>
> If no particular penal statute is directly applicable to an act, then this act will be punished according to that statute whose fundamental idea best fits this same act.[80]

In the end, the judge was responsible for interpreting "the sound perception of the *Volk*." Moreover, the judge had to recognize the fundamental idea of a penal statute and apply this to analogous acts. Thus, the principle of analogy substantially expanded judicial discretion. The sole remaining restriction was that the judge not contrive an arbitrary reading of the fundamental idea of a penal statute – that is, one that completely ignored the content of the legal statute. But as long as the judge claimed to take account of the ethical order and "sound perception of the *Volk*," he was relatively autonomous in determining what counted as a punishable offense. The route to an ideologically distorted jurisdiction was open.

The following examples illustrate the consequences of lifting the ban on analogy. In the first, a Jewish man (the illegitimate child of a Jewish mother) seeking membership in the Nazi Party only entered the names of his non-Jewish foster parents in the application form. On July 28, 1938, a Hamburg court sentenced him for attempted falsification of documents by way of analogy. The court applied § 271 and § 272 of the Criminal Code, simply assuming that the Nazi Party was the equivalent of an official state authority (*amtliche Behörde*). Moreover, the defendant's act was punishable according to the "sound perception of the *Volk*."[81] In the second case, a defendant was sentenced for listening to a non-foreign (that is, German) black transmitter. The sentence again resulted from analogy – the court applied the statute that forbid listening to foreign black transmitters to the case. In justifying its decision, the court held that the legal gap in this case had been closed by applying "§

[79] Ibid., p. 212.

[80] Ibid., pp. 213–214. The amendment was published in the Reichsgesetzblatt RGBL. I (1935), p. 839.

[81] Cited according to Lüken, *Der Nationalsozialismus und das materielle Strafrecht*, pp. 73–74.

2 of the Reich Criminal Code in a lawmaking manner in the interest of material justice."[82]

Several Nazi jurists required an even broader interpretation of the analogy principle so that it not only covered statutory analogy (*Gesetzesanalogie*), but also allowed for analogy of law (*Rechtsanalogie*). Statutory analogy referred to the application of a particular legal regulation to a similar, but legally unregulated act. By contrast, the analogy of law had wider meaning and scope, entailing "the application of an idea (of law) inherent to the whole legal order to a legally unregulated matter of fact which may count as a particular instance of that idea."[83] While a number of Nazi jurists rejected analogy of law, objecting that it would lead to judicial arbitrariness, others argued that in the Führer state analogy of statute and analogy of law simply coincided.[84]

Drawing the line between statutory analogy and analogy of law was indeed difficult because the justification for the permission of statutory analogy – namely, that it allowed the judge to apply the new understanding of law – held equally for analogy of law. Karl Siegert made the following argument in support of permitting analogy of law:

> The *völkisch* Führer principle in particular demands that one acts according to the will of the current lawgiver. This will, which also matches the

[82] Ibid., pp. 74–75.

[83] Siegert, Karl, "Nulla poena sine lege. Kritische Bemerkungen zu den Vorschlägen der amtlichen Strafrechtskommission," in Freisler (ed.), *Deutsches Strafrecht. Strafrecht, Strafrechtspolitik, Strafprozeß*, pp. 376–386, here: p. 380.

[84] The meaning of analogy of law was also discussed in meetings of the Academy for German Law's Criminal Law Committee. See "Protokoll der Sitzung vom 3.4.1936 (Öffentlichkeit des Strafverfahrens. Rechtsanalogie in der Praxis)," and "Protokoll der Sitzung vom 4.4.1936 (Rechtanalogie in der Praxis. Sitzungspolizei. Reformatio in peius)," in *Akademie für Deutsches Recht 1933–1945. Protokolle der Ausschüsse*, vol. VII, pp. 46–64 and pp. 64–80, esp. 64–73. The committee held that analogy of law served to create law in those exceptional cases in which the lawgiver had obviously forgotten to regulate a particular act. However, analogy of law should not be interpreted too extensively, that is, the judge must not replace the supreme lawgiver, that is, the Führer. Ibid., p. 55. Oetker was skeptical toward analogy of law, arguing that § 2 of the revised German Penal Code (1935) only permitted statutory analogy, not analogy of law. See Oetker, "Grundprobleme der nationalsozialistischen Strafrechtsreform," p. 1324. Also Schäfer had reservations against analogy of law. He emphasized that the content of a legal statute could not be ignored, giving the following example. If a statute exists that declares the sexual seduction of minors (defined as under age sixteen) punishable, then a judge could not simply use the principle of analogy to apply the statute to the seduction case of a seventeen-year-old. Ignoring the age limit would contradict the idea of law since the age limit was a constitutive part of the statute. See Schäfer, "Nullum crimen sine poena," p. 205.

> current "end of law," is crucial for the application of a penal law statute. This entails that the application of law has to reach beyond the limits of an interpretation tied to the wording of a statute.[85]

This allowed the judge to abstract from the specific formulation of a statute. By appealing both to the "will of the current lawgiver" and the "*völkisch* principle," the sentences of a judge could be rendered in line with the principles of *Gesetzesanalogie* and *Rechtsanalogie.* It merely required that sentences accord with the ends of the Nazi state.

Siegert also conceded that analogy of law corresponded to the National Socialist understanding of the state insofar as it held that "the conscience of the *Volk* and guidelines of the leadership are also applied aside from legal statutes."[86] Nevertheless, Siegert was skeptical about allowing judges to rely on the analogy of law principle because "the will of the leadership is not clearly recognizable in analogy of law."[87] This warning by a Nazi legal theorist illustrates how obvious the tendency toward normative unboundedness in Nazi criminal law had become.[88]

Some Nazi legal theorists, including Dahm, openly admitted that the permission of analogy and the "abundant use of general clauses and malleable value concepts like the sound perception of the *Volk*"[89] had considerably strengthened judicial authority. Yet Dahm saw no problem in this extension of judicial power given the Führer state's uniform worldview. Only within the subjective, democratic value framework of the Weimar Republic would such a power grab pose a problem. Under liberal conditions, Dahm explained, analogy would favor the perpetrator because the "pre-revolutionary liberal theory of criminal law was not familiar with the legal idea (*Rechtsgedanke*) and did not recognize an idea of justice beyond positive law."[90] Again the message was that democratic societies would lack objectively binding normative standards, and the absence of a strong political authority issuing clear guidelines and values would increase relativism and subjectivism.

According to Dahm, the Nazi legal system's separation between statute and law (law in the sense of justice) allowed for a transpositive assessment

[85] Siegert, "Nulla poena sine lege. Kritische Bemerkungen zu den Vorschlägen der amtlichen Strafrechtskommission," p. 380.

[86] Ibid.

[87] Ibid., p. 381.

[88] For a critical discussion see also Rüthers, Bernd, *Die unbegrenzte Auslegung. Zum Wandel der Privatrechtsordnung im Nationalsozialismus* (Tübingen: Mohr, 1968).

[89] Dahm, "Das Ermessen des Richters im nationalsozialistischen Strafrecht," p. 87.

[90] Ibid., p. 89.

of "the material wrongness" of acts. Dahm enthusiastically commented on these transformations:

> By turning away from liberal legal thinking, law acquires a new function. Its task no longer consists of protecting the individual against the arbitrary power of a mistrusted state. Its task is no longer to implement the separation of power in law-giving and adjudication. The judge is [also] no longer the voice and slave of the law, as the Enlightenment assumed. Rather, legislation and adjudication now have equal standing. Both express the *völkisch* legal idea and the sound perception of the *Volk* as the ultimate transpositive source of law and foundation of legal validity. The legal statute, which in relation to the *Volks*'s perception (*Volksanschauung*) is of no less secondary importance than the decision of the judge, contains merely the general guidelines according to which the judge exerts the perception of the *Volk*.[91]

Freed from the "force of the formal norm," Dahm argued, the judge could renounce abstract legal thinking and turn to the concrete life order (*Lebensordnung*). Accordingly, he not only had a duty to the "order of the *Volk*," but also to the political leadership. As Dahm wrote, "the National Socialist communal idea is inseparably bound up with the idea of authoritarian leadership. It is in the political leadership, especially the Führer, that the *Volk* finds its true representative, which constitutes the basis of the authority of the Führer and the state."[92]

In this way, Dahm tried to avoid the problem that any appeal to the "sound perception of the *Volk*" might grant the judge inordinate discretion. A judge, Dahm explained, could never refuse the application of a statute merely by claiming that it would contradict his understanding of the *Volk*'s intuition. The judge only had "bounded discretion"; he could not presume to determine the people's will. However, Dahm failed to characterize clearly the sound perception of the people, simply calling it "no abstract idea, but a concrete reality of life that is determined and constantly renewed by the given concrete legal convictions."[93]

According to NS legal theorists, two norms were crucial for adjudication: The judge had to consider the "National Socialist idea of justice"; and he must comply with the political leadership. This argument had two parts: First was the postulate that the positive legal statute neither granted legal validity nor was appeal to it sufficient for adjudication; the judge also had to take the "transpositive legal idea" into account. Second, this

91 Ibid.
92 Ibid., p. 90.
93 Ibid., p. 92.

transpositive legal idea was identified with the "sound perception of the *Volk*," which in turn depended upon the Führer's will. Law, Dahm claimed, also was formed by such "extrajuridical expressions of the Führer's will" as literary and programmatic declarations, even if such statements were not couched in legal language and did not directly aim at shaping legal life.[94]

This further opened the door for a political grip on the law. Like other NS officials, the judge was committed to political compliance by constantly finding, interpreting, and considering the Führer's will in all its articulations. This permanent expectation to recognize and meet the leadership's expectations, which often were transmitted in pathetic declarations and programmatic rallies, undermined a judge's striving for independent and impartial judgment.

4.6 The Conception of a Will-Based Criminal Law (*Willensstrafrecht*)

Will-based criminal law was an invention of National Socialist legal theorizing.[95] In its development and justification, NS jurists tried not to ignore completely all standards and matters of juridical know-how. Nevertheless, the will-centered criminal law conception contributed remarkably to the extension of the NS regime's juridical power.

According to the 1871 German Criminal Code (*Reichsstrafgesetzbuch* RStGB), the corpus delicti (*Tatbestand*) was the crucial focus of criminal law. From 1936 on, the view prevailed among NS legal theorists that this traditional conception, which prioritized matters of fact, should be replaced by a law centering on the criminal will.[96] This amounted to a reversal of legal perspectives: While a liberal criminal law focused on securing individual rights and liberties, National Socialism would, wrote Karl Krug, seek to protect the "people's community as such with its ethical order (*Sittenordnung*) and its ideal as well as material *völkisch* goods."[97] The new criminal law should amount to "an ethical postulate."[98]

[94] Ibid., p. 91.
[95] Hartl, *Das nationalsozialistische Willensstrafrecht*, p. 56.
[96] Ibid., p. 37.
[97] Krug, Karl, "Drei Grundprobleme des kommenden Strafrechts," p. 98.
[98] Ibid. According to Gleispach, one of the leading theorists at the time, the will-based criminal law required that the single community member "fulfils his duties and subdues to the living community order." Gleispach, "Willensstrafrecht," p. 1068.

What were the main features of the will-based criminal law? How was it different from a threat-based criminal law (*Gefährdungsstrafrecht*) and an internal attitude-based criminal law (*Gesinnungsstrafrecht*)? How was it related to a perpetrator-based criminal law (*Täterstrafrecht*)?

The core assumption of a will-based criminal law was that the ascription of guilt depended on the will's internal quality. Recall Sauer's statement that, "(j)ust as in Kantian and Fichtean ethics, nothing is good but the good will, so the core of crime lies in the evil will."[99] In this way, a mental element became central to sentencing and punishment, a shift which, Sauer specified, implied giving up the separation of law and morality. The will-based criminal law conception was a clear consequence of the NS thinkers' emphatic moralization of law.

The driving thought was that the state's judiciary should not only react when a legal violation had occurred, but should prevent crime already in its formative stages. According to Freisler, a main advocate of will-based criminal law, the state should intervene "(a)s early as possible and with all available power!"[100] The criminal will should be recognized "as the deepest ground of all punishment rooted in the ethics of the *Volk*."[101]

Will-based criminal law identified atonement as the essence of punishment.[102] Edmund Mezger wrote that the sentence had to be directed at the "will which has rebelled against the people's community."[103] Likewise, criminal law should seek to educate "the sanitary elements in the *Volk* and . . . strengthen the living legal and ethical order."[104] This educational work would bring the single will to fulfil its ethical duties toward the community.

What exactly was meant by "the will"? While NS theoreticians did not provide a precise definition, their descriptions suggest that the will was neither a desire nor a wish. Rather, it constituted the intention to carry out a plan – that is, an active mental element directed at realizing an act. As the motor and source of all successfully accomplished acts, the will was also behind all punishable ones. The combination of intention and concrete action toward executing a plan was essential. After all, NS legal theory maintained that the will should not only be punished if it resulted

[99] Sauer, "Die Ethisierung des Strafrechts," p. 188.

[100] Freisler, "Willensstrafrecht; Versuch und Vollendung," pp. 5–48, here: p. 22.

[101] Ibid., p. 33. The criminal law theorists see their emphasis on the will in the tradition of German philosophy.

[102] Freisler, "Willensstrafrecht; Versuch und Vollendung," p. 15.

[103] Mezger, *Deutsches Strafrecht* (1938), p. 27.

[104] Ibid.

in a successful action, but also if it did no more than lead to an attempted deed (*Tatversuch*).

Freisler identified six stages in the articulation of the will which harmed the people's community: seduction, resolution, preparing the plan, commencing its execution (*Ausführungsbeginn*), successfully carrying out the act, and ensuring its success (*Erfolgssicherung*). The crucial question for Freisler was "at which stage the criminal law should threaten the perpetrator with punishment."[105] Freisler conceded that it did not make sense to punish the mere resolution since any resolution was still open to change. But if a person progressed from resolution to the realization of an act; if he or she set preparatory acts, then preventive action by state institutions was not only justified, it was required.

Freisler saw in the will the element that moved the world. Alluding to Carl Schmitt's basic categories of social life, Freisler stated: "Only a will can be friend or foe!"[106] The enemy of the community was the troublemaker's will, the will that disturbed peace, "the bearer of the asocial ... and anarchic principle on which criminal law's eye" had to be directed.[107] For Freisler, the will-based criminal law was a "combative law," intending "not only to fight the adversary, but to annihilate him."[108] Other Nazi jurists shared this belligerent rhetoric. Gleispach noted that "(t)he culpable will ..., the type of will which rebels against duties, this is the enemy that criminal law has to fight and defeat."[109]

The will-based criminal law thus intervened directly into the sphere of personal attitudes and convictions, aggressively trying to mobilize the ethical self-obligations of the individual. Nevertheless, Nazi legal theorists were eager to downplay the extensive sanctions associated with a will-based criminal law. "The will-based criminal law as such," Freisler claimed, "does not amount to an enhancement of criminal culpability – it amounts to defining the direction criminal law should take in a new way."[110]

Contrary to the Nazis' racial-biological determinism, proponents of a will-based criminal law presupposed freedom of the will.[111] Criminal sentencing should be free from any attempt to mitigate a sentence

105 Freisler, "Willensstrafrecht; Versuch und Vollendung," p. 21.
106 Ibid., p. 15.
107 Ibid., pp. 14–15.
108 Ibid., p. 14.
109 Gleispach, "Willensstrafrecht," p. 1068.
110 Freisler, "Willensstrafrecht; Versuch und Vollendung," p. 19.
111 Gleispach, "Willensstrafrecht," p. 1069.

because of a perpetrator's difficult social circumstances or upbringing. Once again, Freisler emphatically defended indeterminism: National Socialism "does not hear the one who says: I cannot do otherwise, but the one who exclaims in each situation of life: I should, I will, I can!"[112]

According to Freisler, a will-based criminal law should consider the following inner components: the intensity of the will, the manner of the will's exercise (cruelty, irreverence), whether the inner struggle of the perpetrator was weak or fierce, and a perpetrator's readiness for redress and reparation.[113]

Several legal theorists doubted whether adjudication could take these subjective elements into account. Controversy especially swirled over how to ascertain the intensity of the will. Edmund Mezger thought it impossible to take the will's intensity as a marker for the beginning of the deed, arguing that only an objective element could indicate the start of an action.[114] He considered the "natural relation" between the beginning and the execution of an action to be crucial. In response, Freisler explained that it was the post-factum adjudication of the judge that should and could determine the will's articulations. Given the matters of fact in a criminal case, the judge could then infer the modalities of the perpetrator's will.

The defenders of a will-based criminal law required the state to react as early as possible to a violation of law.[115] This obligation to protect the people's community to the highest degree determined, Freisler held, "where the active defense line of the state against the order-denying and order-threatening elements ought to be erected."[116] If possible, the state should already intervene in the planning of a criminal act. When taking the first steps to carry out a planned deed, the perpetrator should face threats of punishment.[117]

According to defenders of a will-based criminal law, two regulations of traditional criminal law in particular obstructed the fight against crime: First, that the judge could only punish someone if the accomplished or attempted deed was legally defined as a crime; and second, that the attempt had to be punished more leniently than the successful deed.[118]

112 Freisler, "Willensstrafrecht; Versuch und Vollendung," p. 15.
113 Ibid., p. 27.
114 Mezger, Edmund, *Deutsches Strafrecht. Ein Leitfaden* (Berlin: Junker & Dünnhaupt, 1936), p. 28. Cited in the following as Mezger, *Deutsches Strafrecht* (1936).
115 Hartl, *Das nationalsozialistische Willensstrafrecht*, p. 92.
116 Freisler, "Willensstrafrecht; Versuch und Vollendung," p. 25.
117 Ibid., p. 26.
118 Ibid., p. 22.

NS jurists insisted that the distinction between attempt and accomplished deed ought to be irrelevant in adjudication because it was often fortuitous whether an attempt resulted in a successful deed or not. But the luck of the circumstances should not, in the NS legal view, determine the line between right and wrong. Since the "will of the perpetrator remains the same in the case of an attempted and a realized crime," noted Karl Krug, will-based criminal law should punish attempt and success equally.[119] The defenders of a will-based criminal law even wanted to punish unsuccessful attempts. In Freisler's view, criminal law adjudication could not change its attitude toward the perpetrator's will merely "because this will used an unfit means" to carry out the intended plan.[120]

In addition to forwarding the state's defense-line chronologically and equating the attempt with the accomplished deed, NS jurists demanded that each person involved in a criminal plan be punished equally. There was to be no difference between punishing incitement, aiding, abetting, or execution of the action. The goal, Krug pointed out, was to grasp and punish the entire will:

> The distinction between whether someone intends to act as a perpetrator or an abettor is irrelevant in comparison with the total criminal will which must be the sole object of conviction – all the more so since practice has shown in manifold ways that a correct assessment of the depth and strength of the criminal will as such cannot be given.[121]

119 Krug, "Drei Probleme des kommenden Strafrechts," p. 99. An example of the radicalization that came with the will-based criminal law (no distinction between the preparation, the attempt and the successful accomplishment of a deed) was a law against car traps (*Autofallengesetz*) which the Nazis introduced on June 22, 1938. The law which was retroactively valid declared the death penalty for erecting car traps to rob other persons. The occasion for its introduction were the robbings of the Götze-brothers between 1934 and 1938. The Götze-brothers were executed two days after the law came into force. See Werle, *Justizstrafrecht und polizeiliche Verbrechensbekämpfung im Dritten Reich*, pp. 200–201. See also Hartl, *Das nationalsozialistische Willensstrafrecht*, p. 379. The *Autofallengesetz* was abolished in 1947.

120 Freisler, "Willensstrafrecht; Versuch und Vollendung," p. 35.

Several Nazi legal theorists argued that the protection of the *völkisch* community required to punish any criminal expression of the will, even if it was a consequence of a factual error of a person (irrespective whether the error concerned the person himself or his circumstances). The *Reichsgericht* followed that line of argument by deciding in a case that a non-Jew, who had wrongly believed to be Jewish and was accused of race defilement (*Rassenschande*), had to be punished. See Hartl, *Das nationalsozialistische Willensstrafrecht*, p. 222.

121 Krug, "Drei Grundprobleme des kommenden Strafrechts," p. 102.

Quite obviously, under the conditions of a totalitarian regime this provision granted extensive leeway to a judge.

Nazi legal theorists tried to establish the independence of the will-based criminal law from a pure internal attitude-based criminal law (*Gesinnungsstrafrecht*), a pure threat-based criminal law (*Gefährdungsstrafrecht*), and a pure perpetrator-based law (*Täterstrafrecht*).

The will-based criminal law was of course close to an internal attitude-based law.[122] However, as Gleispach explained, a will-based criminal law did not punish the "mere will," but rather "the exercise of the evil will" in carrying out a plan. The execution and completion of the deed, as well as the kind of deed, would still be relevant.[123] Mezger clarified that, other than a pure *Gesinnungsstrafrecht*, a will-based criminal law did not punish "the heretical internal attitudes regardless of their external manifestations."[124]

Even a true Nazi like Freisler did not endorse an attitude-based criminal law, thereby refusing to follow the Nazi Party's Legal Office. While he accepted that the lawgiver's attention should be directed toward the criminal will, Freisler felt that inferences about that will could only be reliably drawn by examining matters of fact in the will's articulation. The purely internal mindset, apart from the offense, could not be subject to indictment. There was thus an objective "success-condition": The attempt or action had to be accomplished.

Nazi jurists rejected a purely attitude-based criminal law on the basis of pragmatic considerations rather than skepticism about the state's extensive intervention into the subject's inner sphere. Without objective evidence of the planning and preparation of a deed, or recognizable signs of an attempted action, reliable inferences about the inner attitude, mindset, and intention of the perpetrator were impossible.

Nazi legal theorists sought to separate will-based criminal law from a pure perpetrator-based law that linked crime to the personality of the offender. Although a will-based criminal law would also consider the perpetrator's personality and character, the theorists maintained that adjudication could not rest on a perpetrator-typology alone – the committed offense was still decisive. Freisler defended a connection between will-based and perpetrator-based law by arguing that adjudication should

122 Mezger, for example, noted that the will-based criminal law considered which internal attitudes caused the offense. "Thus a will-based criminal law", he claimed, "is equally an internal attitude-based criminal law." Mezger, *Deutsches Strafrecht* (1936), p. 29.

123 Gleispach, "Willensstrafrecht," p. 1069.

124 Mezger, *Deutsches Strafrecht* (1936), p. 29.

heed the relation between an offense and the corresponding perpetrator-personality. In other words, an appropriate punishment could only be achieved by taking the specific unworthiness of the perpetrator into account.[125]

The NS criminal law expert Paul Bockelmann supported a perpetrator-based law while criticizing traditional criminal law for failing to determine the appropriate punishment according to the perpetrator's specific character and personality. In the case of a criminal offender repeatedly committing crimes, Bockelmann argued, a proper verdict and punishment could not ignore his personal traits.[126]

Interestingly enough, Bockelmann attributed the law's ignorance toward the perpetrator's personal traits to the liberal separation of law and morality, more specifically, to Kant's distinction between an autonomous moral law and a heteronomous principle of law (*Rechtsgesetz*), which restricted the state's interventions to individual's external behaviour. "Only the conceptual separation of law and morality," Bockelmann wrote, "that neutralization of state and law, forbids the assessment of the personality and, thus, reduces law to the punishment of the deed. If the state is deprived of access to the individual's spiritual spheres, then law loses the human being as such."[127]

Ideological radicalization also strengthened the implementation of a perpetrator typology. Increasingly, Nazi legal thinkers tied the crime to the perpetrator's personality, as Mezger's following statement illustrates: "Particular crimes are due to a typical resolution of the will that allows us to characterize specific perpetrator types in their different criminal actions. ... Deed and perpetrator thus form an inextricable unity."[128] Such familiar type categories were the "habitual criminal," the "sexual criminal," the "cheater and defrauder," "the traitor," and the "corrupt criminal." These classic Nazi culprits were increasingly at the center of the state's watchful eye.[129]

125 Freisler, "Willensstrafrecht; Versuch und Vollendung," pp. 27–28.

126 Bockelmann, Paul, *Studien zum Täterstrafrecht, 1. Teil* (Berlin: Walter de Gruyter & Co., 1939), p. 44.

127 Ibid., p. 70.

128 Mezger, *Deutsches Strafrecht* (1936), pp. 29–30.

129 The war intensified law's focus on the perpetrator. A striking example is the reasoning of the SS Judge Norbert Pohl who argued in a letter to his superiors that the perpetrator's personality was paramount for jurisdiction. I discuss Norbert Pohl's letter in Chapter 6 of this book. For a discussion of the Law against Dangerous Habitual Criminals of November 24, 1933 and its effects see Wachsmann, Nikolaus, "From Indefinite Confinement to Extermination. 'Habitual Criminals' in the Third Reich," in

The close connection between a will-based and a perpetrator-based criminal law is also apparent in Mezger's concept of "conduct-of-life-guilt" (*Lebensführungsschuld*):

> Guilt is offense-guilt, but also conduct-of-life-guilt (*Lebensführungsschuld*), and therefore punishment is directed not only at the particular offense, but also at the personality of the perpetrator insofar as one can raise an accusation against the perpetrator. But this does not mean that punishment is solely directed at the personality of the perpetrator and his perilousness.[130]

Defenders of a will-based criminal law refused to equate it with a mere threat-based criminal law, which stressed the endangerment of the ethical stability of the community. Although a will-based criminal law would also emphasize preventive action against threats, NS theorists argued that the center of attention remained the will and its articulations. Nevertheless, a threat-based criminal law would concentrate on posed threats rather than on what actually happened, something Gleispach found "too inscrutable for the community members" and thus detrimental to the clarity of the criminal law.[131] Mezger located the difference between a threat-based and will-based criminal law in the fact that the latter required the intention to violate a statute and not merely to pose a danger. Moreover, each and every punishable articulation of the criminal will was not necessarily connected with an external danger.[132]

4.7 Nazi Criminal Law 1939–1945

The Nazi state applied criminal law brutally. One reason for the turn to pure terror was the rivalry between the judiciary and police, with the judiciary losing competencies. When SS leader Himmler became Chief of the German Police in 1936, he sought to control the whole security apparatus, including the judiciary. Himmler employed the Gestapo in particular to undermine the judiciary and, he hoped, establish the police "as an institution fighting criminality, equal in rank to the judiciary or even higher-ranking."[133] Parallel to the state judiciary, a police judiciary

Gellately, Robert and Stoltzfus, Nathan (eds.), *Social Outsiders in Nazi Germany* (Princeton University Press, 2001), pp. 165–191.

130 Mezger, *Deutsches Strafrecht* (1938), p. 135.

131 Gleispach, "Willensstrafrecht," p. 1069.

132 Mezger, Edmund, *Deutsches Strafrecht* (1938), p. 132.

133 Werle, *Justiz-Strafrecht und polizeiliche Verbrechensbekämpfung im Dritten Reich*, p. 3.

under Himmler emerged that represented, writes historian Eberhardt Schmidt, an "unleashing of police power."[134]

Immediately following the Nazi takeover in 1933, the police began imprisoning political opponents and other "criminals" without legal procedure or litigation. Prison now meant detention in a concentration camp, where inmates were often kept long after having served their sentences and with no chance of returning to civilian life. In the early years of the Third Reich, these police measures were based on the Presidential Decree for the Protection of People and State of February 28, 1933, which allowed state institutions to take extensive security measures under the pretext of ensuring public order and peace. In this period, the judiciary still prosecuted mysterious deaths (suspected killings) in the concentration camps when relatives filed a legal complaint. But after 1936, the judiciary lost control of the concentration camp system to the police.

With the outbreak of the war in 1939, several new or strengthened laws enhanced the power and terror of the NS regime. These included the Decree on Parasites upon the *Volk* of September 5, 1939 (*Volksschädlingsverordnung*); the Decree Against Violent Criminals of December 5, 1939 (*Gewaltverbrecherverordnung*); and the Decree on the Administration of Criminal Law against Poles and Jews of December 4, 1941 (*Verordnung über das Polen- und Judenstrafrecht*).[135] These laws were formulated in the spirit of both a perpetrator-based and will-based criminal law. In some paragraphs, the influence of an internal attitude-based law was also apparent.

The Decree on Parasites upon the *Volk* aimed to prevent a so called "inner front" during the war. The law thus regulated criminal offenses including pilferage (*Plünderung*), crimes in circumstances of air attacks, and crimes against public safety, all of which could be punished by up to fifteen years' imprisonment and even the death penalty. The decree sought to prevent acts that hampered and undermined the resistance capacity of the *Volk* by exploiting wartime conditions.[136] Deterrence constituted the decisive reason for punishment.

The aforementioned criminal offenses constituted breaches of loyalty toward the people's community. The courts focused increasingly on the

[134] Schmidt, Eberhard, *Einführung in die Geschichte der deutschen Strafrechtspflege*, 3rd ed. (Göttingen: Vandenhoeck & Ruprecht, 1965), p. 439.

[135] The full German title was: *Das nationalsozialistische Polenstrafrecht unter besonderer Berücksichtigung der Verordnung über die Strafrechtspflege gegen Polen und Juden in den eingegliederten Ostgebieten vom 4. Dezember 1941.*

[136] Examples were robbing empty apartments or attacking persons during brownout (measures of brownout were extensive during the war).

personality of the perpetrator rather than on the kind of offense. Accordingly, the perpetrator type was at the centre of adjudication: "the public enemy," "the parasite upon the *Volk*" (*Volksschädling*), "the saboteur," and the "loose cannon" (*der gemeingefährliche Täter*) all were to be eliminated from the *völkisch* community. Persons subsumed under these categories were thus subjected to relentless persecution and prosecution.

Moreover, the exceedingly broad definition of the offenses meant that judges had ample discretion when it came to sentencing. In particular, § 4 of the Decree on Parasites upon the *Volk*, which made "exploiting the situation of war" into grounds for intensifying punishment (*Ausnutzung des Kriegszustandes als Strafschärfung*), mandated that all such acts be punished by fifteen years' imprisonment or the death penalty (should the act be found especially detrimental to the sound perception of the *Volk*).[137]

The Decree Against Violent Criminals, which aimed to protect the *Volk* against the so-called "inner front and enemy" in war, was strongly influenced by the idea of a will-based criminal law – that is, the bearer of any intention and expression of will, which posed a risk to domestic security, was slated for annihilation. The decree mandated that any violent criminal offense – sexual violence (*Notzucht*), street robbery, and bank robbery were specified – committed with a weapon ("weapon" here was defined broadly) deserved the death penalty. The law was retroactively valid. Assistance and attempt were also punishable by death.

The Decree on the Administration of Criminal Law Against Poles and Jews of December 4, 1941 strengthened the penalties first introduced in the occupied eastern territories on June 6, 1940. The decree threatened Jews and Poles with the death penalty if they committed a criminal act against the German *Volk*. These "crimes" included public anti-German utterances, removing or damaging the public announcements of German administrative offices and government agencies, and behavior that harmed the German *Volk* by deprecating its standing and reputation. Crucially, this decree also provided a clear example of applying the principle of analogy of law (*Rechtsanalogie*), stating that: "Poles and Jews will also be punished if they violate German criminal legal statutes or commit a deed that, in accordance with the basic idea of German criminal law, deserves to be punished, given state exigencies in the annexed Eastern territories."[138]

[137] Werle, *Justiz-Strafrecht und polizeiliche Verbrechensbekämpfung im Dritten Reich*, p. 234.

[138] Article II, Decree on the Administration of Criminal Law against Poles and Jews from December 4, 1941. For the German text of the Decree on the Administration of Criminal Law against Poles and Jews from December 4, 1941 (*Polen- und Judenstrafrechtsverordnung*

The influence of an internal-attitude based criminal law was apparent in the decree's Article III.2, which stated that a deed displaying an especially disreputable mental attitude was punishable by death. Article III.2 also applied the death sentence to adolescent felons. Article VII of the decree declared that Poles could not recuse German judges. Additionally, Poles could be sentenced to death by court martials for grave uprisings against Germans or endangering German organizational efforts (Article XIII). Court martials could also deliver perpetrators to the Gestapo without any legal proceedings.

The line between politics and law had vanished. The Decree on the Administration of Criminal Law against Poles and Jews was a brutal police instrument that removed all legal security for Poles and Jews.[139] Himmler had won the rivalry between the police and judiciary, which was ultimately decided in the annexed territories. In 1942, he reached an agreement with Justice Minister Thierack that the police would assume penal authority and power in Poland.[140]

4.8 Concluding Remarks

In the realm of criminal law, the legal theorists' complicity with the NS state had particularly chilling effects: They paved the way for the deterioration of the law into an instrument of the regime's political combat.

vom 4. Dezember 1941), see *Deutsches Reichsgesetzblatt* 1941, Part I, Nr. 140, pp. 759–761. For a detailed discussion of this law see Majer, Diemut, *"Non-Germans" under the Third Reich. The Nazi Judicial and Administrative System in Germany and Occupied Eastern Europe, with Special Regard to Occupied Poland, 1939–1945*, transl. by Hill, Peter Thomas; Humphrey, Edward Vance; Levin, Brian (Baltimore and London: The Johns Hopkins University Press, 2003), pp. 412–469.

139 The moralizing guidelines for criminal law were suspended in the Criminal Law Decree against Poles and Jews. It was considered as a purely authoritarian perpetrator-based criminal law for securing the German rule in the Eastern territories, with no connection to the ethical order of the German people's community. See Werle, *Justizstrafrecht und polizeiliche Verbrechensbekämpfung im Dritten Reich*, pp. 373–374.

140 In one of his postwar interrogations by the American CIC, the SS Judge Konrad Morgen remarked on the relationship between the judiciary and the Gestapo in Poland: "In regard to criminal acts of those persons (i.e. Poles and Jews), the authority of the judiciary was completely ruled out." See Morgen, Konrad, American CIC Interrogation, October 12, 1946, p. 7, Interrogation Records Prepared for War Crimes Proceedings at Nuremberg 1945–1947, US National Archives, Record Group 238, Microfilm 1019, Roll 47. Morgen also complained that during the war the rights of the judges were restricted; the judiciary was "at the mercy" of the Gestapo. He added: "Thierack broke the backbone of the judiciary." Ibid., p. 17.

Although legal thinkers minimally tried to keep the transformations of criminal law within certain bounds, their general support of a harsh criminal law system had dramatic consequences for those people perceived as a threat to the regime. The Nazi jurists' attempts for conceptual refinements owed to non-ignorable juridical expertise, and their reservations against a blunt reading of a will-focused criminal law conception collapsed under the political pressure of a totalitarian state.[141]

The war intensified the brutal application of criminal law, as ruthless deterrence and a racialized perpetrator typology became its dominant elements. Punishments, meanwhile, became indistinguishable from the political measures of the authoritarian state. The judge mutated into an executor of the Führer's will. Increasingly, the main question for adjudicators concerned under which type a perpetrator could be subsumed. If a defendant was suspected of an evil mindset endangering the community, even the death penalty was deemed appropriate.

The moralization of criminal law supported its political misuse. What prominent legal theorists claimed to be ethically obligatory and in line with the "sanitary and sound perception of the *Volk*" resulted in countless criminal cases and even deaths for people whose only "crime" was not having shared or met the standards of a *völkisch Sittenordnung.*

The perception of morality as the binding cement for the Aryan people's community supported the erosion of basic normative standards in politically sensitive areas. The Decree on the Administration of Criminal Law against Poles and Jews, for example, constituted part of the German legal order for which the principle of "racial inequality" was fundamental.

[141] A striking example is the increasingly inhuman jurisdiction of the *Volksgerichtshof* under one of the most ferocious defenders of a will-based criminal law, Freisler, from 1942 until Februrary 1945. Freisler was responsible for the death sentences and the execution of the members of the "Weiße Rose," a Munich student group who had distributed regime-critical leaflets in the university. Freisler's conduct of the trial against the defendants in the Stauffenberg plot was so much against all court rules (Freisler, obsessed by prosecuting the "criminal will" and the "honorless mindset" tried to personally humiliate the defendants; he repeatedly screaemd at them and called some of the defendants "Würstchen") that even Justice Minister Thierack, otherwise a fanatic National Socialist, noted in a letter to Martin Bormann on September 8, 1944 that Freisler had undermined the "dignity of the court." Justice Minister Thierack to the Secretary of the Führer Bormann; cited according to Lüken, *Der Nationalsozialismus und das materielle Strafrecht*, pp. 31–32. See also "The Sentencing of Hans and Sophie Scholl and Christoph Probst, 22 February 1943," in Steinweis, Alan E. and Rachlin Robert D. (eds.), *The Law in Nazi Germany. Ideology, Opportunism, and the Perversion of Justice* (New York, Oxford: Berghahn, 2013), Appendices, pp. 204–207(= the sentence was signed by Freisler); see also Rachlin, "Roland Freisler and the Volksgerichtshof. The Court as an Instrument of Terror," in Steinweis and Rachlin (eds.), *The Law in Nazi Germany*, pp. 63–88.

Already, criminal law addressed at the Aryan population confounded law and politics; but this politicization of law became particularly violent when it addressed a population considered to be "unequal" or "inferior."

Although the position of the judiciary was ultimately undermined by Hitler and Himmler's SS and police authority, the legal theorists prepared the groundwork for this power play. An illustrative example appears in Mezger's 1938 explanation of the criminal law's new course: "Apart from intense conflicts of opinion, the orientation of the new law may be characterized as a connection between an ethically founded criminal law and a biologically founded security law, with an emphasis on an evaluative understanding of law and a new total conception of criminal law."[142] Interestingly, some legal theorists later became skeptical of this development of criminal law. In his 1935 article "Verbrechen und Tatbestand,"[143] Georg Dahm had been highly critical of liberal criminal law's focus on the criminal offense and factual matters (namely, the precise appraisal of events). This entailed that only if the committed act was declared to be statutorily illegal could a court take action and sentence a defendant (*nulla poena sine lege*). Dahm outright rejected the liberal principle that required the judge to focus on the corpus delicti in assessing the descriptive elements and features of a deed (*Tatbestand*). He even claimed that "the concept and word of corpus delicti should be removed from criminal law doctrine altogether. The doctrine of the corpus delicti is not only fruitless, but harmful. It obscures the essence and inner nature of crimes."[144]

Consequently, Dahm supported a perpetrator-based criminal law that took into account the relation to the people's community and "the life order of the German *Volk*."[145] In a truly perpetrator-based criminal law, he argued, the offense and the perpetrator formed a unity.[146]

Yet in an article published in 1944, Dahm changed sides and wrote disapprovingly of the developments in Nazi criminal law.[147] In particular,

[142] Mezger, *Deutsches Strafrecht* (1938), p. 19.

[143] Dahm, "Verbrechen und Tatbestand," in Dahm, Georg; Huber, Ernst Rudolf; Larenz, Karl; Michaelis, Karl; Schaffstein, Friedrich; Siebert, Wolfgang, *Grundfragen der Neuen Rechtswissenschaft* (Berlin: Junker & Dünnhaupt, 1935), pp. 62–107.

[144] Ibid., p. 89.

[145] Ibid., p. 85.

[146] Ibid., p. 92.

[147] Dahm, "Gerechtigkeit und Zweckmäßigkeit im Strafrecht der Gegenwart," in Bockelmann, Paul; Dahm, Georg; Dohna, Alexander Graf zu; Engisch, Karl; Exner, Franz; Lange, Richard; Mezger, Edmund; Peters, Karl; Schmidt, Eberhard; Schönke, Adolf; Sieverts, Rudolf; Weber, Hellmuth von; Welzel Hans, *Probleme der Strafrechtserneuerung* (Berlin: Walter de Gruyter & Co., 1944), pp. 1–23.

he bemoaned the moralization of criminal law and its instrumentalization for political and administrative purposes:

> A legal statute is neither a rule of usefulness (*Nützlichkeitsregel*) nor a moral catechism. Hence, there exist boundaries with respect to all those efforts that intersect in such a peculiar way in our time, namely the endeavor to unify law and morality, similarly the inclination to transform law into mere planning, political and technical organization, and the tendency to blur the distinction between state administration and judiciary.[148]

Dahm objected that in such NS legislation as the Decree Against Violent Criminals, for example, the aspect of deterrence superseded that of atonement, resulting in a decree that used punishment for the purposes of deterrence and crime prevention to an extent that "social conscience" could no longer bear.[149] Dahm further maintained that the death sentence could neither be considered a measure of protection nor deterrence: "It contradicts the [death penalty's] ethical meaning and irrational content if one intends to apply it in the sense of a pure rule of expediency (*reine Zweckmäßigkeitsregel*). The death sentence is always a punishment that has to withstand scrutiny not only from the viewpoint of usefulness, but also from the standpoint of justice."[150] In 1944, Dahm was also highly critical of a pure perpetrator-based criminal law, arguing that the corpus delicti was a crucial factor in adjudication. Indeed, he thought it impossible to develop a perpetrator typology that would help the judge to reach a fair verdict beyond "subjective impressions and vague assumptions."[151] A perpetrator-based criminal law, missing the objective standards of an offense-based criminal law, might, Dahm openly warned, merely enhance a judge's arbitrary assessment of the defendant and his personality. A "pure criminological perpetrator-based criminal law," Dahm added remorsefully, "is merely a dream, indeed an ugly dream."[152]

[148] Ibid., p. 2.
[149] Ibid., p. 3.
[150] Ibid., p. 12.
[151] Ibid., p. 18.
[152] Ibid.

5

Racial Legislation

5.1 Introductory Remarks

The Nazi regime's racial ideology, which culminated in the Holocaust, was a constituent part of the Nazi movement since its beginnings. In the Party Program of February 24, 1920, the separation of Jewish from non-Jewish German citizens was one of the NSDAP's political goals. Article 4 stated: "Only a national comrade (*Volksgenosse*) can be a citizen. A national comrade can only be someone of German blood, without consideration of confession. Consequently, no Jew can be a national comrade." Article 5 held that "(w)hoever has no citizenship is only able to live in Germany as a guest and must be under the authority of legislation for foreigners (*Fremden-Gesetzgebung*)." Article 6 excluded Jews from political participation by restricting their right to run for public office and to take part in "determining matters concerning administration and law" to citizens.[1]

With Hitler's nomination to Reich Chancellor in January 1933, the opportunity arrived to implement this program. From the outset, the Führer state deliberately took legal measures for realizing its conception of a racially pure ethnic community, as outlined in the Party program's anti-Jewish directives.

The NS regime's contempt for people who did not meet its criteria for racial purity, strength, and sanity had fatal consequences for other groups as well: At least 80,000 handicapped and mentally ill persons fell victim to the Nazi euthanasia program and nearly 500,000 Sinti and Roma were

[1] *Das Programm der NSDAP und seine weltanschaulichen Grundlagen* (München: Zentralverlag der NSDSAP, Franz Eher Nachfolger, 1935). See online www.documentarchiv.de/wr/1920/nsdap-programm.html.

murdered.[2] But NS racial doctrine was antisemitic at its core. Solving the so-called "Jewish question" topped Hitler's political agenda.

This chapter focuses on Nazi anti-Jewish legislation. After outlining the main theoretical conceptions that influenced and shaped Nazi racial doctrine, it turns to the reception of this ideology by legal theorists. The transition from juridical regulations to the extermination program will then be explored in light of the Nuremberg Laws and their subsequent decrees. As I will show, the administrative regulations enacted during the implementation of the Nuremberg Laws reach deeply into the genocidal period. The concluding remarks address some of the theoretical normative questions this continuity raises.

5.2 Nazi Racial Doctrine

In the late-nineteenth century, highly ideological reinterpretations of biological and anthropological data produced crude theories about races, their composition, and the physical and mental traits of those humans who belonged to them. The racial theories that animated Nazi ideology were a concoction of these pseudoscientific claims, preconceptions, social stereotypes, and prejudices.

Racial anthropologists claimed that "race" was a value-free category of empirical description and classification. De facto, however, the notion of race became a category of normative assessment, specifically when linked to National Socialist standards of superiority and inferiority. "Race" and "racial affiliation" evolved into benchmarks for social acceptance, exclusion, and, ultimately, denigration. These benchmarks established that certain groups of human beings, foremost Jews, were fundamentally

[2] The NS regime also persecuted homosexual and lesbian persons, often sending them to concentration camps where they were treated particularly harshly. Only more recent studies have looked into these victim's fate. See Giles, Geoffrey J., "The persecution of gay men and lesbians during the Third Reich," in Friedman, Jonathan C. (ed.), *The Routledge Handbook of the Holocaust* (London and New York: Routledge, 2011), pp. 385–396 (according to Giles, there was "no gay Holocaust." Ibid., pp. 394–395). Giles, "The Institutionalization of Homosexual Panic in the Third Reich," in Gellately, Robert and Stoltzfus, Nathan (eds.), *Social Outsiders in Nazi Germany* (Princeton: Princeton University Press, 2001), pp. 233–255; Murphy, Melanie, "Homosexuality and the Law in the Third Reich," in Michalczyk, John J. (ed.), *Nazi Law. From Nuremberg to Nuremberg* (London, Oxford et al: Bloomsbury, 2018), pp. 110–124; Zinn, Alexander, *"Aus dem Volkskörper entfernt"? Homosexuelle Männer im Nationalsozialismus* (Frankfurt, New York: Campus 2018).

different from Germans and thus had to be segregated from the mainstream German population.

In her impressive study of the Nazis' administrative implementation of their racial fanaticism, Cornelia Essner reveals two main directions in "the maze of racial thinking."[3] The first, which she calls "contagionistic antisemitism," focused on maintaining "racial purity" by keeping German blood free from alien and corrosive influences. The second prong of racial antisemitism was found in a genetic racism that drew on racial anthropology and biological research on inheritance.[4]

Contagionistic antisemitism was motivated by the fear that fusing German and Jewish blood would lead to the degeneration of future German generations. Any sexual contact between an "Aryan"[5] woman and a Jewish man would make it impossible for the Aryan woman to give birth to a fully Aryan child, even with another father, who was Aryan.

According to Essner, a main inspiration for contagionistic antisemitism was Arthur Dinter's *The Sin Against the Blood* (1918) – a primitive anti-Jewish melodrama that had tremendous public impact.[6] Although Dinter's vulgar fantasies did not meet with the Nazi leadership's approval, the contamination thesis (that sexual intercourse between Jews and Aryans would result in impure Aryan-German blood) continued to exercise great influence.[7] A prominent proponent of this form of

[3] Essner, Cornelia, *Die "Nürnberger Gesetze" oder die Verwaltung des Rassenwahns 1933–1945* (Paderborn, München, Wien, Zürich: Ferdinand Schöningh, 2002), p. 21.

[4] Ibid., pp. 32–49.

[5] "Aryan" was an invented term for racially pure Germanness. See Hitler, Adolf, "Aryan and Jew," in Rabinbach, Anson and Gilman, Sander L. (eds.), *The Third Reich Sourcebook* (Berkely, Los Angeles, London: University of California Press, 2013), pp. 187–191 (extract from Hitler's *Mein Kampf*).

[6] Dinter, Artur, *Die Sünde wider das Blut. Ein Zeitroman* (Leipzig: Matthes und Thost, 1920). For an online version of the 1921 ed. of Dinter's text see https://archive.org/details/Dinter-Artur-Die-Suende-wider-das-Blut_936/page/n1. The story was about an Aryan German and his Jewish wife who died of her own shock at her only being able to give birth to "monstrous" children; the Aryan father eventually found parental peace and happiness when reconnecting with his illegitimate son whom he had fathered with an Aryan girl. The book was hugely popular, in 1921 it appeared already in its 16th ed. Up to 1934, 260,000 copies were sold. See Kren, George M. and Morris, Rodler, F., "Race and Spirituality: Artur Dinter's Theosophical Antisemitism," in *Holocaust and Genocide Studies* 6, 3 (1991), pp. 233–252, p. 238; Hartung, Günther, "Artur Dinter, Erfolgsautor des frühen Nationalsozialismus," in Hartung, Günter, *Deutschfaschistische Literatur und Ästhetik. Gesammelte Studien* (Leipzig: Leipziger Universitätsverlag, 2001), pp. 99–124.

[7] Dinter was expelled from the Nazi Party (NSDAP) on October 11, 1928. Even Dinter's close connection with Streicher could not save him from being shunned by the NSDAP. The main reason for Dinter's exclusion in 1928 was that Hitler did not want to alienate Catholic circles, something Dinter's attacks against Jews certainly provoked. According to

antisemitism was Julius Streicher, the fanatic National Socialist editor of the notorious tabloid *Der Stürmer*.[8]

The contagionistic ideology sought to inhibit sexual relations between Jews and non-Jews. In the first years of Nazi rule, race defilement (*Rassenschande*) was subject to public defamation.[9] With the 1935 Nuremberg Laws, which banned marriages and extramarital sexual intercourse between Jews and Aryan Germans, race defilement became a legal offense which, beginning in 1936, could even be punished with imprisonment.

The second version of antisemitism, genetic racism, originated in the natural sciences in the late-nineteenth century, when biological research began focusing on race. For instance, scientists investigated whether Mendel's laws on heredity aligned with the descent and promulgation of racial features.[10] Seeing race as a specific set of hereditary traits

Ernst Piper, Hitler's accommodating attitude toward Catholic circles was also motivated by his experiences in Austria where the politics of German-nationalists such as Georg von Schönerer (he had aimed at a union of the German-speaking part of the Austrian-Hungarian monarchy with the German Reich) had failed because of its rejection by the Catholic church. See Piper, Ernst, *Alfred Rosenberg. Hitlers Chefideologe* (München: Pantheon, 2007), pp. 167–168.

8 How fanatically Streicher stuck to the contagionistic ideology is confirmed by Bernhard Lösener in his report on his experiences as racial expert (*Rassereferent*) in the Third Reich's Ministry of Interior. See Lösener, Bernhard, "At the Desk of Racial Affairs in the Reich Ministry of the Interior," in *Legislating the Holocaust. The Bernhard Loesener Memoirs and Supporting Documents*, ed. by Schleunes, Karl A., transl. by Scherer, Carol (Boulder, Colorado: Westview Press, 2001), pp. 33–109; here: p. 53. However, Lösener's thesis that the Nuremberg Laws brought some legal certainty for Jews seems to me highly contentious (see section 4 of this chapter).

9 See Gross, Raphael, "Guilt, Shame, Anger, Indignation: Nazi Law and Nazi Morals," in Steinweis, Alan E. and Rachlin, Robert D. (eds.), *The Law in Nazi Germany. Ideology, Opportunism, and the Perversion of Justice* (New York, Oxford: Berghahn Books, 2013), pp. 89–104.

10 A major work of this kind of research was Fischer, Eugen, *Die Rehobother Bastards und das Bastardisierungsproblem beim Menschen* (Jena: Gustav Fischer, 1913; reprint Graz: Akademische Druck- und Verlagsanstalt, 1961). In this book, Fischer discussed his study of people descending from marital and non-marital relations between native black people and European (German) settlers in the German colony of South West Africa, today's Namibia, investigating whether the Mendelian laws of heredity applied to this "mixed population" and whether it amounted to a race with specific characteristics. In the fall of 1908, Fischer stayed four months in South West Africa (his research was funded by the Humboldt Stiftung). The political and cultural context of Fischer's research as well as his terminology (referring to persons of mixed offspring as "Bastards" and using the term "Hottentotten" for the Khoikhoi people and the ethnic group of the Nama) is highly problematic, indeed racist. As Fischer noted in the book's introduction, his interest in the mixed people in South West Africa was aroused by "the great war against the Herero and the Hottentotten from 1904–1907" which had "made wide circles of our *Volk* acquainted

prompted further studies of whether and how genetic endowments were passed on, and what effects this would have for the progeny's racial strength or weakness. A hotly debated issue was the deleterious effect of the mixture of races on hereditary dispositions.

In the wake of Darwinism, the survival and decay of human races became a pressing issue. In the 1921 edition of an influential treatise on human hereditary doctrine and racial hygiene, for instance, the authors Erwin Baur, Eugen Fischer, and Fritz Lenz discussed the possible threat to the "Nordic race" by racial blending.[11] Although the authors refrained from promoting doctrines of racial superiority and inferiority within the German population, they objected to racial "infiltration" from eastern Europeans.[12]

with the situation in German-South West Africa as such, and with its indigenous population, among them 'the Nation of Bastards'." Fischer, *Die Rehobother Bastards und das Bastardisierungsproblem beim Menschen*, p. 2 (cited after the 1961 reprint). The German war against the Herero ended in genocide; at the time of Fischer's stay in 1908, the surviving Herero and Nama were held in concentration camps, exposed to slave labor, mistreatment and cruel medical experiments. Although Fischer did not find any evidence for the claim that a mixture of races would lead to their degeneration, he maintained in the last part of the book that the mixture of races was harmful, which had a tremendous effect on racial hygiene and racial science in Germany. See Weingart, Peter; Kroll, Jürgen; Bayertz, Kurt, *Rasse, Blut und Gene. Geschichte der Eugenik und Rassenhygiene in Deutschland* (Frankfurt am Main: Suhrkamp, 1988), pp. 100–102; see also Essner, *Die "Nürnberger Gesetze" oder die Verwaltung des Rassenwahns 1933–1945*, pp. 41–42. For the connection between racial research before World War I and the racial research under the Nazis see also Lusane, Clarence, *Hitler's Black Victims. The Historical Experiences of Afro Germans, European Blacks, Africans, and African Americans in the Nazi Era* (London and New York: Routledge, 2002), pp. 43–67.

11 See Baur, Erwin; Fischer, Eugen; Lenz, Fritz, *Grundriß der menschlichen Erblichkeitslehre und Rassenhygiene*, vol. II (authored by Fritz Lenz), *Menschliche Auslese und Rassenhygiene* (München: J.F. Lehmanns 1921), pp. 105–108. For an English version of the third ed. of the *Menschliche Erblichkeitslehre* (1927) see Baur, Fischer, Lenz, *Human Heredity*, transl. by Paul, Eden and Paul, Cedar (London: George Allen & Unwin, New York: Macmillan, 1931). The authors mention that they made some changes to the English version. Particularly revealing is ch. XV (authored by Lenz), "Psychological Differences between the Leading Races of Mankind," in *Human Heredity*, pp. 623–699.

12 Lenz, for whom migration from Eastern Europe should be inhibited altogether, recommended instead German migration to the East, foremost Russia. See Lenz, *Menschliche Auslese und Rassenhygiene*, pp. 163–164. In a section on the situation of Jews in Germany, Lenz argued that the acceptance of Jews from Eastern Europe would not be in the interest of German Jews. Ibid., p. 104. Lenz also made inhuman suggestions about the implementation of racial hygiene, including the recommendation of forced sterilization of persons with hereditary diseases, mental disorders and problems such as alcoholism. The political direction of Lenz's views becomes obvious in his statement that "the decisive objective of practical racial hygiene must be that the gifted and the able-bodied will reproduce more strongly than the unfit and inferior." Ibid., pp. 118–119. Lenz also

Research on hereditary racial features in the years before and immediately after the First World War was not yet directed specifically against Jews. That changed in the 1920s.[13] "Racial scientists" (*Rasseforscher*) continued to claim that they were only interested in empirical studies of racial features, traits, and various anthropological differences. Yet racial research and hygiene, which had professed to investigate the preservation of the sane biological substance of populations, increasingly merged with *völkisch* ideology and antisemitism.

The career of Hans F. K. Günther provides a striking example of a *Rasseforscher* cultivating his image as an empirical scientist. Having developed a strong interest in anthropology after studying German literature (he completed his doctorate in 1915), Günther was more of a public writer than an academic thinker. His widely read study on German racial characteristics appeared in 1922, followed two years later by a book on the racial traits of Europeans. In 1930, Günther published a racial study of the Jewish people.[14]

These publications had a tremendous impact on Nazi racial thinking. In particular, Günther's theses that Jews' physical and mental features distinguished them from European races, and thus any mixing of Nordics and Jews should be avoided, became central topoi of Nazi doctrine.

"Race is a concept of natural science applied to human beings," Günther claimed, thus making it a "concept of the descriptive study of human beings (*ein Begriff der beschreibenden Menschenkunde*)."[15] The notion of race would constitute a mere classificatory concept, similar to such categories as family, genus, and species.[16] Günther's definition of "race" as "a human

considered the prohibition of marriages in case one of the partners suffered from venereal disease, but noted that "the rank of our population's ethical views (*sittliche Anschauungen*) is not high enough" to accept such measures. Within a democratic state, he added, racial hygiene legislation could not proceed beyond the endorsement of the major part of the population's ethical conscience. Ibid., pp. 123–124.

13 See Essner, *Die "Nürnberger Gesetze" oder die Verwaltung des Rassenwahns 1933–1945*, p. 49; Weingart, Kroll, Bayertz, *Rasse, Blut und Gene. Geschichte der Eugenik und Rassenhygiene in Deutschland*, pp. 355–366.

14 The titles of the three books are: Günther, Hans F. K., *Rassenkunde des deutschen Volkes* (München/Berlin: J. F. Lehmanns, 1922); Günther, Hans F. K, *Rassenkunde Europas. Mit besonderer Berücksichtigung der Rassengeschichte der Hauptvölker indogermanischer Sprache Rassenkunde des jüdischen Volkes* (München: J. F. Lehmanns, 1924; 3rd revised ed., 1929); Günther, Hans F. K., *Rassenkunde des jüdischen Volkes*, 2nd ed. (München: J. F. Lehmanns, 1930). An English translation of the second edition of *Rassenkunde Europas* appeared as Günther, *The Racial Elements of European History*, transl. by Wheeler, G. C. (London: Methuen & Co., 1927).

15 Günther, *Rassenkunde des Deutschen Volkes* (1922), p. 7.

16 Ibid., p 8.

group, marked off from every other human group through its proper combination of bodily and mental characteristics, which in turn produces only its like," found its way into the Nazi racial law commentaries.[17]

Günther emphasized the distinction between race and *Volk*. While a race was marked by specific biological, anthropological, and mental traits, a *Volk*, he argued, was additionally constituted by its cultural traditions, attitudes, values, and even language. The term "*Volk*" was thus a historical-moral concept, referring to "human beings of the same language and ethical attitudes (*Gesittung*)."[18]

According to Günther, the German people did not correspond to a single race. Rather, it consisted of various races – the Nordic, Mediterranean, Dinaric, Alpine, and East Baltic.[19] Although Günther clearly preferred the Nordic race, his categorical system had to incorporate racial strands associated with southern Germans. He thought the Nordic race to be superior to the other races, particularly the East Baltics.[20] Günther's adoration of Nordic racial traits (tall and slim stature, narrow faces, fair hair, and blue eyes) revealed his racial prejudices and flagrantly contradicted his presumptive self-depiction as an empirical scientist.

Günther saw the strengthening of Nordic racial features (what he called "*Aufnordung*") as the only way to avert further decay of the German *Volk* through migration and the mixture of Germans with non-Germans. "A consequential, pure, and value-creating unfolding of German life," he wrote, "is only possible out of the blood and spirit of the Nordic race."[21] His work Rassenkunde des deutschen Volkes included thoughts on how to enhance Nordic breeding.[22]

17 Günther, *Rassenkunde Europas*, 3rd ed. (1929), p. 8; Günther, *The Racial Elements of European History* (1927), p. 3; a similar definition occurs already in Günther, *Rassenkunde des Deutschen Volkes* (1922), p. 13.

18 Günther, *Rassenkunde des Deutschen Volkes* (1922), p. 7.

19 See Günther, *The Racial Elements of European History*, ch. II. In the third German ed. (1929), Günther presents a slightly different list of European races, that is, the Nordic race, the Western (westisch) race, the dinaric race, the Eastern (ostisch) race, and the East Baltic race; see Günther, *Rassenkunde Europas* (1929), pp. 7–13. Basically the same list (the ostisch race is additionally specified as alpine race) is mentioned in Günther, Hans F. K., *Rasse, Tod und Teufel. Der heldische Gedanke*, 4th ed. (München: J. F. Lehmanns, 1935), p. 178.

20 Günther's preference for the Nordic race might have had personal reasons: he was married to a Norwegian woman and lived in Scandinavia from 1923 until 1929.

21 Günther, *Rassenkunde des deutschen Volkes* (1922), p. 349.

22 One of Günther's suggestions is that nordic children from poor, child-reach families should be adopted by economically better off nordic people with a firm nordic mental attitude. See Günther, *Rassenkunde des deutschen Volkes*, 1922, p. 357.

In his 1920 text *Ritter, Tod und Teufel*, Günther had already expressed the urgency of leading the German people back to the Nordic worldview.[23] In stressing the importance of committing to a Nordic existence, he postulated a racial moral law similar to Kant's categorical imperative: "Act so, that you can always think the direction of your will as a foundational directive of Nordic-racial legislation."[24] Günther offered the following explanation for the directive's philosophical background: Other than Kant, Fichte had taken the step toward a *Volk*-bound legislation. However, Fichte still had no insight into "the nexuses of blood" (*Blutzusammenhänge*). This was only available, according to Günther, when nineteenth-century thinkers abandoned cosmopolitanism's "ideal of humanity" and "universal legislation," a step supported by racial science. The study of races, Günther added, would ultimately lead from natural science into the sphere of ethical values.[25]

The pernicious character of Günther's work became yet more apparent in his racial study of the Jewish people. Just as Germans were supposedly composed of different races, Günther maintained that Jews were a mix of racial elements, foremost Near Eastern and Oriental races. He divided these two groups into Israelites and Hebrews. The former had lived in Palestine, while the Hebrews had lived in Egypt, Africa, and northern parts of the Near East, from where they migrated to Palestina (Canaa) and mixed with Jews there. Günther further argued that the Jewish people was shaped by Western, Hamite, Nordic, and Negro races.[26]

23 Günther, *Ritter, Tod und Teufel*, 4th ed. (1935), p. 191. Added to the the fourth edition is Günther's postscript (*Nachwort*) to the book's third edition of 1928 in which he states that he made only some slight changes in terminology, style and in shortening of repetitive passages, but otherwise left the text in the form of its first publication in 1920. Since Günther added no further postscript, one can assume that also the fourth edition is in its substance identical to the 1920 text. An online version of *Ritter, Tod, und Teufel*, 4th ed. (1935), is available under https://archive.org/details/RitterTodUndTeufelDerHeldische Gedanke.

Günther's reflections in *Ritter, Tod und Teufel* (4th ed. 1935) are in alignment with Nazi racial and political ideology. Take, for example, the following statements: "Morals (*Gesittung*) is a shaping of one's conduct of life that each national comrade (*Volksgenosse*) perceives as a duty." Günther, *Ritter, Tod und Teufel*, 4th ed. (1935), p. 111; "Heroic statecraft will only emanate from a hero, not from ministers or representatives of a majority, and not from envoys of the masses." Ibid., p. 152.

24 Günther, *Rassenkunde des deutschen Volkes* (1922), p. 365. The same formulation of the racial-ethical imperative is in Günther, *Ritter, Tod und Teufel* (4th ed. 1935), p. 191.

25 Günther, *Rassenkunde des deutschen Volkes* (1922), p. 366.

26 Günther, *Rassenkunde des jüdischen Volkes*, pp. 63–115. In this book, Günther distinguished between the following European races: the Nordic, Phalic, Estern, Western, Dinaric, and East Baltic one. See also Steinweis, Alan E., *Studying the Jew. Scholarly*

Apart from his reflections on Jewish racial history, Günther devoted a chapter of *Rassenkunde des jüdischen Volkes* to an extensive discussion of contemporary Jews' physical and behavioral characteristics. His description was chock-full of negative stereotypes and racial prejudices, despite his vow to avoid judging the Jewish people, let alone ascribing them inferiority. Günther claimed his book merely described the Jews' otherness (*Andersartigkeit*) – that is, their mental-spiritual difference. Yet by confounding the descriptive and evaluative, he attributed the advent of the so-called "Jewish question" to this otherness – a problem whose solution required in his view the strict separation of Jews and non-Jews.[27]

The normative subtext of Günther's book belies his insistence on racial science (*Rassenkunde*) as just a branch of descriptive natural science. Nevertheless, he successfully upheld his nimbus as a mere value-neutral anthropologist and racial expert both during and after the Nazi era. Despite being one of the major inspirations for the regime's racial fanaticism, Günther managed to avoid postwar legal proceedings.[28]

Besides the two forms of antisemitism distinguished by Essner, namely contagionistic and biological-hereditary antisemitism, one could identify a culturally based form that built on the accomplishments of German culture and philosophy. The idolization of Germanic virtues and values (inspired by Günther's adoration of the Nordic race) gave rise to a kind of racially grounded ethical perfectionism that not only advocated breeding and cultivating a racially noble species, but considered this goal to be ethically obligatory.

Max Gerstenhauer's text *Das ewige Deutschland* (The eternal Germany) provides a striking example of this form of racial ethics.[29]

Antisemitism in Nazi Germany (Cambridge, MA and London: Harvard University Press, 2008), pp. 28–33.

[27] See Günther, *Rassenkunde des deutschen Volkes*, p. 433 (Appendix: Das Judentum).

[28] Günther was in an internment camp after the war, but eventually he was classified as a mere Nazi Follower (*Mitläufer*).

[29] Gerstenhauer, Max, *Das ewige Deutschland. Idee und Gestalt* (Leipzig: Armanen 1940); a part of Gerstenhauer's book (pp. 58–68; slightly shortened) is reprinted in Pauer-Studer, Herlinde and Fink, Julian (eds.), *Rechtfertigungen des Unrechts. Das Rechtsdenken im Nationalsozialismus in Originaltexten* (Berlin: Suhrkamp, 2014), pp. 398–410. Another work of cultural racism is Hildebrandt, Kurt, *Norm, Entartung und Verfall. Bezogen auf den Einzelnen/Die Rasse/Den Staat* (Stuttgart: W. Kohlhammer 1934, 2nd ed. 1939). This book was a revised edition of two texts Hildebrandt, a National Socialist philosophy professor in Kiel (he also held a doctorate in medicine) had published in 1920. Although Hildebrandt's book included a chapter on race, racial degeneration, and racial hygiene, it did not indulge in the aggressive anti-Jewish rhetoric displayed in similar works of the time.

According to Gerstenhauer, racial science as he viewed it (that is, based on biological and anthropological doctrine) was internally connected with a *völkisch* worldview, thus yielding a "new system of ethics" that relied on a harmony of ethical and racial-physical laws.[30] For Gerstenhauer, a person's essence (that is, a person's will and mental and ethical attitudes) were inherited. "Race itself is Geist," Gerstenhauer claimed, but also "life-giving power, essence, and the law of development."[31] The German *Volk* was obligated to sustain this racial ethics. "The preservation of the purity of blood and of *völkisch* particularity," he wrote, "is a *moral duty*, an *obligation of ethics*."[32] The unity of race, blood, essence, and particularity constituted a special form of Germanic spirit. A *Volk* that spoiled its particularity and uniqueness by racial mixture was thus acting against "its law of development, against the godly will of the creator."[33]

A major work of cultural racism was Alfred Rosenberg's *The Myth of the 20th Century*.[34] Given the active political role of its author in the Nazi era, particularly as Reich Minister of the Occupied Eastern Territories (the Baltic States, Belarus, Ukraine) from July 1941, Rosenberg's book, though not uncontroversial among Nazi leaders, had a special status within Nazi racial literature.

Although Rosenberg understood race in a spiritual-cultural rather than a biological sense, he still elevated the Nordic race.[35] What interested him were neither the racial anthropologists' focus on physical features nor race science's fascination with hereditary traits but the Nordic racial spirit and soul. For Rosenberg, racial nobility was expressed in a Germanic will shaped by Germanic art and mysticism. He saw the Nordic race in an existential fight with the Jewish race.

The Myth of the 20th Century attempted to cover all of German philosophy's contributions to a racially based axiology and conception of the state. Yet Rosenberg's lengthy and tedious expositions did not

[30] Gerstenhauer, *Das ewige Deutschland*, pp. 60–61.

[31] Ibid., p. 65 (italics in the original).

[32] Ibid., p. 63 (italics in the original).

[33] Ibid.

[34] Rosenberg, Alfred, *Der Mythus des 20. Jahrhunderts. Eine Wertung der seelisch-geistigen Gestaltenkämpfe unserer Zeit* (München: Hoheneichen, 1930, 2nd ed. 1931). Rosenberg already had a finished book manuscript in the mid-twenties, but could not find a publisher until 1931 (even J. F. Lehmanns, a well-known publisher for Nazi books, rejected the publication of the manuscript). See Piper, Ernst, *Alfred Rosenberg. Hitlers Chefideologe* (München: Pantheon, 2007), pp. 183–184.

[35] Piper, *Alfred Rosenberg. Hitlers Chefideologe*, pp. 194–196.

amount to a substantial thesis. As Victor Klemperer succinctly put the point in his famous diary notes: "[Rosenberg] frequently repeats himself, for he knows only *one* sentence: The Nordic Race, Nordic blood are the bearers of *all* culture, of *all* that is good – every mixing of blood produces something inferior."[36]

The acceptance of Germanic racial mythology had its limits. When Rosenberg's book was first published in 1930, public reaction to the author's quasi-religious Nordic race-cult was fierce: Southern Germans felt downgraded and humiliated; ecclesiastical circles protested vehemently. Rosenberg's talk of a racial soul and, especially, his thesis of God's revelation in this soul, were rejected by the churches.[37]

Always eager to avoid open conflict with the churches, Hitler urged Rosenberg to back off from religiously provocative racial doctrines that also estranged non-Nordic populations in Germany. On the Führer's express order, Rosenberg wrote in the *Völkischer Beobachter* (February 17, 1931) that *The Myth of the 20th Century* was not the Party line, but his private opinion.[38] Hitler also ordered NS authors to refrain from provoking the churches and to abstain from internal superiority/inferiority comparisons among the Aryan German *Volk*. This strategic compromise notwithstanding, the racial stereotypes continued to shape public discourse and political life.

The controversies over Rosenberg's book persisted after the Nazis took power in 1933.[39] Although Hitler was anything but impressed by Rosenberg's metaphysical raves and mystical ideology, he never took action against Rosenberg. On the contrary, he appointed Rosenberg as Leader of the Foreign Policy Office of the NSDAP in 1933, and, one year later, made him commissioner for the surveillance of the Party's entire spiritual and ideological education.[40]

[36] Klemperer, Victor, *I will Bear Witness 1942–1945. A Diary of the Nazi Years* (New York: Random House, 2001), p. 77 (italics in the original).

[37] Rosenberg was particularly critical of the Roman Catholic Church in ch. 4 (The Nordic-German Law) and ch. 5 (German *Volkskirche* and Education) of Book 3 of the *Myth of the Twentieth Century*, 2nd ed., pp. 531–596. See also Piper, *Alfred Rosenberg. Hitlers Chefideologe*, pp. 184–190.

[38] Piper, *Alfred Rosenberg. Hitlers Chefideologe* p. 171, p. 680, note 38 (referring to Rosenberg, "In eigener Sache," in *Völkischer Beobachter*, February 17, 1931).

[39] The harsh critique from the Catholic side resulted in Rosenberg's book being listed on the Pope's Index of forbidden books in 1934.

[40] Rosenberg's political offices, particularly his role as Reich Minister for the Occupied Territories brought Rosenberg to stand trial as one of the major war criminals in Nuremberg; he was sentenced to death and executed on October 16, 1946.

Still, Hitler distanced himself from Rosenberg's spiritual racism. In a speech at the cultural conference of the 1938 NS Party rally, he declared:

> National Socialism is a sober reality-based doctrine (*Wirklichkeitslehre*), of sharpest scientific insights and their conceptual manifestation. We have now opened our people's heart to this doctrine; but we do not want to fill its heart with a mysticism outside our doctrine. Most of all, National Socialism is in its organization arguably a people's movement, but under no circumstances a cult movement.[41]

To the extent that Hitler was interested in the theoretical underpinnings of antisemitism, he saw biological research, anthropology, and population development studies as more important than pseudo-philosophical reflections on Germanic and Nordic virtues.[42]

Racial research also secured its place institutionally. By the final years of the Weimar Republic, an unholy alliance between racial anthropology/hygiene and National Socialism had emerged. The first attempts to instrumentalize racial researchers also occurred before the Nazi seizure of power, with Hans F. K. Günther playing a vital part.

In 1930, Günther was appointed Professor for Social Anthropology and Racial Science (*Rassenkunde*) at the Jena Institute for Anthropology by the Thuringen provincial government's Minister of Education, the National Socialist Wilhelm Frick (who went on to become the Third Reich's first Interior Minister).[43] Although the university faculty protested Günther's promotion because of his lacking academic credentials,

41 Domarus, Max, *Hitler. Reden und Proklamationen 1932–1945. Kommentiert von einem Zeitgenossen*, vol. 1 Triumph, Zweiter Halbband 1935–1938 (München: Süddeutscher Verlag, 1965), p. 893; also discussed in Piper, *Alfred Rosenberg. Hitlers Chefideologe*, p. 195. The speech was not given by Hitler himself, but read by Adolf Wagner on September 6, 1938 at the cultural conference that was part of the Nazi Party rally in Nuremberg. According to Richard Weikart, Hitler endorsed a "scientific racism"; see Weikart, Richard, *Hitler's Ethic. The Nazi Pursuit of Evolutionary Progress* (Basingstoke: PalgraveMacmillan, 2009), pp. 55–82.

42 In the same vein, Hitler was always skeptical of Himmlers "*Germanenschwärmerei.*" However, in *Mein Kampf* Hitler endorsed not only a genetic form of antisemitism focused on biologically sane and pure procreation, but also a contagionistic form of antisemitism, focusing on the prevention of racial blending. See Weingart, Kroll, Bayertz, *Rasse, Blut und Gene. Geschichte der Rassenhygiene und Eugenik in Deutschland*, pp. 367–381. Cornelia Essner argues that Hitler also was open to the Nordic form of racial science and its concept of "Aufnordung" but did not accept the mythical side of the Nordic racial science. See Essner, Cornelia, *Die "Nürnberger Gesetze" oder Die Verwaltung des Rassenwahns 1933–1945*, pp. 55–61.

43 The National Socialists were part of the coalition government in Thuringen from 1929 on. Frick (Minister of Interior in the Third Reich from 1933–1943) became the first National Socialist minister in a provincial government. For a detailed analysis of Frick's career see

the nomination succeeded due to the Nazi leadership's political backing.[44] Hitler and Göring even attended Günther's inaugural lecture in Jena in November 1930. Once the Nazis reached power, Günther's career advanced rapidly. In 1935, he became professor at the University of Berlin and Director of the Institute for Racial Science, People's Biology, and Sociology (*Anstalt für Rassenkunde, Völkerbiologie und ländliche Soziologie*). His books reached a wide audience.[45]

The Kaiser-Wilhelm-Institute of Anthropology, Human Heredity, and Eugenics that was founded in 1927, played a major role in the scientific support of racial doctrine. The institute's history, and particularly that of its director, Eugen Fischer, is paradigmatic of how racial science came under the political influence of National Socialism. In the pre-Nazi era, Fischer presented himself as an empirical researcher on hereditary laws, eugenics, and anthropology. He defined anthropology as the scientific study of the complex relations between heredity and the environment, emphasizing that "pure anthropology doesn't issue any value judgments."[46] At the time, Fischer was not affiliated with the Nazi Party.

From 1933 on, the Kaiser-Wilhelm-Institute came under the NS regime's control and Fischer deferred to the new political powers. In 1936, he hailed the Nuremberg Laws as an opportunity for geneticists to undertake research in the service of the *Volk*. And in a meeting of the Prussian Academy of Science in 1937, he noted that he was honored to have made contributions to the Third Reich's racial and hereditary

Neliba, Günther, *Wilhelm Frick. Der Legalist des Unrechtsstaates. Eine politische Biographie* (Paderborn, München, Wien, Zürich: Ferdinand Schöningh, 1992).

44 The Nazis considered the establishment of a professorship for Social Anthropology and Racial Science a crucial step in the implementation of their racial-political program. Academics immediately reacted with harsh open criticism. In a critical analysis of *völkisch* racial theory, the German historian Walter Goetz called Günther's nomination as university professor in Jena "a devastation of our intellectual life." Günther was for him a dilettante, merely promoted by the Nazi Party's political favoritism. See Goetz, Walter, "Die Rassenforschung," *Archiv für Kulturgeschichte* 22 (1932) pp. 1–20, here: p. 17. In this essay, Goetz rejected the idea of enduring racial traits, arguing that science at most could locate certain features of human beings or groups of human beings shaped by environment and history. Goetz was Professor for History at the University of Leipzig and a Reichstag deputy of the German Democratic Party (DDP) from 1920 to 1928; the Nazis forced him into retirement after their seizure of power. After the war, Goetz took a position at the University of Munich.

45 In 1940, Günther moved to the University of Freiburg where he taught until 1945.

46 Cited after Weingart, Kroll, Bayertz, *Rasse, Blut und Gene. Geschichte der Eugenik und Rassenhygiene in Deutschland*, p. 243. Fischer's remark appeared in an article he published in 1926 on the tasks of anthropology, human heredity, and eugenics.

population policy, particularly through his discovery that racial attributes were hereditary.[47]

Hans F. K. Günther was not the only racial expert to make a university career. After the Nazi seizure of power, racial science, anthropology, and hygiene entered the academic mainstream. At several universities, professorships were created for these new subjects. Always on the lookout for career opportunities, racial researchers pushed hard for the legitimation of race science, thereby pursuing their personal interests in the service of the regime's dreadful ideology. In June 1933, an Advisory Board for Population and Race politics was established at the Interior Ministry (Hans F. K. Günther was a member). Additionally, the Academy for German Law (founded by Hans Frank in 1933) established a panel for legal questions regarding population politics. Yet the political standing and influence of those committees were limited.[48]

[47] See Weingart, Kroll, Bayertz, *Rasse, Blut und Gene. Geschichte der Eugenik und Rassenhygiene in Deutschland*, p. 412; see also pp. 407–424 for the Nazi's political pressure on the Kaiser-Wilhelm-Institute of Anthropology, Human Heredity, and Eugenics. See also Schmuhl, Hans-Walter, *The Kaiser Wilhelm Institute for Anthropology, Human Heredity, and Eugenics 1927–1945. Crossing Boundaries*, transl. by O'Hagan, Sorcha (Dordrecht: Springer 2008), pp. 117–139.

[48] The Expert Advisory Board for Population- and Racial Politics which was situated at the Interior Ministry (*Sachverständigenbeirat für Bevölkerungs- und Rassenpolitik im Reichsministerium des Innern*) had its first meeting on June 28, 1933 with an opening speech by Interior Minister Wilhelm Frick. See "Niederschrift über die Sitzung des Sachverständigenbeirats für Bevölkerungs- und Rassenpolitik am 28.6. 1933," in *Akademie für Deutsches Recht 1933–1945. Protokolle der Ausschüsse*, ed. by Schubert, Werner, vol. XII, Ausschuss für Rechtsfragen der Bevölkerungspolitik (1934–1940) und Ausschuß für Kolonialrecht zusammen mit den Entwürfen des Kolonialpolitischen Amts (1937–1941). Sachverständigenbeirat für Bevölkerungs- und Rassenpolitik im Reichsministerium des Inneren (1933/1939) (Frankfurt am Main: Peter Lang, 2001), pp. 257–267 (Frick's speech is reprinted on pp. 262–267). As the available protocols of the board's meetings show, the members suggested a purely administrative way for pursuing the NS regime's racial ends; they urgently recommended, for example, "to immediately establish a Reich office ordered to set up a kinship card file (*Reichssippenkartei*) with the aim of clarifying, registering, and documenting the ancestry of all of the German population." "Niederschrift über die Sitzung der Arbeitsgemeinschaften II und III am 3.8. 1933," in *Akademie für Deutsches Recht 1933–1945. Protokolle der Ausschüsse*, vol. XII, pp. 291–295, here: p. 295. In the meetings of June 6, 1940 and November 21, 1940 the jurist and expert for racial hygiene Falk Ruttke suggested building up an archive for legal questions of population politics on which legislators could rely. These were obviously the panel's last official meetings, no further protocols exist. See "Niederschrift über die Sitzung vom 12.6.1940," in *Akademie für Deutsches Recht 1933–1945. Protokolle der Ausschüsse*, vol. XII, pp. 239–242; "Protokoll der Sitzung vom 21.11.1940," ibid., pp. 243–256. The complicated bureaucratic procedures recommended by the Expert Advisory Board conflicted with the radical political policies pushed by the Nazi Party, let alone the SS. A striking example how the advisory committees for racial questions

More politically significant were the offices for Racial and Jewish Questions (*Rassen- und Judenreferate*), which were established at various state institutions. The juridically most important one was founded in 1933 at the Interior Ministry. Led by the racial expert Bernhard Lösener, this office, which from 1935 was under the supervision of State Secretary Wilhelm Stuckart, played a crucial role in the preparation and enactment of the Nuremberg Laws. Stuckart and his staff were also involved in the administrative process that accompanied the successive radicalization of the regime's anti-Jewish policies and culminated in the genocide of the Jews.

Since this study concerns how racial ideology shaped Nazi laws and legal theory, it is essential to examine the ways in which different antisemitic threads merged into the NS state's anti-Jewish legislation. The common ground was preserving the *Volk*'s racial substance by protecting it from alien elements. However, the question of whether legal measures drew on considerations of contagionistic or biological-hereditary antisemitism, or even incorporated ideas of Germanic-Nordic racism, often depended on political strategy, if not rivalries, between state institutions and the Party.

5.3 Racial Ideology and Legal Theory

Legal theoreticians who identified with National Socialism adopted Nazi racial doctrine to an appalling extent. Concepts such as racial homogeneity, racial-*völkisch* unity, racial values, racial equality, racial law, racial

were superseded by the political developments can be found in the protocol of the meeting of the Academy of German Law's Panel on Legal Questions of Population Politics (*Akademieausschuss für Rechtsfragen der Bevökerungspolitik*) on November 23, 1939. In a discussion about the committee's mission and future tasks during the war, the members noted (as if with resignation) that the Reichsführer SS (Himmler) had already received a special order for the resettlement of Germans in occupied Poland and had already started with executing the order. The committee concluded that the Jewish question might be a future topic to engage in and then discussed the possible establishment of an institute which would support legislation by relevant preliminary work. See "Protokoll der Sitzung vom 23. 11. 1939 (Umsiedlungsfragen im Osten. Institut für Bevölkerungspolitik und Bevölkerungswissenschaft)," in *Akademie für Deutsches Recht 1933–1945. Protokolle der Ausschüsse*, vol. XII, pp. 228–238. The conflicts between the NS state's political representatives who shared and upheld the NS ideology and the racial experts for whom the state's authority took precedence over the Nazi Party led in two well-known cases to the dismissal of the racial experts – on the pretext of having violated § 175 of the German Criminal Code (referring to homosexuality, which was a criminal offense at the time). The jurist Helmut Nicolai, author of a book on racial legislation and another one on the future constitution of the NS state and a founding member of Hans Frank's Academy for German Law, lost his position as official in the Interior Ministry in 1935; the racial scientist Achim Gercke was similarly dismissed (de facto he was taken in custody and later sent to the Eastern front).

blood ties, racial purity, and race treason (*Rassenverrat*) were common in the contemporary juridical literature.[49]

Many legal commentaries explicitly endorsed Günther's definition of "race" as a "group of humans differing from all other human groups by its typical physical features and spiritual characteristics."[50] These differences determined the boundaries between equality and otherness in kind (*Artgleichheit and Artfremdheit*), a distinction that eventually implicated who had or didn't have legal rights.[51]

The NS jurists also adopted Günther's distinction between people (*Volk*) and race. While Günther associated the term "race" with hereditary biological features, the concept of "*Volk*" included cultural values. In the NS legal theorists' view, these notions were interconnected, as any given people could only consist of individuals belonging to certain races.

Let us now examine some passages in the NS jurists' texts. According to Georg Dahm, "German law is the German people's order of life," whereby racial sameness was constitutive of this life order.[52] As Forsthoff wrote in *The Total State*, "*Volk* is a community based on an ontological, generic homogeneity (*seinsmäßige, artmäßige Gleichartigkeit*). This homogeneity results from the homogeneity of race and the *Volk*'s fate."[53] Adopting Günther's definition of race as a "hereditarily identical group of humans," Helmut Nicolai held that there exist no "raceless humans."[54]

Günther's influence is also apparent in Ernst Rudolf Huber's statement that the constitution of the NS state could only be *völkisch* in the racial sense. "The political *Volk*," Huber wrote, "is formed by the unity of kind (*Einheitlichkeit der Art*). Race is the natural foundation of the *Volk*. Race is a community of ancestry marked by specific bodily and mental traits."[55]

49 See Huber, Ernst Rudolf, "Neue Grundbegriffe des hoheitlichen Rechts," in Dahm, Georg; Huber, Ernst Rudolf; Larenz, Karl; Michaelis, Karl; Schaffstein, Friedrich; Siebert, Wolfgang, *Grundfragen der neuen Rechtswissenschaft* (Berlin: Junker & Dünnhaupt, 1935), pp. 143–188, esp. pp. 151–157.

50 Stuckart, Wilhelm and Globke, Hans, *Kommentare zur deutschen Rassengesetzgebung*, vol. 1 (München und Berlin: C. H. Beck, 1936), p. 1.

51 See Walz, Gustav Adolf, *Artgleichheit gegen Gleichartigkeit. Die beiden Grundprobleme des Rechts* (Hamburg: Hanseatische Verlagsanstalt, 1938).

52 Dahm, Georg, "Verbrechen und Tatbestand," in Dahm, Huber, Larenz, Michaelis, Schaffstein, Siebert, *Grundfragen der neuen Rechtswissenschaft*, pp. 62–107, here p. 85.

53 Forsthoff, Ernst, *Der totale Staat* (1933), p. 38.

54 Nicolai, Helmut, *Rasse und Recht* (Berlin: Hobbing, 1933), p. 7. See also Nicolai, Helmut, *Die rassengesetzliche Rechtslehre. Grundzüge einer nationalsozialistischen Rechtsphilosophie* (München: Franz Eher Nachf., 1932), p. 26f.

55 Huber, Ernst Rudolf, *Verfassungsrecht des Großdeutschen Reiches*, 2nd ed. (Hamburg: Hanseatische Verlagsanstalt, 1939), p. 153.

Otto Koellreutter justified a racial grounding of law thus: "The national rule of law state as a *völkisch* life order builds on the *Volk*; its preservation in its racial substance and as a body of physically healthy members is the foundation of any political and cultural progress."[56] Accordingly, Koellreutter approved of legal measures that "hinder the influx of racially alien elements."[57] And he considered it vital to anchor political authority in *völkisch* commonality. The political form of the Führer state, Koellreutter claimed, was "determined by the people's racial and territorial conditionalities and by the essence of the *Volk*'s spirit (*Volksgeist*)."[58]

Koellreutter had no qualms about specifying the radical consequences of his conception of the state's foundations and governance. "Leadership," he wrote, "amounts to the complementary ordering of a homogeneous group of humans and the keeping at bay, possibly the destruction, of enemy forces. Thus, any leadership needs the power of creating inner order and of using its own strengths to ward off disruptive influences."[59]

NS jurists claimed that racially alien individuals could neither ethically nor legally comply with German law and justice. They thus had to be excluded from the German community. The jurists also directly linked racial-biological factors to crime.[60] Crime prevention entailed the racial protection of the German community.

In 1935, Erich Becker argued for a "Volk-directed form of politics in line with racial and eugenic viewpoints."[61] In an article on the concept of race in the *Dictionary of Criminology* in 1936, Max Hagemann deemed it self-evident that law, as "an expression of an entire way of life and conduct of a people," should display a specific *völkisch* character.[62] And

56 Koellreutter, Otto, *Grundriß der Allgemeinen Staatslehre* (Tübingen: J.C.B. Mohr [Paul Siebeck]), p. 50.

57 Ibid. p. 51. Here Koellreutter quotes approvingly the Law for the Restoration of the Professional Civil Service of April 7, 1933.

58 Koellreutter, *Grundriß der Allgemeinen Staatslehre*, p. 163.

59 Ibid., p. 54.

60 Already in the first edition of his *Rassenkunde des deutschen Volkes* (1922), Günther had an extended section on the alleged connection between crime and Jewishness. See Günther, *Rassenkunde des deutschen Volkes*, pp. 379–381. He continued exposing his prejudiced views in *Rassenkunde des jüdischen Volkes*, pp. 276–280.

61 Becker, Erich, *Diktatur und Führung* (Tübingen: J.C.B. Mohr [Paul Siebeck], 1935), p. 32 (italics in the original).

62 Hagemann, Max, "Rasse," in Elster, Alexander and Lingemann, Heinrich (eds.), *Handwörterbuch der Kriminologie und der anderen strafrechtlichen Hilfswissenschaften*, vol. 2 (Berlin and Leipzig: Walter de Gruyter, 1936), pp. 454–460, here: p. 454.

in their commentary on the Nuremberg Laws, Wilhelm Stuckart and Hans Globke wrote: "Over and against the doctrines of universal human equality and the principally unrestricted freedom of the individual vis-à-vis the state, National Socialism sets the harsh but necessary recognition of the natural inequality and heterogeneity of humans."[63] Stuckart and Schiedermair's commentary on racial legislation confirms this rejection of human equality:

> The liberalistic era did not recognize any racial question. It had fallen into the fateful error that anyone with a human face was equal. Hence the state leadership at the time did not see the racial question as a state political task. The legislation of the liberal era thus did not cope with the racial question. *National Socialism,* however, *puts the racial question at the center of its worldview.*[64]

Legal theorists could not have been oblivious to the direction in which the Nazi regime's racial ideology would develop. The first anti-Jewish legislation already made it clear that the regime's fierce antisemitism extended beyond aggressive rhetoric to establish realities that deleteriously affected Jewish lives. On April 7, 1933, the Law for the Restoration of the Professional Civil Service (*Gesetz zur Wiederherstellung des Berufsbeamtentum*) ruled that all Jewish officials were to be removed from state service. § 3.1 stated: "Civil service officials of non-Aryan descent are to be retired; honorary civil service officials (*Ehrenbeamte*) are to be dismissed from office."[65]

The law's consequences were striking, particularly for the legal discipline. Jewish university professors and state jurists lost their positions. Deprived of their livelihoods, they were forced into emigration. NS loyal theoreticians scooped up the posts of abruptly dismissed Jewish law professors and legal officials.[66]

[63] Stuckart and Globke, *Kommentare zur deutschen Rassengesetzgebung*, p. 25.

[64] Stuckart, Wilhelm and Schiedermair, Rolf, *Rassen- und Erbpflege in der Gesetzgebung des Dritten Reiches*, 1st ed. (Leipzig: Kohlhammer, 1938), p. 9 (italics in the original).

[65] See "Law for the Restoration of the Professional Civil Service," in *The Third Reich Sourcebook*, p. 53 (transl. slightly changed, H.P. St.) In response to a request by Hindenburg, § 3 Sect. 2 stipulated an exception for Jewish civil servants who had served during World War I. In amendments of this law after Hindenburg's death, this exception was annulled. For a detailed discussion of the development and effects of this law see Mommsen, Hans, *Beamtentum im Dritten Reich. Mit ausgewählten Quellen zur nationalsozialistischen Beamtenpolitik* (Stuttgart: Deutsche Verlags-Anstalt, 1966).

[66] Kelsen lost his professorship at the University of Cologne and Hermann Heller his chair in Frankfurt on the Main, which was taken over by Ernst Forsthoff. On this see Rüthers, Bernd, *Entartetes Recht. Rechtslehren und Kronjuristen im Dritten Reich*

The Law for the Restoration of the Professional Civil Service was a dramatic first step in the bureaucratic implementation of racial ideology. It demonstrated that the NS regime was determined to introduce a completely new juridical criterion – "racial affiliation" – for the recognition or denial of rights. It came to designate a specific *normative* status.

NS jurists tried to conceal this remarkable shift from the empirical to the normative. "I think it is important to point out that race is not a political, but *per se* a natural-scientific concept," stated Koellreutter, echoing Günther's definition of race.[67] By maintaining that discourse about race and racial affiliation was merely empirical-scientific, NS jurists sought to circumvent explaining normatively why *racial affiliation* had suddenly become the benchmark for social rights and opportunities. They thus reasoned that a "natural-scientific" grounding of the racial doctrine would silence critics. Biological facts would speak for themselves, amounting to irrefutable empirical truths. By referring to supposedly natural-scientific facts, the jurists obscured their *normative* use of "race," which in turn called for a *normative* justification (which of course was never given).

How could legally trained thinkers, perfectly familiar with the difference between the factual and the normative, openly endorse such a fallacy? The NS jurists were at least aware of the problem and faced it head-on by vehemently criticizing the *is/ought* dichotomy as a mere construct of legal positivism (one of the "artificial abstractions of the Vienna School"), which they claimed was incompatible with the premises of *völkisch* legal thinking.[68] The thesis was apparently that in a *völkisch* jurisprudence, whose starting point was the given *völkisch* order of life and thus the laws of being (*Sein*), the spheres of the empirical and the

(München: C.H. Beck, 1998), pp. 129–132. On Heller's fate see also Dyzenhaus, David, "Hermann Heller and the 'Jewish Element' in German Public Law Theory," in Epple, Moritz; Fried, Johannes; Gross, Raphael; Gudian, Janus (eds.), "*Politisierung der Wissenschaft.*" *Jüdische Wissenschaftler und ihre Gegner an der Universität Frankfurt am Main vor und nach 1933* (Göttingen: Wallstein 2014), pp. 209–248. The Law Faculty at the University of Kiel became a center of National Socialist legal theory. Among the professors were Georg Dahm, Ernst Rudolf Huber, Karl Larenz, Karl August Eckhardt, Friedrich Schaffstein. For a detailed discussion see Wiener, Christina, *Kieler Fakultät und "Kieler Schule." Die Rechtslehrer an der Rechts- und Staatswissenschaftlichen Fakultät zu Kiel in der Zeit des Nationalsozialismus und ihre Entnazifizierung* (Baden-Baden: Nomos, 2013).

[67] Koellreutter, *Grundfragen unserer Volks- und Staatsgestaltung* (Berlin: Junker & Dünnhaupt, 1936), p. 11.

[68] Larenz, Karl, *Deutsche Rechtserneuerung und Rechtsphilosophie* (Tübingen: J.C.B. Mohr [Paul Siebeck], 1934), p. 18.

normative would merge and the difference between *is* and *ought* vanish. Georg Dahm provides a telling example of such reasoning:

> All acting and being only make sense if they arise from the community which is neither a structure of norms nor an outward way of being together, but a real, living, inner order ... The community is not organized externally, from the outside, but bears its law within. That is why any kind of thinking that assumes a duality of value and reality, of *ought* and *is*, is wrong, though empirical reality may certainly contradict the *völkisch* and racial order. But our *völkisch* being is order rather than chaos. It bears its standard of evaluation (*Maßstab*) within, thus it cannot be assessed and judged from a standpoint beyond reality, and also not by means of independent norms.[69]

This unification of the factual and the normative gave legal theorists discretion in their use of the race concept. The Nazi thinkers often moved from the empirical to the normative level without recognizing the distinction between *is* and *ought*, and, if it served their ideology, they simply confounded the two levels. According to their thinking's inner logic, it was perfectly acceptable to derive normative conclusions and ought-statements from "natural-scientific" premises. This strategy gave subsequently passed racial laws a pseudoscientific underpinning.

5.4 The Nuremberg Laws

The next major move in the Third Reich's racial legislation came with the Nuremberg Laws, specifically, the Reich Citizenship Law and the Law for the Protection of German Blood and German Honor. The Reichstag passed these constitutional laws on September 15, 1935, during a special session of the Nazi Party rally in Nuremberg.

The Reich Citizenship Law distinguished between "citizens of the Reich" (*Reichsbürger*) and "subjects of the state" (*Staatsangehörige*). Article 2.1 stated that a "citizen of the Reich is only that subject of the state who is of German or kindred blood and who, through his conduct, proves that he is both willing and able to faithfully serve the German people and Reich." According to Article 1.1, a "subject of the state is a person who belongs to the protective union of the German Reich, and who therefore has particular obligations toward the Reich." Article 2.3

[69] Dahm, Georg, "Verbrechen und Tatbestand," in Dahm, Huber, Larenz, Michaelis, Schaffstein, Siebert, *Grundfragen der neuen Rechtswissenschaft*, pp. 85–86 (italics, H.P.-St.).

specified that "(o)nly the citizen of the Reich enjoys full political rights in accordance with the provisions of the law."[70]

The full consequences of the Reich Citizenship Law only became apparent with the subsequent decrees. The First Supplementary Decree to the Reich Citizenship Law (November 14, 1935) denied Jewish Germans the right to vote: "A Jew cannot be a citizen of the Reich. He has no right to vote on political matters and cannot hold public office" (Article 4.1).[71] Article 4.2 ruled that all Jews still in civil service were subject to retirement by December 31, 1935. This also affected Jewish officials who had served in World War I and thus far been spared dismissal on Hindenburg's personal request. While the First Supplementary Decree granted Jewish officials their salaries through retirement age, a directive from the Reich and Prussian Interior Ministries (December 20, 1935) held that Jewish officials' mandatory retirement, effective on December 31, 1935, did not automatically entail their receiving retirement payments. Such payments would, so the cryptic formulation, depend on whether the dismissed Jewish officials "deserve it according to the relevant statutory provisions."[72] The directive included those officials who fought in World War I.

These regulations denied Jews any certainty about legal guarantees, as successive and rapidly enacted provisions overruled earlier ones. Moreover, the constantly changing provisions came with substantial bureaucratic hassles.

The Law for the Protection of German Blood and German Honor intervened heavily into the private lives of Germans. Article 1.1 banned marriages between "Jews and state subjects of German or of related

[70] See "Reich Citizenship Law," in *The Third Reich Sourcebook*, p. 209.

[71] See "First Supplementary Decree to the Reich Citizenship Law (November 14, 1935)," in *Legislating the Holocaust. The Bernhard Loesener Memoirs and Supporting Documents*, Appendix: Nazi Legislation, pp. 155–157. For a German version, see "Erste Verordnung zum Reichsbürgergesetz vom 14. November 1935," in Gütt, Arthur; Linden, Herbert; Maßfeller, Franz, *Blutschutz- und Ehegesundheitsgesetz. Gesetz zum Schutze des deutschen Blutes und der deutschen Ehre und Gesetz zum Schutze der Erbgesundheit des deutschen Volkes nebst Durchführungsverordnungen sowie einschlägigen Bestimmungen* (München: J. F. Lehmanns, 1936), pp. 245–247.

[72] "Runderlaß des Reichs- und Preußischen Ministeriums des Inneren from December 20, 1935," in Gütt, Linden, Maßfeller, *Blutschutz- und Ehegesundheitsgesetz. Gesetz zum Schutze des deutschen Blutes und der deutschen Ehre und Gesetz zum Schutze der Erbgesundheit des deutschen Volkes nebst Durchführungsverordnungen sowie einschlägigen Bestimmungen*, p. 251. The Reich Ministry of Interior had been united with the Prussian Ministry of Interior on November 1, 1934.

blood."[73] It also voided all previous marriages, even if the marriage was conducted abroad. Article 2 forbade "extramarital affairs between Jews and nationals of German or related blood." Article 3 prohibited Jews from employing in their households "female nationals of German" or related blood younger than forty-five.

The Nuremberg Laws combined political discrimination (Jews lost their status as citizens and the right to run for political office) with social exclusion. The laws strictly separated Jews from the non-Jewish population. The Law for the Protection of German Blood and Honor illustrates well the influence of contagionistic antisemitism: In forbidding marriages and sexual relations between Jews and Aryan Germans, it was motivated by bizarre biological ideas of preserving the purity of the *Volk* and keeping Aryan blood free from contamination.

The loss of individual rights caused by the Nuremberg Laws, as well as the brutality with which they and their subsequent decrees were enforced, reveal the cynicism of the Nazi legal theorists' contention that the racial policies of the NS state did not mean to downgrade or disgrace Jews but simply to separate the Aryan and Jewish races on an equal basis.

Regarding the promulgation of the Nuremberg Laws and their impact on German Jews, three oft-held theses require critical discussion. The first is that the state bureaucracy was not involved in the preparation of the Nuremberg Laws but was taken aback by the regime's sudden plans and did its level best to alleviate the laws' effects. According to the second thesis, the Jewish population received the Nuremberg Laws with some relief, as they brought normative clarity to what Jews were and were not allowed. The third thesis is that the Nuremberg Laws were not responsible for the later radicalization of anti-Jewish policy under the wartime conditions that culminated in the Holocaust.

All three theses must be viewed with skepticism. They are based on the autobiographical notes of the special adviser in race matters (*Rassereferent*) at the Reich Ministry of the Interior, Bernhard Lösener, which were first published in the *Vierteljahreshefte für Zeitgeschichte* in 1961, and in English translation in 2001.[74]

[73] "Law for the Protection of German Blood and German Honor," in *The Third Reich Sourcebook*, p. 209.

[74] Lösener, Bernhard, "Als Rassereferent im Reichsministerium des Innern," ed. by Strauß, Walter in *Vierteljahreshefte für Zeitgeschichte* 9, 3 (1961), pp. 264–313; English version: Loesener, Bernhard, "At the Desk for Racial Affairs in the Reich Ministry of the Interior," in *Legislating the Holocaust. The Bernhard Loesener Memoirs and Supporting Documents*, pp. 33–109. Lösener was racial expert from 1933 up to the end of 1942. He left the Interior

In his report, Lösener claimed that the Nuremberg Laws had been hastily drafted under pressure from Hitler by officials in the Reich Interior Ministry, including himself, who unexpectedly had been summoned to the Nuremberg Party rally in September 1935. The reason for the rush was that the Führer wanted to end the uncontrolled Jew-baiting and pogrom-like actions that Streicher and Propaganda Minister Goebbels had recently provoked, and which were threatening both the German economy and the regime's already notorious external reputation.

According to Lösener, the Interior Ministry had been completely sidelined in all deliberations leading to the Nuremberg Laws, for which he blamed the Nazi Party, the SS, and the Security Service (*Sicherheitsdienst*) under Heydrich. Lösener's report described in detail how he and other ministry officials, all of whom allegedly had been repulsed by the previous months' antisemitic excesses, pushed back at Nuremberg against Streicher and leading SS and SD representatives by, for example, exempting so-called half-Jews from the regulations.

With respect to the reception of the Nuremberg Laws that Hitler allegedly had ordered "without a moment's notice," Lösener also noted the following:

> After they became public, they were not always seen exclusively as laws of persecution. Many people who had in no way been adherents of the Nazi system, and even those directly affected, welcomed them with a certain relief because they ended the state of complete legal uncertainty. At least now one knew where one stood, and a wide, previously threatened circle of people drew a deep breath, especially the one's of "Jewish offspring" (*Judenstämmlinge*) and spouses in mixed marriages, because until this point the extremists had demanded the legal separation of mixed marriages. Likewise, civil servants, especially those in the Ministry of the Interior, viewed the Nuremberg Laws in this light.[75]

Lösener emphatically denied that the Nuremberg Laws "marked the beginning of the actual persecution" of the Jewish population, culminating in the

Ministry after a conflict with his superior Wilhelm Stuckart over the Nazi regime's murder of Jews. Lösener, so his version of the story, had learned about executions of Jews in Riga in December 1941, and when he then informed Stuckart, his superior merely reacted by informing him that the executions had been ordered from the highest ranks of the Nazi leadership. Lösener was shortly imprisoned by the Nazis in November 1944 since he had allowed one of the conspirator's in the attack on Hitler in July 1944 to stay for a few days in his apartment. Lösener was excluded from the Nazi Party, but was set free shortly before the end of the war.

[75] Loesener, Bernhard, "At the Desk for Racial Affairs in the Reich Ministry of the Interior," p. 54 (transl. slightly changed, H.P.-St.).

Holocaust. He even claimed that drawing a connection between these laws and "other atrocities committed against the Jews," let alone the extermination, constituted "a misjudgment of historical truth," reversing "the relationship between cause and effect in the chain of historical events."[76] As he explained:

> For me, given my knowledge of many facts that never became publicly known, or, what's more, by remembering those facts that have today slipped from memory, it is a simple statement of objective fact to point out the following: the completely hellish form of the persecution of Jews in later years became horrible reality *not as a result of, but rather despite the Nuremberg Laws.*[77]

Historians take such statements with a grain of salt, not least because of the report's history.[78] After all, Lösener's former superior in the Interior Ministry, Wilhelm Stuckart, participated in the notorious Wannsee conference on January 20, 1942, and was prosecuted in the Ministries Trial (*US* v. *Weizsäcker, et al.*) that took place from November 1947 until April 1949. Lösener, who exonerated Stuckart as a witness for the defense, was asked by jurist Walter Strauß to record his experiences as a racial expert in the Interior Ministry.[79] Lösener's report, which Strauß (with Lösener's consent) handed to the Munich *Institut für Zeitgeschichte* in 1950, was only published in the Institute's journal in 1961 (years after Lösener's death and with introductory remarks by Strauß). The background for the report's publication seems to have been an effort by the Adenauer government to silence public criticism of its personnel policy, which was fairly lenient toward former NS officials. (At the center of controversy was State Secretary Hans Globke, Stuckart's coauthor of an

[76] Ibid. pp. 55, 52.

[77] Ibid. p. 55 (italics in the original).

[78] See Essner, Cornelia, *Die "Nürnberger Gesetze" oder die Verwaltung des Rassenwahns 1933–1945*, pp. 113–154; Wildt, Michael, "Einleitung," in Wildt (ed.), *Die Judenpolitik des SD 1935 bis 1938. Eine Dokumentation* (München: Oldenbourg, 1995), p. 25; Jasch, Hans-Christian, "Civil Service Lawyers and the Holocaust: The Case of Wilhelm Stuckart," in Steinweis, Alan E. and Rachlin, Robert D. (eds.), *The Law in Nazi Germany. Ideology, Opportunism, and the Perversion of Justice*, pp. 37–61, esp. pp. 48–50; Koonz, Claudia, *The Nazi Conscience* (Cambridge, MA and London: Harvard University Press, 2003), pp. 190–192.

[79] Walter Strauß was Jewish and survived the NS rule because he was married to a German woman; but he was condemned to forced labor. From 1949 until 1963 he served as State Secretary in the Justice Ministry of the Federal Republic of Germany. See Apostolow, Markus, *Der "immerwährende Staatssekretär." Walter Strauß und die Personalpolitik im Bundesministerium der Justiz 1949–1963* (Göttingen: Vandenhoeck & Ruprecht, 2019).

NS commentary on the Third Reich's racial laws).[80] In line with his testimony as witness at Stuckart's trial, Lösener's report created the myth that the Interior Ministry had actively tried to hamper the persecution of the Jews.

Although Lösener's report is partial and self-serving, his contentions are not only important for understanding the dreadful interlocking of law, administrative decrees, and extermination orders, but also for better grasping the Third Reich's complex structure generally.

Lösener's assertion that he and other Interior Ministry officials neither had expected the Nuremberg Laws nor had been involved in their planning is simply false. Using documentary evidence, historians have proven that the laws were systematically prepared in Nazi Party and Ministry circles.[81]

Already on August 20, 1935, a meeting on the economic consequences of the intensified combat against Jewry took place in the Reich's Ministry of Economy. Besides Economy Minister Hjalmar Schacht, who chaired the meeting, the attendees included: Interior Minister Wilhelm Frick; the Minister of Justice, Franz Gürtner; Finance Minister Graf Schwerin von Krosigk; Prussian Minister of Finance, Johannes Popitz; the *Gauleiter* and Bavarian Minister of the Interior, Adolf Wagner (in his function as representative of the Führer's deputy Rudolf Hess); several state secretaries, and representatives of the NSDAP's Race-Political Office (*Rassenpolitisches Amt*), the Gestapo and the Security Service (SD). Lösener himself wrote a protocol of this meeting – a fact omitted in his report.[82]

80 See Essner, *Die "Nürnberger Gesetze" oder die Verwaltung des Rassenwahns 1933–1945*, pp. 114–116.

81 See Kulka, Otto Dov, "Die Nürnberger Rassengesetze und die deutsche Bevölkerung im Lichte geheimer NS-Lage- und Stimmungsberichte," in *Vierteljahreshefte für Zeitgeschichte* 32, 4 (1984), pp. 582–624, esp. pp. 615–620.

82 Ibid., p. 616. There are different protocols of this meeting in existence. A first protocol was written on August 22, 1935 (= "Niederschrift über die Chefbesprechung am 20. August 1935, 3:30 im Reichswirtschaftsministerium ueber die wirtschaftlichen Auswirkungen der verstaerkten Bekaempfung des Judentums"). This protocol was a document at the International Military Tribunal Trial in Nuremberg (Document IMT-NG 4607, State Archive Nuremberg). The signature initials of this protocol, which supposedly was written by the Ministry of Economy, are not legible. For a long time, historical research considered only this protocol as the relevant source. According to Kulka, a final version of the meeting's protocol was written and signed by Lösener on August 27, 1935 and was kept in the Secret State Archive (GStA, Rep. 320, Nr. 513); see Kulka, "Die Nürnberger Rassengesetze und die deutsche Bevölkerung im Lichte geheimer NS-Lage- und Stimmungsberichte," p. 616, note 116. A further version of the protocol was, as Kulka notes, written by the Ministry of Exterior Affairs. Kulka mentions that

The meeting considered how to cope with the so-called Jewish problem without causing uncontrollable outbreaks of aggression that would shock foreign countries and likely have economic consequences. The participants agreed to give anti-Jewish measures legal form. Frick called for a decree allowing police to take strong action against illegal anti-Jewish riots to be passed immediately. And Schacht held that the implementation of the anti-Jewish articles in the Nazi Party's program should be done on a legal basis. Justice Minister Gürtner also emphasized the importance of pursuing the Führer state's ends legalistically.

The meeting's protocol of August 22, 1935 reveals that the ministry representatives called for legal regulations in order to control unruly forms of antisemitism, rather than requesting to forbid antisemitic actions altogether. None of the participants openly rejected the regime's antisemitism.[83]

Interior Minister Frick's presence at the meeting refutes Lösener's claim that the Nuremberg Laws came as a complete surprise to Interior

Lösener's version of the protocol is different from the other two versions, reporting statements of participants that are neither part of the August 22, 1935 protocol (Document IMT-NG 4607) nor of the Ministry of Exterior Affairs protocol. The historian Michael Wildt has added an important detail to the meeting of August 20, 1935: Heydrich's presence at this meeting was overlooked by those historians who only consulted the meeting's protocol from August 22, 1935 (IMT-NIG 4607) which did not mention Heydrich. However, Heydrich's presence at this conference is, as Wildt shows, confirmed by a letter Heydrich addressed to the meeting's participants on September 9, 1935 in which he articulated crucial restrictions on Jews, also anticipating the Nuremberg Laws, for example, the prohibition of marriages between Jews and Aryans and the ban on extramarital sexual relations between Jews and Aryan Germans. See "Heydrich an die Teilnehmer der Chefbesprechung im Reichswirtschaftsministerium, 9. September 1935 (Sonderarchiv Moskau 500/1/1939)," in Wildt (ed.), *Die Judenpolitik des SD 1935 bis 1938. Eine Dokumentation*, pp. 70–73, here: p. 71f.

83 Schacht vehemently criticized the actions against Jews, but for their negative effects on the economy. Protocol (dated August 22, 1935) of the Meeting at the Reich Ministry of Economy on August, 20, 1935 (IMT-NG 4607, State Archive Nuremberg). Already on May 3, 1935, Schacht authored a memorandum to Hitler in which he asked for a special legislation on the Jewish question to prevent antisemitic riots. In this memorandum, as Kulka explains, Schacht signaled his agreement with "labeling the Jews as inhabitants/persons with inferior legal status and fewer rights by relevant legal regulations" but added that "for those rights one still gave them, Jews should enjoy the state's protection against fanatics and uneducated ones." See Kulka, "Die Nürnberger Rassengesetze und die deutsche Bevölkerung im Lichte geheimer NS-Lage- und Stimmungsberichte," p. 619, note 126. In a speech in Königsberg on August 8, 1935 Schacht again emphasized that special legal regulations concerning the treatment of Jews were necessary as well as laws defining their status in accordance with Articles 4 and 5 of the Nazi Party Program of 1920. See Kulka, "Die Nürnberger Rassengesetze und die deutsche Bevölkerung im Lichte geheimer NS-Lage- und Stimmungsberichte," p. 619, note 126.

Ministry officials, let alone Lösener's own summary of the meeting from August 27, 1935. The protocol also challenges Lösener's assertion that the state bureaucracy, foremost the Interior Ministry, had tried to exempt so-called *Mischlinge* from the Nuremberg Laws. Wagner, for example, suggested applying the planned laws only to full Jews, so that the question of how to include the *Mischlinge* would not disrupt or stall the planned legislative process.[84]

Equally problematic is Lösener's assumption that the Jewish population perceived the Nuremberg Laws as at least granting them some security. How realistic is that? Can people who are deprived of their citizenship and political rights actually feel that way? Even if the regime's desire to end the violent street riots in spring/summer 1935 mitigated the brutality, the shift to formalizing antisemitism legally can hardly be considered an improvement given the altogether dire situation of Germany's Jews.

Admittedly, the Nuremberg Laws' classification of Jewishness was milder than that of the Law of the Restoration of the Civil Service in April 1933. While the so-called Aryan paragraph in this law's first supplementary decree (April 11, 1933) classified a person with one Jewish grandparent as non-Aryan, the First Supplementary Decree to the Reich Citizenship Law of November 14, 1935 made him/her into a *Mischling*, which exempted one from certain anti-Jewish regulations. However, Lösener's contention that "those directly affected welcomed [the Nuremberg Laws] with a certain relief" is belied by his description of desperate, terrified Jews trying to figure out whether or not the supplementary regulations applied to them.[85] Lösener himself notes in his report how Jewish *Mischlinge* who wanted to marry "had to subject themselves to weeks and weeks of humiliating inquiries by various offices into all aspects of their lives, only to receive the inevitable flat-out no."[86]

[84] Ibid., p. 618.

[85] Lösener writes in his memoirs that the "immediate effect of the two 'First Decrees' [the one of November 14, 1935, the other from December 21, 1935] was that I was showered with petitions aimed at gaining exemptions from their oppressive provisions." Loesener, "At the Desk of Racial Affairs in the Reich Ministry of the Interior," p. 62. Article II, paragraph 7 of the First Supplementary Decree of November 14, 1935 stated: "The Führer and Reich Chancellor can grant exemptions from the regulations laid down in this supplementary decree." See *Legislating the Holocaust*, p. 157.

[86] Loesener, "At the Desk of Racial Affairs in the Reich Ministry of the Interior," p. 64; see also Jasch, Hans-Christian, *Staatssekretär Wilhelm Stuckart und die Judenpolitik. Der Mythos von der sauberen Verwaltung* (München: Oldenbourg, 2012), p. 245.

5.5 From the Nuremberg Laws to the Holocaust

What about Lösener's contention that there was no direct connection between the Nuremberg Laws and the "hellish form of the persecution of the Jews," culminating in the Holocaust? Two claims seem to be at stake here. One concerns the historical facts. The other claim relates to the relevant state institutions' role and responsibility in this development. It merits closely examining these aspects of Lösener's disconnection-thesis in order to understand better the Nazi dictatorship's normative structure.

How plausible is Lösener's thesis in light of actual historical developments? When the Nuremberg Laws were enacted, the regime's progress toward the destruction of European Jewry could by no means be predicted. A decisive factor in the collapse of all normative and moral standards was the Nazis' decision to wage aggressive war on neighboring countries. In particular, the "war of annihilation" against the Soviet Union came with brutal destruction and mass murder: During the summer of 1941, large-scale shootings of Jews, including women and children, were organized in the wake of the invasion. The decision to systematically murder all Jews in specifically designed death camps was made some time between the late summer and fall of 1941, when the NS leadership realized that initial plans to expel Jews from German territory could not be achieved. In late fall 1941, the regime's intentions turned from deporting Jews to occupied territories in the East (probably conquered areas in the Soviet Union) to extinction.[87]

Lösener does not actually mention the difficulty of foreseeing those events; recall his claim that they became "a dreadful reality *not as a result of, but rather despite the Nuremberg Laws*." Yet it seems fair to ask how legal regulations that denied Jews formerly held entitlements as citizens

[87] The exact point of time when the decision was made to murder all European Jews is a matter of debate among historians. Christopher Browning argues that by "the end of October 1941 the conception of the Final Solution had taken shape." Browning, Christopher (with contributions by Jürgen Matthäus), *The Origins of the Final Solution. The Evolution of Nazi Jewish Policy, September 1939-March 1942* (Lincoln: University of Nebraska Press, Jerusalem: Yad Vashem, 2004), p. 374; see also pp. 352–373 on the developments in the preceding months. Longerich claims that "the intention behind the deportations and planning of autumn 1941 was still to deport all European Jews to camps in the occupied Soviet Union, after victory had been achieved." Longerich, Peter, *The Unwritten Order: Hitler's Role in the Final Solution* (Stroud: Tempus, 2003), pp. 134–135. The first deportations of Jews from Germany and Austria to the East happened on October 15 and November 5, 1941. Ibid., p. 132. On the developments in the fall of 1941 see also Longerich, Peter, *Heinrich Himmler*, transl. by Noakes, Jeremy and Sharpe, Lesley (Oxford: Oxford University Press, 2012), pp. 541–553.

could be seen as a hindrance to intensified persecution. Would not the loss of rights and separation from the population put people at risk of aggravated discriminatory measures? The only way to construe Lösener's statement is counterfactually: Had the Nazi leadership's actions against the Jews not continued beyond the enactment of legal norms made public in the *Reichgesetzblatt*, then the terrible persecution would not have occurred. Perhaps, but the history tells a different tale: The Nuremberg Laws were anything but the end of persecution.

Lösener's disconnection-thesis implies a specific view on the institutions partaking in the persecution of Jews. As historians have noted, his memoirs have been crucial in creating the myth of the "clean bureaucracy," detaching it from the Nazi state's center of power – the Party, the SS, the Security Service, and the Gestapo. According to this viewpoint, only the latter organizations, not the ministerial bureaucracy, were responsible for executing the regime's racial ideology right through to mass murder.

Certainly, the decision to murder the Jews was made in the innermost circles of Nazi power, apart from the ministries and the administration, and at a time (late summer to fall 1941) when cabinet meetings had long stopped taking place and ministers had increasingly less access to Hitler.[88] The order for the so-called "Final Solution" (by which time meant death, not expulsion) came from Hitler, though in oral rather than in written form, according to historians. This command went from Hitler to Himmler, the Reichsführer SS and Chief of the German Police, who transferred it to the *Einsatzgruppen*, the Higher SS and Police Officers and special command units charged with organizing the deportations and killings.[89] According to Ian Kershaw, during the summer of 1941 the whole situation of how to make sense of and carry out the regime's anti-Jewish plans and policies was still marked by "a high degree of confusion and contradictory interpretations of anti-Jewish policy by the Nazi authorities."[90] However, by December 1941, the program had the clear contours of a full-scale extermination.

88 Cabinet meetings ended around 1937–1938. A consequence was that ministers had less direct access to Hitler. Interior Minister Frick, for example, was explicitly sidelined by Hitler and in August 1943 Frick was dismissed as Interior Minister, but installed as Reich Protector in Bohemia. See Neliba, *Wilhelm Frick. Der Legalist des Unrechtsstaates. Eine politische Biographie*, pp. 324–333.

89 The SS and Police Leader of Lublin, the Austrian Odilo Globocnik, was ordered by Himmler to organize the murders in the extermination camps of Belzec, Sobibor, and Treblinka (the so-called "Aktion Reinhard").

90 Kershaw, Ian, *The Nazi Dictatorship. Problems and Perspectives of Interpretation*, 4th ed. (London: Arnold, 2000), p. 120.

Although the ministerial bureaucracy was not directly involved in the decision-making to commit large-scale industrial mass murder, it is untenable to contend that there was no connection between the administration and the Final Solution. There was a legalistic subtext to the planned extermination of Jews that was shaped and written by the bureaucrats, foremost the jurists in the Interior Ministry. Instead of hindering the genocide, administration jurists facilitated it.

The Wannsee Conference of January 20, 1942 was the de facto link between the role of the SS (Reich Security Main Office, Security Service, SS Race- and Settlement Office) and the ministerial bureaucracy in the Final Solution. Besides high-ranking SS officers, several jurists attended the meeting, including Roland Freisler (Justice Ministry), Friedrich Wilhelm Kritzinger (Reich Chancellery), and Wilhelm Stuckart (Interior Ministry).[91] Since the decision to murder the Jews had already been made by the time of the conference, the main issue concerned how to carry it out.

Security Service Chief Reinhard Heydrich, who had convened the meeting, opened it by informing participants that Reich Marshal Herman Göring "had appointed him as delegate for the preparations for the Final Solution of the Jewish question in Europe" and that Himmler would lead this undertaking "without regard to geographic borders."[92] Although the transcript does not indicate the change of meaning in "handling the Final Solution," it must have been clear to the participants what was at stake when Heydrich exposed the plans to evacuate eleven million Jews to the East. "Final Solution" no longer referred to expulsion, but to outright extermination.

Heydrich also announced special regulations for *Mischlinge*. As noted in the conference protocol, first-degree Jewish *Mischlinge* (that is, Jews with two Jewish grandparents) would be considered Jews, which meant

91 For the complete list of participants see "Wannsee Protocol Section I," in *The Third Reich Sourcebook*, p. 752. The German document version of the Wannsee conference protocol is available on www.ghwk.de/fileadmin/user_upload/pdf-wannsee/dokumente/protokoll-januar1942_barrierefrei.pdf.

A reprint is in Kampe, Norbert and Klein, Peter, *Die Wannsee-Konferenz am 20. Januar 1942. Dokumente, Forschungsstand, Kontroversen* (Köln, Weimar, Wien: Böhlau, 2013), pp. 40–54. This version of the protocol (the sixteenth copy of altogether thirty copies that were handed to the participants of the Wannsee conference) was the only one found after the war; it was found in the office of Martin Luther, Undersecretary of State in the Ministry of Exterior. See Jasch, *Staatssekretär Wilhelm Stuckart und die Judenpolitik. Der Mythos von der sauberen Verwaltung*, p. 320.

92 "Wannsee Protocol, Section II," in *The Third Reich Sourcebook*, p. 752.

their inclusion in the deportations. The protocol, however, exempted first-degree *Mischlinge* who were married to Germans and had children with partners of German blood, as well as those "for whom the highest offices of Party and State have already issued exemption permits in any sphere of life."[93] The protocol further specified that every case was to be assessed on an individual basis, with a possible unfavorable outcome for the *Mischling*.[94]

The reaction of State Secretary Wilhelm Stuckart is paradigmatic of the interaction between the ministerial apparatus and the SS. Stuckart objected that the proposed regulations would create "endless administrative work" and suggested instead forced sterilization of all half-Jews. With respect to mixed marriages, Stuckart recommended that the legislator should simply declare: "These marriages have been dissolved."[95]

Stuckart's recommendations have been the subject of much controversy. While he defended himself after the war by arguing that he had tried to save the *Mischlinge* (first and second degree) from deportation at the Wannsee conference, others have interpreted his interventions as bowing to Heydrich's plans. The protocol's author himself, Adolf Eichmann, supported this latter view at his trial in Jerusalem, confessing his surprise that Stuckart, normally a stickler for the statutes, would devise radical measures that were inconsistent with the legal paragraphs.[96]

Stuckart's interventions at the Wannsee conference should be interpreted as an effort to maintain the Interior Ministry's competencies

93 "Wannsee Protocol, Section IV," in *The Third Reich Sourcebook*, p. 756.

94 Ibid.

95 Ibid., p. 757. On March 16, 1942, the Interior Minister sent a letter, signed by Stuckart to the participants of the Wannsee conference, requesting that Jewish *Mischlinge* of first degree should be exempted from the deportations since otherwise also "German blood would be halfway abandoned." See Reichsminister des Innern (gez. Stuckart), "Brief vom 16. März 1942," Document NG-2586, State Archive, Nuremberg (the document was part of the so-called Ministries Trial against Stuckart and other leading ministry officials, November 1947–April 1949); reprinted in *Rechtfertigungen des Unrechts. Das Rechtsdenken im Nationalsozialismus in Originaltexten*, pp. 438–443, here: p. 441.

96 In the trial in Jerusalem, Eichmann stated the following with respect to the Wannsee conference (July, 24 1961): "(J)ust look at Stuckart, who was always regarded as a legal pedant, punctilious and fussy, and now what a different tone! The language being used here was very unlegalistic." When asked what was the subject, Eichmann added that the discussions had been about "killing, elimination, and annihilation." Cited according to Jasch, Hans-Christian, "Wilhelm Stuckart. Reich Interior Ministry: 'A Legal Pedant'," in Jasch, Hans-Christian and Kreutzmüller, Christoph (eds.), *The Participants. The Men of the Wannsee Conference* (New York, Oxford: Berghahn, 2017), pp. 301–320, here: p. 301. For calling Stuckart a legal pedant, Eichmann used the term "*Gesetzesonkel*" which literally means "uncle of law."

within the intensely competitive NS state structure. According to historian Hans-Christian Jasch, Heydrich's request to deport first-degree *Mischlinge* and to decide exemptions on a case-by-case basis directly challenged the Interior Ministry's authority in regulating Jewish matters by administrative decree.[97] As early as 1935, Hitler threatened to transfer responsibility for the "Jewish question" to the SS Security Service and the Nazi Party. And beginning with the forced emigration of Jews (systematically first carried out by Eichmann in Vienna), the SS had been increasingly assertive in Jewish matters. The administrative agencies, foremost Stuckart's department for racial matters, had a vital interest in maintaining their relevancy in anti-Jewish policy, even in executing the Final Solution.

While Lösener's report and Stuckart's narrative created the "myth of the clean administration," the true story may well have been very different: Eager to preserve their status, Stuckart and his staff did everything they could to prove their indispensability in Jewish matters. The Supplementary Decrees to the Reich Citizenship Law are good examples of this compliance, as they were drafted by the Interior Ministry (supposedly Stuckart and his staff) and reached deep into the period of mass murder.

The Eleventh Supplementary Decree to the Reich Citizenship Law (November 25, 1941) stated that Jews were no longer German subjects and that Jewish property would thus fall to the Reich.[98] Article 4 of the Twelfth Supplementary Decree (April 25, 1943) ruled that "Jews and Gypsies cannot become state subjects (*Staatsangehörige*)" nor even "provisional state subjects or protected subjects," which meant they had no security whatsoever. The bureaucracy's willingness to go along with the Party and the SS is also apparent in Article 5, which specified that the necessary "legal and administrative orders" for the decree's implementation were to be issued by the Reich Minister of the Interior in agreement with the Leader of the Party Chancellery, the Reichsführer SS, and the Reich Commissioner for the Strengthening of Germandom.[99]

Further escalation in anti-Jewish legal codes came with the Thirteenth Supplementary Decree of July 1, 1943, by which all legal violations by

[97] Jasch, *Staatssekretär Wilhelm Stuckart und die Judenpolitik. Der Mythos von der sauberen Verwaltung*, p. 330ff.

[98] See "Eleventh Supplementary Decree to the Reich Citizenship Law (November 25, 1941)," Paragraph 1 and Paragraph 3.1, in *Legislating the Holocaust*, pp. 170–171.

[99] See "Twelfth Supplementary Decree to the Reich Citizenship Law (25 April, 1943)," Paragraph 4 and Paragraph 5, in *Legislating the Holocaust*, p. 172.

Jews were to be punished by the police and Jews would no longer be subject to the Penal Law for Poles and Jews of December 4, 1941 – in other words, Jews were now outside the competencies of state jurisdiction and the courts. Paragraph 2.1 stated bluntly that "(u)pon the death of a Jew, his property is forfeited to the Reich."[100] This vicious combination of murder and expropriation was signed by the Minister of the Interior (Frick), the Reich Minister of Justice (Thierack), the Reich Minister of Finance (Schwerin von Krosigk) and the Leader of the Party Chancellery (Bormann).

While the Supplementary Decrees to the Reich Citizenship Law were drafted but not signed by Stuckart and his officials, the commentaries on racial legislation clearly bear Stuckart's signature. The commentary that Stuckart co-authored with Hans Globke, published in 1936, had no further editions and was out of use by 1942.[101] However, the commentary on racial legislation that Stuckart published with Rolf Schiedermair, *Rassen- und Erbpflege in der Gesetzgebung des Dritten Reiches*, underwent five successive editions, the first appearing in 1938, and the final one in 1944.[102] A comparative examination of the crucial passages in these editions reveals the legal subtext to the Holocaust.

A striking difference between the Stuckart/Schiedermaier commentary's first edition (1938) and its second, expanded edition (1939) is the section entitled "The elimination of Jews from the German economy," which specified restrictions of Jewish businesses, property, and assets.[103]

[100] See "Thirteenth Supplementary Decree to the Reich Citizenship Law (July 1, 1943)," Paragraph 2.1, in *Legislating the Holocaust*, p. 172.

[101] See Lommatzsch, Erich, *Hans Globke (1898–1973). Beamter im Dritten Reich und Staatssekretär Adenauers* (Frankfurt am Main, New York: Campus, 2009), p. 74. Note that Lommatzsch tends to exonerate Globke (providing, for example, a euphemistic description of Globke's activities in the Reich Ministry of Interior, see pp. 43–103).

[102] Stuckart, Wilhelm and Schiedermair, Rolf, *Rassen- und Erbpflege in der Gesetzgebung des Dritten Reiches* 1st ed. (Leipzig: Kohlhammer, 1938); 2nd ed. 1939, 3rd ed. 1942, 4th ed. 1943, 5th ed. 1944 (note that the second, third, fourth, fifth editions have the title *Rassen- und Erbpflege in der Gesetzgebung des Reiches*).

[103] Just to mention the most important of these restrictions: Jews were forbidden from retail trade; Jewish businesses were excluded from public procurement; Jewish enterprises were controlled by the state and could be dissolved by state force; Jews could not become managers; existing contracts with Jewish managers could be dissolved within 6 weeks; no new Jewish enterprises could be established. See Stuckart and Schiedermair, *Rassen- und Erbpflege in der Gesetzgebung des Dritten Reiches*, 2nd ed. (1939), pp. 57–71. In addition, Jews had to register their property and the worth of their assets; they were forbidden from acquiring new land property and existing Jewish land property was put under state control and its worth could be legally reduced; all their stocks and securities had to be deposited in a bank licensed for foreign exchange; moreover, Jewish ownership of stocks

The background for these regulations was the "Night of Broken Glass" (*Kristallnacht*), an orgy of violent attacks on Jews, Jewish institutions, and businesses that forced thousands of Jews to flee the Reich.[104] The pretext for this wave of violence was the murder of a German Embassy official in Paris, Ernst vom Rath, by a Jewish student, Herschel Grynszpan. The 1939 edition of the commentary required the whole German Jewish community to make a "reparation payment" of one billion German Marks as compensation (*Sühneleistung*) "for the hostile attitude of Jews against the German *Volk* and *Reich*, which had led to the murder of the Embassy employee Vom Rath in Paris."[105] In other words, the NS regime made the Jewish victims pay for the damage inflicted upon them.

Additionally, the second edition (1939) restricted Jews from certain public spaces. All Jewish passports were invalidated by October 5, 1938, replaced thereafter by a special Jewish identity card (*Kennkarte*) that had to be carried at all times.[106] While the formulations of these regulations in the second (1939) and third (1942) editions of the Stuckart/Schiedermair commentary are identical, the fourth edition (1943) subjected Jews' residences and whereabouts to surveillance (based on an Interior Ministry Police Decree from November 1, 1941). Moreover, Jews (except *Mischlinge*) had to wear the Jewish star in public and needed the written permission of their local police agency to leave their municipality.[107]

The most telling changes with regard to the Jews' heightened persecution occur in the fourth edition (1943). The subsections of the commentary's first section of part I ("Foundations of Racial Legislation") had the

and securities could be transferred into German property by way of legal enforcement. Ibid., pp. 71–75. Jews were also forbidden to acquire assets such as diamonds, jewelry and art objects or sell such assets; Jews had to hand over to pawn offices controlled by municipalities objects of gold, platin and silver and diamonds and pearls until March 31, 1939. Ibid., pp. 75–77.

104 After the Anschluss of Austria in March 1938, Jews in Vienna were forced into emigration. The expulsion of Austrian Jews (organized by Adolf Eichmann and his staff) became a model for other areas in the Reich.

105 Stuckart and Schiedermair, *Rassen- und Erbpflege in der Gesetzgebung des Dritten Reiches*, 2nd expanded ed. (1939), p. 77.

106 See Stuckart and Schiedermair, *Rassen- und Erbpflege in der Gesetzgebung des Dritten Reiches*, 2nd expanded ed. (1939), p. 79.

107 See Stuckart and Schiedermair, *Rassen- und Erbpflege in der Gesetzgebung des Reiches*, 4th revised ed. (1943) p. 77. The third (1942) and fourth edition (1943) also contained a section on rental regulations with Jews, stating that Jews should only live with Jews and, furthermore, stating that apartments in Berlin, Munich, and Vienna which became free after Jews had left, had to be registered with the authorities and could only be rented given a permission by the authorities.

same headers and content in the 1938, 1939, and 1942 editions, but the fourth edition replaced the first two subsection titles in the former editions.[108] Instead of "The racial-political requirements," the commentary now referenced "The racial-political task." Likewise, "The German racial problem" was replaced by "The goal of racial laws."[109]

In all three editions (1938, 1939, and 1942), the section on "The racial-political task" stressed that the liberal era did not recognize any racial question. This was followed shortly thereafter by the boldened sentence: "**By contrast, National Socialism puts the racial question at the center of its worldview.**" After this sentence, the 1938 and 1939 editions continued: "**(l)egislation** in the Third Reich soon began **to realize** the **racial-political requirements** ensuing from the National Socialist worldview by issuing generally binding norms."[110]

In the fourth revised edition of 1943, this sentence was replaced by the phrase: "The National Socialist state leadership soon began also to fulfill the racial requirements following from the National Socialist worldview in a practical way."[111] This clearly indicated that legislation in the form of "generally binding norms" had been replaced by concrete actions – actions that in this case meant murder.

Crucially, the 1943 edition also added a section on the goal of the racial laws, that is, a "Jew-free Germany."[112] While the word "deportation" was not used, it was referenced implicitly in explanations that neither emigration nor expulsion were feasible means for solving the "Jewish question" (defined as "an order of *völkisch* self-preservation and self-defense [*Notwehr*])" because potential receiving countries only allowed small quotas of Jews to enter and tried to stop the Jewish influx through tightened immigration laws.[113] The commentary further stated

[108] The titles in the first, second and third editions are "Racial-Political Requirements" (*Die rassenpolitischen Forderungen*), "The German Racial Problem" (*Das deutsche Rassenproblem*), "The Legal Definition of Concepts" (Die gesetzlichen Begriffsbestimmungen).

[109] See Stuckart and Schiedermair, *Rassen- und Erbpflege in der Gesetzgebung des Reiches*, 4th ed. (1943) pp. 9, 12.

[110] The sentence was slightly changed in the third edition of 1942, that is, the phrase "(l)egislation in the Third Reich" is replaced by "National Socialist legislation." See Stuckart and Schiedermair, *Rassen- und Erbpflege in der Gesetzgebung des Reiches*, 3rd ed. (1942), p. 9 (bold letters in the original).

[111] Stuckart and Schiedermair, *Rassen- und Erbpflege in der Gesetzgebung des Reiches*, 4th ed. (1943), p. 9.

[112] Ibid., p. 12.

[113] Ibid., p. 11.

that "expulsion was unfeasible since a suitable host country was not available."[114]

In these eerie formulations, the authors based the NS regime's internal decision for murder on the external obstacles to emigration created by their own anti-Jewish policies. According to the commentators, political developments had required special provisions (*Sondervorschriften*) for Jews which were no longer necessary:

> **The goal of racial legislation** can be considered as having been **already achieved,** and racial legislation therefore largely finalized. It [racial legislation] has, as already mentioned, led to a preliminary solution of the Jewish question and has, at the same time, essentially prepared its Final Solution. Many regulations will lose their practical significance as Germany approaches the ultimate goal of the Jewish question.[115]

To summarize: Racial legislation had proven so successful in preparing the ground for the "ultimate solution" – the elimination of the Jews – that it no longer had a role to play in 1943. The fourth edition of Stuckart and Schiedermair's commentary appeared in 1943, when a large part of European Jewry had already been killed in the extermination camps Belzec, Treblinka, Sobibor, and Auschwitz-Birkenau.

5.6 Concluding Remarks

This chapter has outlined the ideological foundations of racial legislation and the role of law in the NS regime's relentless persecution of Jews. Nazi rule came with a veneer of legality and Nazi jurists upheld this façade even when the regime turned toward murderous policies.

The prewar writings of NS legal theoreticians shared the regime's fierce antisemitism and easily accommodated its anti-Jewish discrimination. Legal thinkers not only appreciated the 1935 Nuremberg Laws, but they assigned them constitutional status. Moreover, there were professional ties between university law professors and jurists in the ministerial bureaucracy. Both groups met to discuss National Socialist law reform and sat on high-ranking commissions to bring law in line with the political principles of National Socialism; they both followed their respective publications (recall Koellreutter's enthusiastic assessment of Stuckart and Globke's 1936 commentary on racial lawgiving).

114 Ibid., p. 12.

115 Ibid., p. 14 (bold letters in the original). The same formulations occur in the 5th ed. (1944).

Yet the thinking of academic legal theorists and high-ranking government jurists drew apart, as those in the ministerial bureaucracy came closer to the political power centers for anti-Jewish policies than the university professors did. The relevant administrative bodies were informed of the extermination program and provided the legal subtext to force, terror, and murder. But decision-making was in the hands of the highest political authority and the core institutions backing this system of totalitarian power: the Party and, foremost, the SS.

What insights about the normative structure of the NS state can we gain from our examination of the role of the Party and SS, on the one hand, and the ministerial bureaucracy, on the other?

The Party/SS and the ministerial bureaucracy sought to realize the political ends of the NS state in strikingly different ways. While administrative officials implemented the state's policies legally, the Party and SS were ruthless in executing their understanding of National Socialism's political mission. This involved not merely exerting considerable pressure on the content of laws, but all too often violating and even rejecting outright the Reich's legal framework. The means chosen by the Party and the SS for achieving their political goals were dictated by mere expediency – a brutal instrumentalism that ended in mass murder. Especially during the war, political criminality replaced law.

The bifurcation of roles in these two institutional systems – the ministerial bureaucracy and the Party/SS complex – evokes Ernst Fraenkel's famous characterization of the National Socialist state as a "dual state," that is, a political body consisting of the normative state and the prerogative state. While the normative state still functioned by law, the prerogative state exercised its authority via arbitrary interventions, measures, and orders. The guiding principle of the prerogative state was pure discretionary force. In Fraenkel's own words: "There are no legal rules governing the political sphere. It is regulated by arbitrary measures (*Massnahmen*) in which the dominant officials exercise their discretionary prerogatives. Hence the expression 'Prerogative State' (*Massnahmenstaat*)."[116]

To be sure, Fraenkel was not suggesting that the Third Reich was evenly split into law-governed institutions (the ministerial and administrative

[116] Fraenkel, Ernst, *The Dual State. A Contribution to the Theory of Dictatorship*, with an introduction by Meierhenrich, Jens, transl. by Shils, E. A. (Oxford: Oxford University Press, 2017) p. 3 (italics in the original).

apparatus) and the law-violating Party and SS.[117] Rather than carving out distinct state entities within the regime, the concepts of normative state and prerogative state are best understood as two modes of exercising state authority – one that still complied with what was left of the rule-of-law state; the other operating through so-called measures that amounted to arbitrary, if not capricious, uses of power. Fraenkel himself clarified that the NS state had no reliable legal structure, so that, at any moment, arbitrariness, if not despotism, could break into the allegedly stable legal framework to override and revoke laws.

Of course, we can observe a strong tendency in such ideological core institutions as the Party and the SS to apply measures with brute force. But as a general analysis of the NS state, the assumption of its being divided into two separate state units would be misleading. As we saw in the second chapter, the program of *Gleichschaltung* between 1933 and 1934 resulted in an institutional fusion of state and Party. The merger of these power centers was constitutive for the authoritarian Führer state.[118]

Our discussion of racial policies and lawgiving also engages legal theory. Although the commentaries on racial legislation in the Third

[117] A warning that Fraenkel's formula of the dual state might invite a potentially misleading impression of the Nazi state came from another German law theorist who, like Fraenkel, had to leave Germany: Franz Neumann. In his famous 1942 analysis of the NS state, *Behemoth*, Neumann rejected the idea "that National Socialism is a dual state, that is, in fact, one state within which two systems are operating, one under normative law, the other under individual measures, one rational, the other the realm of prerogative." Neumann, Franz, *Behemoth. The Structure and Practice of National Socialism 1933–1944*, with an introduction by Hayes, Peter (Chicago: Ivan R. Dee, 2009), pp. 467–468. For Neumann normative law had no place in National Socialism; he held that "there is no realm of law in Germany, although there are thousands of technical rules that are calculable." Ibid., p. 468. Neumann disputed that the Third Reich was a state at all, because it missed the constitutive features of a state, namely being able "to coordinate and integrate hundreds and thousands of individual and group conflicts" by a process "accomplished in a universally binding manner, that is, through abstract rational law or at least through a rationally operating bureaucracy." Ibid. He denied that one can "detect in the framework of the National Socialist political system any one organ which monopolizes political power." Ibid., p. 469. The overall merits of Neumann's study notwithstanding, I think that Fraenkel's analysis is illuminating; there were indeed constant tensions between the normative and the prerogative, between what Meierhenrich calls "the remnants of the Rechtsstaat" and the arbitrary force of the Party and the SS. See Meierhenrich, Jens, *The Remnants of the Rechtsstaat. An Ethnography of Nazi Law* (Oxford: Oxford University Press, 2018).

[118] See also Meierhenrich, Jens, "An Ethnography of Nazi Law: The Intellectual Foundations of Ernst Fraenkel's Theory of Dictatorship," in Fraenkel, *The Dual State*, pp. xxii–lxxxi, here: xli. Meierhenrich emphasizes that according to Fraenkel State and Party were "institutionally fused, virtually indistinguishable in conceptual terms." Ibid.

Reich built a framework of norms, regulations, and administrative directives around the Holocaust, somehow attempting to cope with the "unspeakable," the authors themselves finally had to concede that the NS state pursued its racial agenda in ways that transcended legality. The regime's "practical way" of realizing "the racial requirements" of National Socialism sidelined legal norms and robbed them of their significance, as Stuckart and Schiedermair noted in 1943. Not only were the political forces at the core of power stronger than the administration, but their means and measures could not be translated into "generally binding norms." There was no way to legalize terror, mass murder, and annihilation. The "rupture in civilization" for which the Holocaust stands could not be couched in legal concepts.[119]

What lessons can we draw from the fact that, when faced with mass murder, the law ultimately failed, as crucial passages in the racial law commentaries indicate? How does this shape our understanding of legality and the formal features of a legal order?

There is a striking distinction to be made between the Nuremberg Laws and the Nazi regime's turn toward mass murder. Their dreadful content notwithstanding, the Nuremberg Laws were published in the *Reichgesetzblatt* and their content was thus accessible to all affected by them. Yet the order to eliminate the Jews was made so surreptitiously that even SS officers operating in the vicinity of the murders did not know about the extermination program.[120] The mere notion that the Third Reich would announce its plan to annihilate European Jewry via general norms in the *Reichsgesetzblatt* seems outrageous to us.[121] And yet this

[119] The thesis defended here seems contrary to David Fraser's argument that law was present in Auschwitz. Fraser writes: "But the Law was in fact not absent from Auschwitz. It was not a lawless time or place. Auschwitz was lawful, it was full of law – lawful prescriptions of 'Aryan' and 'Jew', lawful sterilizations and euthanasia to protect the blood, lawful orders, from lawyers and doctors, for the removal, isolation, and then extermination of those enemies of the State, those parasites who would infect the *Volksgemeinschaft*." See Fraser, David, *Law after Auschwitz. Towards a Jurisprudence of the Holocaust* (Durham: Carolina Academic Press, 2005), p. 13, see also pp. 19–49. I think that Fraser's point is correct as far as administrative orders are concerned, but fails with respect to law in the sense of procedurally enacted legal norms (officially announced and made public).

[120] As the case of Konrad Morgen shows, it was even difficult for an SS judge to get knowledge about the working of the "Aktion Reinhard." See Pauer-Studer, Herlinde and Velleman, J. David, *Konrad Morgen. The Conscience of a Nazi Judge* (Basingstoke: Palgrave Macmillan, 2015), pp. 74–81, 86–87.

[121] Rundle, Kristen, "The Impossibility of an Extermination Legality," in *University of Toronto Law Journal* 59, 1 (2009), pp. 65–125.

reveals something important about the constitutive conditions of a legal order.

In *The Morality of Law,* Lon L. Fuller formulated eight criteria for the law – namely, that a legal system must consist of general rules (not decisions on an ad hoc basis); those rules must be made public; they must be understandable; reliable (not changing too frequently); not contradictory; not impossible to satisfy; they must not hold retroactively, and there must be congruence between announced rules and their actual administration.[122] The publication and transparency of legal norms, particularly for those directly affected by them, were Fuller's core requirements for a system of rules that qualified as a legal order.

The development and radicalization of the Third Reich's racial policies, in particular their transformation from published laws into a secret program of industrial mass murder, provide a striking example of the relevance of Fuller's conditions.[123] The strength of the promulgation requirement is tested with the surreptitious implementation of the Nazis' extermination plan. Could the decision to destroy European Jewry have been promulgated in the *Reichsgesetzblatt?* In all likelihood, no – at least not without undermining the plan itself. And the impossibility we encounter here has a remarkable consequence: The simple requirement to publish all of its regulations might have prevented the Nazi regime's worst excesses.

That the law was running out in the face of mass murder also says something about legality: Law and legal norms simply come in a specific form, one displayed neither by arbitrary measures nor secret orders and oral commands.

[122] See Fuller, Lon L., *The Morality of Law*, revised ed. (New Haven and London: Yale University Press, 1969), p. 39.

[123] Fuller problematically claimed that his criteria formed the inner morality of law, whereas they neither amount to moral principles nor do some of those conditions exempt legal norms that meet them from having morally odious ends. This point was emphasized by H. L. A. Hart. See Hart, H. L. A., "The Morality of Law by Lon L. Fuller," in *Harvard Law Review* 78, 6 (1965), pp. 1281–1296, here: p. 1287. According to Hart, there is, for example, "no special incompatibility between clear laws and evil." Ibid. In my view, Hart's objection does not cast doubt on the constitutive relevance of Fuller's principles. However, Hart's critique is justified in so far as it is directed against Fuller's claim that the mentioned conditions constitute the inner morality of law. In my view, it makes more sense to read Fuller's conditions as being constitutive for a system of rules that can be called a legal order – that is, requirements that result from our experience with political systems that govern through arbitrary measures and terror. For a more elaborate discussion of this point see Chapter 8.4 of this book.

Finally, one might criticize the argument that the regime's extermination program transcended legality by arguing that the sources of legality (in the sense of given positive law) were considerably broader in the Third Reich. In other words, one could emphasize the breadth and strength of the leadership principle. The Führer, according to this objection, not only united all power in his hands, but ruled both by measures and enacted legal norms.

This exact question of whether Hitler's legislative authority extended to declarations and announcements was controversial among NS jurists. Indeed, a forceful objection to conferring legal status to Führer declarations came from one of the Third Reich's highest jurists, Justice Minister Franz Gürtner. In a committee consultation on how to reform law in agreement with National Socialist principles, Gürtner stated:

> I am ready to accept any of the Führer's declarations of will, as far as it is a means for the recognition of the aim of a law and its content. However, any attempt to treat this will as equal to the will given in legislative form seems to me highly questionable, especially as the form in which such an extralegal declaration of will occurs is a question that deserves additional consideration.[124]

Gürtner's concerns indicate that, from a jurisprudential viewpoint, there were limits to granting legality to all articulations of the Führer's power – limits that several high-ranking jurists in the Third Reich were still endorsing. However, the NS state was a totalitarian political system

[124] *Quellen zur Reform des Straf- und Strafprozeßrechts*, II. Abteilung NS-Zeit (1933–1939) – Strafgesetzbuch, Band 2, Protokolle der Strafrechtskommission des Reichsjustizministeriums, 3. Teil, 2. Lesung: Allgemeiner Teil. Besonderer Teil, 56. Sitzung, 22. März 1935, ed. by Regge, Jürgen and Schubert, Werner (Berlin, New York: Walter de Gruyter, 1990), p. 11. There is documentary evidence that Gürtner tried to mitigate the legal implementation of Nazi radical antisemitism. In a meeting of the Official Criminal Law Commission on June 5, 1934 on the topic of protection of race (*Rasseschutz)*, Gürtner raised concerns about introducing specific criminal law regulations for the protection of the Aryan race. He rejected, for instance, criminal sanction of extramarital sexual relations between Jewish and non-Jewish Germans – thereby provoking harsh objections from Freisler who noted in the discussion: "Herr Reich Minister, I cannot stand it that the inclusion of race protection (*Rasseschutz)* in the new criminal law finds no support at all in this circle." *Quellen zur Reform des Straf- und Strafprozeßrechts*, II. Abteilung NS-Zeit (1933–1939) – Strafgesetzbuch, Band 2, Protokolle der Strafrechtskommission des Reichsjustizministeriums, 2. Teil, 1. Lesung: Allgemeiner Teil (1989), 37. Sitzung, 5. Juni 1934, pp. 223–276, here: p. 229. On Gürtner's skepticism toward the legal implementation of the regime's antisemitism see also Whitman, James Q. *Hitler's American Model. The United States and the Making of Nazi Race Law* (Princeton: Princeton University Press, 2018), pp. 87–113.

with the highest authority enjoying unlimited power. That power, moreover, could be exerted both through legislation that promulgated legal norms and measures, orders, announcements, and commands. Although all of Hitler's normative power covered all of his political avowals, not all articulations of his will amounted to law. Not every Führer declaration had the normative status of a legal norm. This is highlighted in Fraenkel's notion of the dual state, with its two systems of power – one that operated normatively via legislation, the other via arbitrary measures that belonged to the political rather than the legal sphere. It was precisely this duality of governance that made the NS state so fearsome, unpredictable and dangerous for those who did not meet the racial criteria for enjoying basic state protections.

6

Police Law

6.1 Introductory Remarks

The Third Reich was characterized by a constant power struggle between state institutions and National Socialist core organizations, notably the Nazi Party and the SS. A crucial issue concerned which side could claim authority over the police.

In the Weimar Republic, police matters were in the hands of the federal states. The strongest federal police unit was the Prussian police, which from 1931 relied on a codified police law – the Prussian Law on Police Administration (*Preußisches Polizeiverwaltungsgesetz*, or PVG). Considered as *the* model for organizing the police by the rule of law (not least since it allowed for administrative judicial review of police measures), the PVG gave the Prussian Interior Minister control over the police (including the political police).

Two articles of the Prussian Law on Police Administration played important roles in restricting police power – § 14 of section IV ("The Tasks of Police Authorities") and § 41 of section VIII ("Police Orders"). PVG § 14 broadly defined the task of police authorities as the prevention of danger to public security and order "within the framework of valid laws" and "after due consideration."[1] § 41 stipulated that, to protect public security and order, "such means [have to] be chosen that will least impair the concerned persons and the public."[2] These guarantees

[1] "Preußisches Polizeiverwaltungsgesetz vom 1.6.1931," in *Recht, Verwaltung und Justiz im Nationalsozialismus. Ausgewählte Schriften, Gesetze und Gerichtsentscheidungen von 1933 bis 1945*, ed. by Hirsch, Martin; Majer, Diemut; Meinck, Jürgen (Köln: Bund-Verlag, 1984), pp. 322–323.

[2] Ibid., p. 318, note 2.

were still valid in the period of presidential dictatorship in the last months of the Weimar Republic.[3]

With the Nazis' accession to power in late January 1933, the police's legal framework abruptly changed. At the constitutional level, this affected how police understood their responsibilities and authority. The Reichstag Fire Decree of February 1933 allowed for police interventions into basic personal rights. The regime's claim of restoring public order provided a pretext for persecuting political opponents. Such new measures as protective custody strengthened police power.[4]

Although the PVG remained valid after the Nazi seizure of power, it merely functioned as a negative foil for how to redesign police law in an authoritarian Führer state. The general clause of § 14 that restricted the means of police power was reinterpreted such that the police's central duty was to combat political opposition perceived as threatening Nazi rule.

In a rule-of-law system, the police adhere to the state administration (usually the Interior Ministry). But the National Socialists contested placing the police force into a framework of legal norms and administrative regulations. When Hitler appointed Reichsführer SS Heinrich Himmler as Chief of the German Police on June 17, 1936, an executive state body was brought under the direct control of an organization intensely committed to National Socialist ideology. Indeed, Himmler aimed to align the police with the political mission of the SS by making it into a tool of "inner warfare."[5]

In what follows, I show how these normative changes in police power came about and were justified theoretically in the NS state.

6.2 The Struggle over Police Control 1933–1936

Since Prussia was the Reich's largest federal state, control over its police force was crucial for the distribution of power in National Socialist Germany. Hitler thus nominated Hermann Göring as Reich Commissioner for the Prussian Interior Ministry on January 30, 1933, giving the long-time Nazi and World War I hero full authority over the Prussian police.

[3] See Schwegel, Andreas, *Der Polizeibegriff im NS-Staat. Polizeirecht, juristische Publizistik und Judikative 1931–1944* (Tübingen: Mohr Siebeck 2005), p. 39f.

[4] Werle, Gerhard, *Justiz-Strafrecht und polizeiliche Verbrechensbekämpfung im Dritten Reich* (Berlin/New York: Walter de Gruyter, 1989), pp. 2–3.

[5] Frei, Norbert, *Der Führerstaat. Nationalsozialistische Herrschaft 1933–1945*, 6th ed. (München: Deutscher Taschenbuch Verlag, 2001), p. 147.

On March 3, 1933, Göring considerably extended police competencies with a circular decree on the implementation of the Reichstag Fire Decree of February 28, 1933, which had already suspended many basic rights in the Weimar Constitution.[6] Göring's decree allowed police to take action beyond the limits set by PVG § 14 and § 41 by, for example, suspending the principle of proportionality in the application of police measures. Historian Jürgen Meinck sees Göring's decree as a striking example of breaking legal rules and restrictions via administrative executive orders.[7]

Göring's power grew with his nomination to Prime Minister of Prussia on April 10, 1933. On April 26, he founded the Secret State Police Office (Gestapa)[8] by enacting the first Gestapo Law. Tasked with recording any activities in the Reich that might endanger the state, the Gestapo was crucial to the NS regime's quest for unlimited power.[9]

Eager to maintain his authority, Göring undermined Interior Minister Frick's attempts to control the Gestapo by passing a second Gestapo Law on November 30, 1933 which subordinated the political police directly to the Prussian Prime Minister – Göring himself.

The rivalry between Göring and Frick paled in comparison with Himmler's ambitions. After obtaining authority over the Bavarian political police in April 1934, Himmler assumed control over the political police forces in all the federal states except Prussia and Schaumburg-Lippe. The Reichsführer SS then pressed to win authority over the Prussian police. In April 1934, Göring gave in and appointed Himmler as the Gestapo's highest Inspector and the latter's confidant, Reinhard Heydrich, as its head.

The position of the SS, and thereby the Gestapa, was strengthened by the murders of SA chief Ernst Röhm and other leading SA members in

[6] "Durchführung der Verordnung zum Schutz von Volk und Staat vom 28. 2. 1933," Runderlaß des Ministeriums des Inneren (Circular Decree of the Interior Ministry) vom 3.3. 1933, in *Recht, Verwaltung und Justiz im Nationalsozialismus*, p. 319 (= *Ministerialblatt für die Preußische innere Verwaltung* 1933, I, p. 233).

[7] Meinck, Jürgen, "Polizeirecht," in *Recht, Verwaltung und Justiz im Nationalsozialismus*, pp. 317–319, here p. 318.

[8] Until 1936, the Secret State Police Office was called Gestapa (*Geheimes Staatspolizeiamt*), from then on the term "Gestapo" was used for the entire Secret Political Police apparatus.

[9] See "Gesetz über die Errichtung eines Geheimen Staatspolizeiamts. Vom 26. 4. 1933," in *Recht, Verwaltung und Justiz im Nationalsozialismus*, pp. 326–327, note 11. This first Gestapo Law replaced the previous police authorities of the federal states by state police authorities and, moreover, required all district police authorities to directly inform the state police authorities about all important political activities and observations. Spying on political opponents was thus declared legal, marking a clear step toward a totalitarian police state. Ibid., p. 327.

late June 1934 (the "Night of the Long Knives").[10] Under Heydrich, the Gestapo helped to plan the SS action, after which Himmler and the SS enjoyed Hitler's favor and trust.

In November 1934, Göring gave Himmler responsibility for the Prussian Gestapo. Himmler also prevailed in the raging conflict between the Interior Ministry and the SS over ultimate control of the Gestapo. When, in addition to his leadership of the SS, Himmler became Chief of the German Police on June 17, 1936, the Gestapo was de facto beyond the Interior Ministry's authority. The SS was now fully in charge of the concentration camps as well.[11]

Already before Himmler's appointment as Chief of the German Police, a third Gestapo Law was passed in February 1936.[12] Drafted by Gestapo legal counsel Werner Best, the law aimed to undercut loyalties toward any still existing rule of law principles in the administrative apparatus and to secure the SS influence on the administration. In the mid-1930s, parts of the ministerial bureaucracy assumed that the measures backed by the Reichstag Fire Decree could be recalled or at least limited, as the political state of emergency had supposedly given way to order and stability. The imposition of protective custody was thus particularly controversial among ministry officials.

An enabling clause (*Ermächtigungsklausel*) included in § 1 of the third Gestapo Law tasked the Gestapo "to investigate and fight any subversive attempts in the entire state territory, to collect and evaluate the results of [said] investigations, to inform the state government and other authorities concerning any evidence they might deem important."[13] This invalidated the core idea of the former Prussian Police Law, expressed in its § 14, that the police should protect the general public and

10 The pretext for the elimination of its leadership was that the SA had become too powerful and had challenged the direction in which the National Socialist state under Hitler developed.

11 For a detailed account of the conflicts between Göring, Frick, and Himmler see Schwegel, *Der Polizeibegriff im NS-Staat*, pp. 41–59. See also Herbert, Ulrich, *Best. Biographische Studien über Radikalismus, Weltanschauung und Vernunft 1903–1989* (Bonn: J. H. W. Dietz Nachfolger, 2001) (= Studienausgabe der Originalausgabe von 1996), pp. 133–147.

12 See Best, Werner, "Gesetz über die Geheime Staatspolizei. Vom 10. Februar 1936," in *Recht, Verwaltung und Justiz im Nationalsozialismus*, pp. 329–330 (= *Preußische Gesetzessammlung* 1936, pp. 21–22).

13 See "Gesetz über die Geheime Staatspolizei. Vom 10. Februar 1936," § 1, in *Recht, Verwaltung und Justiz im Nationalsozialismus*, p. 329. § 1 also stipulated that the Chief of the Gestapo, in agreement with the Minister of the Interior, decided which tasks exactly were transferred to the Gestapo.

individuals such that they respected each person's defensive rights against the state. The 1936 law required the Gestapo to actively defend the state against all possible dangerous political movements. In other words, protection of the state replaced its obligation to safeguard the public and individuals. While § 14 PVG had bound the averting of danger to the prevailing legal regulations, the Gestapo Law allowed for a wide discretion in interpreting the principle of safeguarding the state.[14] In line with the tendency to expand the political police's scope of action, § 7 of the third Gestapo Law specified that "(o)rders concerning matters of the Secret State Police are not subject to judicial review by the administrative courts."[15]

Another significant piece of legislation was the Decree for the Implementation of the III. Gestapo Law.[16] Its § 2 permitted the Gestapo to carry out police investigations in cases of high crime, treason, and offenses involving explosives. § 4 stipulated that, in supporting the Gestapo, police authorities at the district and local levels may restrict the right of assembly and association and, moreover, confiscate printed materials. Most remarkable was the decree's § 2, section 4, which placed the Secret State Police Office "in charge of administering the state concentration camps."[17] Since the third Gestapo Law ruled out judicial review of Gestapo measures, it ensconced SS despotism in the concentration camps and the legal defenselessness of camp prisoners.

The Justice Ministry repeatedly tried to intervene against Nazi brutality and violence. It even attempted to restrict how the SS and the SA handled protective custody (that is, internment in a concentration camp). In April 1934, a Justice Ministry decree sought to shut down unauthorized concentration camps erected by the SA and SS. The implementation decree of February 10, 1936 sidestepped these Nazi organizations by giving the Gestapo authority over protective custody. Ironically, however, this regulation would soon benefit the SS. When Himmler gained control over the German Police and the Gestapo in June 1936, it enabled him to claim that the SS had the "legal power" to order preventive custody.[18]

[14] See Schwegel, *Der Polizeibegriff im NS-Staat*, p. 153.

[15] See "Gesetz über die Geheime Staatspolizei. Vom 10. Februar 1936," § 7, p. 330.

[16] See "Verordnung zur Ausführung des Gesetzes über die Geheime Staatspolizei. Vom 10. Februar 1936," in *Recht, Verwaltung und Justiz im Nationalsozialismus*, pp. 330–331 (in *Preußische Gesetzesssammlung 1936*), pp. 22–23.

[17] Ibid., p. 330, § 2.4.

[18] Siehe Schwegel, *Der Polizeibegriff im NS-Staat*, pp. 53–55.

By that time, the Justice Ministry's position vis-à-vis the regime had considerably weakened. Justice Minister Gürtner had not even dared to condemn openly the Röhm murders. Instead, he retroactively authorized the action against the SA by legislation passed in July 1934.[19] Given such extensive concessions to the Führer state, it would have been incoherent of the Justice Ministry to insist, two years later, on restricting SS police power by statutes and administrative regulations. The Ministry had already too willingly backed the NS state to raise effective objections against Himmler's rise to power.

Himmler's nomination to Chief of the German Police on June 17, 1936 sealed the administration's power loss. The SA crisis of 1934 had taught Hitler, who already mistrusted jurists and the ministerial bureaucracy, how important it was to back up his authority with a loyal NS organization.

The combined office of "Reichsführer SS and Chief of the German Police" created an institution under the Führer's direct executive power. Although the Interior Minister was formally authorized to issue instructions to the Chief of the German Police, his competence was de facto preempted by the dictatorial structure. Sovereign power in the Third Reich rested with Hitler. In conflicts over how to lead the police, the Reich Minister of the Interior could "neither appeal to his ministry's legal competence nor assert his authority vis-à-vis his personal and direct 'subordinate' [Himmler]," as he thus would have opposed the Führer's authority, emphasized historian Hans Buchheim.[20]

6.3 The Ideological Foundations of Police Power

In the early stages of the Third Reich, the extension of police power relied on the special measures permitted for a state of emergency by the Reichstag Fire Decree of February 28, 1933. Gradually, however, comprehensive police powers were justified merely by appealing to the Nazi worldview. Identifying the police's primary function in terms of establishing and securing a total Führer state led to a wide interpretation of executive competency.

19 See Gruchmann, Lothar, *Justiz im Dritten Reich 1933–1940. Anpassung und Unterwerfung in der Ära Gürtner* (München: R. Oldenbourg, 1988), pp. 448–455.

20 See Buchheim, Hans, "The SS-Instrument of Domination," in Krausnick, Helmut; Buchheim, Hans; Broszat, Martin; Jacobsen, Hans-Adolf, *Anatomy of the SS-Staate*, transl. by Barry, Richard (New York: Walker and Company, 1968) pp. 127–301, here: p. 163.

The theoretical writings of NS jurists reflect these remarkable developments. NS legal theorists primarily saw the police as a state surveillance tool. Under the influence of NS racial ideology, the executive's role went so far as to include shielding the Aryan ethnic community from "racial-biological infiltration."

According to Walter Hamel, an expert on NS police law, police authority was necessarily determined in line with the union of state and society. The police should act as the "guardian of the community," tasked with "checking that everyone fulfills his duties to the people and observes his function in the maintenance and creation of the *Volk*'s values (*Volkswerte*)."[21]

Propagating a kind of ethical-perfectionist conception of the *völkisch* Führer state, Hamel argued:

> Both poles – the freedom of the *völkisch* comrades (*Volksgenossen*) and the shaping of this freedom by the state – are today oriented toward preserving the substance of the people: the *völkisch* comrade is obliged to use his freedom for developing the concrete ethical and material values of the people. And the state, the sovereign power of the community, shapes these service obligations, ensures that they are fulfilled in the best possible manner, and protects the thus created goods in order to drive the people's community to its utmost perfection. Thus, the special material sovereign right of the police – to avert danger from the liberal society – has become irrelevant. . . . Restricting the police to averting danger was just an artificial fantasy of rationalist ideology, which considered this [averting danger] as the state's only meaning. Basically, the task of the police is always the task of the state in general.[22]

In Hamel's view, the competence of the police could no longer be regulated by positive law. He claimed that "the nature of state sovereignty and the way in which it is shaped by the Führer and Reich Chancellor" were the only legal police foundations in the NS state.[23]

Hamel's arguments, particularly that the state should force citizens to promote communal ethical values, show how NS police law was shaped by the moralization of law which was typical for Nazi Germany. The police had to partake in the "ethical program" of the *völkisch* state, the implementation of which, Hamel emphasized, required extending such

[21] Hamel, Walter, "Wesen und Rechtsgrundlagen der Polizei im nationalsozialistischen Staate," in Frank, Hans (ed.), *Deutsches Verwaltungsrecht* (München: Zentralverlag der NSDAP, Franz Eher Nachf., 1937), pp. 381–398, here: p. 385.

[22] Ibid., p. 384.

[23] Ibid., p. 389.

coercive measures as protective custody. He thus considered the authorization for protective custody as "a natural part of the police's office" that neither could nor did derive from a statute.[24]

Yet, in the end Hamel avoided giving any clear definition of the scope of police authority, let alone of its limits. The office of the police, he wrote,

> can neither be determined nor subdivided, because the tasks of the state cannot be completely divided according to any rational purposes or subject areas. Certain tasks or certain subjects may indeed be separated from the state's general sovereignty; but there will always remain an irrational core that defies restriction, interferes with any determination of aims and subjects, and whose scope continually changes with the situational context. This irrational core of state sovereignty is represented by the police. Any general definition of the police's office would amount to a rationalization of the state. . . . If the sovereignty of the National Socialist state cannot be rationally limited, there also must exist a last indeterminable substance within the state administration.[25]

Such rhetoric associating the police with the irrational and indefinable aspects of state authority supported its transformation into an ideologically malleable tool in Himmler's hands. Moreover, NS jurists did not object to the police no longer preventing violations of individual rights, while supporting a state ready to commit precisely such violations in its pursuit of comprehensive power.

Other publications on police law similarly offered vague descriptions of the police's role. In one programmatic article, SS jurist Reinhard Höhn argued that National Socialism had its own conception of the police and its tasks, with the protection of the people's community as its ultimate goal. "The decisive change of police law would not consist in altering the scope of competencies," he wrote, "but in altering the police's essence."[26] Höhn thus rejected the restrictions set by § 14 of the Prussian Police Law as outdated positivistic legal thinking that did not match the new role of the police in the Führer state. The obligation to preserve the communal order, he asserted, required extensive preventive measures that conflicted with liberal principles. Accordingly, the third Gestapo Law introduced a "new police principle" whereby the political police functioned as the

[24] Ibid., p. 395.
[25] Ibid., p. 386.
[26] Höhn, Reinhard, "Altes und neues Polizeirecht," in Frank, Himmler, Best, Höhn, *Grundfragen der deutschen Polizei* (Hamburg: Hanseatische Verlagsanstalt, 1937), pp. 21–34, here: p. 33.

Führer state's protective corps and assigned the criminal police to "eradicate an asocial phenomenon as such, namely professional criminality."[27]

With Himmler's nomination to Chief of the German Police, police power transcended all remaining normative boundaries. For example, the political police could now order protective custody (that is, internment in a concentration camp) with no legal backing. The mission of protecting the *völkisch* order simply exceeded all statutes.

In a 1936 essay on the legal foundations of protective custody Hans Tesmer (an official in the Gestapa) summarized this normative change: While the Reichstag Fire Decree had considered protective custody as a measure against political opponents, foremost against the communists' "subversive violent actions," by 1936 protective custody was imposed on "all elements ... whose harmful behavior toward the state and *Volk* endangers the German people's reconstruction work."[28] In other words, divergent political convictions were already also regarded as detrimental to the *Volk*'s well-being. In another 1936 article, Gestapo judicial advisor Werner Best forcefully postulated how rigorously the Secret State Police was expected to persecute those who did not or could not identify with the "ideological-political" principles of National Socialism:

> With the establishment of the *National Socialist Führer state*, a political rulership has emerged in Germany that, for the first time, derives its legitimacy from a living idea and wards off attack on its current leadership with all means of state power. The political totality principle of National Socialism, which matches the worldview principle of organic and inseparable national unity, does not tolerate any political will formation in its sphere that does not align with the general will. Any attempt to enforce or merely maintain another political view will be extinguished as an illness threatening the general unity of the undivided organism of the people, [and] without regard for the subjective will of its bearers.[29]

In defining "the idea and ethos of the Political Police in the racial Führer state," Best also linked the police's mission with racial hygiene: "[The Political Police] is an institution that carefully supervises the political

[27] Ibid., pp. 29, 31. See also the discussion of Höhn's views in Schwegel, *Der Polizeibegriff im NS-Staat*, pp. 214–225.

[28] Tesmer, Hans, "Die Schutzhaft und ihre rechtlichen Grundlagen (1936)," in *Recht, Verwaltung und Justiz im Nationalsozialismus*, pp. 331–332, here: p. 331.

[29] Best, "Die Geheime Staatspolizei," in *Deutsches Recht* 6 (1936), pp. 125–128, here pp. 125–126 (italics in the original); see also the discussion in Herbert, *Best*, pp. 163–168.

sanity of the German body politic . . . [by] recognizing in a timely manner each symptom of disease and identifying the germs of destruction – whether they developed through inner corrosion or were imported externally by willful poisoning – and extinguishing them by whatever means appropriate."[30] Best's publications were not the mere outpourings of an ideologically deluded SS jurist – they were the leading contemporary official commentaries on police law. Indeed, his 1940 book *The German Police,* which distinguished between the individualistic-humanitarian state (an invention of the consensual will of individuals) and the *völkisch* state, became a police handbook.[31] In the former state form, Best asserted, the police protected individual citizens by means of principles, regulations, and statutes. Conversely, the *völkisch* state aimed to preserve and enhance the *Volk* as a "transpersonal, time-transcending totality of uniform blood and spiritual character."[32] For Best, the police amounted to a kind of "order and security service" for "protecting the *völkisch* order against disruption and destruction."[33] The Gestapo Law of February 10, 1936, drafted by Best himself, followed this guideline by defining the Secret State Police's function as observing, persecuting, and suppressing all tendencies that might endanger the state.

Best insisted that his delineation of the role of the police was supported by a *völkisch* law conception by which the Führer's will, in all its articulations, was the source of all law. This thus eliminated the differences between stronger and weaker norms, constitutional law and ordinary legal norms, statutes, decrees, and administrative orders, and between public and private law.[34] Best quoted approvingly a 1935 decision of Saxony's Higher Administrative Court that configured the law in the Führer state "as the law of the community – that is, the order, in which the *Volk* leads its communal life, which, furthermore, is prioritized over the legal statutes."[35]

In order to understand how the police under Himmler could assume such vast powers outside of the state's ministerial bureaucracy, one must first acknowledge these radical legal transformations. The identification of legality with the Führer's decisional authority, as Best's texts on police law remarkably illustrate, explains the normative unboundedness of police actions: in the NS state, all police activities could in principle be

[30] Best, "Die Geheime Staatspolizei," p. 126 (in bold letters in the original quote).
[31] Best, *Die Deutsche Polizei* (Darmstadt: L.C. Wittich, 1940).
[32] Ibid., p. 12.
[33] Ibid., p. 14.
[34] Ibid., p. 15.
[35] Ibid., p. 19.

justified with reference to the political leaderships' plans, intentions, and will.

The new understanding of law also explains why SS ordered police actions could not be challenged, let alone prevented, by the ministerial bureaucracy. Although ministry officials who still thought in the classical categories of *Beamtenstaat* and the *Beamtenethos* were, time and again, puzzled by the "legality" of many police measures and protested against the omission of administrative procedures and regulations, they were ultimately running up against a new normative order – a system that had changed state structures much more radically than they were able to fully recognize in the prewar period.

6.4 The Extension of Police Power under Himmler

Himmler used his power as Chief of the German Police to reorganize the institution. Just days after his appointment in June 1936, he divided the police into two branches – the Order Police under Kurt Daluege (consisting of the constabulary, the *Gendarmerie*, and the municipal police) and the Security Police commanded by Reinhard Heydrich (including the Office of Administration and Law, the Criminal Investigation Department, and the Political Police Office).[36]

By separating ordinary police matters from so-called *political* police affairs, Himmler could build up a security apparatus. He filled leading positions in the Security Police with SS members, gave the Gestapa in Berlin authority over the political police in the entire Reich (as opposed to just Prussia), and nominated the ruthless SS mastermind Reinhard Heydrich as head of the Gestapa and the Security Police. For his part, Heydrich fully supported Himmler's plans to turn the police into a safeguard of the Führer state. According to Heydrich, the "eternal principles [. . .] of the worldview enacted by the Führer should be embodied in both the police as well as in the SS," and serve as a "merciless sword" against opponents.[37]

[36] Hans Buchheim considers the division into Order Police and Security Police as a crucial step in Himmler's overall plan of integrating all of the police into the SS. It established the political police as an independent office of the German police and aligned it organizationally with the criminal police. See Buchheim, "The SS-Instrument of Domination," pp. 165–166.

[37] Cited according to Werle, *Justiz-Strafrecht und polizeiliche Verbrechensbekämpfung im Dritten Reich*, p. 486. Werle refers here to Heydrich, Reinhard, *Wandlungen unseres Kampfes* (München, Berlin: Eher 1935), p. 18.

Such harsh pronouncements were soon put into practice. On December 14, 1937, a police decree on preventing crime permitted the unrestricted surveillance of suspects. Although Interior Minister Frick signed the Himmler-initiated decree, its "legality" rested upon an institutional Führer authorization.[38] Moreover, the surveillance measure, which was directed at so-called professional and habitual criminals, was not subject to judicial review. Defendants could only plead for mercy (that is, suspension of surveillance) with the Reich Criminal Police Office. In the last instance, repealing the measure depended also upon Himmler's consent.

The December 14, 1937 decree served as the legal basis for various "special police actions" against criminals and so-called asocials (defined as persons unwilling to work, vagabonds, gypsies, and those unworthy of military service).[39] As Chief of the German Police, Himmler decided which police department would handle these actions, ordering the Gestapo (rather than the Criminal Police) to carry them out by taking suspects into protective custody (which meant detention in a concentration camp).[40]

The Reichsführer's police directives were legal as long as Himmler could claim to be acting on the basis of a Führer order. Since Hitler's will counted as a source of legality, its articulations could come in various forms – a statute, decree, an administrative regulation, and a written or even oral order. It was precisely this scope and variability of Führer authorizations that made Himmler's authority so powerful and terrifying for suspects.

Protective custody was a particularly crushing instrument of Gestapo terror. On January 25, 1938, a Decree on Protective Custody concealed the whole procedure leading to confinement in a concentration camp.

[38] The NS jurist Theodor Maunz explained the concept of "institutional authorization" (*institutionelle Ermächtigung*) in the following way: "The general order of the Führer to the police to function as state protection corps, is called the 'institutional authorization' of the police. It is of fundamental significance constitutionally and with respect to police law." Maunz, Theodor, *Gestalt und Recht der Polizei* (Hamburg: Hanseatische Verlagsanstalt, 1943), p. 27.

[39] The action against asocial people was carried out on April 21, 1938; another action against asocial people (including previously committed Jews) occurred from June 13 to June 18, 1938. See Werle, *Justiz-Strafrecht und polizeiliche Verbrechensbekämpfung im Dritten Reich*, pp. 522–523.

[40] According to Werle, those actions possibly served to supply the labor force for concentration camps rather than combatting crime. See Werle, *Justiz-Strafrecht und polizeiliche Verbrechensbekämpfung im Dritten Reich*, pp. 524–525.

Defendants could neither be represented by lawyers nor access their indictment files. Replacing all former protective custody regulations, the decree relied on the "general assignment given to the German Police in general and to the Secret State Police in particular in the course of reconstructing the National Socialist state."[41] Increasingly, protective custody was directed not only against enemies of the state, but also against persons who did not meet National Socialist norms of social behavior.

Although § 1. II of the 1938 Decree on Protective Custody held that criminal acts should be sentenced by the courts and that "protective custody may not be imposed for the purpose of punishment or as a substitute for imprisonment," many defendants faced a different reality. Even when their trials ended in acquittal, they were regularly taken into custody by the Gestapo and immediately sent to a concentration camp.

The justice system was largely helpless against such "sentence corrections." Although jurists protested repeatedly against the Gestapo's arrest of acquitted defendants, the Justice Ministry could not intervene in arrests justified as crime prevention measures since it had no authority over protective custody cases. Curt Rothenberger, President of the Hamburg Higher Regional Court, summarized the Justice Ministry's position in an address to Hamburg jurists on February 1, 1939: "The Ministry holds, and we approve, that protective custody measures cannot be challenged as long as they have a preventive character. However, correction measures must not become habitual."[42] In the end, the judiciary lost its fight with the Gestapo and Justice Minister Gürtner could merely advise the courts to have the Gestapo at least wait outside the courtroom before arresting acquitted defendants – a shallow formality that did not compensate for the justice system's humiliation.[43]

The judiciary also had no competence over execution verdicts made outside of judicial procedures. Again, the state's totalitarian structure was decisive. As the highest court instance in the Third Reich, Hitler could order executions even when the courts had issued prison sentences. The execution

[41] Cited according to Werle, *Justiz-Strafrecht und polizeiliche Verbrechensbekämpfung im Dritten Reich*, p. 544.

[42] Ibid., p. 573. For Rothenberger's critique of the Gestapo practice see Gruchmann, *Justiz im Dritten Reich 1933–1940. Anpassung und Unterwerfung in der Ära Gürtner*, pp. 563–564; see also 599–603. Rothenberger was State Secretary in the Justice Ministry from August 1942 until December 1943.

[43] Werle, *Justiz-Strafrecht und polizeiliche Verbrechensbekämpfung im Dritten Reich*, p. 574 (referring to an advice by Gürtner to court presidents from January 24, 1939).

orders came either directly from the Führer or from Himmler via a Führer delegation of power. The outbreak of war increased the number of execution orders, which also served to reprimand the judiciary for acting too mildly in the eyes of the NS leadership.[44] Hitler's authority over the judiciary was further strengthened by a law passed on September 16, 1939, granting him the right to appeal court sentences and order a new trial.[45]

During the war, as the fight against state enemies and political opponents intensified, the justice system lost yet more power to the police. Himmler's strategy was to send all persons displaying a hostile attitude toward Nazi Germany to concentration camps. The invasion of the Soviet Union aggravated these police measures. In an August 1941 circular, Heydrich reported that the Reichsführer SS had ordered communists and German-hostile Poles and Czechs to be interned in concentration camps for an extended period of time.[46] A special agreement between Justice Minister Thierack (Gürtner's successor) and Himmler in September 1942 affirmed that criminal procedures against Poles, Jews, Russians, Ukrainians, and Gypsies would be handled by the Reichsführer SS rather than the courts. Asocial elements were to be transferred from ordinary prisons to concentration camps geared toward "destruction by work" (*Vernichtung durch Arbeit*).[47]

At the outset of World War II, the police received an ominous brief – to realize the Nazi vision of a greater Germany in the East through involvement in what we now call the Holocaust. On September 27, 1939, Himmler established the Reich Security Main Office (RSHA), which centralized SS power by uniting the Secret State Police, the Criminal Police (KriPo), and the Security Service (SD). With Heydrich at its head, the RSHA became the main institution for organizing administration in the invaded territories, securing German dominion, and implementing the NS regime's genocidal racial program.[48]

[44] Until August 1942, Hitler ordered in at least twenty-five to thirty cases that defendants were handed to the Gestapo for being executed. See Werle, *Justiz-Strafrecht und polizeiliche Verbrechensbekämpfung im Dritten Reich*, p. 577.

[45] Ibid., p. 580.

[46] Ibid., pp. 553–554.

[47] See Longerich, Peter, *Heinrich Himmler*, transl. by Noakes, Jeremy and Sharpe, Lesley (Oxford: Oxford University Press, 2012), p. 637. Longerich writes that based on this agreement 17,307 convicted persons were transferred from prisons to concentration camps from the fall 1942 until the middle of 1943; by April 1, 1943, already 5935 transferred judicial prisoners had died. Ibid.

[48] Heydrich died on June 4, 1942 (due to an attack by Czech resistance fighters on May 27, 1942). On January 30, 1943 Ernst Kaltenbrunner became Head of the RSHA.

The murderous methods for creating an enlarged, racially pure German Reich were geared up prior to the attack on Poland with the formation of five special SS mobile units (SS *Einsatzgruppen*) each consisting of 500 men selected by the Security Police Main Office. By a decree on July 31, 1939, the SS mobile units were directed to combat "all elements hostile to the Reich and to Germany."[49]

Initially, military leaders and the Chief of the Security Police agreed that the special SS units, which were to follow the Wehrmacht into Poland, should not mistreat the population in the invaded territories. Yet once hostilities began it became clear that Himmler and Heydrich had no intention of honoring this agreement. The SS and police units killed both Jews and Polish prisoners of war.[50] When Wehrmacht officers inquired into or outright protested these mass killings, SS leaders referred them to a "special order" from Hitler to Himmler to stabilize the occupation by "the harshest means" necessary, including summary executions.[51]

With the attack on the Soviet Union in June 1941, SS and police atrocities increased in both number and horror. Four large SS *Einsatzgruppen*, tasked to annihilate the "bolshevist-Jewish intelligentsia," murdered over 200,000 Jewish men, women, and children in the occupied zones. Several leaders of these mobile SS units served in the RSHA: Arthur Nebe, Chief of the Criminal Police Department, commanded Einsatzgruppe B, which murdered approximately 45,000 Jews in the Baltic States; Otto Ohlendorf, a high-ranking academic, directed Einsatzgruppe D, which killed 90,000 Jews in the southern region of the Soviet Union, as Ohlendorf himself confessed after the war.[52]

The RSHA planned these operations well before the invasion of the Soviet Union. In talks with army representatives, the RSHA determined that the mobile units should operate independently from the Wehrmacht, though with the latter's full knowledge.[53] In special cases, military

[49] Wildt, Michael, *An Uncompromising Generation. The Nazi Leadership of the Reich Security Main Office*, transl. by Lampert, Tom (Madison, Wisconsin: The University of Wisconsin Press, 2009), p. 220.

[50] Ibid., pp. 221–225.

[51] Ibid., pp. 229–230. Himmler relied, as Wildt notes, on a special assignment by Hitler for directly ordering shootings by SS and police units, bypassing the military altogether. However, the Wehrmacht generals considered the danger of insurrections to be so great that they did not sufficiently protest against the SS and police actions (in some cases the Wehrmacht collaborated with the SS).

[52] See Sowade, Hanno, "Otto Ohlendorf," in Smelser, Roland and Zitelmann, Rainer (eds.), *The Nazi Elite* (New York: NYU Press, 1993), pp. 155–164.

[53] Wildt, *An Uncompromising Generation*, pp. 268–271.

commanders-in-chief had the right to prohibit an *Einsatzgruppen* action – a concession that could de facto be overruled since the units were commanded by the Chief of the Security Police and the Security Service (SD) Heydrich, who was always backed by Himmler (who in turn could appeal to a special Führer order).

Order Police Chief Kurt Daluege had taken part in the preparatory meetings for the SS and police actions in the Soviet Union.[54] As a result, several Order Police battalions were assigned to support the *Einsatzgruppen* in the mass shootings in the summer and fall of 1941. Other units participated in hunting down and murdering the remaining Jewish population in Poland. The best known Order Police unit is Reserve Police Battalion 101, which operated in Poland from July 1942. Its actions have been meticulously reconstructed by historian Christopher Browning in his now famous study of how ordinary men could become mass murderers.[55]

6.5 Concluding Remarks

The National Socialist state had no codified police law – after all, specifying the scope of police authority in a fixed legal framework would have restricted the dictatorship's political ambitions. The Gestapo Law, the only law drafted by a National Socialist jurist, merely sought to strengthen the political police by freeing it from the ministerial bureaucracy.

Nazi legal publications gave theoretical sustenance to the transgression of traditional normative boundaries. NS jurists intensely discussed police law, but their efforts served mainly to rethink the police's mission in light of the NS worldview.[56]

[54] Ibid., p. 269. On the involvement of the Order Police see also Browning, Christopher R. (with contributions by Matthäus, Jürgen), *The Origins of the Final Solution. The Evolution of Nazi Jewish Policy, September 1939–March 1942* (Lincoln: University of Nebraska Press, and Yad Vashem, 2004), pp. 230–234.

[55] Browning, Christopher R., *Ordinary Men. Reserve Police Battalion 101 and the Final Solution in Poland* (London: Penguin Books, 2001) p. 17 (first published Harper Collins, 1992). The Penguin edition of *Ordinary Men* contains an afterword (pp. 101–223) in which Browning discusses Daniel J. Goldhagen's controversial book *Hitler's Willing Executioners. Ordinary Germans and the Holocaust* and replies to Goldhagen's critique of his study.

[56] In his address at the founding session of the Academy of German Law's Committee of Police Law in October 1936, Best declared: "As necessary manifestations and activities of the National Socialist state, the tasks of the police ultimately must be newly derived from the concept of state and *Volk* and thus from the National Socialist worldview." Cited according to Schubert, Werner, "Introduction," in *Akademie für Deutsches Recht*

The incompatibility between a codified police law and the totalitarian Führer state is strikingly illustrated by the fruitless attempts of the German Law Academy's Committee for Police Law to create a National Socialist legal police code. On June 21, 1934, the first committee for NS police law was established within the Academy.[57] After Himmler's advancement to Chief of the German Police in June 1936, the committee was reorganized under the leadership of Werner Best and his deputy Reinhard Höhn. At its founding meeting on October 11, 1936, Himmler and Hans Frank (President of the Academy for German Law) gave programmatic speeches that disappointed the expectations of committee members.[58] In the end, the committee met irregularly and was dissolved in May 1938 with little to show for itself. Yet examining this failed enterprise reveals why efforts to invent a systematic NS police law were doomed in the first place.[59]

1933–1945. Protokolle der Ausschüsse, ed. by Schubert, Werner, vol. VIII, Ausschüsse für Strafrecht, Strafvollstreckungsrecht, Wehrstrafrecht, Strafgerichtsbarkeit der SS und des Reichsarbeitsdienstes, Polizeirecht sowie für Wohlfahrts- und Fürsorgerecht (Bewahrungsrecht) (Frankfurt am Main: Peter Lang, 1999), pp. XI–LVIII, here: p. XXXV; see also Best, Werner, "Die Politische Polizei des Dritten Reiches," in Frank, Hans (ed.), *Deutsches Verwaltungsrecht*, pp. 417–430.

57 The head of this first committee was Ludwig Grauert, State Secretary in the Prussian Ministry of Interior. See Schubert, "Introduction," in *Akademie für Deutsches Recht 1933–1945. Protokolle der Ausschüsse*, vol. VIII, p. XXXIV. Grauert was a founding member of the Academy for German Law, he was also a member of the SS. Nevertheless he held that central principles of the PVG were still decisive for police law in the Third Reich. See Schwegel, *Der Polizeibegriff im NS-Staat*, pp. 120–126. On July 1, 1936, Grauert was forced to retire.

58 The speeches by Frank, Himmler, along with the speeches of Best and Höhn (chairman and vice-chairman of the Committee on Police Law) are published in Frank, Hans; Himmler, Heinrich; Best, Werner; Höhn, Reinhard, *Grundfragen der deutschen Polizei. Bericht über die konstituierende Sitzung des Ausschusses für Polizeirecht der Akademie für Deutsches Recht am 11. Oktober 1936* (Hamburg: Hanseatische Verlagsanstalt, 1937). The committee's members were (among others): Werner Best, Reinhard Höhn, Wilhelm Stuckart, Arthur Nebe (Chief of the Reich Criminal Police Office), Heinrich Müller (from 1939 on Chief of the Gestapo), and the law professors Georg Dahm and Paul Ritterbusch.

59 Usually the committees of the Academy for German Law kept extended protocols of their meetings. According to Werner Schubert, no protocols of the Committee on Police Law could be found in the archives. However, reports and notifications of the Chairman Best to the committee members and also some lectures and talks by committee members as well as their written comments have been preserved. See Schubert, "Introduction," in *Akademie für Deutsches Recht 1933–1945. Protokolle der Ausschüsse*, vol. VIII, p. XXXIV–XXXVIII. The preserved materials of the Committee on Police Law are published in vol. VIII, pp. 489–533.

On Best's request to reconceptualize the police, committee members offered such suggestions as: "'Police' is the power that must carry out the task set by the state leadership, namely to serve the preservation and development of the *Volk* through protection of the inner leader order and communal order, also by exerting force" (Arthur Nebe); "The police must provide inner protection of the people's community. The specific kind, form, and means of police actions are determined by given necessities" (Heinrich Müller); and "The police serves the inner protection of the people's community . . . and is called upon to execute lawful orders of other instances, insofar as their execution requires force" (Reinhard Höhn).[60]

In his report on the committee's second session on June 2, 1937, Best condensed the committee's proposals into the formula: "The police is the protective corps of the Reich, destined to secure the German *Volks*' order against inner disruption and destruction through the prompt execution of all necessary measures."[61]

How far this definition transcended classical notions of legal normativity is clear from the enthusiastic comment by committee member Danckwerts (an Interior Ministry official), who clearly had internalized NS ideology: "First, I may notice that the use of the concept '*Volk's* order' seems to me most felicitous. It certainly enables the necessary, norm free application of state authority. It means to depart from a 'formal lawfulness' (*Formalgesetzmäßigkeit)* that is no longer bearable."[62]

Best agreed that the political nature of the police in National Socialism conflicted with a system of positive legal norms. In a 1938 publication, he conveyed just how uneasy NS jurists (even those actively engaged in the project) felt about the impending "German Police Order."[63] Yet their worries were premature: The codification never occurred. Instead, the Führer's absolute power regulated police matters, as Best conceded:

[60] For all these quotes see "Vorschläge von Ausschußmitgliedern zum Polizeibegriff," in *Akademie für Deutsches Recht 1933–1945. Protokolle der Ausschüsse,* vol. VIII, pp. 510–511.

[61] See "Bericht von Werner *Best* über die 2. Arbeitssitzung am 2.6.1937," in *Akademie für Deutsches Recht 1933–1945. Protokolle der Ausschüsse,* vol. VIII, pp. 512–513, here: p. 512 (italics in the original).

[62] "Stellungnahme von Ministerialrat Dr. Danckwerts vom 18.9.1937," in *Akademie für Deutsches Recht 1933–1945. Protokolle der Ausschüsse,* vol. VIII, p. 513.

[63] Best, Werner, "Werdendes Polizeirecht," in *Deutsches Recht* 8 (1938), pp. 224–226, here: p. 226.

> The unwritten "police" law, which is not codified in legal statutes [and] today determines all "police" actions, not only consists of pure "legal ideas" rooted in the *Volk*, but [also] of many regulations and rules which in various forms – statutes, administrative decrees and singular commands, organizational regulations and regulations of competences – are set by the supreme leadership of the Reich or with the leadership's approval.[64]

The texts of NS jurists clearly indicated that the police was in the hands of the true power centers in the National Socialist state, the Führer and Reichsführer. "The police," Best wrote, "never acts 'lawlessly' or 'against the law', as far as the police acts in conformity with the rules set by its superiors, up to the highest leadership."[65] In his book *Form and Law of the Police*, Theodor Maunz further claimed that the police had to adjust to the orders of the Reichsführer and, ultimately, the Führer himself, even if they exceeded positive law. "The Führer," he wrote, "is not restricted to the path of legal statutes, but may announce his will in other ways, including in very general outlines. Even then the police has the task of fulfilling this will."[66]

Nonetheless, the ministerial bureaucracy was not eliminated. While the quasi-personalized form in which the Führer's will was translated by loyal National Socialists preceded the state administration, the latter provided a crucial continuity of traditional legal security that helped stabilize the Nazi state. In his 1936 article "The Secret State Police," Best himself supported a connection between the Gestapo and state administration.[67]

The dual character of Himmler's office – that is, the interlocking of an SS-governed political police apparatus and the state administration – call to mind Ernst Fraenkel's analysis of the NS state in terms of the prerogative and the normative state. In the preface to *The Dual State*, Fraenkel wrote that Martin Gauger, a legal counsel of the Lutheran Church with whom Fraenkel had discussed his work, "seized the opportunity to casually explain to Best the theory of the dual state" during a meeting concerning the return of funds confiscated by the Gestapo to

64 Ibid., p. 20.

65 Ibid.

66 Maunz, Theodor, *Gestalt und Recht der Polizei*, p. 27.

67 The link between the Gestapo and the state administration was, Best thought, established by a certain distribution of decisional authority: while the Gestapa, as the highest political police office, had the right to issue directives to the local district presidents, those instances of the civil administration had the right to issue directives to the local Gestapo departments in their districts. Best, "Die Geheime Staatspolizei," p. 127.

the Confessing Church (a branch of the Lutheran Church). According to Fraenkel, he and Gauger "came to view it as a macabre confirmation of our theoretical efforts when Best, in a [1937] contribution to the *Jahrbuch der Akademie für Deutsches Recht* (Yearbook of the Academy for German Law) developed an argument that largely rehearsed ideas that Gauger had shared with him."[68]

Fraenkel's remarks should be viewed in a larger context. Best, after all, was as familiar with Fraenkel's categories as Fraenkel was with Best's own theoretical writings from 1934 to 1937.[69] Yet independently of political opponents, the Gestapo's legal expert had sufficient insight into the NS state to realize that the police must transcend traditional forms of legality in order to serve the regime's political goals, while maintaining the bare minimal ties to the *Beamtenstaat* that lent it the appearance of legitimacy.

[68] Fraenkel, Ernst, "Preface to the 1974 German Edition," in Fraenkel, Ernst *The Dual State. A Contribution to the Theory of Dictatorship*, with an introduction by Meierhenrich, Jens; transl. by Shils, E. A. (Oxford: Oxford University Press, 2017), p. XX. The article Fraenkel refers to is Best, "Neubegründung des Polizeirechts," in *Jahrbuch der Akademie für Deutsches Recht* 4 (1937), pp. 132–138. Best argues that the future regulation of police law in the NS state must be based on the assumption "that the police must, in a norm-free application of state authority, take all measures necessary for the fulfilment of its task." Ibid., p. 136. Best added that the Reichstag Fire Decree from February 28, 1933 already enabled the political police to act outside legal restrictions (that is, outside norms), but this extended power should also apply to the entire police forces.

[69] See also Herbert, *Best*, pp. 177–180.

7

The SS Jurisdiction

7.1 Introductory Remarks

In his August 6, 1946 witness testimony at the Trial of the Major War Criminals before the International Military Tribunal (IMT) in Nuremberg,[1] former Chief Judge of the SS Judiciary Günther Reinecke (witness for the SS defense), stated the following:

> The SS, from the beginning of its formation, fought against crime on principle and at all costs, and it had a perfectly orderly administration of justice. . . .
>
> Training in the SS was systematically directed toward decency, justice, and morality. Institutions existed which guaranteed that this training was carried out in full. Not only was the law, including international law, taught in the Junker schools of the SS, but legal proceedings were held openly before entire units. The head office "SS Courts," as this legal system's central unit, issued its own literature to insure that these principles of decency and justice became firmly established among all SS members. The legal training as it was handled in the SS was the exact opposite of the Prosecution's assertion. . . .
>
> The SS was bound by so-called fundamental laws to observe a particular moral conduct. Offenders in the SS who infringed on a law incurred heavier guilt and therefore deserved severer punishment. And that explains the more severe punishment of SS members in comparison with members of the Armed Forces or German civilians.[2]

[1] The IMT trial took place from November 14, 1945 until October 1, 1946.

[2] Reinecke, Günther, "Witness Testimony, International Military Tribunal Trial against Major War Criminals at Nuremberg," August 6, 1946, One Hundred Ninety-Sixth Day, online: https://avalon.law.yale.edu/imt/08-06-46.asp (cited according to the English version); in German: http://www.zeno.org/Geschichte/M/Der+Nürnberger+Prozeß/Hauptverhandlungen/Einhundertsechsundneunzigster+Tag.+Dienstag,+6.+August+1946/Nachmittagssitzung, pp. 466–467, 468. Note that the English transcript lists the

As an attempt to exonerate the SS, Reinecke's hubristic claims fell flat. The International Military Tribunal indicted the entire SS as a criminal organization. But Reinecke's testimony at Nuremberg offers insight into the normative self-understanding of the organization most responsible for carrying out the NS regime's unspeakable crimes.

The SS (*Schutzstaffel*) was founded in 1925 as a bodyguard for Hitler. In 1929, Heinrich Himmler took command of the SS and set about shaping it into a paramilitary safeguard of the National Socialist movement. From 1931, Reinhard Heydrich built up a counterintelligence service within the SS, the Security Service (SD).

According to historian Hans Buchheim, by 1933 the SS "had turned from a Party cadre into something more resembling a refined version" of the much larger SA (*Sturmabteilung*) led by Ernst Röhm.[3] The men who applied for membership in the SS mostly just wanted to join a National Socialist organization without having to devote much time to political service. With a monthly financial contribution, one could be a sponsoring member of the SS.

The turning point for the SS came in the Röhm-Putsch in late June 1934, when SS men killed SA leader Ernst Röhm and more than 100 of his men on the pretext that the SA had become a potential danger to Hitler's authority.[4] Subsequently, the SS gained eminent political power, evolving into a state within the Nazi state.[5]

Until 1939, the General SS, a quasi-Party organization, was the main unit of the SS. Yet considerable efforts were made by the SS leadership (in the period 1935 to 1938) to build up a military arm – the SS Dispositional Troop (*SS-Verfügungstruppe*).[6] With the outbreak of war in 1939, the SS

cited passage from Reinecke's testimony as part of the morning session of August, 6, 1946, the German transcript, however, as part of the afternoon session of August 6, 1946. With respect to content, there is no difference between the English and the German version of the cited passage.

[3] Buchheim, Hans, "The SS-Instrument of Domination," transl. by Barry, Richard, in Krausnick, Helmut; Buchheim, Hans; Broszat, Martin; Jacobsen, Hans-Adolf, *Anatomy of the SS State* (New York: Walker and Company, 1968), pp. 127–301, p. 142.

[4] Although many SA members were dissatisfied with the results of the "National Socialist revolution" (they had expected a more radical change of social structures in favor of disadvantaged social groups), there is no historical evidence that Röhm had planned a coup d'état.

[5] See Reitlinger, Gerhard, *The SS. Alibi of a Nation 1922–1945* (Melbourne, London, Toronto: Heinemann, 1956), pp. 253–288.

[6] See Wegner, Bernd, *Hitlers politische Soldaten. Die Waffen-SS 1933–1945. Leitbild, Struktur und Funktion einer nationalsozialistischen Elite*, 7th ed. (Paderborn, München, Wien, Zürich: Ferdinand Schöningh, 2006), pp. 103–123.

Dispositional Troop was incorporated into the so-called Waffen SS (since November 1939 this was the official term for the armed SS troops that served in combat or where reserve units).[7] Similarly, most members of the General SS were conscripted into the Waffen SS.

The SS was a complex organization.[8] During the war, the most powerful SS offices (aside from Himmler and his personal staff) were the Reich Security Main Office (RSHA) under Reinhard Heydrich and the SS Main Economic and Administrative Office (WVHA) under Oswald Pohl. While the RSHA, founded on September 27, 1939, handled state security matters, the WVHA was responsible for the SS's economic enterprises, including the economic administration of the concentration camps.

Recent studies provide a more nuanced depiction of the SS than the immediate postwar literature, which largely portrayed SS men as primitive and brutalized social outcasts who had failed professionally.[9] This description might well be accurate for most SS camp guards and some notorious Waffen SS units, though not for the high-ranking SS officers responsible for planning and executing Nazi racial policies. The RSHA staff, for example, was composed of numerous academics, above all jurists.[10]

Ideology ran high in the SS. Himmler intended to make it into a tight-knit and highly elite "fraternity" committed to the NS worldview.[11] His

[7] Ibid., pp. 263–317. Informative also is Weingartner, James J., *Hitler's Guard. The Story of the Leibstandarte SS Adolf Hitler 1933–1945* (Carbondale and Edwardsville: Southern Illinois University Press, 1974).

[8] The main SS offices were: the Personal Staff Reichsführer SS under Karl Wolff; the SS Main Office (*SS Hauptamt*) under Gottlob Berger; the SS Leadership Main Office (*SS Führungshauptamt*) under Hans Jüttner; the SS Race and Settlement Main Office (*SS Rasse- und Siedlungshauptamt*) under Richard Hildebrandt, the Main Office SS and Police Jurisdiction (*Hautpamt SS- und Polizeigerichtsbarkeit*) under Paul Scharfe, from 1942 Franz Breithaupt; the SS Main Office for Personnel (*SS-Personal Hauptamt*) under Maximilian von Herff; the Main Office Order Police (*Hauptamt Ordnungspolizei*) under Kurt Daluege; the SS Main Economic and Administrative Office (*Wirtschafts- und Verwaltungshauptamt*) under Oswald Pohl. Himmler was also assigned as Reich Commissioner for the Strengthening of Germanism (*Reichskommissar für die Festigung des deutschen Volkstums*). As historians have argued, the SS was not an all-powerful monolithic institution, but a partially disparate organization seeking the cooperation with other institutions of the Nazi state. The power of the Gestapo, for example, was for a good part due to an extensive readiness of the population to denounce others.

[9] See Kogon, Eugen, *The Theory and Practice of Hell. The German Concentration Camps and the System behind them* (New York: Farrar, Straus and Giroux, 1950), esp. ch. 22.

[10] See Wildt, Michael, *An Uncompromising Generation. The Nazi Leadership of the Reich Security Main Office*, transl. by Lampert, Tom (Madison Wisconsin: The University of Wisconsin Press, 2009).

[11] See Longerich, Peter, *Heinrich Himmler*, transl. by Noakes, Jeremy and Sharpe, Lesley (Oxford: Oxford University Press, 2012), pp. 255–298; see also Hambrock, Michael,

historical romanticism went so far as to stylize the SS as a "knightly order" in the tradition of the Teutonic Order (*Deutscher Ritterorden*), thereby aligning the SS with the latter's colonization of the East.[12]

SS men were expected to uphold the SS ethos of "decency, honor, and manliness," to demonstrate loyalty to the Führer, and to obey higher orders unconditionally. Severely infringing upon these norms could result in exclusion from the SS. Rather than securing compliance by external sanctions, the SS relied on the SS man's "ethical fulfillment" of duties – that is, the internally motivated obedience to standards. An article on the best education of young SS men, published in the regular memoranda of the SS Jurisdiction's Main Office, held that education in the SS should be "tackled from the ethical side": "The SS man must not be educated such that he follows orders merely for fear of punishment, but rather so that he gradually reaches the point of fulfilling his duties out of a voluntary commitment resting on a deep conviction."[13]

These normative principles also applied to the Waffen SS, whose active members ranked as "political soldiers" charged with fighting for the expansion of National Socialism in a greater German Reich. Waffen SS combatants were thus subject to military commands and ideological directives. Apart from their "formal command/compliance relationship," these two types of orders had nothing in common, as Hans Buchheim emphasized.[14] Although after the war many Waffen SS fighters claimed they acted as mere soldiers, the Waffen SS divisions were notorious for committing atrocities.[15]

"Dialektik der 'verfolgenden Unschuld.' Überlegungen zur Mentalität und Funktion der SS," in Schulte, Jan Erik (ed.), *Die SS, Himmler und die Wewelsburg* (Paderborn, München, Wien, Zürich: Ferdinand Schöningh, 2009), pp. 79–101.

12 The Teutonic Order (*Deutscher Ritterorden*) played a crucial role in the colonization of Eastern Prussia, parts of Poland, Latvia, and Lithuania. For Himmler's cultivation of historical ideals see Reinicke, Wolfgang, *Instrumentalisierung von Geschichte durch Heinrich Himmler und die SS* (Neuried: ars et unitas, 2003), ch. 4. See also Schulte, "Zur Geschichte der SS. Erzähltraditionen und Forschungsstand," in Schulte (ed.), *Die SS, Himmler und die Wewelsburg*, pp. XI-XXXV; see also Smelser, Ronald and Syring, Enrico, "Annäherungen an die 'Elite unter dem Totenkopf'," in Smelser, Ronald and Syring, Enrico (eds.), *Die SS: Elite unter dem Totenkopf. 30 Lebensläufe*, 2nd ed. (Darmstadt: Wissenschaftliche Buchgesellschaft, 2003), pp. 9–27.

13 See "Zur Erziehung und Belehrung von SS-Rekruten," in *Mitteilungen des Hauptamts SS-Gericht*, vol. II, 3, (1942), p. 85 (U.S. National Archives, Record Group 242, microfilm T175A, roll 3).

14 Buchheim, Hans, "Command and Compliance," transl. by Barry, Richard, in Krausnick; Buchheim; Broszat; Jacobsen, *Anatomy of the SS State*, pp. 305–396, here: p. 312.

15 Historical studies have meanwhile shown that Wehrmacht troops were also involved in war crimes, thus correcting the myth of the "respectable Wehrmacht." See

Formally, Waffen SS units were under Wehrmacht command. Establishing a special SS jurisdiction for Waffen SS soldiers and SS police units exempted them from being tried by the Wehrmacht's military courts for war crimes and other atrocities.[16]

7.2 The SS Court System. Between Legal Standards and SS Ethos

On October 17, 1939, just weeks after the start of World War II, the SS and Police Judiciary (*SS- und Polizeigerichtsbarkeit*) assumed jurisdiction for criminal offenses committed by Waffen SS men, SS task forces (*Einsatzgruppen*), and police units serving in the war.[17] The pretext was

Messerschmidt, Manfred, *Die Wehrmacht im NS-Staat. Zeit der Indoktrination* (Hamburg: R v. Decker, G. Schenck, 1969); Sheperd, Ben, "The Clean Wehrmacht, the War of Extermination, and Beyond," in *The Historical Journal* 52, 2 (2009), pp. 455–473; Wette, Wolfram, *The Wehrmacht. History, Myth, Reality*, transl. by Schneider, Deborah Lucas (Cambridge, MA and London: Harvard, University Press, 2006), pp. 90–131. Equally, historians have relativized the picture of the Waffen SS as a tight fraternity, held together by special bonds and virtues of decency and honor. Rivalries, conflicts of interests and intrigues were also common in the Waffen SS. If there was anything like a spirit of solidarity and fraternity, it was, as more recent historical accounts suggest, due to the common experience of harsh combat at the front and less to special SS virtues. See Kühne, Thomas, "Zwischen Männerbund und Volksgemeinschaft. Hitlers Soldaten und der Mythos der Kameradschaft," in *Archiv für Sozialgeschichte* 38 (1998), pp. 165–189.

16 Early in the invasion of Poland, members of the Wehrmacht lodged complaints about the atrocities committed by SS units. These complaints were based partly on moral grounds, but also on grounds that these activities would adversely affect the discipline of the troops. See "Notes of Eastern Territories Commander Johannes Blaskowitz," in Klee, Ernst; Dressen, Willi; Riess, Volker (eds.), *The Good Old Days. The Holocaust as Seen by Its Perpetrators and Bystanders*, transl. by Burnstone, Deborah (New York: The Free Press, 1988), pp. 4–5. The question whether the SS judiciary was established to prevent military prosecutions of the Waffen SS was raised at the IMT trial in Nuremberg, in connection with the prosecution's indictment of the SS as a criminal organization. See Reinecke, Günther, "Witness Testimony, International Military Tribunal Trial against Major War Criminals at Nuremberg," August 6 1946, One Hundred Ninety-Sixth Day, https://avalon.law.yale.edu/imt/08-06-46.asp, in German: www.zeno.org/Geschichte/M/Der+Nürnberger+Prozeß/Hauptverhandlungen/Einhundertsechsundneunzigster+Tag.+Dienstag,+6.+August+1946/Nachmittagssitzung, p. 429.

17 The creation of the SS judiciary on October 17, 1939 was announced in the *Reichsgesetzblatt*, October 30, 1939 (RGBl 1939, I, Nr 214, p. 2107). See Vieregge, Bianca, *Die Gerichtsbarkeit einer "Elite". Nationalsozialistische Rechtsprechung am Beispiel der SS- und Polizei-Gerichtsbarkeit* (Baden-Baden: Nomos, 2002), Appendix, p. 247. Plans for introducing a special SS judicial system existed already since the establishment of the first armed task forces in the SS in 1934. On May 31, 1938, a working group on the introduction of a special SS jurisdiction was established within the Academy for German Law. Reinecke gave a talk about its possible structure, See "Arbeitsgemeinschaft für Fragen der Strafgerichtsbarkeit der SS und des Reichsarbeitsdienstes," (protocols of the meetings on May 31, 1938, November 11

that the standard military courts could not grasp the political mentality and worldview of SS men enough to try them.

Yet Himmler's creation of a special judicial system within the SS was not merely to shield Waffen SS soldiers and SS task force members from the Wehrmacht's military courts. Law in the hands of an SS court system was also designed to strengthen the SS's position in the Third Reich's power structure. Himmler planned for the SS to be the backbone of the coming greater Germany – an end he pursued both with brute force and ideologically perverted forms of morality and legality.

Several SS courts were soon established at the headquarters of the Higher SS and Police leaders in major German cities and the annexed territories.[18] Local court authorities could order criminal investigations and, depending on the outcome, an SS court trial. An SS judge (someone with a formal legal education) presided over these trials, which typically included two assisting judges, a prosecuting counsel, and possibly a defense. The verdict was reached by majority vote.

The highest SS court was the SS Judiciary Main Office (*Hauptamt SS-Gericht*) in Munich. Hitler was the supreme judicial authority and nominated the SS court judges. Yet otherwise the Führer delegated his power to Himmler, who oversaw the judges as Waffen SS men.[19]

The SS judiciary acknowledged the judge's independence – a formality that, historians argue, was de facto undermined by Himmler.[20] While Himmler could not directly intervene in court proceedings, he had the authority to quash sentences and reorder a trial. In

and 12, 1938), in *Akademie für Deutsches Recht 1933–1945. Protokolle der Ausschüsse 1933–1945*, vol. VIII, Ausschüsse für Strafrecht, Strafvollstreckungsrecht, Wehrstrafrecht, Strafgerichtsbarkeit der SS und des Reichsarbeitsdienstes, Polizeirecht sowie für Wohlfahrts- und Fürsorgerecht (Bewahrungsrecht) (Frankfurt am Main: Peter Lang, 1999), pp. 471–488.

18 In 1944 there existed twenty-nine SS and police courts. See Buchheim, "The SS-Instrument of Domination" in Krausnick, Buchheim, Broszat, Jacobsen, *Anatomy of the SS State*, p. 252.

19 Formally, Hitler himself was the highest court authority, but he had referred the authority to Himmler. See Buchheim, "The SS-Instrument of Domination," p. 253; Vieregge, *Die Gerichtsbarkeit einer "Elite,"* pp. 37–40.

20 See Theel, Christopher, "'Parzifal unter den Gangstern'? Die SS- und Polizeigerichtsbarkeit in Polen 1939–1945," in Schulte, Jan-Erik; Lieb, Peter; Wegner, Bernd (eds.), *Die Waffen SS. Neuere Forschungen* (Paderborn: Schöningh, 2014), pp. 61–79, here: pp. 63–65. Nevertheless, SS judges insisted on the independence of the judge. For example, when Himmler wanted to send Konrad Morgen to a concentration camp in May 1942, the SS Main Office intervened, arguing that Himmler could re-order a trial, but not punish the judge. Eventually, Morgen was sent to the Eastern front.

politically sensitive cases, Himmler used his authority to uphold or dismiss a verdict.[21]

There existed no specific SS penal code. The courts relied on official military law and the Criminal Code of 1871 (still valid in the Third Reich).[22] Materially, however, the SS judiciary was heavily influenced by prevailing SS values.

Officially, SS judges were required to have a university law degree and to be formally qualified as judges. They also had to be SS members. Most of the SS judges had previously worked as attorneys or public prosecutors, which familiarized them with pre–Nazi rule-of-law traditions. But in the SS, their judicial role entailed a commitment to the regime's ideological values. In the words of historian James Weingartner, the SS judge was "expected to conduct himself in a manner fundamentally different from that of the traditional judge. No slave to the letter of the law, he was, ideally, a political fighter and educator to whom principle took precedence over paragraph."[23]

In a directive from August 1, 1942, Himmler dictated that the head of the SS judiciary should have a military rather than a legal background. Franz Breithaupt (not a lawyer), nominated as Chief of the SS Judiciary Main Office in Munich in August 1942, thus defined the SS jurisdiction's mission:

> The SS judiciary's task is to ruthlessly intervene should an SS man selfishly forget his duties toward the community, thereby violating our community's laws. SS judges are not "jurists," but rather SS leaders familiar with the law. They also show understanding for indiscretions (*Unbesonnenheiten*), provided the man's core is in good order. However, they must take uncompromising action against offenses caused by petty selfishness. Whoever in our community does not support the Führer with his last strength, does not belong to the elite of our people. Weaklings who have failed before the tasks of our time . . . will be hit by the harsh punishment they deserve.[24]

Such rhetoric might well have turned off SS jurists with a formal university education. Nor would they all have appreciated Breithaupt's

[21] Himmler also delayed indictments of high-ranking officers (he protected, for example, Waffen SS General Hermann Fegelein).

[22] Though there were plans for a specific codification of SS law, they were never put into practice. See Vieregge, *Die Gerichtsbarkeit einer "Elite"*, pp. 81–85.

[23] Weingartner, James J., "Law and Justice in the Nazi SS. The Case of Konrad Morgen," in *Central European History* 16 (1983), pp. 276–294, here: p. 280.

[24] Breithaupt, Franz, "An die Führer der SS und Polizei," in *Mitteilungen Hauptamt SS-Gericht*, vol. II, 3 (1942), p. 73.

announcement that the SS judiciary should be in the hands of "young, fresh SS leaders" rather than "over aged and senile jurists."[25]

Nevertheless, SS judges were spellbound by the SS ethos and its ideological guidelines, which were published in regular memoranda (*Mitteilungen*) by the Main Office. The notion of a "higher law" expressing "the right and the just" served as a handy means of reinterpreting military law statutes to suit SS ideology. Criminal offenses were redefined accordingly.[26]

Particularly, § 92 of the Military Penal Code, which regulated military disobedience, allowed SS ideology to enter into SS criminal law.[27] Homosexuality, adultery, and alcohol abuse eventually all constituted infringements of § 92. The SS judiciary interpreted § 92 so broadly, in fact, that practically every violation of Himmler's orders could be classified as military disobedience. As Bianca Vieregge argues, the SS jurisdiction entered juridically new territory by allowing SS judges to create law.[28]

This had grave consequences, as Himmler held the SS to a stricter standard than ordinary citizens. For example, whereas the first Nuremberg Law – the Law for the Protection of German Blood and German Honor – forbade citizens of "German or related blood" to have sexual relations with Jews, SS members were forbidden to have relations with any person of other races, including, for example, non-Jewish Poles. This restriction was spelled out in Himmler's "Order of *völkisch* self-respect" (*Befehl über völkische Selbstachtung*), the infringement of which counted as military disobedience under § 92.[29] And

[25] Bundesarchiv Berlin-Lichterfelde, NS7/13 "Bericht über die Dienstbesprechung der Chefs der SS- und Polizeigerichte am 7. Mai 1943 in München," pp. 13–21, p. 14.

[26] See Vieregge, *Die Gerichtsbarkeit einer "Elite"*, pp. 92–94.

[27] § 92 of the Military Penal Code (§ 92 MStGB) stated: "(1) Whoever does not follow an order in official matters (*Dienstsachen*) and who thereby intentionally or by negligence causes either a considerable disadvantage, or a danger to human life, or a significant danger to the property of others, or a danger to the security of the Reich or the vigour or training of the military troops, will be punished by severe detention (no less than a week) or imprisonment or fortress detention (*Festungshaft*) of up to ten years. (2) If the deed is committed in military combat or constitutes an especially grave case, it can be punished by either the death penalty or lifelong or temporary arrest." For the German original see Vieregge, *Die Gerichtsbarkeit einer "Elite"*, p. 96, note 162.

[28] Vieregge, *Die Gerichtsbarkeit einer "Elite"*, p. 68, p. 95.

[29] Himmler reiterated this order in a memo to Friedrich-Wilhelm Krüger, the Higher SS and Police Leader in Kraków, dated 30 June 1942. See Heiber, Helmut (ed.), *Reichsführer! Briefe an und von Himmler* (Stuttgart: Deutsche Verlagsanstalt, 1968), document 120, p. 125. Here Himmler explicitly stated that violations were punishable as military disobedience. On Himmler's order see also Vieregge, *Die Gerichtsbarkeit einer "Elite"*, pp. 107–109.

whereas the penalty for sexual relations with Jews was imprisonment, violators of § 92 could be sentenced to death.

SS jurisdiction also aligned § 92 with a narrower interpretation of military disobedience – that is, as violations of orders and other hierarchical disruptions. When members of the Waffen SS and police units acted without higher orders, they could not simply justify their actions by appeal to the SS worldview. This was particularly sensitive for cases of unordered killings. Given the murderous implementation of the NS racial program in the East, some SS men assumed that their task was to kill Jews on their own initiative. Several of these cases were prosecuted by the SS jurisdiction.[30]

Altogether, SS judges faced a complicated normative framework that created potentially conflicting demands. As SS members, they belonged to a political organization bound by Himmler's directives. Yet as formally schooled judges, they were also constrained by legal standards and principles. On the one hand, SS judges were expected to affirm the SS ethos, which granted them a high degree of discretion. On the other, however, they had to follow preexisting rules of military law and the German Penal Code. This commitment at once to legal statutes and the worldview and "ethical principles" of the SS produced considerable tension. As we will see below, some judges were torn between their ideological mission and self-understanding as lawyers.

7.3 Transcending Legal Statutes. The Theoretical Reflections of SS Judge Norbert Pohl

The changes in NS criminal law theory – including the turn to a will-based criminal law, the approval of a perpetrator typology, and the permission of analogy – all visibly affected the SS judiciary. Along with the unity of law and morality, SS judges decided cases according to the SS ethos. This is strikingly illustrated in a long letter from Norbert Pohl, Chief Judge at the SS court in Kraków, to Paul Scharfe, head of the SS Judiciary Main Office in Munich.[31]

[30] A striking case was the indictment of Max Täubner. See Büchler, Robert Yehoshua, "'Unworthy Behavior': The Case of SS Officer Max Täubner," in *Holocaust and Genocide Studies* 17, 3 (2003), pp. 409–429.

[31] Bundesarchiv Berlin-Lichterfelde NS7/318, "Letter of Norbert Pohl to Paul Scharfe," January 22, 1942, Bundesarchiv Berlin-Lichterfelde, NS7/318, p. 4. From July 1940 until March 1942, Norbert Pohl (1910–1968) was Chief SS judge at the SS and Police Court VI in Kraków; he then served as division SS judge with the SS tank division "Wiking,"

Pohl's letter of January 22, 1942 protested the Main Office's frequent repeal of sentences handed down by SS trial judges, which he felt had created a crisis of confidence in the SS judiciary.[32] In rescinding a sentence, Pohl complained, the Main Office relied on experts who had merely studied the facts in the case files. And while a sentence might seem too mild to a judicial expert examining the files, Pohl argued that it was fully justified by the defendant's positive character and firm demeanor. A mild sentence could also be appropriate because an uneducated defendant lacked insight into the nature of his offense. Yet such details were only obvious through the direct contact of judge and defendant.

For Pohl, the impression a defendant made on the judge was crucial to rendering a fair verdict. He even went so far as to place character above legal norms, asserting that "the defendant's personality, not first and foremost the legal statute, dictates the finding of justice."[33] Obviously "no slave to the letter of the law," Pohl described his own adjudication in these terms: "In deliberating a sentence, I start with the question: What punishment must the perpetrator receive for an offense whose occurrence has been established at trial? Only if clarity has been attained on this point are legal statutes consulted, which are then subsumed under the decision reached."[34] Here Pohl turned judicial reasoning on its head by rejecting the common procedure of deriving a sentence from the general norm, with the facts of a case as the specific instance. If the judge "falls back on the facts of the case as set out in the records, neatly subsumes them under the legal statute, and then concludes that a man who has so thoroughly violated the law can only be penalized with the harshest punishment," then this judge's procedure, Pohl argued, "is nothing but a regression to law-bound, liberal adjudication."[35]

For Pohl, statutes, although an important source of legal knowledge, "remain bloodless (*blutleer*) and degrade the judge to a mechanical instrument if the personality of the defendant and his community-relatedness . . .

operating in the Soviet Union (several SS judges had to serve in the field). The SS Court was located in Kraków, because it was the site of the German administration of the General Gouvernement, that is, that part of occupied Poland which was not incorporated into the German Reich.

32 Bundesarchiv Berlin-Lichterfelde, NS7/318, "Letter of Norbert Pohl to Paul Scharfe," January 22, 1942, p. 4.

33 Ibid.

34 Ibid., p. 6.

35 Ibid., p. 5.

are not also consulted."[36] He briskly concluded that a reviewer in the SS Judiciary's Main Office simply lacked the evidence to assess the appropriateness of a punishment.

Pohl invoked Nazi legal theory to support his view, asserting: "A radical change of enormous proportions is taking place in criminal law before our very eyes - today, and for the foreseeable future, the perpetrator's personality is not only the pivot of a trial, but of finding justice altogether."[37] Pohl praised criminal law theorist Georg Dahm for replacing the traditional deed-based criminal law with a perpetrator-based criminal law. While the civil criminal law courts would already use "a criminological perpetrator type," Pohl argued that the SS jurisdiction should embrace Dahm's notion of a "normative perpetrator type."[38]

Pohl took that suggestion even further: Other than the criminological approach, which focused on the specific criminal features of an individual perpetrator type (the drunkard, the habitual thief, the murderer, etc.), the normative approach assessed the perpetrator in light of the *general* features of the group to which he/she belonged. This opened the door to an array of racial and ethnic prejudices in sentencing. It is thus telling that Pohl, who served at a court in the General Gouvernement, would endorse an understanding of perpetrator typology so broad that even some NS jurists rejected it as a juridical guideline.[39]

Pohl also criticized the legal experts in the SS Main Office in Munich for their unfamiliarity with the situation in the General Gouvernement and the enormous challenges this posed for the Kraków court:

> Anyone who has experienced only fleetingly the indescribable chaos of these first months in Poland knows that hardly any officer or man - whether from

[36] Ibid., p. 6. Pohl's critique recalls Karl Schäfer's remark that liberal adjudication would reduce the judge to a "subsumption machine." See Schäfer, Karl, "Nullum Crimen sine Poena (Das Recht als Grundlage der Bestrafung. Zeitliche Geltung der Strafgesetze)," in *Das kommende deutsche Strafrecht. Allgemeiner Teil*, ed. by Gürtner, Franz (Berlin: Franz Vahlen, 1935), pp. 200–218, here: p. 202.

[37] Bundesarchiv Berlin-Lichterfelde, NS7/318, "Letter of Norbert Pohl to Paul Scharfe," 22 January 1942, p. 4.

[38] For a discussion of the criminal and the normative perpetrator type see See Bockelmann, Paul, "Der Tätergedanke im Strafrecht. Bemerkungen zum Buch von Georg Dahm," in *Zeitschrift der Akademie für Deutsches Recht* 7, 20 (1940), pp. 311–314.

[39] Bockelmann objected that the normative perpetrator type could not be clearly defined in accordance with a legal norm. See Bockelmann, "Der Tätergedanke im Strafrecht. Bemerkungen zum Buch von Georg Dahm," p. 312. As mentioned in Chapter 4.8 of this book, Dahm later changed his mind about character-based adjudication. In 1944, Dahm conceded that it was impossible to develop a perpetrator typology, warning that a perpetrator-based criminal law might merely reflect a judge's subjective impressions.

> the Army, the SS, the police, or the civil administration – has behaved in a way he could justify to himself. The situation of absolute lawlessness, famine, confusion, and the hostility of the population has led top-ranked commanders and others to bow to the circumstances. Everyone knows that only a small percentage of those (officers) received a just punishment.[40]

Nevertheless, in 1941 alone the SS court in Kraków, with merely four judges, investigated 1,341 grave cases and issued 365 trial sentences, according to Pohl. Additionally that year, the SS judges in Kraków examined and assessed 3,000 court marital sentences against Poles. They also traveled to other courts (Pohl mentions Tarnopol, Lublin, Warsaw, and Lemberg) for legal proceedings and trials.[41]

In one particular case of large-scale corruption, Pohl writes that the judges were confronted during the ten-day trial with an "abyss of filth and dishonesties" that confirmed "his already established opinion that Poland in the first months after the invasion was a morass of corruption and trafficking (*Schiebertum*) so extensive that the highest administrative offices were also involved."[42]

The case in question was Georg von Sauberzweig. As chief of the Waffen SS warehouse in Warsaw, Sauberzweig had profited greatly by selling Aryanized Jewish property on the black market. The SS Court in Kraków sentenced him to death. Yet because of Sauberzweig's high position, the judgment caught the attention of the SS Main Office. In an effort to avert repeal, Pohl justified the court's decision in a letter to Scharfe that named the assisting SS judge: Konrad Morgen.[43] Morgen had not only incisively investigated Sauberzweig and his cronies, but as Pohl stressed he had pursued and tried other SS offenders in the General Gouvernement. Morgen's activities illustrate the extent to which the NS

40 Bundesarchiv Berlin-Lichterfelde, NS7/318, "Letter of Norbert Pohl to Paul Scharfe," 22 January 1942, p. 16.

41 Ibid., pp. 10–11.

42 Ibid., p. 25.

43 Pohl mentioned in his letter to Scharfe that the trial and sentence against von Sauberzweig was "a highly political decision," so that the justification of the sentence could not be legally documented and protocolled. Pohl complained that SS Judge Reinecke who was not sufficiently familiar with the case, had brought the von Sauberzweig indictment to the attention of Himmler. And he added that "death sentences and their execution are no small thing so that one has to understand that someone in such a situation does nothing except his duty with all his strength, so that even a critical superior must have some understanding for oversights and mistakes which otherwise would have been inconceivable." Bundesarchiv Berlin-Lichterfelde, NS7/318, "Letter of Norbert Pohl to Paul Scharfe," 22 January 1942, p. 15.

state's political-legal framework undermined efforts to achieve judicial integrity.

7.4 "A Fanatic for Justice." The SS Judge Konrad Morgen[44]

Konrad Morgen (1909–1982) studied law at the Universities of Frankfurt, Rome, Berlin, The Hague, and Kiel. In May 1933, he joined the NSDAP and became an SS member.[45] From 1934–1938, he did his legal training in the German judiciary system. In 1936, Morgen published his dissertation on "War Propaganda and War Prevention."[46] Two years later, he passed the second state exam, which qualified him to serve as a judge. Morgen came into conflict with his superiors at a court in Stettin and was dismissed from the civil jurisdiction by the Reich's Ministry of Justice.[47] After a one-year stint in the Waffen SS, Morgen applied in 1940 for a position in the SS jurisdiction. Following brief training, he was transferred on January 1, 1941, to the SS and Police Court in Kraków.

Morgen's career as an SS judge can be divided into two periods: his service at the SS court in Kraków (January 1941 to May 1942), where in addition to prosecuting mundane violations of military law he tried to

[44] Morgen used this self-description ("fanatic for justice") in a postwar interrogation by American officers. "Interrogation of Konrad Morgen by the American CIC," Nuremberg September 4, 1946, p. 7. Morgen was in American custody from September 1945 until May 1948, and interrogated repeatedly by the American Counter Intelligence Corps (CIC). See "Interrogations of Konrad Morgen by the American CIC," in Interrogation Records Prepared for War Crimes Proceedings at Nuremberg 1945–1947, US National Archives, Record Group 238, Microfilm 1019, Roll 47.

[45] In his interrogations after the war, Morgen claimed that his parents, particularly his mother, had urged him to join the Nazi Party. See for example "Interrogation of Konrad Morgen by the American CIC," Nuremberg, August 30, 1946, p. 1.

[46] Morgen, Konrad *Kriegspropaganda und Kriegsverhütung* (Leipzig: Robert Noske, 1936). Morgen's dissertation displayed an interest in International Law, foremost of how to promote peace by transnational agreements and contracts. The Nazi Party objected to the publication of Morgen's dissertation.

[47] In one of his postwar interrogations in Nuremberg, Morgen described the details of the case. The defendant was a schoolteacher who was accused of illegal excessive corporeal punishment. During the trial, in which he was one of the assisting judges, Morgen gained the impression that all evidence in favor of the defendant was dismissed by the presiding judge. Morgen suspected that the defendant was treated unfairly because he was not a member of the Nazi Party and that the Hitler Youth had somehow initiated the proceedings. Morgen refused his consent to the verdict, thereby causing a scandal and his removal as a judge. See "Interrogation of Konrad Morgen by the American CIC," Nuremberg, August 30, 1946, pp. 3–5. After he left the civil jurisdiction, Morgen worked as legal advisor for the German Labour Force (*Deutsche Arbeitsfront*), an NS organization representing laborers in court proceedings with respect to salary and vacation disputes.

indict high-ranking SS officers for financial corruption; and, from June 1943 to the end of the war, his investigation of embezzlement and "illegal killings" – that is, killings outside of administrative orders – in the concentration camps. During the latter investigations, Morgen detected the so-called "Final Solution" – the mass extermination of European Jewry.[48]

In May 1942, Himmler demoted Morgen to army private and dismissed him from the SS judiciary on the grounds that he acquitted a defendant who had confessed to racial defilement (*Rassenschande*). But the real reason was that Morgen's corruption investigations in the General Gouvernement implicated powerful SS officers, who used their connections to Himmler to get Morgen out of the way.[49] Morgen was sent to the Eastern front in late December 1942. Yet in May 1943, Himmler reinstalled him as an SS judge in the Reich's Main Criminal Office in Berlin.[50] Himmler now needed Morgen to help him fight the enormous corruption in the concentration camps.

In July 1943, Morgen began investigating a corruption case in the concentration camp Buchenwald that also involved "illegal killings." On August 24, 1943, Morgen arrested former camp commandant Karl Otto Koch and camp physician Dr. Waldemar Hoven on charges of embezzlement and the unauthorized murder of prisoners.[51]

48 For a detailed discussion see Pauer-Studer, Herlinde and Velleman, J. David, *Konrad Morgen. The Conscience of a Nazi Judge* (Basingstoke: Palgrave MacMillan, 2015), ch. 12.

49 Especially strained were the relations between Morgen and Oswald Pohl, the Chief of the Reich's Main Economic and Administrative Office (WVHA). Pohl who was himself involved in corruption was eager to protect SS members against Morgen's investigations. See "Interrogation of Konrad Morgen by the American CIC," Nuremberg, August 30, 1946, pp. 7–12; see also "Interrogation of Konrad Morgen by the American CIC," Nuremberg, September 4, 1946, p. 47. In one of his Nuremberg interrogations, Morgen stated that he learned from the SS Jurisdiction Main Office in Munich that there existed a secret order by Himmler to send him to a concentration camp for two–three years. Due to interventions by the SS judges in the Main Office who objected that this way the independence of a judge would be violated, Himmler decided that Morgen should be sent to the Eastern front. See "Interrogation of Konrad Morgen by the American CIC, Nuremberg," August 30, 1946, pp. 18–20.

50 See "Interrogation of Konrad Morgen by the American CIC," Nuremberg, August 30, 1946, p. 20; Interrogation of Konrad Morgen by the American CIC," Nuremberg, September 4, 1946, pp. 4–5. Morgen held now a double position: He was still an SS judge, but he also was now a member of the Criminal police enabling him to investigate also civilian persons besides members of the Waffen SS and the police.

51 Also Koch's wife Ilse and the SS camp guard Sommers were arrested. Koch's wife was accused of cruelty against concentration camp prisoners, and for profiting from her husband's embezzlements. Sommers was accused of illegal killings.

Morgen also conducted investigations in the Lublin, Oranienburg, Sachsenhausen, Herzogenbosch, Auschwitz, Kraków-Plaszow, and Dachau camps. In fall 1943, he learned of the mass extermination of Jews in Lublin and Auschwitz.[52] Morgen visited Auschwitz to gather direct evidence of the industrial murder methods. By November 1943, he also had firsthand knowledge about mass shootings of Jews in the Lublin district.[53] Morgen eventually recognized that Himmler had ordered these crimes.

While Morgen realized that he was powerless to prosecute the instigators of the extermination program, Hitler and Himmler, he sought professional means to indict lower level perpetrators for secondary crimes. After his inspection of Auschwitz in November 1943, Morgen arrested Auschwitz Gestapo Chief Maximilian Grabner for 2,000 cases of killing prisoners outside of administrative orders.[54] Morgen even persuaded the SS court in Berlin to issue an arrest warrant for Adolf Eichmann on charges of misappropriating diamonds.[55]

In fall 1944, Morgen's prosecutions culminated in an SS trial in Weimar against former Buchenwald commandant Karl Otto Koch, Buchenwald camp physician Waldemar Hoven, and arrested Auschwitz Gestapo Chief Grabner.[56] Koch and Hoven were sentenced to death. Koch was executed in early April 1945, while Hoven was released from prison that March. The trial against Grabner came to nothing. Himmler

[52] See "Interrogation of Konrad Morgen by the American CIC," Nuremberg, September 4, 1946, p. 29.

[53] On November 3 and 4 1943, 42,000 Jews were shot in Majdanek (Lublin) and the nearby camp Poniatowa. Himmler had ordered the mass murder.

[54] Although Grabner was not directly involved in the mass extermination of Jews in Auschwitz-Birkenau, he supported the terror and the murderous system in Auschwitz in his role as the camp's Gestapo Chief.

[55] For the details see Pauer-Studer and Velleman, *Konrad Morgen. The Conscience of a Nazi Judge*, ch. 15.

[56] On August 17, 1944 Morgen had authored a bill of indictment against the former commandant of Buchenwald, Karl Otto Koch, the camp physician Dr. Waldemar Hoven, Koch's wife Ilse Koch, and the camp guard Sommers. See Morgen, "Anklageverfügung Koch," Prien August 17, 1944, SS and Polizeigericht z.b.V., Dodd Archive, University of Connecticut (uconn_asc_1994-0065_box288_folder7343 - 7344). The bill of indictment rested on Morgen's extended summary of his investigations, dated April 11 1944 (= Koch *Ermittlungsergebnis*, dated April 11, 1944). IMT Document NO 2366, U.S. National Archives. Record Group 238, Identifier 597043 / MLR Number NM70 174. After the war, Morgen handed over his personal copy of the detailed summary of the result of his investigations against Koch, dated 11 April, 1944, to the American authorities.

used the Weimar proceedings to send a stark warning to fraudulent concentration camp commandants.[57]

In late November 1943, Morgen applied to create a special SS court to prosecute so-called "political crimes" (coded language for the murder of Jews) in the camps.[58] Although Himmler approved the court in April 1944, he otherwise obstructed Morgen's activities, eventually closing the pending cases and halting further investigations. In November 1944, Morgen was again sent to the SS court in Kraków, which was relocated to Breslau in January 1945. There his career as an SS judge ended in May 1945.[59]

Morgen was in American custody from September 1945 to May 1948. Interrogated intensively about his wartime activities by the American Counter Intelligence Service (CIC), he also testified at the International Military Tribunal (IMT) and two American Military Tribunals in 1947.[60] After his de-Nazification case was closed in 1950, Morgen became a lawyer in Frankfurt am Main.[61]

At considerable personal risk, Konrad Morgen had gone much further than other SS judges in fighting corruption and crimes in the SS. Indeed,

[57] Morgen described this in a postwar interrogation in the following way: "Koch should be sentenced. One had planned this in the following way: Himmler wanted to give a harrowing speech in front of Koch's dangling feet. All concentration commandants should be assembled." See "Interrogation of Konrad Morgen by the American CIC," Nuremberg, September 4, 1946, p. 21.

[58] Bundesarchiv Berlin-Lichterfelde, NS 7/128, "Letter of the Chief of the SS Jurisdiction Main Office to Himmler," dated December 13, 1943. The meaning of "political crimes" was due to the notorious memo from the fall of 1942, in which Himmler had issued that killings (shootings) of Jews for "political motives" but not for "sadistic motives" were permitted. See "Letter of SS Judge Horst Bender to the SS Jurisdiction Main Office," dated October 26, 1942, in Heiber (ed.), *Reichsführer! Briefe an und von Himmler*, document 165, pp. 164–165. Bender was Himmler's personal legal advisor.

[59] See "Interrogation of Konrad Morgen by the American CIC," Nuremberg, August 30, 1946; see also "Interrogation of Konrad Morgen by the American CIC," Nuremberg, September 16, 1946.

[60] Morgen testified on behalf of the defense of the SS at the International Military Tribunal trial against the Major War criminals in Nuremberg (IMT trial). Morgen was a defense witness in the trial against Oswald Pohl, Chief of the SS Main Economic and Administrative Office, and in the trial against Waldeck, the Higher SS and Police leader in Kassel. He was a prominent witness (this time for the prosecution) in the Auschwitz trial in Frankfurt am Main, which took place from December 1963 to August 1965.

[61] The reasons for Morgen's problems after the war are discussed in Pauer-Studer and Velleman, *Konrad Morgen. The Conscience of a Nazi Judge*, pp. 64, 105–106. Morgen was in American custody in Nuremberg from September 1945 until May 1948 and then handed to the German authorities for his de-Nazification procedures. Although Morgen was released from German internment in September 1948, he only passed denazification in 1950 when all pending cases were closed.

he claimed in his postwar interrogations to have investigated more than 800 cases, 200 of which came to trial. He took credit for the arrest of five concentration camp commandants, two of whom were executed.[62]

Morgen repeatedly tested the limits of his authority as an SS judge. He even sought to enlarge his legal scope for prosecuting crimes in the camps, including the killing of Jews. Unsurprisingly, his investigations provoked his superiors. At the SS trial in Weimar, high-ranking SS officers attacked Morgen so severely for prosecuting Koch and Hoven that they basically branded him a "dead man."[63] Nevertheless, Morgen's professional status as an SS judge tied him closely to the elite Nazi organization.

Morgen's attitude toward the SS was highly ambivalent. On the one hand, he was attracted to its value system of "decency, honor, manly uprightness, and honesty."[64] Yet at the same time, Morgen was disillusioned by SS criminality and deeply shocked when confronted with direct evidence of the mass extermination of the Jews. His mindset was constantly in flux: Sometimes he endorsed SS virtues, at others he expressed disapproval and even disdain for the SS code, contemptuously referring to "SS ideology." As Morgen explained in a postwar interrogation: "The resistance that confronted me from the central authorities I answered

[62] See Morgen, Konrad, "Witness testimony, International Military Tribunal Trial against Major War Criminals at Nuremberg," vol. 20, August 7, 1946, One Hundred and Ninety-Seventh Day, accessible online http://avalon.law.yale.edu/imt/08-08-46.asp, p. 488,; in German: www.zeno.org/Geschichte/M/Der+Nürnberger+Prozeß/Hauptverhandlungen/Einhundertsechsundneunzigster+Tag.+Dienstag,+6.+August+1946/Nachmittagssitzung, p. 532, Koch was sentenced to death at the trial in Weimar in September 1944, but he was executed only beginning of April 1945, one week before the Americans liberated the concentration camp Buchenwald on April 11, 1945. The order to shoot Koch came from Waldeck, the Higher SS and Police leader in Kassel who had authority to manage Buchenwald. Waldeck's motives for ordering Koch to be executed remain open; he probably tried to improve his reputation and standing vis-á-vis the Americans.

[63] See "Interrogation of Konrad Morgen by the American CIC," Nuremberg, January 18, 1947, p. 5. Morgen learned from his colleague, SS Judge Gerhard Wiebeck, that Himmler had already issued a secret order for sending him to a concentration camp.

[64] Himmler's horrible interpretation of these ideological principles came to the fore in his notorious Posen speeches from October 4, 1943 and October 6, 1943. See Himmler, Heinrich, "Rede vor den Reichs- und Gauleitern in Posen am 6.10.1943," in *Heinrich Himmler Geheimreden 1933 bis 1945*, ed. by Smith, Bradley and Peterson, Agnes F. (Frankfurt am Main, Berlin, Wien: Propyläen, 1974), pp. 162–183. See Harvard Law School Library, *Nuremberg Trials Project: A Digital Document Collection*, HLSL Item No. 3790, HLSL Item No. 2974; accessible online http://nuremberg.law.harvard.edu/.

with SS-ideology: 'Don't you want to have absolute purity in the SS? Etc. Then they were of course always beaten and had to say 'Yes'."[65]

Nevertheless, SS norms often determined how Morgen distinguished between what was "permissible" and "forbidden," frequently distorting his moral perception. For example, while serving in the General Gouvernement (1941–1942), Morgen tried to prosecute the notorious Waffen SS General Oskar Dirlewanger, whose brigade committed terrible atrocities. Morgen spoke extensively about Dirlewanger's crimes in his postwar interrogations by the Americans. Yet he also condemned Dirlewanger for not respecting SS standards by keeping a young Jewish mistress, even introducing her to visiting SS officers.[66]

Twenty years after detecting the extermination program at Auschwitz, Morgen still seemed spellbound by the SS code of decency. In his March 1964 testimony at the Auschwitz Trial in Frankfurt am Main, he related his shock as an SS officer when, after inspecting the extermination machinery in Birkenau, he found the guard room of responsible SS personnel in disarray, with men dozing on couches and eating potato pancakes served by Jewish girls wearing civilian clothes rather than prison uniforms.[67] His observations about infringements of SS standards paralleled his testimony that the night before, while he was traveling to Auschwitz, "several thousand people, several trains full with people, had been gassed and turned into ashes."[68]

Morgen's judicial activities were deeply flawed, his courage and risks notwithstanding. Even a brief glance at Morgen's personal statements on his role as SS judge indicates that he faced a considerable problem in depicting how what he was doing matched the actual juridical practice in which he was involved.

Morgen emphasized repeatedly that he was a judge with a university education in law. In a postwar interrogation by the CIC, he described his bewilderment when, on assignment to the SS court in Kraków as a jurist "somewhat familiar with the German civil service tradition," he encountered the effects of the German occupation: "What one saw there made

65 "Interrogation of Konrad Morgen by the American CIC," Nuremberg, October 21, 1946, p. 129.

66 "Interrogation of Konrad Morgen by the American CIC," Nuremberg, August 30, 1946, p. 22.

67 See Auschwitz trial, "Witness testimony Konrad Morgen," March 9, 1964, 25th day of trial, in *Der Auschwitz-Prozess. Tonbandmitschnitte, Protokolle, Dokumente*, ed. by Fritz-Bauer-Institute Frankfurt am Main and the Staatliches Museum Auschwitz-Birkenau, 25. Verhandlungstag, 9. März 1964, pp. 5557–5570.

68 Ibid., p. 5567.

one's hair stand on end. It was as if a swarm of locusts had descended to devour the land. . . . On the one hand there was the poverty of the populace, which was obvious; on the other was the carousing and extravagance and – corruption."[69]

In March 1942, Morgen wrote to the personnel chief of the SS Judiciary Main Office in Munich to request transfer from the General Gouvernement to an area with a "healthier atmosphere," preferably Norway: "The corruption in the General Gouvernement is so great, and the number of capital crimes and noxious offenses so high, that I am utterly convinced that any judge would in time become jaded and thus risk injuring his natural sense of justice."[70]

Morgen wrote here as if he operated in a rule-of-law system. A similar understanding seemed to drive his August 1944 bill of indictment against former Buchenwald commandant Karl Otto Koch and camp physician Waldemar Hoven, which he prepared for the SS trial in Weimar. Relying on Paragraphs 211 and 212 of the German Penal Code from 1871, Morgen charged both men with murder and manslaughter of camp prisoners.

However, Morgen's attempt to portray his professional identity as that of an ordinary judge pursuing a moral ideal of justice fails miserably. Nor could his claim to be a kind of rule-of-law judge be sustained given what he himself had to say about the political and legal framework of Nazi Germany:

> Law in the National Socialist state was several things: First, as in former times, it was the sum of legal norms in place, including common law. But then [it was] also the Führer's orders. The Führer in the National State united all authority in his person. He was not only head of state, but also the highest lawgiver and supreme judge.[71]

69 "Interrogation of Konrad Morgen by the American CIC," Nuremberg, August 30, 1946, pp. 6–7.

70 "Letter of Konrad Morgen to Eberhard Hinderfeld," dated March 27, 1942 in NO-2366, US National Archives ARC Identifier 597043/MLR Number NM70 174. One might wonder whether Morgen, by speaking of "capital crimes," also referred to the murder of Jews. There is evidence that Morgen also was willing to prosecute the killing of Jews. For example, he sought to prosecute Dirlewanger, a notorious Waffen SS General who was also suspected of having murdered at least forty-two Jews in Lublin. Morgen asked his higher court authority in Kraków to arrest Dirlewanger, but the arrest failed because Dirlewanger was not subject to the SS jurisdiction.

71 "Interrogation of Konrad Morgen by the American CIC," Nuremberg, September 19, 1946, pp. 7–8; see also "Interrogation of Konrad Morgen by the American CIC," Nuremberg, October 11, p. 82.

In his witness testimony at the IMT, Morgen explained why he could not take legal action against the instigators of the mass extermination:

> The circumstances prevailing in Germany during the war were no longer normal in the sense of state legal guarantees. Besides, the following must be considered: I was not simply a judge, but I was a judge of military penal justice. No court-martial in the world could bring the Supreme Commander, let alone the head of state, to court.[72]

Clearly, Morgen was aware of the distorted legal regime in Nazi Germany. What he did not recognize was that this system severely limited his claim to a morally sound professional self-understanding. Morgen's attempt at cultivating a rule-of-law identity as a judge was incoherent to say the least. In his operative framework, the constitutive normative standard of a rule-of-law jurisdiction, namely justice, was simply not in place.

Likewise, Morgen's self-portrayal as a "judge of military penal justice" is untenable. As a military court system, the SS jurisdiction was part of the German military machinery that launched wars of aggression on its neighbors. The main purpose of the SS judiciary was to prosecute violations of military law by the notorious combatants of the Waffen SS. To suppose that justice could be enforced in such a system amounts to willful self-deception.

An agent's professional identity depends upon his compliance with the practice-rules of the profession.[73] Thus, partaking in a specific practice not only shapes one's professional role and self-understanding, it also links an agent to the institution or organization in which the practice is embedded. Although on critical reflection an agent might not endorse all of the

[72] Konrad Morgen, "Witness testimony in International Military Tribunal Trial against Major War Criminals at Nuremberg," vol. 20, August 8, 1946, One Hundred and Ninety-Eighth Day, accessible online http://avalon.law.yale.edu/imt/08-08-46.asp, p. 505; in German: www.zeno.org/Geschichte/M/Der+Nürnberger+Prozeß/Hauptverhandlungen/Einhundertachtundneunzigster+Tag+Donnerstag,+8.+August+1946/Vormittagssitzung, p. 552. In his testimony at the Auschwitz trial in Frankfurt am Main on November 27, 1964, the presiding judge in the SS trial against Maximilian Grabner in Weimar 1944, SS Judge Werner Hansen, stated: "It was a fact, that this action (the mass murder of Jews) was outside the jurisdiction's power sphere. It would have been impossible to open proceedings because of these mass killings against the highest state leadership. The indictment against Grabner was the utmost what the SS judiciary could do." Auschwitz trial, "Witness testimony Dr. Werner Hansen," 116th day of trial, November 27, 1964, in *Der Auschwitz-Prozess: Tonbandmitschnitte, Protokolle, Dokumente,* 116. Verhandlungstag, 27 November, 1964, pp. 26049–26054, here: p. 26050.

[73] We have to make room for rule-violations that do not amount to a complete rejection of the rules. Thus, acceptance of the practice rules does not require full compliance, however, compliance beyond a certain threshold.

organization's constitutive aims, he is nonetheless tied to the organization as long as he partakes successfully in its activities and practices.

The incongruity in Morgen's self-depiction is obvious. He claimed to have a professional identity (as a rule-of-law judge) tied to a practice that required the constitutive standard of justice to be operative. In other words, by definition the actions of a rule-of-law judge aim at justice. Yet at the same time the SS juridical system made it impossible to draw on this standard.[74]

There was thus a constitutive failure in Morgen's effort to describe his actions in terms of justice (in the sense of a rule-of-law system). A constitutive failure might be described as an attempt to justify one's actions according to a standard that is external to the practice in which one is actually engaged.[75] In Morgen's case, the constitutive failure was yet more extreme: He did not merely assume a practice-external standard (namely, justice in the sense of the rule of law), but one corrupted by the institution in which the practice was situated. Morgen's futile attempt to invoke a constitutive aim or standard, which was undermined by the very practice rules in which he was engaged, explains both why his judicial practice was flawed and, more generally, why the SS jurisdiction was "a sham."[76]

Morgen did not outright reject the ideal of justice. Rather, he was incapable of seeing that justice was not and could not be the SS jurisdiction's constitutive aim and standard, given the institutional setting of the Third Reich. He also lacked a clear understanding of what justice required – his moral sense was tainted by his SS membership. For example, neither during the war, nor in his depositions at postwar trials against former SS officers, nor in his interrogations by the CIC did Morgen clearly censure Nazi Germany's military aggression.[77]

[74] For a more detailed exposition of this argument see Pauer-Studer, Herlinde, "Complicity and Conditions of Agency," in *Journal of Applied Philosophy* 35, 4 (2018), pp. 643–660.

[75] For such a definition of "constitutive failure" see Schapiro, Tamar, "Compliance, complicity, and the nature of non-ideal conditions," in *The Journal of Philosophy* 100, 7 (2003), pp. 32–55, particularly p. 336.

[76] See Schapiro, "Compliance, complicity, and the nature of non-ideal conditions," p. 339. Schapiro gives a slightly different explanation for practices turning into a sham than the account offered here. While my account locates what is going wrong foremost in the missing constitutive standard of the practice, Schapiro tries to locate the failure in how the misconduct of others changes the practice rules such that participation in the practice no longer counts "as participation in the form of activity that is, ideally, defined by those rules." Ibid., p. 339.

[77] He never used the formula "war of aggression." Also with respect to the attack on the Soviet Union, which Nazi leaders had planned with the clear intention of ignoring established war conventions, Morgen just said in a court testimony that the war had led to terrible cruelties on both sides.

Morgen tried hard to salvage his favorable self-portrayal. Besides measuring his judicial actions according to a normative parameter that exceeded the professional practice in which he was engaged, he sought to detach his activities from the political and legal background of Nazi Germany. For instance, Morgen once addressed his American interrogator thus: "I don't know why I should be in prison, as I was never a criminal but have investigated war crimes just as you are doing now."[78]

But Morgen pursued crimes within the disreputable SS. And his most noteworthy achievement, the SS trial in Weimar, was only sanctioned by Himmler to deter concentration camp commandants from corruption.

In one postwar deposition, Morgen alleged that his first thought after detecting the Final Solution in the fall 1943 was to flee to Switzerland. But he gave up the plan for fear of the consequences.

Morgen could not produce a single explanation for his activities that transcended the SS's normative framework. In fact, he never even cut ties with the SS despite this being essential to his ability to ascribe himself a normative identity as a rule-of-law judge. By performing actions within a practice, one automatically confirms the constitutive standards of said practice. In his actions as an SS judge, Morgen both implicitly and explicitly endorsed the constitutive standards of the SS jurisdiction—standards created in light of the disastrous ideological mission of the SS.

In the end, Morgen had to concede that the very workings of the SS jurisdiction undermined his judicial efforts, however laudable they seemed from a first-personal normative standpoint. He thus explained his bill of indictment against former Buchenwald commandant Koch in these terms:

> Koch was the test case for the SS jurisdiction. I tried to make it easy for [the jurisdiction] through the formulation of my bill of indictment, which in order to succeed had to be framed in accordance with Nazi law. But it was only half successful. After all, the rest did not care or desire to change the system and establish, in this test case, that a man's life is holy.[79]

7.5 Concluding Remarks

After the war, when the crimes, atrocities, and horrors of the NS regime became apparent, many blamed the legal profession for blindly following the Nazis out of a commitment to the principle of "the law is the law." Yet

78 "Interrogation of Konrad Morgen by the American CIC," Nuremberg, April 4, 1947, p. 3.

79 Konrad Morgen, "Short remarks to the bill of indictment against Standartenführer Koch," part of document file NO-2366, 10/11/10, p. 3.

our examination of the SS jurisdiction indicates that the reasons for the jurists' failures were more complex and varied. Konrad Morgen did not simply follow his superiors' directives – he sought ways to circumvent them, and sometimes ignored their orders altogether. Nor did Morgen uncritically hold to established legal regulations. Rather, the problem was his complacency as a judge, which prevented him from seeing that the political context of his legal activities undermined their aim and purpose. While Morgen tried to stylize himself an advocate of a high ideal of justice, the legal system within which he operated adhered to the organization responsible for the worst crimes of the NS regime.

The SS jurisdiction was shot through with a moralizing ideology embracing the very unification of law and morality that defined Nazi legal theory. And the SS judges (at least those cited in this chapter) took that perverted form of ethics to heart. Reinecke boasted of the ethical education and conscience in the SS. Pohl gave his personal impression of the defendant – did his demeanor live up to SS virtues? – precedence over legal statutes. Even Morgen judged SS men according to how well their behavior aligned with SS standards.

The very challenge posed by an ideologically deformed ethical code like that of the SS jurisdiction is that its concepts seem so familiar. Abstracted from the social and legal background, the principles and virtues that constituted this code – honesty, decency, trustworthiness, rectitude, loyalty, fidelity – also belong to our uncorrupted understanding of morality. Only by placing their meaning into a specific context can we lay bare semantic distortions and distinguish between moralization and morality.[80]

Moral concepts, principles, and virtues all need to be socially articulated – in other words, they must be given a relevant interpretation and be applied by agents with a relatively intact moral awareness, recognizing morally relevant situations. Typically, situations of moral relevance are those in which persons' status as persons is at stake in terms of fair consideration and respectful treatment (that is, not being deceived, abused, or mistreated). Conventional morality acknowledges and follows these indicators of moral salience.[81]

80 Roughly stated, "moralization" refers to using moral concept and principles as a means of pursuing reprehensible purposes (for example, manipulation of others, suppression of critique, gaining power over others, etc.).

81 Barbara Herman talks of "rules of moral salience," see Herman, Barbara, "The Practice of Moral Judgment," in Herman, *The Practice of Moral Judgment* (Cambridge, MA and

However, serious deviances and deformations in the gauges of moral salience can occur, as clearly happened in the Third Reich. The Nazi regime reinterpreted the standards of right and wrong, good and bad. Indeed, it so completely redefined such concepts as decency, honor, uprightness, loyalty, and fidelity that acceptable behavior, as proscribed by conventional morality in a rule-of-law society, was distorted out of recognition. In thus transforming the moral order, the Nazi state, and the SS in particular, created a normative world in which duty was confused with unconstrained warfare and, even, political murder.

This new normative world was not one of complete amoralism or boundless criminality – rather, it was an inverted order in which criminal acts and murder equated with living up to ethical duties and requirements. As Hannah Arendt chillingly put it:

> This "new order" was exactly what it said it was – not only gruesomely novel, but also and above all, an order. The widespread notion that we deal here with nothing more than a gang of criminals who in conspiracy will commit just any crimes is grievously [sic] misleading. ... Equally misleading is the common notion that we deal here with an outbreak of modern nihilism, if we understand the nihilistic credo in the sense of the nineteenth century: "all is permitted." The ease with which consciences could be dulled was partly the direct consequence of the fact that by no means all was permitted.[82]

The SS judges found themselves precisely at the fulcrum of this new order, assigned to protect it legally by punishing infringements of its norms. And by and large they indulged themselves, deriving their "professional integrity" from fulfilling their prescribed assignments. Yet, the system could not completely silence their former sense of right and wrong and their residual affiliations to the rule of law. Their conscience was awoken – Pohl revolted against the "abyss of filth and dishonesties" in the General Gouvernement; Morgen leaped into action when confronted with Koch's orders to kill witnesses of his embezzlements, Hoven's killing of camp inmates by phenol

London: Harvard University Press, 2007), pp. 51–78. However, also feelings of empathy and care are crucial for moral awareness, that is, for opening one's heart to what one sees.

[82] Arendt, Hannah, "Personal responsibility under dictatorship," in Arendt, *Responsibility and Judgment*, ed. with an introduction by Kohn, Jerome (New York: Schocken Books, 2003), pp. 17–48, pp. 41–42.

injections, Grabner's shootings of prisoners in the Gestapo bunker in Auschwitz, and, above all, with the mass murder of the Jews.

In the end, however, their legal powers were not strong enough to overcome their consciences. Or as Konrad Morgen succinctly put it: No judge in the SS jurisdiction could bring the head of state, who also was "highest lawgiver and supreme judge," to court.

8

The Moralization of Law in National Socialism

8.1 NS Legal Thinkers' Attack on Legal Positivism

In his seminal article "Statutory Lawlessness and Supra-Statutory Law" (1946), Gustav Radbruch delivered a crushing verdict on legal positivism's role during Nazi rule: "Positivism, with its principle that 'a law is a law,' has in fact rendered the German legal profession defenceless against statutes that are arbitrary and criminal. Positivism is, moreover, in and of itself wholly incapable of justifying the validity of statutes."[1] For Radbruch, legal positivism's main weakness consisted in its sharp separation of law and morality, respectively justice. The upshot of Radbruch's criticism in short: By raising an entire generation of jurists in the spirit of keeping law apart from morality, positivism had prepared the juridical ground for the NS system.

Yet a close examination of the original texts of Nazi legal thinkers casts considerable doubt on Radbruch's argument. Indeed, National Socialist legal theorists firmly rejected legal positivism and endorsed the unity of law and morality.

[1] Radbruch, Gustav, "Statutory Lawlessness and Supra-Statutory Law," in *Oxford Journal of Legal Studies* 26, 1 (2006), pp. 1–11; transl. by Litschewski Paulson, Bonnie and Paulson, Stanley L., p. 6. (transl. of the second sentence slightly changed, H.P.-St.). Litschewski Paulson and Paulson translated the sentence as "Positivism is, moreover, in and of itself wholly incapable of establishing the validity of statutes." My translation (using "justifying the validity of statutes" instead of "establishing the validity of statutes") is closer to Radbruch's original German formulation "Dabei ist der Positivismus gar nicht in der Lage, aus eigener Kraft die Geltung von Gesetzen zu begründen." Radbruch, Gustav, *Gesetzliches Unrecht und übergesetzliches Recht* (Baden-Baden: Nomos, 2002), p. 10 (reprint of Gustav Radbruch, "Gesetzliches Unrecht und übergesetzliches Recht," in *Süddeutsche Juristen-Zeitung* 1946).

The Nazi jurists' biting critique targeted legal positivism's most prominent academic exponent at the time: Hans Kelsen.[2] Karl Larenz, a law professor at the University of Kiel, called Kelsen's *Pure Theory of Law* "a manifestation of intellectual foreign infiltration (*geistige Überfremdung*)."[3] His colleague, Ernst Forsthoff, blamed legal positivism of being responsible for the ethical disorientation and relativism that, in his view, had afflicted Germany during the Weimar period.[4]

In particular, the objections focused on Kelsen's claim that law and morality must be treated as separate normative spheres. Larenz asserted that legal positivism stripped law of "*its natural connection with national mores and morals.*"[5] Conversely, he hailed Carl Schmitt for having revived and highlighted "the nature and essence of the political," that is, "the simple reality of political life vis-à-vis the artificial abstractions of the Vienna School."[6]

Altogether, NS legal thinkers agreed that positivism's allegedly formalistic conception of law should be replaced by a material understanding of law that is based on a unity of law and morality. This call to merge law with morality[7] was given succinct expression by Georg Dahm:

[2] See also Dreier, Horst; Müßig, Ulrike; Stolleis, Michael; Korb, Axel-Johann, *Kelsens Kritiker. Ein Beitrag zur Geschichte der Rechts- und Staatstheorie (1911–1934)* (Tübingen: Mohr Siebeck, 2010).

[3] Larenz, Karl, *Deutsche Rechtserneuerung und Rechtsphilosophie* (Tübingen: J.C.B. Mohr [Paul Siebeck], 1934), p. 11. Larenz's remark has racial connotations: the term "foreign infiltration" alluded to the fact that Kelsen was Austrian and Jewish. Kelsen's first edition of the *Reine Rechtslehre* appeared in 1934.

[4] See e. g. Forsthoff, Ernst, *Der totale Staat* (Hamburg: Hanseatische Verlagsanstalt, 1933), p. 13ff.

[5] Larenz, *Deutsche Rechtserneuerung und Rechtsphilosophie*, p. 12 (italics in original). Following Hegel, Larenz wrote: "The objective spirit of a *Volk*, as it encounters us in its objectivations as the language, mores, law, and culture of *this Volk* and as it lives within it, cannot be only understood psychologically . . .; for the objective spirit is never owned by the single individual as such, but indeed inheres in the community as the living entirety (*das Lebensganze*). Thus it is always also the spirit of a *specific Volk that is internally formed by blood and fate*." Ibid. p. 16 (italics in the original).

[6] Ibid., p. 11.

[7] For purposes of clarity: When the terms "ethics" and "ethical" refer to the Nazi theorists' concept and understanding of ethics, this is in a purely descriptive sense. This use of the terms is not to be confused with a universalistic understanding of ethics, which attempts to establish universally valid criteria of right and wrong. Some authors distinguish between the terms "ethics" and "morality." In that case, "ethics" and "ethical" refer to personal attitudes, convictions, and virtues; "morality" to social morality, that is, moral concepts of justice and virtue. The term "*Sittlichkeit*" as it was chosen by the NS jurists has a broad sense, covering both ethics (in the personal sense) and morality (in the sense of social morality). That is why in the following I use "ethics" for "*Sittlichkeit*" in the same sense as "ethics" or "morality." If in the following I speak of abandoning the separation of law and

> We recognize today the independence and neutralization of law, the separation and opposition of law and state, law and politics, law and the people's intuition (*Volksanschauung*), law and morality as the core of this evil [that is, the positivism-induced degeneration of law]. Overcoming these antagonisms and creating unity within law is virtually a precondition for a true renewal of our legal life.[8]

In other words, the basic values of National Socialism and the moral sense of the people's community should form the new foundations of law. The German people's healthy intuition (*gesunde Volksanschauung*) ought to determine what counted as decent and right versus that which had to be criminalized and punished. The result was a blending of legal and moral norms. In the words of Roland Freisler: "There can be no divide between a requirement of law and a requirement of morality. For requirements of law are requirements of decency; but what is decent is determined by the conscience of the *Volk* and its members."[9] In a publication on NS police law, the lawyer Walter Hamel blatantly proclaimed that "any distinction between a moral duty and a legal obligation for action . . . can no longer be made."[10]

Legal positivism indeed endorses the strict separation of law and morality. For legal positivists, morality sets external standards for assessing legal systems and legal norms.[11] Positivists argue that those external moral standards should motivate legal reform and the revision of statutes that generate unacceptable consequences. Moreover, moral principles and considerations should guide a judge's legal decision-making in hard cases when positive law runs out (that is, when a decision cannot be directly inferred from enacted positive legal norms).

morality, the term "morality" refers both to personal ethical attitudes and to principles of social morality or justice. For reasons of terminological simplicity, however, I just speak of the separation of law and morality and not of law and ethics.

8 Dahm, Georg, "Die Erneuerung der Ehrenstrafe," in *Deutsche Juristen-Zeitung* 39, 13 (1934), pp. 822–832, here p. 826.

9 Freisler, Roland, *Nationalsozialistisches Recht und Rechtsdenken* (Berlin: Spaeth & Linde, 1938), p. 56.

At the time of this publication, Freisler was State Secretary in the Reich Ministry of Justice.

10 Hamel, Walter, "Wesen und Rechtsgrundlagen der Polizei im nationalsozialistischen Staate," in Frank, Hans, (ed.), *Deutsches Verwaltungsrecht* (München: Zentralverlag der NSDAP Eher, Franz Nachf., 1937), pp. 381–398, here p. 384.

11 This holds particularly for the legal positivism of H. L. A. Hart and Joseph Raz. See Hart, H. L. A., *The Concept of Law*, 3rd ed. (Oxford: Clarendon Press, 2012); Raz, Joseph, *The Authority of Law. Essays on Law and Morality*, 2nd ed. (Oxford: Clarendon Press, 2009).

It was just such an understanding of the relationship between morality and law that was untenable to NS legal theorists. In their view, moral ideals should form an integral part of the law. Yet NS lawyers' concept of morality was ideologically distorted. Consequently, ethical concepts such as "decency," "honor," and "loyalty" were transformed into legal concepts.

The texts of SS jurist Reinhard Höhn are illustrative of those remarkable normative shifts. Law, Höhn claimed, is "not simply a technique of applying independent ethical principles. Rather, law can only mean the lived morality or decency (*gelebte Sittlichkeit*) of a *Volk*."[12] In his view, law may not be reduced to general principles and formal procedures. The dualism of statutory law and a higher principle of justice – that is, one transcending statutes – had to be overcome. As Höhn described the core of his conception: "*According to German legal doctrine, law is neither a system of norms nor a sum of values, law is the expression of the community order.* Justice is not outside the law."[13]

The notion of a people's community (*Volksgemeinschaft*) was fundamental to the National Socialist moralization of law. As Höhn wrote: "(T)he community under the new German concept of law is not only a social fact, but also a legal principle."[14] In this way, the ideologically and racially coined value notions associated with the ideal of the *Volksgemeinschaft* found their way into law. "Honor and loyalty, race and soil" had not only been revived in National Socialism, they were actually incorporated into law.[15] Only an "individualistic legal system" could classify such concepts as "unlawful."[16]

Raising the people's community to a source of law and a legal precept had striking normative implications. For instance, such characteristic elements of the myth of the homogenous people's community as the principle of "generic equality" (*Artgleichheit*) and "generic sameness of experience" (*artgleiches Erleben*) began shaping NS legal discourse. The

[12] Höhn, Reinhard, "Volk, Staat und Recht," in Höhn, Reinhard; Maunz, Theodor; Swoboda, Ernst (eds.), *Grundfragen der Rechtsauffassung* (München: Duncker & Humblot, 1938), pp. 1–27, here p. 13. Höhn demands that ideas of justice, other than in legal positivism, may not be reduced to "ethical values . . . which cannot be directly expressed by a legal norm but are supposed to be taken into consideration in law-making and in the application of law." Ibid. p. 12. According to Höhn, the positivist separation of morality and law entails that "the idea of justice is (never) able to immediately penetrate positive law." Ibid.

[13] Höhn, "Volk, Staat und Recht," p. 9 (italics in the original).

[14] Ibid.

[15] Ibid.

[16] Ibid.

notion of "blood unity" became a prerequisite "for experiencing law within the community."[17] As Höhn noted:

> The development of the communal spirit is subject to certain preconditions, particularly the condition of generic equality (*Artgleichheit*) of those persons who form the community. Consequently, the German understanding of law builds on the facts of racial doctrine. *Identical thinking, feeling, and acting in a people is necessarily conditioned by common generic predispositions.*[18]

Such arguments firmly anchored the National Socialist racial doctrine in the law. Indeed, in claiming that the establishment and preservation of a "racially pure community" was a legal obligation, NS jurists laid the groundwork for the regime's explicit racial legislation.

In a similar manner, Otto Koellreutter emphasized the bond between law, morality, and communal values. For him, the community member's sense of justice was implicit in NS law:

> Just as the political experience of Volk and nation . . . must be alive in each member of the *Volk* in the *völkisch* state, so must the *völkisch* idea of law be alive in the sense of justice of each *Volksgenosse*. . . . This means above all that each member of the *Volk* recognizes all other members as legal comrades, and that the personality and honor of each *Volksgenosse* is an inviolable legal good.[19]

NS legal experts thus ascribed the power of deciding questions of law and ethics to members of the Aryan people's community – their judgment determined what was right or wrong, worthy or worthless, just or unjust. The communal spirit was thought to enhance and grant proper moral and legal judgment. In Koellreutter's words: "If communal feeling is awakened and kept alive within each member of the *Volk*, then the "correct" *völkisch* feeling of justice will develop . . . The *völkisch* concept of justice thus stems from the same roots as the *völkisch* view of the essence of the political."[20] For NS theoreticians, a fundamental flaw of legal positivism was its lack of a supra-positive idea of law. Law had to incorporate an idea of justice and would thus exceed written positive law. In other words, the positive legal order should be a means of "realizing the concept and idea of law (*Rechtsidee*)."[21] NS legal experts thus stressed

[17] Ibid., p. 13.
[18] Ibid., p. 8 (italics in the original).
[19] Koellreutter, Otto, *Deutsches Verfassungsrecht. Ein Grundriss*, 3rd ed. (Berlin: Junker & Dünnhaupt, 1938), p. 12.
[20] Ibid., p. 11.
[21] Ibid., p. 56.

the importance of distinguishing between law and legal statutes, *Recht* and *Gesetz*.

A striking example is again Höhn: For him, the "new German understanding of law" aimed to overcome "the dichotomy between the idea of justice and statutory law" by connecting law and morality in a racially defined community. Law was thereby "lived and known as a concrete order of life."[22]

In Koellreutter's view, legal positivism failed precisely because it did not endorse a notion of law "that culminates in the demand for justice."[23] Justice remained tied to the community's understanding of right: Hence, only those norms were just "that have made it their mission to protect and develop the people's national order of life."[24] Although Koellreutter restricted the principles of justice to NS ideology, he did not shy away from claiming that "the National Socialist rule of law state is both a just state and an order state."[25]

What are we to make of the above passages? What should we infer from the fact that NS legal theory erased the line between law and morality?

In what follows, I outline the theoretical implications of the NS jurists' endorsement of the unification of law and morality and then flesh out the insights gained from their original texts. We should, as I argue, uphold the distinction between law and morality. Although morality should be separated from law, it might well function as a source for constitutive requirements of a legal system that complies with the rule of law.

8.2 The Disappearance of Internal Freedom

The unification of law and morality in NS legal theory must be understood in its political context. The Third Reich was a totalitarian state striving for complete control over its citizens. A core feature of political authoritarianism is a comprehensive value system that aims to regulate all aspects of social life. The totalitarian state thus permeates all societal

[22] Höhn, "*Volk, Staat und Recht*," p. 13.

[23] Koellreutter, *Deutsches Verfassungsrecht*, p. 55.

[24] Ibid., p. 11.

[25] Ibid., p. 56. Koellreutter first declares a normative standard to be justified in terms of NS ideology, and then he goes on to state the universal validity of this parameter. Proceeding this way is necessary to uphold coherency in his overall arguments, given that he criticized legal positivism of being relativist. Thus, he had to conceive of the internal NS point of view as the general criterion for "right" or "wrong."

spheres, restricting personal autonomy by literally defining "the good life" for its citizens.

The normative ambitions of National Socialism involved what John Rawls has called a fully comprehensive moral and political doctrine – that is a normative order that "covers all recognized values and virtues within one rather precisely articulated system."[26] A "fully comprehensive doctrine" is thus unreasonable in so far as it makes a fundamentalist claim to absolute truth – the state's view of what is true and good is beyond criticism. "(T)he religiously true, or the philosophically true," as Rawls writes, overrides "the politically reasonable."[27]

All this contrasts sharply with a liberal-democratic political system in which the state is constitutively neutral toward personal values, religious convictions, and worldviews. In the democratic state, citizens are free to pursue their individual conception of a well-lived life within an established framework of rights. There is no need for the state to intervene and constrict personal values as long as these value commitments respect the rights of others. Diverse individual conceptualizations of a good, well-lived life are the cornerstones of democratic society.

It is precisely this principle of tolerance that is discarded when a state moves toward totalitarianism.[28] In a totalitarian system, individual freedom succumbs to an all-encompassing normative ideological order. The

[26] Rawls, John, *Political Liberalism* (New York: Columbia University Press, 1993), p. 152, note 17; see also pp. 153–160. Due to its irrational elements and its negation of general human rights, National Socialism is an unreasonable doctrine; it does not belong to those political conceptions which Rawls connects with the "idea of public reason."

[27] See Rawls, John, *The Law of Peoples with "The Idea of Public Reason Revisited"* (Cambridge, MA and London: Harvard University Press, 1999), p. 178. Because of its encompassing conception of what is right and good, a political ideology such as National Socialism gets into conflict with the "idea of public reason," that is, the idea that, different value conceptions and religious doctrines notwithstanding, an overlapping consensus on the basic principles of the social order can still be reached. Some comprehensive doctrines are, in Rawls's view, reasonable in so far as they recognize basic individual rights (as examples he mentions Mill's and Kant's liberalism). Rawls criticizes that these liberal comprehensive doctrines do not sufficiently acknowledge pluralism, that is to say, the diversity of worldviews and religions).

[28] Of course, this neutrality toward different worldview conceptions does not allow for all possible ideological background conceptions, but only for those which do not flagrantly contradict a democratic constitution and its guarantee of fundamental personal rights and liberties. One of the National Socialists' strategies was to interpret the neutrality principle, which is constitutive for liberal-democratic states, as complete indifference toward all political ideas – a move enabling them then to claim that democracy is directionless.

NS state strategically developed a fully comprehensive moral doctrine in order to keep the people's community in line – indeed, NS law was steeped in this moral doctrine.

NS legal theorists' emphatic call for merging law with morality and ethical decency sought to expand the state's sphere of action. In eliminating the difference between legal and ethical norms, the NS state's authority encompassed not only the sphere of outer freedom but also the sphere of inner freedom – that is, of personal ethical values, convictions, and attitudes. The state now impinged upon a normative territory that is (ideally) foreclosed to it in a democratic system.

A look at philosophy reveals what is at stake in this normative shift. The Enlightenment philosophers, foremost Immanuel Kant, drew attention to the destructive effects of blurring the lines between law and morality. Kant sharply distinguished law from ethics, not least to delineate the limits of state authority. For him, the state had to regulate human relationships in outer space – that is, the sphere of external freedom. Although the state might require citizens to obey its statutes, by means of force, if necessary, the motives compelling individuals to comply with the state's legal norms were not the state's business. The domain of inner freedom – that is, the sphere of ethical dispositions, attitudes, and motives – was subject to self-legislation, not to state legislation.

Commitment to ethical values and principles is thus a matter of personal autonomy. While a person's obedience to the laws might be based on ethical considerations, such a form of ethical self-commitment is up to the person herself. Acting out of ethical motives concerns an individual's ethical self-perfection and ethical virtuousness and may not be enforced by the state.

The major differences between Kant's ethics and his philosophy of right reside in the roles played by *motivation* and *coercion* in the two normative spheres. Kant's ethics maintains a close connection between motivation and normativity. The point of his ethical philosophy is to reveal the principle of a good will – which for him is the categorical imperative. Acting morally, thus, is to act out of respect for the moral law, that is, to act out of duty. The morally good person makes the moral law – the categorical imperative – her or his principle of action by acting only on maxims that can be thought or willed as a universal law. Hence the inner motive (the incentive in

Kant's terminology) is decisive for the morality or immorality of an individual's ways of acting.[29]

Things work differently in the sphere of right. For Kant it is crucial *that* people follow laws and statutes that in the ideal case conform with the principle of right, which requires to respect the equal external freedom of others.[30] The motivational reasons *why* individuals comply with laws are legally irrelevant. Outer conformity is sufficient for the fulfillment of juridical obligations.[31]

Ethics and law also differ in relation to coercion. For Kant, ethics is a matter of assessing the maxims underlying individual actions. The relevant test is whether maxims can be universalized, or whether acting on them violates the human dignity of others. As subjective principles of action, maxims are associated with setting ends. Setting one's ends and directing one's incentives, Kant argues, is a matter of autonomous choice and internal freedom: No person or no state institution has the right to force anyone to adopt specific incentives and internal ends.

But regulating the outer relations of freedom requires enforcement – that is, persons have to be prevented from violating others' bodily integrity and external space. According to Kant, the principle of equal freedom as the guiding norm of the public sphere entails that citizens

[29] See Kant, Immanuel, "Groundwork of the Metaphysics of Morals (1785)," in Kant, *Practical Philosophy* (Cambridge: Cambridge University Press, 1996), pp. 37–108. Kant's ethics is an ethic of maxims: the point is to test one's maxims (= the subjective principles underlying our actions) in light of the categorical imperative. For testing our maxims two forms of the categorical imperative are crucial: the Formula of Universal Law (whether one's maxims can be universalized without a contradiction in thinking or a contradiction in willing) and the Formula of Humanity (whether acting on our maxims does not violate the principle that human beings should not be treated as mere means but as an end, that means as beings having absolute worth (dignity).

[30] Kant's Universal Principle of Right holds: "Any action is *right* if it can coexist with everyone's freedom in accordance with a universal law, or if on its maxim the freedom of choice of each can coexist with everyone's freedom in accordance with a universal law." Kant, Immanuel, "The Metaphysics of Morals (1797)," in Kant, *Practical Philosophy*, pp. 353–603, here: p. 387, MS AA 6:230 (italics in the original).

[31] As Kant famously expresses this distinction between ethical and legal lawgiving:

> All lawgiving can therefore be distinguished with respect to the incentive ... That lawgiving which makes an action a duty and also makes this duty the incentive is *ethical*. But that lawgiving which does not include the incentive of duty in the law and so admits an incentive other than the idea of duty itself is *juridical*. Kant, "The Metaphysics of Morals (1797)," p. 383. MS AA 06:218, 06:219 (italics in the original).

have rights whose protection justifies coercion.[32] Coercion is hence legitimately used when it is directed at securing the equal freedom of all.

In a condition of rightful mutual relations, however, individuals themselves may not use coercion. Rather, public rightfulness requires that coercion is exercised by proper public institutions. Kant, therefore, transfers the power of coercion to a commonly accepted authority – the state. To coercively remove a "*hindering of a hindrance to freedom*"[33] is the state's prerogative.

In Kant's view, reasonable individuals would consent to the state's coercive authority, given that they would otherwise face a condition of "external lawless freedom," a so-called state of nature.[34] The move to a civil and rightful condition is justified since each member of society would, if reasonable, agree to the normative principles of "lawful freedom." Kant's claim that a rightful condition is tied to "the idea of a will

[32] Right is, as Kant holds, "connected with an authorization to use coercion." Kant, "The Metaphysics of Morals (1797)," p. 388, MS AA 6:231. Although Kant claims that from the perspective of equality every individual "member of a commonwealth" has "coercive rights against every other," no individual has the right to turn that right into action since it is "the head of state, by whom alone any rightful coercion can be exercised." Kant, "On the common saying: That may be correct in theory, but it is of no use in practice," in Kant, *Practical Philosophy*, pp. 273–309, here: p. 292, TP AA 8:291. Only in a state of "externally lawless freedom" would an individual be "authorized to use coercion against someone who already, by his nature, threatens him with coercion." Kant, "The Metaphysics of Morals (1797)," p. 452, MS AA 6:307, 6:308. Kant claims that such a condition of "externally lawless freedom" has to be overcome since it is "a condition that is not rightful, that is, in which no one is assured of what is his against violence." Ibid., MS AA 6:308. According to Kant, we have to leave the state of nature and consent to "a rightful condition" of public justice that guarantees and protects rights. As Kant writes: "A rightful condition is that relation of human beings among one another that contains the condition under which alone everyone is able to *enjoy* his rights, and the formal condition under which this is possible in accordance with the idea of a will giving laws for everyone is called public justice." Kant, "The Metaphysics of Morals (1797)," p. 450, MS AA 6:306. For a discussion of the separation between Kant's ethics and Kant's philosophy of right see Ripstein, Arthur, *Force and Freedom. Kant's Legal and Political Philosophy* (Cambridge, MA and London: Harvard University Press, 2009), pp. 355–388; see also Pauer-Studer, Herlinde, "A Community of Rational Beings," in *Kant-Studien* 107, 1 (2016), pp. 125–159.

[33] Kant, "The Metaphysics of Morals (1797)," p. 388, MS AA 6:231 (italics in the original).

[34] The transition to a rightful condition requires, as Kant argues, a state based upon a constitution all citizens could accept, since it secures their rights: "Public *right is therefore a system of laws for a people, that is, a multitude of human beings, or for a multitude of peoples, which, because they act on one another, need a rightful condition under a will uniting them, a constitution (constitutio)*, so that they may enjoy what is laid down as right." Kant, "The Metaphysics of Morals (1797)," p. 455, MS AA 6:311 (italics in the original).

giving laws for everyone" indicates that individuals share the normative ground for obtaining a condition of public justice in which "everyone is able to *enjoy* his rights."[35] Kant thus outlines the public normative conditions for rightful interpersonal relations, that is, relations that respect others' rights.

Kant provides a careful justification of why we may not confound ethics and law. Respect for personal and public autonomy requires keeping the two normative spheres separate. Other than ethics, which is directed at an agent's inner freedom, law should preserve an agent's external freedom – his or her autonomy in the public sphere. Thus, the larger message we can derive from Kant's practical philosophy is that law should be an enabling condition for free agency. That is to say, in normatively proper circumstances, law is directed at preserving an agent's inner as well as outer freedom.[36]

The preceding philosophical digression allows us to perceive the fatal role of the moralization of law in NS legal theory. With their seemingly innocent call for the unification of morality and law, NS jurists supported a major normative transgression: the state's deliberate demand upon its subjects' ethical self-obligation. NS legal ideology required an individual not only to comply with legal norms, but to abide by the state's orders and legal rules out of inner ethical commitment. The strategy of dispensing with the state's neutrality toward an agents' motivating reasons for obeying law enhanced the state's possibilities of exercising political control.

The attempt to eliminate any distinction between morality and law strengthened the regime's power. An attitude of inner commitment and loyalty served the goals of the Führer state more than mere obedience of the laws. As historians have argued, the "ethical acceptance" of Führer orders was fundamental for the internal stability of the Third Reich in the

[35] Ibid., p. 450, MS AA 6:306 (italics in the original).

[36] That law is directed at agents' autonomy is the central assumption of Jürgen Habermas's discourse theory of law. Habermas assumes that from a general discourse principle, which is anchored in relations of mutual recognition, a principle of democracy can be derived. In the legal sphere, this principle of democracy is spelled out in terms of basic rights that secure an individual's private autonomy, but also (via basic rights of political participation) the person's public autonomy. See Habermas, Jürgen, *Between Facts and Norms. Contributions to a Discourse Theory of Law and Democracy*, transl. by Rehg, William (Cambridge and Malden: Polity Press, 1996), pp. 118–131. Note, however, that Habermas is keen to separate his account of law (which keeps law and morality apart) from Kant's practical philosophy because he assumes (I think wrongly) that Kant subordinates law to morality.

years before the war. In his fascinating study of the effects of the Nazi civil service law that went into effect on April 7, 1933, Hans Mommsen noted:

> State administration is a fundamental element of historical continuity, and – this also holds for the Third Reich – the precondition for any lasting intrinsic or extrinsic display of power. Without the work and dutifulness of an apparatus of loyal civil servants, the considerable initial successes of the Third Reich and its relatively high degree of inner stability could not be explained. Apart from the Reichswehr, civil servants were the strongest traditional and stabilizing factor of the Third Reich's power structure.[37]

Through its early legal measures in February and March 1933 (the Reichstag Fire Decree and the Enabling Act, respectively), the NS regime had already set harsh restrictions on outer freedom. But the Nazi's totalitarian ambitions went further than curtailing such civil rights and liberties as the freedom of movement and assembly, and the right to vote, to join political parties, and to run for office. They sought total power by also controlling the minds of their subjects. The price for belonging to an ethically superior communal unity was forfeiting one's freedom of conscience and allowing the regime access to one's innermost evaluative attitudes.

8.3 Is Nazi Law Invalid Law?

Let us return to Radbruch's damning judgment on legal positivism. Clearly, the reasoning we find in the Nazi original texts suggests that Radbruch somehow missed the point in trying to pin responsibility for the German jurists' pandering to the NS system on legal positivism. Not only did the NS thinkers vehemently criticize legal positivism, but when considered in abstraction from the political context the conditions they imposed on law – that is, that law and morality should form a unity, with justice internal to law – were similar to those articulated by postwar critics of positivism.

Our discussion in the preceding section indicates that legal theory should take seriously the distinction between inner and outer freedom and recognize that morality and law amount to separate normative spheres. To keep law and morality apart is, to repeat the point, crucial for agents' freedom and autonomy. Just because legal positivism propagates the separation of law and morality, it hardly deserves Radbruch's

[37] Mommsen, Hans, *Beamtentum im Dritten Reich. Mit ausgewählten Quellen zur nationalsozialistischen Beamtenpolitik* (Stuttgart: Deutsche Verlags-Anstalt, 1966), p. 13.

sharp rejection. Seen this way, H. L. A. Hart's critical remark that Radbruch "has only half digested the spiritual message of liberalism which he is seeking to convey to the legal profession" gets right to the point.[38]

Yet, a closer look at Radbruch's article "Statutory Lawlessness and Supra-Statutory Law" shows that the author was not focused on rejecting positivism's separability thesis *as such*. Rather, Radbruch was foremost concerned about the consequences it had for legal positivism's conception of legal validity. He suspected that positivism neither could nor did question the validity of the Nazi legal system because it had relegated justice to an external evaluative standard. His critique of the separation between law and morality was prompted by his concern that legal positivism might restrict us to saying only that the Nazi legal system was morally bad law. In essence, it was positivism's stance on the *validity* of Nazi law that provoked Radbruch's damning judgment.

Legal positivism indeed holds that wicked law is still law. As legal positivists repeatedly emphasize, the fact that a legal system fails to meet standards of morality does not entail that its statutes are legally invalid; it still has authority over its subjects. "(T)he validity of a positive legal order," Hans Kelsen wrote, "does not depend on its conformity with some moral system."[39] Similarly, Hart maintained that a law's evilness does not entail its invalidity. In his seminal article "Positivism and the Separation of Law and Morals," he cites approvingly John Austin's statement that "the existence of law is one thing; its merit or demerit is another."[40]

[38] Hart, H. L. A., "Positivism and the Separation of Law and Morals," in *Harvard Law Review* 71, 4 (1958), pp. 593–629, here p. 618.

[39] Kelsen, Hans, *Pure Theory of Law*, transl. by Knight, Max (Berkeley and Los Angeles: University of California Press, 1967), p. 67.

[40] Hart, "Positivism and the Separation of Law and Morals," p. 596. And in response to legal philosophers' claim that "if human laws conflicted with the fundamental principles of morality then they cease to be laws," Hart, not without irony, illustrates the power of positive law by the following quote from John Austin: " … the court of justice will demonstrate the inconclusiveness of my reasoning by hanging me up, in pursuance of the law of which I have impugned the validity." Ibid., p. 616; see also Hart, *The Concept of Law*, Ch. IX, pp. 185–212. Although Hart says that an intact legal system should have a minimal content of natural law, the minimum principles of natural law he mentions (human vulnerability, equal strength [as much as possible], limited degree of altruism, limited resources, limited knowledge and limited willpower) present facts of human nature which must be taken into consideration by an intact legal system but are not genuine moral principles. According to Hart's positivism, ethical considerations in jurisdiction are relevant particularly in hard cases, that is, if the law does not clearly stipulate a decision, or does not allow to infer a decision from legal statute but leaves it to

Kelsen's plea for keeping law and morality apart derives from his larger project of providing a scientific theory of law. The aim of the pure theory of law, he wrote, is "to answer the question what and how the law *is*, not how it ought to be."[41] In order to save law's impartiality, Kelsen argued that law should be free from such "alien elements" as ethics and politics.[42] Only in its "pure" form could law, in his view, live up to its role as a neutral arbiter of political and ideological strife.

Kelsen's descriptive approach to law influenced his account of legal validity. For Kelsen, a norm was legally valid within a particular legal system if and only if it had been generated in conformity with the system's established procedures for creating valid legal norms.[43] Legal validity was thus defined and assessed solely on legal grounds, independent of all criteria of political or moral correctness.

Although Kelsen was a staunch defender of the separation thesis, he still valued morality and justice: For him, they constituted external standards for assessing legal systems. Indeed, Kelsen deemed the separation of law and morality to be indispensable for the revision of morally deficient legal statutes and for legal reform generally. The demand that law should fulfill requirements of justice and morality only made sense, Kelsen emphasized, if law and justice were not conceptually intertwined.[44]

The puzzling thing about Kelsen's position is that he was a relativist for whom it was impossible to prove moral values or norms to be universally valid, let alone true. Such a claim, he argued, amounted to lingering religious dogma – in other words, a form of absolutism that Kelsen considered to be incompatible with democracy's tolerance of value diversity.[45]

the judge's discretion to decide the case. Kelsen equally supports this claim, however, the role of morality is more complicated in Kelsen's work as he openly supports moral subjectivism and relativism. See Kelsen, *Pure Theory of Law*, pp. 63–65.

41 Kelsen, *Pure Theory of Law*, p. 1 (italics in the original).

42 Ibid. Thus, Kelsen's plea for keeping law and morality apart was not primarily driven by Kantian-inspired reflections on the importance of preserving inner freedom vis-à-vis the state, but by Kelsen's commitment to a scientific description of law's working.

43 Kelsen, *Pure Theory of Law*, p. 198. "The norms of a legal order," Kelsen wrote, "must be created by a specific process." Ibid.

44 Ibid., p. 66.

45 In a nutshell, Kelsen's relativism amounts to the following argument:

a. To assess a norm and the value stated by the norm as objectively valid and therefore as good, the norm must emanate from a superhuman authority, that is, from God or from a natural order created by God.

This radical form of relativism, rather than his separation of law and morality, is the weak point of Kelsen's version of legal positivism. It also conflicts with his thesis that morality and justice constitute external standards for assessing legal systems and legal norms. Kelsen's relativism invited the sharp critique of NS legal thinkers who then decried democracy's lack of stable value foundations. What Kelsen failed to see is that relativism is anything but a viable metaethical stance if one wants to reject such moralized ideologies as National Socialism.

Radbruch's postwar distance to positivism might have been fueled by the tight bond between positivism and relativism. Of course, it is not necessary to link legal positivism to relativism and subjectivism. Judging moral standards as right or wrong commits one neither to value absolutism nor to a platonic form of value realism, as Kelsen assumed. But Kelsen's thesis that liberal democracy's value pluralism entailed relativism had shaped democratic legal thinking in the Weimar years.[46]

b. The object of a scientific theory of value are only norms (and the values constituted by these norms) enacted by a human will.
c. Therefore: It is not possible to assess the norms and values enacted by a human will to be objectively valid (if we operate in the framework of a scientific theory of value).

Kelsen, however, offers no argument for the first premise. The dichotomy – that values are absolute and based on the will of God or they are manmade, based on human willing and therefore relative – is just presupposed. Kelsen rules out by definition that there might be norms and values that are the result of human willing and construction and that can be justified by rational deliberation and argument as objectively, that is, intersubjectively, valid. Though Kelsen was an antagonist of natural law, especially religion-based natural law, he was obviously still in the grip of religious thinking when it came to explaining the objectivity of values. Kelsen's relativism is thoroughgoing. We are of course familiar with conflicting value judgments: What A judges to be good, B can claim to be bad. A and B can also hold conflicting moral norms to be valid: A maintains that norm x is valid; B claims that norm not-x is valid. Kelsen's relativism, however, is not restricted to admitting that individuals might entertain different value judgments and moral norms, and that therefore conflicts of value among individuals might occur. Kelsen thinks it impossible to rationally resolve the question which of two conflicting norms is the correct one, as the following passage shows: "For example, a norm could be valid forbidding to commit suicide or to lie under all circumstances, and another norm could be valid permitting or even commanding suicide or lies under certain circumstances, yet it would be impossible to prove rationally that only one of these two norms, but not the other, is the truly valid one." Kelsen, *Pure Theory of Law*, p. 18. See also Pauer-Studer, Herlinde, "Kelsen's Legal Positivism and the Challenge of Nazi Law," in Galavotti, Maria Carla; Nemeth, Elisabeth; Stadler, Friedrich (eds.), *European Philosophy of Science – Philosophy of Science in Europe and the Viennese Heritage* (Dordrecht: Springer, 2014), pp. 223–240.

46 In the first edition of *Vom Wesen und Wert der Demokratie* (1920), Kelsen claimed that "relativism is the worldview presupposed by the idea of democracy." Kelsen, Hans, *Vom*

And while Radbruch himself had endorsed a form of relativism during Weimar democracy, his experience with National Socialism made him understand justice as an objective standard that could not be relativized to a particular worldview or a specific practical-political standpoint. In Radbruch's view, the internal connection between law and justice was indispensable for correcting the Nazi misuse of law.

In my view, Radbruch's postwar critique of legal positivism confounded two separate issues: the de facto validity of legal statutes and norms relative to a particular legal system, and, how to assess a legal system's moral worth, that is, it's moral appropriateness in terms of its conformity with justice and the rule of law. Let me explain.

Important to notice is that Radbruch's objections to positivism were also motivated by a specific problem in postwar Germany – namely, the treatment of court cases in which those accused of having committed monstrous deeds in the Nazi era asserted that their actions had been legal under the NS regime. Legal positivism, Radbruch argued, did not offer the means for indicting odious actions under Nazi rule, including reporting persons to the Nazi authorities for criticizing the regime.

Radbruch's article "Statutory Lawlessness and Supra-Statutory Law" opens with just such a case: Puttfarken, a clerk in the justice department, had reported the merchant Göttig to Nazi authorities for having written on the wall of a public restroom that Hitler was a mass murderer and responsible for the war. Göttig was sentenced to death and executed by the Nazis. After the war, Puttfarken was tried by a court in Thuringen (the Russian zone) and sentenced to life in prison for being an accomplice to murder.

From this case, Radbruch concluded that justice superseded positive law. Rather than simply holding that a legal statute lost its validity for being unjust, Radbruch explained that in the interest of legal certainty, positive legislation preceded justice, "unless the conflict between statute and justice reaches such an intolerable degree that the statute, as 'flawed law' must yield to justice."[47] Based upon this reasoning, the so-called

Wesen und Wert der Demokratie (Tübingen: J.C.B. Mohr [Paul Siebeck], 1920), p. 36. Kelsen repeated that point in the book's second edition (1929).

47 Radbruch, "Statutory Lawlessness and Supra-Statutory Law," p. 7. Note also Radbruch's further argument: "Where there is not even an attempt at justice, where equality, the core of justice, is deliberately betrayed in the issuance of positive law, then the statute is not merely 'flawed law', it lacks completely the very nature of law. For law, including positive law, cannot be otherwise defined than a system and an institution whose very meaning is to serve justice. Measured by this standard, whole portions of National Socialist law never

"Radbruch Formula," Radbruch suggested that such informer cases could only be decided by declaring National Socialist law to be invalid law. Yet, Radbruch need not have gone that far. Informers could still be judged guilty without declaring whole portions of Nazi law to be invalid or maintaining that certain Nazi statutes were not legal. Indeed, in his own article on the Puttfarken case, Radbruch quoted extensively to this effect from the court's Chief Public Prosecutor, Dr. Friedrich Kuschnitzki: "The defendant's contention that his belief in National Socialism had led him to inform on Göttig is legally insignificant. Whatever one's own political convictions, there is no legal obligation to denounce anyone. Even during the Hitler years, no such legal obligation existed."[48] The Chief Public Prosecutor's reasoning confirms that the Radbruch Formula – that Nazi Law was invalid and must give way to justice – did not factor into establishing why he thought the defendant guilty of accessory to murder.[49] The Chief Public Prosecutor relied on the extant positive laws, which did not obligate citizens to commit such odious acts as reporting persons to the authorities. The Chief Prosecutor's argument also undermines the familiar defense line in informer cases.

Typically, accused informers maintained that Nazi laws had compelled them to report persons who had mocked, criticized, or verbally attacked the NS regime. Postwar prosecutors, however, argued that the system had not legally forced them to do so; their acts exceeded what was legally required and were usually carried out for malicious personal reasons.[50]

attained the dignity of valid law." Ibid. What Radbruch should have said is that large parts of Nazi law never attained the dignity of the rule of law, or of morally non-odious law.

48 Radbruch, "Statutory Lawlessness and Supra-Statutory Law," p. 2.

49 Ibid., p. 2.

50 This also holds for the famous Grudge Informer Case discussed by Hart in "Positivism and the Separation of Law and Morals," pp. 618–621. During the war, a woman had reported her husband to the local Nazi authorities for having made disrespectful remarks about Hitler and Hitler's war. The remarks were made in private. The husband was sentenced to death, but eventually sent to the Eastern front. In 1949, the woman was indicted by a West German court though she claimed that what she had done was lawful at the time. The court of appeal upheld the judgment. Hart presents the case as if the court had simply sentenced the woman because what she had done "was contrary to the sound conscience and sense of justice of all decent human beings." Hart, "Positivism and the Separation of Law and Morals," p. 619. Hart, however, misread the Grudge Informer Case. In an illuminating article on the case, David Dyzenhaus has shown that the court's major argument for indicting the woman was that the laws of the time had in no way obligated the woman to report on her husband – which exactly mirrors the judgment of the Chief Public Prosecutor in the Puttfarken case. See Dyzenhaus, David, "The Grudge Informer Case Revisited," in *New York University Law Review* 83 (2008), pp. 1000–1034.

Given the political circumstances in Nazi Germany, the defendants knew well that defeatism or accusing the Führer of mass murder would lead to severe punishment, if not the death sentence.

Postwar courts handling informer cases often appealed to pre-Nazi era legal statutes that were still valid during Nazi rule such as the German Penal Code of 1871. The postwar courts' sentences were on safer legal ground if they were based on these preexisting statutes rather than dependent upon arguments against the validity of Nazi law. In other words, the courts often tried to evade the high moral ground of the Radbruch Formula – that is, that in grave conflicts between justice and positive law, the latter had to give way to justice.

However, there was another dimension to postwar court sentences highlighted in Radbruch's article. The postwar courts were often faced with the task to correct former injustices and communicate why they, but not the NS jurisdiction, could legitimately claim to exercise justice. This required courts to uncover and name the distortions in the NS legal system. Again, the Chief Public Prosecutor's reasoning in the Puttfarken case is illuminating:

> The decisive question is whether the defendant acted in the interest of the administration of justice, a question presupposing that the judicial system is in a position to administer justice. *Fidelity to statutes, a striving toward justness, legal certainty – these are the requirements of a judicial system.* And all three are lacking in the politicized judicial system of the Hitler regime.[51]

In this passage, the prosecutor specifies prerequisites for a proper legal system which, generally speaking, constitute provisions for the rule of law. Thus the rule of law entails that subjects understand what the law requires from them. They must also have reason to expect that courts do not sentence arbitrarily, that they respect the principle of equality before the law, and that they apply the given law impartially. Only if a legal framework does not ignore these conditions, but rather strives to live up to them, can those making use of it claim to have acted in the name of justice.

However, to argue that a legal system does not fulfill basic requirements of the rule of law is different from arguing that it is not valid law – at least, that is, if "validity of law" refers to positive *legal* validity, that is, validity in the sense of being a statute of positively given law that is actually in force. Of course, we might understand "validity of law" in

[51] Radbruch, "Statutory Lawlessness and Supra-Statutory Law," p. 2 (italics in the original).

a *moral* sense – that is, of meeting standards of justice and morality. But this meaning is better expressed by the term "legitimacy" than by "legal validity." *Legal* validity depends upon compliance with the defined procedures of law-creation, not on conformity with moral standards. Conflicts with justice, even grave ones, do not invalidate positive law. Wicked legal systems still preserve de facto authority over their subjects.

Still, a larger question looms: How can understanding what was *legally* wrong in the Nazi legal system enable us to prevent the law from being instrumentalized by a criminal political regime? In what follows, I will address this question by outlining an account of constitutive conditions of a rule-of-law system that combines insights from legal positivism and its opponents, and that does not commit us to side with one of those traditions.

8.4 Conditions of the Rule of Law

Previously, I have defended a core assumption of legal positivism: the separation of law from morality. The defense rested on a normative argument:[52] to keep law and morality apart is crucial for preserving individuals' autonomy. Yet one might further question whether the dreadful experiences with Nazi law compel us to assume more of a connection between law and morality as just claiming them to be distinct normative spheres. Does not the law's misuse in the Third Reich make us think more deeply about the role of justice in an appropriate legal system?

[52] Jeremy Waldron has suggested to categorize views holding that "separability of law and morality, or this separability of legal judgment and moral judgment, is a good thing, perhaps even indispensable (from a moral, social, or political point of view) and certainly something to be valued and encouraged" as forms of normative positivism. See Waldron, Jeremy, "Normative (or Ethical) Positivism," in Coleman, Jules (ed.), *Hart's Postscript. Essays on the Postscript to the* Concept of Law (Oxford: Oxford University Press, 2001), pp. 411–433, here: p. 411. It is, however, crucial to spell out (that is, provide the normative reasons for) why the separation is valuable. This is why I make the connection to law's autonomy-preserving function.

Interestingly enough, already Franz Neumann provided a normative argument for the separation of law and morality, noting that "an identity of law and morality can be maintained only in a fully homogenous society." And he adds that in a society allowing for differences in moral convictions an identity of law and morality "is merely a way of terrorizing man's conscience." Neumann, Franz, *Behemoth. The Structure and Practice of National Socialism, 1933–1944*, with an introd. by Hayes, Peter (Chicago: Ivan R. Dee, 2009), p. 444.

Indeed, the separability thesis does not absolve us from reflecting further upon the relationship between law, morality, and justice, even if some legal positivists have failed to flesh out those connections. For example, in the 1967 English edition of his *Pure Theory of Law*, Hans Kelsen wrote:

> The legal order of totalitarian states authorizes their governments to confine in concentration camps persons whose opinions, religion, or race they do not like; to force them to perform any kind of labor; even to kill them. While such measures may be violently condemned from a moral standpoint, they cannot be considered as taking place outside the legal order of these states.[53]

More than two decades after the war, Kelsen had little more to say about law in the Nazi era other than reaffirming that Nazi legal orders and statutes had been positive law. Similarly, Hart maintained that it "is in no sense a necessary truth that laws reproduce or satisfy certain demands of morality, though in fact they often have done so."[54] Undeniable as these points are, we should be able to say more about the NS legal system than that it was morally odious.

Opponents of legal positivism urge us to reflect on the *legal* failures of Nazi law. In such a legal framework, David Dyzenhaus reminds us, something "goes wrong not only morally speaking, but also . . . legally speaking."[55]

NS law indeed displayed grave structural deficiencies – failures connected to the regime's worst crimes. Apart from politically motivated retroactive legislation, the greatest havoc was wreaked by the secretive nature of the Führer's orders (both verbal and in the form of letters). For example, there was no written order, let alone a legal statute, for the murder of the Jews.[56] And the "legal foundation" of the National Socialists' euthanasia program, which claimed an estimated 70,000 victims, was an informal letter from Hitler to the head of the Führer Chancellery, Philipp Bouhler, and his personal physician, Karl Brandt. Dated September 1, 1939, the missive empowered them to inform

53 Kelsen, *Pure Theory of Law*, p. 40.

54 Hart, *The Concept of Law*, pp. 185–186.

55 Dyzenhaus, David, "Legality without the Rule of Law? Scott Shapiro on Wicked Legal Systems," in *Canadian Journal of Law and Jurisprudence* 25, 1 (2012), pp. 183–200, here: p. 184. On the same line, John Finnis has argued that legal systems which violate basic demands of morality and justice cannot qualify to be genuine law, but are, in his words, "peripheral" and "watered-down versions" of the central cases of law. Finnis, John, *Natural Law and Natural Rights* (Oxford: Oxford University Press, 2011), p. 11.

56 See Longerich, Peter, *The Unwritten Order. Hitler's Role in the Final Solution* (Stroud: Tempus, 2003).

"selected physicians" that "in all probability incurably ill people may be granted mercy death after the most scrupulous judgment of their state of illness."[57]

The Nazis' racial laws, the so-called Nuremberg laws enacted on September 15, 1935, were officially published in the *Reichsgesetzblatt*. Yet the regime did not dare to issue orders for euthanasia or the extermination of the Jews and other ethnic groups (Roma and Sinti) in the form of a legal statute, let alone to publicize those measures in the *Reichsgesetzblatt*. Secrecy is one of the main instruments of a totalitarian system's exercise of power and political criminality. The mere requirement to promulgate Führer orders would have prevented the worst excesses of the Nazi regime.[58]

This argument can be generalized thus: A legal system that recognizes and aims to meet normative conditions such as publicity, transparency, understandability, reliability, predictability, consistency, and avoidance of arbitrary retroactive legislation, does not lend itself to totalitarian power. At the purely legal level, the horrendous crimes of the Third Reich seem impossible when a legal system aligns itself with those requirements.

The aforementioned normative conditions are basically those principles that Lon L. Fuller developed in his story of the well-meaning sovereign (Rex) who confused citizens with his erratic legislation.[59] Fuller suggested that legal rules and norms should be general and made known to the affected subjects (promulgation). Moreover, they should be prospective rather than retroactive, clear and understandable, and free from contradictions. In short, legal rules and norms should not require that which is impossible; they should not be constantly changed; and there should be congruence between enacted law and official actions.

Fuller called those principles which defined a proper form of legislation the "inner morality of law."[60] His terminology and his

[57] Hitler, Adolf, "Schreiben an Reichsleiter Bouhler und Dr. med. Brandt, Berlin 1.9. 1939," Document NS-630; www.ns-archiv.de/medizin/euthanasie/ befehl.php.

[58] Some NS legal theorists even held that Führer speeches amounted to law. See Chapter 3.6 of this book.

[59] See Fuller, Lon L., *The Morality of Law*, rev. ed. (New Haven and London: Yale University Press, 1969), pp. 39–41.

[60] Ibid. Fuller sometimes called those conditions "principles of legality," which is potentially misleading. Fuller, *The Morality of Law*, pp. 197, 200. In order to avoid confusion one has to keep in mind that Fuller's notion of "legality" does not refer to given positive law; it is not a descriptive term, but a normative term. When Fuller talks of "principles of legality," he refers to conditions a legal system ought to meet (morally speaking), not to criteria for determining whether a norm or statute is positive law. In order to avoid misunderstanding,

understanding of the outlined principles thus blurred the line between law and morality in ways that I have criticized. He came close to a unification of law and morality which I think problematic.

Fuller's conditions for appropriate legal systems – publicity, transparency, understandability, reliability, predictability, consistency/coherence, and freedom from arbitrary retroactive legislation – are neither full-fledged moral principles nor inner moral elements of the law. Rather, they constitute normative requirements that stand between law and morality. As neither legal nor moral principles, they are best seen as constitutive conditions of a legal system that does not openly violate the rule of law. These conditions result from translating moral insights (insights about the consequences of law in the hands of erratic, let alone tyrannical, sovereigns) into normative requirements of a legal system that complies with the rule of law. Such a legal order might come closer to the ideal of a morally proper legal system. Requirements of the rule of law link law and morality without erasing the distinction between those normative spheres.

How should we understand this? Instead of striving for an inner unity of law and morality that might be open to ideology-driven moralization, it is preferable to convert available moral insights about the malfunctioning of legal systems into normative requirements that function as constitutive conditions of a formally intact legal system (that is, one that does not openly violate the rule of law). Such insights into the conditions of an intact legal system, one that is focused on agent autonomy, can be gained by reflecting on the likely consequences when law serves an authoritarian or totalitarian regime to control and suppress individuals.

Fuller's parable of legislator Rex is illustrative. However, real-world historical cases like Nazi rule can evidently inform us of the actual consequences when a legal system serves as a mere instrument of political ideology and does not meet the aforementioned conditions of publicity, transparency, understandability, reliability, predictability, consistency, coherence, and freedom from arbitrary retroactive legislation.

Fuller paid dearly for reading those principles as the inner morality of law. Although he had an accurate understanding of what went wrong in

I chose to name those principles "conditions of the rule of law." "Rule of law" just refers to certain features (virtues) a legal system ought to have. Note that compliance with the rule of law is, as Joseph Raz emphasizes, a "matter of degree." See Raz, Joseph, "The Rule of Law and its Virtue," in Raz, Joseph, *The Authority of Law. Essays on Law and Morality* 2nd ed. (Oxford: Oxford University Press, 2009), pp. 210–229, here: p. 222.

the Nazi legal system, Fuller's theoretical contributions were not well received by legal theorists, who felt that they erased the line between law and morality. Hart, for whom the separation thesis was indispensable, argued that "the classification" of Fuller's principles as "a form of morality breeds confusion."[61] He therefore reduced Fuller's requirements to mere instrumental rules "reached solely through a realistic consideration of what is necessary for the efficient execution of the purpose of guiding human conduct by rules."[62] But Hart's critical reading of Fuller's conditions misjudged their normative significance, which becomes apparent as soon as we read them as constitutive conditions of a rule-of-law system, that is, a legal system oriented toward agents' autonomy.[63]

The Nazi legal system amounted to a purely hierarchical exercise of force. Fuller called it "a one-way projection of authority, emanating from an authorized source and imposing itself on the citizen."[64] Nazi law was not merely about control – it used brutal terror on its subjects in the process. The NS state, particularly with respect to Jews, political opponents, and handicapped persons, dispensed with all criteria of a rule-of-law system. Nazi Germany granted one individual unlimited power, abolished basic liberties and rights, willfully imprisoned and killed dissidents, and sought to eliminate whole groups of people. And the law adapted to this dictatorial political system.

Law that respects agents' inner and outer freedom is structured differently. Instead of brute force "imposing itself upon citizens," such law amounts to a social practice that seeks to protect agents' autonomy

[61] Hart, H. L. A., "Review of *The Morality of Law by Lon L. Fuller*" in *Harvard Law Review* 78, 6 (1965), pp. 1281–1296, here: p. 1284.

[62] Ibid.

[63] In her excellent study of Fuller's legal philosophy, Kristen Rundle argues that Fuller's legal theory was tied to promote legal subjects' "capacity for agency" (agency in the sense of being a self-determined "bearer of dignity"), thus granting them the status of citizen "as an active participant in the legal order." See Rundle, Kristen, *Forms Liberate. Reclaiming the Jurisprudence of Lon L. Fuller* (Oxford and Portland, Oregon: Hart Publishing Company, 2012), pp. 8, 100. Note the Kantian ring in Rundle's interpretation of Fuller. Scott Shapiro also suggests to read Fuller's requirements as conditions of the rule of law. However, for Shapiro the central value of the rule of law consists in enabling social planning and planning agency (Shapiro builds his account on Michael Bratman's conception of planning agency), whereas the approach I defend focuses on a normatively richer conception of agential autonomy than mere planning agency. See Shapiro, Scott J., *Legality* (Cambridge, MA and London: Harvard University Press, 2011), pp. 392–400. Shapiro is very sensitive to the problem that ideological moralization might undermine law's capacity to enable social planning, and he therefore insists on a strict separation of law and morality. Ibid., pp. 273–277.

[64] Fuller, "The Morality of Law," p. 192.

by setting regulative rules for coordination, cooperation, and conflict solving, thus normatively structuring relations between subjects. Law in this sense embodies the means to create regulative rules of social interaction.

As Hart famously argued, law as social practice is a system of primary and secondary rules. Primary rules not only tell us what do to, they enable us to do certain things (for example, making contracts). Secondary rules define how to invent primary rules. But social practices need a constitutive standard that both informs us of the practice's aim and enables us to assess what counts as compliance with the practice rules, what merely violates said rules, and what amounts to a complete dismissal of the practice.[65] And here is where we discover the proper role of justice as the constitutive aim or standard for a rule-of-law system. Justice is a parameter for assessing good or bad legal practice.

In a legal context, the concept of justice foremost comprises impartiality, equality before the law, due process, fair procedures, and exclusion of legally irrelevant factors (such as the religious or political views of defendants, their ethnic backgrounds, etc.). Justice thus is an additional constitutive element to the aforementioned conditions of a rule-of-law system (publicity, generality, clarity, coherence, etc.).

For justice to be in place, a legal system must also enhance and promote rightful conditions, rather than serve political suppression, and, even, crime. Law that is embedded in a rightful state order is shaped by different constitutive conditions than law in a totalitarian state order.

Law should enhance agential freedom by making possible future-oriented planning, social coordination, and cooperation. A legal system should create rules and regulations for handling social conflicts nonviolently, and preferably by reasonable deliberation and negotiation. Overall, law should secure agents' internal and external freedom. In order to achieve these aims, law should avoid becoming contested moral and ideological ground.

The NS legal system provides a striking historical example of how law can completely fail to meet these requirements. Law turned into an instrument of political despotism, and the misuse was covered up by an ideological moralization of law.

[65] See Pauer-Studer, Herlinde, "Complicity and Conditions of Agency," in *Journal of Applied Philosophy* 35, 4 (2018), pp. 644–660, here: pp. 648–650.

8.5 Concluding Remarks

What conclusions should we draw from our analysis of Nazi law? One result is certainly that the distortions of Nazi law pose a challenge to legal philosophy that requires us to move beyond the legal positivism and natural law theory divide.

At first sight it may appear that the NS jurists' understanding of law aligned with natural law theory. Proponents of a natural law position have strongly defended the tight connection between law and morality, and they have vigorously argued that justice and morality are integral to law. All of this was shared by NS theorists, as our examination of the original texts confirms. Of course, natural law theorists were and are a long way from promulgating a conception of law that could turn it into a mere means of a totalitarian regime. When they stressed the significance of a tight connection between law and morality, they did so precisely to prevent an ideological abuse of law.

However, as our discussion sought to show, all attempts at diminishing, let alone erasing the line between morality and law should be met with skepticism, if not outright rejection, since they fail to recognize that separating these normative spheres is crucial for securing agential freedom. Since morality and law have different regulatory tasks, they follow different normative principles. Simply pursuing a congruence of law and morality is inappropriate for correcting such distortions as those found in the NS legal system.

Radbruch's postwar critique of legal positivism has often been interpreted as a victory of natural law over legal positivism. This is implausible. Positivism is right that wicked legal systems still preserve their authority and that their statutes remain legally valid and in force. But natural law theorists are also right to remind us that there is more to say about the connections between justice, morality, and law than just asserting that law may be morally bad and unjust.

The account I have offered, namely to read justice as a constitutive aim and standard of a rule-of-law legal system, along with further conditions such as generality, promulgation, clarity, and reliability, is in direct response to Radbruch's assertion that the connection between justice and law is important for preventing the deterioration of a legal system. The suggested understanding of the relation between law and morality – via constitutive conditions of a rule of law system – pays tribute to legal positivism's claim that law and morality amount to distinct normative spheres, while also taking seriously natural law theorists' arguments.

Let us then return to this chapter's core question: What follows from the moralization of law in National Socialism? What is implied by the fact that the NS theoreticians endorsed the unification of law and morality?

One possible answer is that nothing profound follows other than recognition that the NS theoreticians had an ideologically perverted idea of morality. In other words, if the moralization of law rests on the "correct," or "true," morality, then the ideological misuse of law as under Nazi rule will not occur.

Besides ignoring our extended justification for why morality and law should be treated as distinct normative spheres, this suggestion ignores the fact that societies do not always have in view what moral philosophy arrogantly considers "true morality" – that is, clearly recognizable and a priori detectable moral principles. Morality, if it claims to be relevant for our social behavior and intertwined with our interactions, cannot be limited to a few purely abstract formulas and rules determined to be a priori true. Moral truths (insofar as we are speaking of those at all), as well as moral rules and principles, require that their meaning be interpreted via social practices and contexts. And in a context like the NS state, it is precisely at this level where the distortion, indeed perversion, of the moral takes place.[66]

A particular danger is the close proximity of the normative categories of a politically deformed understanding of morality to those of an ideology-free morality. We thus find virtues as honesty, truthfulness, self-obligation, and immunity to corruption not only in our ordinary understanding of morality, but also in the NS context. Taken as such, abstracted from their social and political embeddedness, these moral concepts are pure schemata. This complicates efforts to distinguish between an intact morality and a morality that has been perverted. Indeed, the differences between a viable form of morality and a politically deformed one can only be identified by taking into account how these moral formulas and concepts are interpreted and made use of in a particular social and political context.

The NS regime developed its own interpretation of moral principles, rules, and virtues. In particular, ideology-driven organizations of the NS state such as the SS were permeated with perverted morality. Heinrich Himmler propagated his own reading of virtues of "honesty and

[66] See Pauer-Studer, Herlinde and Velleman, J. David, "Distortions of Normativity," in *Ethical Theory and Moral Practice* 14, 3 (2011), pp. 329–356; Pauer-Studer, Herlinde, "Law and Morality under Evil Conditions. The Case of SS Judge Konrad Morgen," in *Jurisprudence* 3, 2 (2012), pp. 367–390.

truthfulness," of "bravery, loyalty, and courage," and of how the principles of the "sanctity of property" and the "rules of manly discipline" were to be understood and implemented politically.[67]

Law should be a means for coping with social and moral conflicts rather than a crushing moral problem itself. The ideological misuse of morality in the Nazi legal system suggests that morality might best fulfill its role as a critical parameter for assessing a legal system when it acts as a source for defining the constitutive conditions of the rule of law. And compliance with the requirements of the rule of law defines an intact legal order.

[67] See Himmler, Heinrich, "Rede vor den Reichs- und Gauleitern in Posen am 6.10.1943," in *Heinrich Himmler Geheimreden 1933 bis 1945*, ed. by Smith, Bradley and Peterson, Agnes F. (Frankfurt am Main, Berlin, Wien: Propyläen, 1974), pp. 162–183. See also Gross, Raphael, *Anständig Geblieben. Nationalsozialistische Moral* (Frankfurt am Main: S. Fischer, 2010). See also the contributions by Wolfgang Bialas; Werner Konitzer; Ernst Tugendhat and Rolf Zimmermann in Konitzer, Werner and Gross, Raphael (eds), *Moralität der Bösen. Ethik und nationalsozialistische Verbrechen* (Frankfurt/M., New York: Campus, 2009).

BIOGRAPHICAL NOTES

Erich Becker (1906–1981): political engagement for National Socialism; 1941 Professor at the Reich University Posen.

Werner Best (1903–1989): since 1929 active in the National Socialist movement; 1931 entry into the SS; professional employment in the Security Service (*Sicherheitsdienst*, SD); 1935 Legal Counsel of the Gestapo; 1939 assigned to the Reich Security Main Office (*Reichssicherheitshauptamt*, RSHA); 1940 Best left the RSHA over conflicts with Reinhard Heydrich. 1940–1942 service in the German military administration in occupied France; 1942–1945 Reich Commissioner (*Reichsbevollmächtigter*) for occupied Denmark. 1948 trial in Denmark (Best was first sentenced to death, but then released from prison).

Karl August Eckhardt (1901–1979): 1931 entry into the NSDAP and SA; 1933 entry into the SS. 1933 Professor at the University of Kiel; 1934 Consultant in the Reich Ministry of Science (in charge of university professorship appointments); 1936 Professor at the University of Berlin; 1937 Professor for German Legal History at the University Bonn. 1936–1938 editor of the Journal *Deutsche Rechtswissenschaft*.

Manfred Fauser (1906–1981): NS jurist, official in the Wurttemberg State Ministry, 1937–1945 official in the Reich Ministry of the Interior.

Ernst Forsthoff (1902–1974): student of Carl Schmitt, 1933 Professor for Public Law in Frankfurt am Main; 1935 Professor in Hamburg, 1936 Professor in Königsberg, 1941 Professor in Vienna; 1943 Professor in Heidelberg; 1952–1967 Professor in Heidelberg.

Hans Frank (1900–1946): 1923 member of the NSDAP and member of the SA; 1928 Founder of the Association of German Jurists; Head of the Legal Department of the NSDAP. 1934–1942 President of the Academy for German Law. 1939 General Gouverneur of occupied Poland (the so-called General Gouvernement). 1945–46 Defendant at the International Military Tribunal in Nuremberg (sentenced to death and executed in October 1946).

Roland Freisler (1893–1945): 1925 member of the NSDAP; 1934 State Secretary in the Reich Ministry of Justice; 1942–1945 President of the People's Court. Freisler was notorious for his harsh sentences (for instance, against members of the "White Rose", a non-violent student resistance group, and against officers involved in the Stauffenberg plot against Hitler on July 20, 1944). Freisler was killed in a bomb raid on Berlin in February 1945.

Max Robert Gerstenhauer (1873–1940): ministry official in Thuringen, from 1921 until 1940 he was engaged in the *Deutschbund*, an anti-semitic *völkisch* association. Due to Gerstenhauer's influence, from 1930 the members of the Deutschbund were obligated to work together with the NSDAP.

Wenzel von Gleispach (1876–1944): Austrian criminal law expert. 1907 Professor in Prague; 1915 Professor in Vienna; 1934 Professor for Criminal Law in Berlin and Director of the Criminalist Institute in Berlin. Member of the Academy for German Law, member of the Official Commission for Criminal Law Reform (headed by Justice Minister Franz Gürtner).

Reinhard Höhn (1904–2000): 1933 entry into the NSDAP and the SS; 1935 Associate Professor for Constitutional Law in Heidelberg and Berlin; 1939 Professor at the University Berlin. From 1936 Deputy Head of the Committee for Police Law at the Academy for German Law. 1939 Department Head in the Reich Security Main Office. (*Reichssicherheitshauptamt*). 1956 Head of the Academy for Managers in Bad Harzburg.

Ernst Rudolf Huber (1903–1990): student of Carl Schmitt; 1926 Doctorate, 1931 Habilitation in Economic Administrative Law; 1933 Professor in Kiel; 1937 Professor in Leipzig and from 1941–1944 Professor in Strasbourg. With Georg Dahm, Karl Larenz, Friedrich Schaffstein, and Franz Wieacker Huber formed the so-called *Kieler Schule*, a group of National Socialist professors at the University of Kiel. After the war Huber was banned from university teaching until 1956. 1957 Professor for Social Science in Wilhelmshaven and then at the University of Göttingen. Between 1957 and 1990 Huber wrote an eight-volume compendium on German Constitutional Law (*Deutsche Verfassungsgeschichte*).

Otto Koellreutter (1883–1972): constitutional law expert; 1921 Professor at the University Jena; 1933 entry into the NSDAP; 1933

Professor at the University of Munich and member of the Academy for German Law. After the war, Koellreutter was in the course of de-Nazification first classified as Lesser Offender. In 1947 he was taken in custody for thirteen months because of his Nazi past. In 1949 he was forced to retire from the University; 1952 official retirement as emeritus professor.

Karl Larenz (1903–1993): expert in civil law and philosophy of law. From 1933 he was teaching at the University of Kiel; 1935 Professor for Legal Philosophy at Kiel University. 1937 membership in the NSDAP. From 1948 Larenz taught again in Kiel; in 1960 he became Professor at the University of Munich.

Konrad Morgen (1909–1982): jurist and judge; 1933 entry into the NSDAP and the SS. From January 1941 until Mai 1942 he was SS Judge at the SS and Police Court in Kraków. May 1942, demotion by Himmler; in December 1942 Morgen was sent to the Eastern front. Reordered by Himmler in May 1943; assignment to investigate corruption in the concentration camp Buchenwald. Morgen's investigations resulted in an SS trial in Weimar (September 1944) against the former commandant of Buchenwald, Karl Otto Koch, and the camp physician Waldemar Hoven. 1945–1948, Morgen was in American custody. He testified in several postwar trials (also in the Auschwitz trial in Frankfurt am Main in 1964).

Falk Ruttke (1894–1955): jurist; 1932 entry into the NSDAP and 1933 entry into the SS. Member of the Expert Council for Population and Racial Politics at the Reich Interior Ministry. 1935 Lecturer for racial law at the University Berlin; 1940 special assignment for strengthening Germanness in the Warthegau; 1942 Professor at the University of Jena. Internment from 1945–1948.

Rolf Schiedermair (1909–1991): jurist and official; member of the NSDAP and the SS; expert for racial questions in the Reich Ministry of Interior. He co-authored with Stuckart a commentary on racial legislation, *Rassen- und Erbpflege in der Gesetzgebung des Dritten Reiches* (five editions from 1938–1944).

Ulrich Scheuner (1903–1981): 1933 Professor for Public Law in Jena; 1940 Professor at the University Göttingen; 1941 Professor at the University Strasbourg. 1950 University of Bonn.

Carl Schmitt (1888–1985): 1933 entry into the NSDAP, member of the Academy for German Law; in July 1933 Hermann Göring nominated Schmitt to State Councillor for Prussia. 1933 Professor at the University of Cologne and then at the University Berlin; editor of the

Deutsche Juristen-Zeitung. 1937 Schmitt resigned from political offices (due to attacks in the SS Journal *Das Schwarze Korps*); he retained his professorship in Berlin and his title as Prussian State Councillor. After the war Schmitt was banned from university positions.

Wilhelm Stuckart (1902–1953): jurist and official; 1922 entry into the NSDAP, 1926 legal counsel of the NSDAP; 1932 member of the SA; 1933 State Secretary in the Prussian Ministry for Culture; 1934 State Secretary in the Reich Ministry of Science; 1935 State Secretary in the Reich Ministry of Interior; 1936 entry into the SS; participant at the Wannsee Conference in January 1942. 1947 defendant in the Ministries Trial (*Wilhelmstraßenprozess)*, Stuckart was sentenced to three years of imprisonment. 1953 Stuckart died in a car accident.

Gustav Adolf Walz (1897–1948): 1927 Habilitation at the University Marburg; 1931 entry into the NSDAP. 1933 Professor at the University Breslau; 1938 Professor at the University Cologne; 1939 Professor for Constitutional Law and Philosophy of Law at the University Munich.

BIBLIOGRAPHY

NS Literature 1933–1945

Best, Werner, "Die Politische Polizei des Dritten Reiches," in Frank, Hans (ed.), *Deutsches Verwaltungsrecht* (München: Zentralverlag der NSDAP, Franz Eher Nachf., 1937), pp. 417–430.

"Die Geheime Staatspolizei," in *Deutsches Recht* 6, 1936, pp. 125–128.

Die Deutsche Polizei (Darmstadt: Wittich, 1940; 2nd ed. 1941).

Bockelmann, Paul, *Studien zum Täterstrafrecht, 1. Teil* (Berlin: Walter de Gruyter & Co., 1939).

Dahm, Georg, "Die Erneuerung der Ehrenstrafe," in *Deutsche Juristen-Zeitung* 13, 39 (1934), pp. 822–832.

"Das Ermessen des Richters im nationalsozialistischen Strafrecht," in Freisler, Roland (ed.), *Deutsches Strafrecht. Strafrecht, Strafrechtspolitik, Strafprozeß* (Berlin: R. v. Decker, G. Schenck, 1934), pp. 87–96.

"Verbrechen und Tatbestand," in Dahm, Georg; Huber, Ernst Rudolf; Larenz, Karl; Michaelis, Karl; Schaffstein, Friedrich; Siebert, Wolfgang, *Grundfragen der Neuen Rechtswissenschaft* (Berlin: Junker & Dünnhaupt, 1935), pp. 62–107.

"Gerechtigkeit und Zweckmäßigkeit im Strafrecht der Gegenwart," in Bockelmann, Paul; Dahm Georg; Dohna, Alexander Graf zu; Engisch, Karl; Exner, Franz; Lange, Richard; Mezger, Edmund; Peters, Karl; Schmidt, Eberhard; Schönke, Adolf; Sieverts, Rudolf, Weber, Hellmuth von; Welzel Hans, *Probleme der Strafrechtserneuerung* (Berlin: Walter de Gruyter & Co., 1944), pp. 1–23.

Dahm, Georg and Schaffstein, Friedrich, *Liberales oder autoritäres Strafrecht?* (Hamburg: Hanseatische Verlagsanstalt, 1933).

Dinter, Artur, *Die Sünde wider das Blut. Ein Zeitroman* (Leipzig: Matthes und Thost, 1920).

Fauser, Manfred, "Das Gesetz im Führerstaat," in *Archiv des öffentlichen Rechts*, N. F. 26 (1935), pp. 129–154.

Forsthoff, Ernst, *Der totale Staat* (Hamburg: Hanseatische Verlagsanstalt, 1933; 2nd ed. 1934).

Frank, Hans (ed.), *Nationalsozialistisches Handbuch für Recht und Gesetzgebung* (München: Zentralverlag der NSDAP, Franz Eher Nachf., 1935).

(ed.), *Deutsches Verwaltungsrecht* (München: Zentralverlag der NSDAP, Franz Eher Nachf., 1937).

"Einführung: Nationalsozialismus und Verwaltungsrecht," in Frank, Hans (ed.), *Deutsches Verwaltungsrecht* (München: Zentralverlag der NSDAP, Franz Eher Nachf., 1937), pp. XI–XXIII.

Frank, Hans, Reichsleiter/Reichsrechtsamt der NSDAP (eds.), *Nationalsozialistische Leitsätze für ein neues deutsches Strafrecht. 1.Teil*, 4th ed.(Berlin: Deutsche Rechts- und Wirtschaftswissenschaft Verlags-Ges., 1935).

Frank, Hans, Reichsleiter/Reichsrechtsamt der NSDAP (eds.), *Nationalsozialistische Leitsätze für ein neues deutsches Strafrecht. 2. (Besonderer) Teil* (Berlin: Deutsche Rechts- und Wirtschaftswissenschaft Verlags-Ges., 1936).

Freisler, Roland (ed.), *Deutsches Strafrecht. Strafrecht, Strafrechtspolitik, Strafprozeß* (Berlin: R. v. Decker, G. Schenck, 1934).

Schutz des Volkes oder des Rechtsbrechers? Fesselung des Verbrechers oder des Richters? Einiges über das zweckmäßige Maß der Bindung des Richters an gesetzliche Straftatbestände (Berlin: R. v. Decker, G. Schenck, 1935).

"Willensstrafrecht; Versuch und Vollendung," in Gürtner, Franz (ed.), *Das kommende deutsche Strafrecht. Bericht über die Arbeit der amtlichen Strafrechtskommission. Allgemeiner Teil*, 2nd revised ed. (Berlin: Franz Vahlen, 1935), pp. 5–48.

"Aufbau und Aufgabe des Besonderen Teils. Gestaltung seiner Tatbestände. Einbau des Schutzes der Bewegung in das Gesetz," in Gürtner, Franz (ed.), *Das kommende deutsche Strafrecht. Bericht über die Arbeit der amtlichen Strafrechtskommission. Besonderer Teil*, 2nd revised ed. (Berlin: Franz Vahlen, 1936), pp. 13–77.

Nationalsozialistisches Recht und Rechtsdenken (Berlin: Spaeth & Linde, 1938).

Freisler/Oetker/Dürr/Schwarz/Schoetensack/Thierack/Noack/Mayer/Strauß, *Grundzüge eines Allgemeinen Deutschen Strafrechts. Denkschrift des Zentralausschusses der Strafrechtsabteilung der Akademie für Deutsches Recht über die Grundzüge eines Allgemeinen Deutschen Strafrechts* (Berlin: R. v. Decker, G. Schenck, 1934).

Gerstenhauer, Max, *Das ewige Deutschland. Idee und Gestalt* (Leipzig: Armanen Verlag, 1940).

Günther, Hans F. K., *Rassenkunde Europas. Mit besonderer Berücksichtigung der Rassengeschichte der Hauptvölker indogermanischer Sprache* (München: J. F. Lehmanns, 1924; 3rd revised ed., 1929).

Rassenkunde des jüdischen Volkes, 2nd ed. (München: J. F. Lehmanns, 1930).

Ritter, Tod und Teufel. Der heldische Gedanke (München: J. F. Lehmanns, 1920; 4th ed. 1935).

Gürtner, Franz (ed.), *Das kommende deutsche Strafrecht. Allgemeiner Teil. Bericht über die Arbeit der amtlichen Strafrechtskommission*, 2nd revised ed. (Berlin: Franz Vahlen, 1935).

(ed.), *Das kommende deutsche Strafrecht. Besonderer Teil. Bericht über die Arbeit der amtlichen Strafrechtskommission*, 2nd revised ed. (Berlin: Franz Vahlen, 1936).

Hamel, Walter, "Wesen und Rechtsgrundlagen der Polizei im nationalsozialistischen Staate," in Frank, Hans (ed.), *Deutsches Verwaltungsrecht* (München: Zentralverlag der NSDAP, Franz Eher Nachf., 1937), pp. 381–398.

Himmler, Heinrich, "Rede vor den Reichs- und Gauleitern in Posen am 6. 10.1943," in Smith, Bradley F. and Peterson, Agnes F. (eds.), *Heinrich Himmler Geheimreden 1933 bis 1945* (Frankfurt am Main, Berlin, Wien: Propyläen, 1974), pp. 162–183.

Hitler, Adolf, "Aryan and Jew," in Rabinbach, Anson and Gilman, Sander L. (eds.), *The Third Reich Sourcebook* (Berkeley, Los Angeles, London: University of California Press, 2013), pp. 187–191.

Höhn, Reinhard, *Die Wandlung im staatsrechtlichen Denken* (Hamburg: Hanseatische Verlagsanstalt, 1934).

Rechtsgemeinschaft und Volksgemeinschaft (Hamburg: Hanseatische Verlagsanstalt, 1935).

"Altes und neues Polizeirecht," in Frank, Hans; Himmler, Heinrich; Best, Werner; Höhn, Reinhard, *Grundfragen der deutschen Polizei* (Hamburg: Hanseatische Verlagsanstalt, 1937), pp. 21–34.

"Volk, Staat und Recht," in Höhn, Maunz and Swoboda, Ernst (eds.), *Grundfragen der Rechtsauffassung* (München: Duncker & Humblot, 1938), pp. 1–27.

Höhn, Reinhard; Maunz, Theodor; Swoboda, Ernst (eds.), *Grundfragen der Rechtsauffassung* (München: Duncker & Humblot, 1938).

Huber, Ernst Rudolf, *Reichsgewalt und Staatsgerichtshof* (Oldenburg i. O.: Gerhard Stalling, 1932).

"Die Totalität des völkischen Staates," in *Die Tat* 26, 1 (1934), pp. 30–42.

Verfassungsrecht des Großdeutschen Reiches, 2nd ed. (Hamburg: Hanseatische Verlagsanstalt, 1939).

Kerrl, Hanns (ed.), *Nationalsozialistisches Strafrecht. Denkschrift des Preußischen Justizministers* (Berlin: R. v. Decker, G. Schenck, 1934).

Koellreutter, Otto, *Der nationale Rechtsstaat. Zum Wandel der Deutschen Staatsidee* (Tübingen: J. C. B. Mohr [Paul Siebeck], 1932).

Vom Sinn und Wesen der nationalen Revolution (Tübingen: J. C. B. Mohr [Paul Siebeck], 1933).

Grundriß der Allgemeinen Staatslehre (Tübingen: J. C. B. Mohr [Paul Siebeck], 1933).

Volk und Staat in der Weltanschauung des Nationalsozialismus (Berlin: Pan Verlagsgesellschaft, 1935).

Grundfragen unserer Volks- und Staatsgestaltung (Berlin: Junker & Dünnhaupt, 1936).

Deutsches Verfassungsrecht. Ein Grundriss, 3rd ed. (Berlin: Junker & Dünnhaupt, 1938).

Krug, Karl, "Drei Grundprobleme des kommenden Strafrechts," in *Zeitschrift der Akademie für Deutsches Recht* 2 (1935), pp. 98–102.

Larenz, Karl, *Rechtserneuerung und Rechtsphilosophie* (Tübingen: J. C. B. Mohr [Paul Siebeck], 1934).

Maunz, Theodor, "Das Verwaltungsrecht des nationalsozialistischen Staates," in Frank, Hans (ed.), *Deutsches Verwaltungsrecht* (München: Zentralverlag der NSDAP, Franz Eher Nachf., 1937), pp. 27–48.

Gestalt und Recht der Polizei (Hamburg: Hanseatische Verlagsanstalt, 1943).

Mayer, Hellmuth, *Das Strafrecht des deutschen Volkes* (Stuttgart: Ferdinand Enke, 1936).

Mezger, Edmund, *Deutsches Strafrecht. Ein Leitfaden* (Berlin: Junker & Dünnhaupt, 1936).

Deutsches Strafrecht. Ein Grundriss (Berlin: Junker & Dünnhaupt, 1938).

Morgen, Konrad, *Kriegspropaganda und Kriegsverhütung* (Leipzig: Universitätsverlag von Robert Noske, 1936).

Nicolai, Helmut, *Grundlagen der kommenden Verfassung. Über den staatsrechtlichen Aufbau des Dritten Reiches* (Berlin: Reimar Hobbing, 1933).

Rasse und Recht. Vortrag gehalten auf dem Deutschen Juristentag des Bundes nationalsozialistischer deutscher Juristen am 2. Oktober 1933 in Leipzig (Berlin: Reimar Hobbing, 1933).

Oetker, Friedrich, "Grundprobleme der nationalsozialistischen Strafrechtsreform," in Frank, Hans (ed.), *Nationalsozialistisches Handbuch für Recht und Gesetzgebung* (München: Zentralverlag der NSDAP, Franz Eher Nachf., 1935), pp. 1317–1361.

Sauer, Wilhelm, "Die Ethisierung des Strafrechts. Über die Prinzipien der Strafrechtserneuerung und ihre praktische Auswirkung," in Freisler, Roland (ed.), *Deutsches Strafrecht. Strafrecht, Strafrechtspolitik, Strafprozeß* (Berlin: R. v. Decker, G. Schenck, 1934), pp. 177–190.

Schäfer, Karl, "Nullum Crimen sine Poena (Das Recht als Grundlage der Bestrafung. Zeitliche Geltung der Strafgesetze)," in Gürtner, Franz (ed.), *Das kommende deutsche Strafrecht. Allgemeiner Teil. Bericht über die Arbeit der amtlichen Strafrechtskommission*, 2nd revised ed. (Berlin: Franz Vahlen, 1935), pp. 200–217.

Schaffstein, Friedrich, "Ehrenstrafe und Freiheitsstrafe in ihrer Bedeutung für das neue Strafrecht," in Freisler, Roland (ed.), *Deutsches Strafrecht. Strafrecht, Strafrechtspolitik, Strafprozeß* (Berlin: R. v. Decker, G. Schenck, 1934) pp. 273–282.

Scheuner, Ulrich, "Die nationale Revolution. Eine staatsrechtliche Untersuchung," Part I, in *Archiv des öffentlichen Rechts* NF 24 (1934), pp. 166–220.

"Die Rechtstellung der Persönlichkeit in der Gemeinschaft," in Frank, Hans (ed.), *Deutsches Verwaltungsrecht* (München: Zentralverlag der NSDAP, Franz Eher Nachf., 1937), pp. 82–98.

Schmitt, Carl, *Staat, Bewegung, Volk. Die Dreigliederung der politischen Einheit* (Hamburg: Hanseatische Verlagsanstalt, 1933).

"Der Führer schützt das Recht. Zur Reichstagsrede von Adolf Hitler vom 13. Juli 1934," in *Deutsche Juristen-Zeitung*, 39, 15 (1934); reprinted in Schmitt, Carl, *Positionen und Begriffe im Kampf mit Weimar-Genf-Versailles 1923–1939* (Hamburg: Hanseatische Verlagsanstalt, 1940), pp. 199–203; English: Schmitt, Carl, "The Führer Protects the Law. On Adolf Hitler's Reichstag Address 13 July 1934," in Rabinbach, Anson and Gilman, Sander L. (eds.), *The Third Reich Sourcebook* (Berkeley, Los Angeles, London: University of California Press, 2013), pp. 63–67.

"Der Rechtsstaat," in Frank, Hans (ed.), *Nationalsozialistisches Handbuch für Recht und Gesetzgebung* (München: Zentralverlag der NSDAP, Franz Eher Nachf., 1935), pp. 3–10.

"Was bedeutet der Streit um den Rechtsstaat?," in *Zeitschrift für die gesamte Staatswissenschaft/Journal of Institutional and Theoretical Economics* 95, 2 (1935), pp. 189–201.

Der Leviathan in der Staatslehre des Thomas Hobbes. Sinn und Fehlschlag eines politischen Symbols (Hamburg: Hanseatische Verlagsanstalt, 1938).

Positionen und Begriffe im Kampf mit Weimar-Genf-Versailles 1929–1939 (Hamburg: Hanseatische Verlagsanstalt, 1940).

Siegert, Karl, "Nulla poena sine lege. Kritische Bemerkungen zu den Vorschlägen der amtlichen Strafrechtskommission," in Freisler, Roland (ed.), *Deutsches Strafrecht. Strafrecht, Strafrechtspolitik, Strafprozeß* (Berlin: R. v. Decker, G. Schenck, 1934), pp. 376–386.

Tesmer, Hans, "Die Schutzhaft und ihre rechtlichen Grundlagen (1936)," in Hirsch, Martin; Majer, Diemut; Meinck, Jürgen (eds.), *Recht, Verwaltung und Justiz im Nationalsozialismus. Ausgewählte Schriften, Gesetze und Gerichtsentscheidungen von 1933 bis 1945* (Köln: Bund-Verlag, 1984), pp. 331–332.

Thierack, Otto Georg, "Sinn und Bedeutung der Richtlinien für die Strafrechtsreform," in National-Sozialistischer Rechtswahrer-Bund (ed.), *Deutscher Juristentag 1936, 5. Reichstagung des Bundes National-Sozialistischer Deutscher Juristen* (Berlin: Deutscher Rechts-Verlag, 1936), pp. 25–30.

Triepel, Heinrich, "Die nationale Revolution und die deutsche Verfassung," in *Deutsche Allgemeine Zeitung* 2. April 1933; reprinted in Hirsch, Martin; Majer, Diemut; Meinck, Jürgen (eds.), *Recht, Verwaltung und Justiz im*

Nationalsozialismus. Ausgewählte Schriften, Gesetze und Gerichtsentscheidungen von 1933 bis 1945 (Köln: Bund-Verlag, 1984), pp. 116–119.

von Gleispach, Wenzel, "Willensstrafrecht," in Elster, Alexander and Lingemann, Heinrich (eds.), *Handwörterbuch der Kriminologie und der anderen strafrechtlichen Hilfswissenschaften*, vol. 2 (Berlin and Leipzig: Walter de Gruyter & Co., 1936), pp. 1067–1079.

Literature

Anschütz, Gerhard, *Die Verfassung des Deutschen Reichs vom 11. August 1919. Ein Kommentar für Wissenschaft und Praxis*, Vierte Bearbeitung, 14th ed. (Berlin: Georg Stilke, 1933).

Apelt, Willibalt, *Geschichte der Weimarer Verfassung*, 2nd ed. (München and Berlin: C. H. Beck, 1964).

Arendt, Hannah, *Eichmann in Jerusalem. A Report on the Banality of Evil* (New York: Penguin Books, 2006).

"Personal Responsibility under Dictatorship," in Arendt, Hannah, *Responsibility and Judgment*, ed. with an introduction by Kohn, Jerome (New York: Schocken Books, 2003), pp. 17–48.

The Origins of Totalitarianism, with an introduction by Powers, Samantha (New York: Schocken Books, 2004).

Baur, Erwin; Fischer, Eugen; Lenz, Fritz, *Grundriß der menschlichen Erblichkeitslehre und Rassenhygiene*, vol. II, Fritz Lenz, *Menschliche Auslese und Rassenhygiene* (München: J. F. Lehmanns, 1921).

Baur, Erwin; Fischer, Eugen; Lenz, Fritz, *Human Heredity*, transl. by Paul, Eden and Paul, Cedar (London: George Allen & Unwin, New York: Macmillan, 1931).

Bendersky, Joseph W., *Carl Schmitt. Theorist for the Reich* (Princeton: Princeton University Press, 1983).

Blasius, Dirk, *Carl Schmitt. Preußischer Staatsrat in Hitlers Reich* (Göttingen: Vandenhoeck and Ruprecht, 2001).

Boberach, Heinz (ed.), *Richterbriefe. Dokumente zur Beeinflussung der deutschen Rechtsprechung 1942–1944* (Boppard am Rhein: Harald Boldt Verlag, 1975).

Bollmeyer, Heiko, *Der steinige Weg zur Demokratie. Die Weimarer Nationalversammlung zwischen Kaiserreich und Republik* (Frankfurt am Main: Campus, 2007).

Brecht, Arnold, *Prelude to Silence. The End of the German Republic* (New York: Howard Fertig, 1968).

Browning, Christopher R., *Ordinary Men. Reserve Police Battalion 101 and the Final Solution in Poland* (London: Penguin Books, 2001).

(with contributions by Matthäus, Jürgen), *The Origins of the Final Solution. The Evolution of Nazi Jewish Policy, September 1939–March 1942* (Lincoln: University of Nebraska Press, and Yad Vashem, 2004).

Buchheim, Hans, "The SS-Instrument of Domination," in Krausnick, Helmut; Buchheim, Hans; Broszat, Martin; Jacobsen, Hans-Adolf, *Anatomy of the SS State*, transl. by Barry, Richard (New York: Walker and Company, 1968), pp. 127–301.

"Command and Compliance," in Krausnick, Helmut; Buchheim, Hans; Broszat, Martin; Jacobsen, Hans-Adolf, *Anatomy of the SS State*, transl. by Barry, Richard (New York: Walker and Company, 1968), pp. 305–396.

Büchler, Robert Yehoshua, "'Unworthy Behavior'. The Case of SS Officer Max Täubner," in *Holocaust and Genocide Studies* 17, 3 (2003), pp. 409–429.

Caldwell, Peter C., "National Socialism and Constitutional Law. Carl Schmitt, Otto Koellreutter, and the Debate over the Nature of the Nazi State, 1933–1937," in *Cardozo Law Review* 16 (1994), pp. 399–427.

"Ernst Forsthoff in Frankfurt. Political Mobilization and the Abandonment of Scholarly Responsibility," in Epple, Moritz; Fried, Johannes; Gross, Raphael; Gudian, Janus (eds.), *"Politisierung der Wissenschaft." Jüdische Wissenschaftler und ihre Gegner an der Universität Frankfurt am Main vor und nach 1933* (Göttingen: Wallstein, 2013), pp. 249–283.

Das Strafgesetzbuch für das Deutsche Reich, ed. by Oppenhoff, Th. F., 7th ed. (Berlin: G. Reimer, 1879).

Domarus, Max, *Hitler. Reden und Proklamationen 1932–1945. Kommentiert von einem Zeitgenossen*, vol. I Triumph, Erster Halbband 1932–1934 (München: Süddeutscher Verlag, 1965).

Hitler. Reden und Proklamationen 1932–1945. Kommentiert von einem Zeitgenossen, vol. I Triumph, Zweiter Halbband 1935–1938 (München: Süddeutscher Verlag, 1965).

Hitler. Reden und Proklamationen 1932–1945. Kommentiert von einem Zeitgenossen, vol. II Untergang, Erster Halbband 1939–1940 (München: Süddeutscher Verlag, 1965).

Hitler. Reden und Proklamationen 1932–1945. Kommentiert von einem Zeitgenossen, vol. II Untergang, Zweiter Halbband 1941–1945 (München: Süddeutscher Verlag, 1965).

Dreier, Horst and Pauly, Walter (eds.), *Die deutsche Staatsrechtslehre in der Zeit des Nationalsozialismus* (Berlin/New York: Walter de Gruyter, 2001).

Dreier, Horst; Müßig, Ulrike; Stolleis, Michael; Korb, Axel-Johann, *Kelsens Kritiker. Ein Beitrag zur Geschichte der Rechts- und Staatstheorie (1911–1934)* (Tübingen: Mohr Siebeck, 2010).

Dyzenhaus, David, "'Now the Machine Runs Itself'. Carl Schmitt on Hobbes and Kelsen," in *Cardozo Law Review* 16, 1 (1994), pp. 1–19.

Legality and Legitimacy. Carl Schmitt, Hans Kelsen and Hermann Heller in Weimar (Oxford: Oxford University Press, 1997).

"Legal Theory in the Collapse of Weimar. Contemporary Lessons?" in *The American Political Science Review* 91, 1 (1997), pp. 121–134.

"The Grudge Informer Case Revisited," in *New York University Law Review* 83 (2008), pp. 1000–1034.

"Legality without the Rule of Law? Scott Shapiro on Wicked Legal Systems," in *Canadian Journal of Law and Jurisprudence* 25, 1 (2012), pp. 183–200.

Essner, Cornelia, *Die "Nürnberger Gesetze" oder die Verwaltung des Rassenwahns 1933–1945* (Paderborn, München, Wien, Zürich: Ferdinand Schöningh, 2002).

Finnis, John, *Natural Law and Natural Rights* (Oxford: Oxford University Press, 2011).

Fischer, Klaus P., *Nazi Germany. A New History* (New York: Continuum, 1995).

Fraenkel, Ernst, "Die repräsentative und die plebiszitäre Komponente im demokratischen Verfassungsstaat," in Fraenkel, Ernst, *Deutschland und die westlichen Demokratien*, 9th ed., with an introduction ed. by Brünneck, Alexander von (Baden-Baden: Nomos, 2011), pp. 165–207.

The Dual State. A Contribution to the Theory of Dictatorship, with an introduction ed. by Meierhenrich, Jens, transl. by Shils, E. A. (Oxford: Oxford University Press, 2017).

Fraser, David, *Law after Auschwitz. Towards a Jurisprudence of the Holocaust* (Durham: Carolina Academic Press, 2005).

Frei, Norbert, *Der Führerstaat. Nationalsozialistische Herrschaft 1933–1945*, 6th ed. (München: Deutscher Taschenbuch Verlag, 2001).

Fuller, Lon L., *The Morality of Law*, rev. ed. (New Haven and London: Yale University Press, 1969).

Gellately, Robert and Stoltzfus, Nathan (eds.), *Social Outsiders in Nazi Germany* (Princeton: Princeton University Press, 2001).

Giles, Geoffrey J., "The Persecution of Gay Men and Lesbians during the Third Reich," in Friedman, Jonathan C. (ed.), *The Routledge Handbook of the Holocaust* (London and New York: Routledge, 2011), pp. 385–396.

Graver, Hans Petter, *Judges Against Justice. On Judges when the Rule of Law is Under Attack* (Berlin, Heidelberg: Springer, 2015).

"Why Adolf Hitler Spared the Judges. Judicial Opposition Against the Nazi State," in *German Law Journal* 19, 4 (2018), pp. 845–877.

Gross, Raphael, *Anständig Geblieben. Nationalsozialistische Moral* (Frankfurt am Main: S. Fischer, 2010).

"Guilt, Shame, Anger, Indignation. Nazi Law and Nazi Morals," in Steinweis, Alan E. and Rachlin, Robert D. (eds.), *The Law in Nazi* Germany. *Ideology, Opportunism, and the Perversion of Justice* (New York, Oxford: Berghahn, 2013), pp. 89–104.

Gruchmann, Lothar, "Rechtssystem und nationalsozialistische Justizpolitik," in Broszat, Martin and Möller, Horst (eds.), *Das Dritte Reich. Herrschaftsstruktur und Geschichte* (München: C. H. Beck, 1983), pp. 86–87.

Gruchmann, Lothar, *Justiz im Dritten Reich 1933–1940. Anpassung und Unterwerfung in der Ära Gürtner* (München: R. Oldenbourg, 1988).

Günther, Klaus, "Von der Rechts- zur Pflichtverletzung," in Institut für Kriminalwissenschaften (ed.), *Vom unmöglichen Zustand des Strafrechts* (Frankfurt am Main: Peter Lang, 1995), pp. 445–460.

Habermas, Jürgen, *Between Facts and Norms. Contributions to a Discourse Theory of Law and Democracy*, transl. by Rehg, William (Cambridge and Malden: Polity Press, 1996).

Hambrock, Michael, "Dialektik der 'verfolgenden Unschuld.' Überlegungen zur Mentalität und Funktion der SS," in Schulte, Jan Erik (ed.), *Die SS, Himmler und die Wewelsburg* (Paderborn, München, Wien, Zürich: Schöningh, 2009), pp. 79–101.

Hart, H. L. A., "Positivism and the Separation of Law and Morals," in *Harvard Law Review* 71, 4 (1958), pp. 593–629.

"Review of *The Morality of Law* by Lon L. Fuller" in *Harvard Law Review* 78, 6 (1965), pp. 1281–1296.

The Concept of Law, 3rd ed. (Oxford: Clarendon Press, 2012).

Hartl, Benedikt, *Das nationalsozialistische Willensstrafrecht* (Berlin: Weißensee, 2000).

Hartung, Günther, "*Artur Dinter, Erfolgsautor des frühen Nationalsozialismus,*" in Hartung, Günther (ed.), *Deutschfaschistische Literatur und Ästhetik. Gesammelte Studien* (Leipzig: Leipziger Universitätsverlag, 2001), pp. 99–124.

Hegel, G. W. F., *Elements of the Philosophy of Right*, ed. by Wood, Allen W., transl. by Nisbet, H. B. (Cambridge: Cambridge University Press, 1991).

Heiber, Helmut (ed.), *Reichsführer! Briefe an und von Himmler* (Stuttgart: Deutsche Verlagsanstalt, 1968).

Herbert, Ulrich, *Best. Biographische Studien über Radikalismus, Weltanschauung und Vernunft 1903–1989* (Bonn: Dietz, 2001).

Herman, Barbara, "The Practice of Moral Judgment," in Herman, Barbara, *The Practice of Moral Judgment* (Cambridge, MA and London: Harvard University Press, 2007), pp. 51–78.

Hiden, John W., *The Weimar Republic* (London: Longman, 1974).

Hippel, Ernst von, "Das richterliche Prüfungsrecht," in Anschütz, Gerhard and Thoma, Richard (eds.), *Handbuch des deutschen Staatsrechts*, Band 2 (Tübingen: J. C. B. Mohr [Paul Siebeck], 1932), pp. 546–563.

Hirsch, Martin; Majer, Diemut; Meinck, Jürgen (eds.), *Recht, Verwaltung und Justiz im Nationalsozialismus. Ausgewählte Schriften, Gesetze und Gerichtsentscheidungen von 1933 bis 1945* (Köln: Bund-Verlag, 1984).

Hoefer, Frederick, "The Nazi Penal System I," in *Journal of Criminal Law and Criminology* 35, 6 (1945), pp. 385–393.

Huber, Ernst Rudolf, "Carl Schmitt in der Reichskrise der Weimarer Endzeit," in Quaritsch, Helmut (ed.), *Complexio Oppositorum. Über Carl Schmitt.*

Vorträge und Diskussionsbeiträge des 28. Sonderseminars 1986 der Hochschule für Verwaltungswissenschaften Speyer (Berlin: Duncker & Humblot, 1988), pp. 33–50.

Jacobson, Arthur J. and Schlink, Bernhard (eds.), *Weimar. A Jurisprudence of Crisis* (Berkeley and Los Angeles: The University of California Press, 2001).

Jasch, Hans-Christian, *Staatssekretär Wilhelm Stuckart und die Judenpolitik. Der Mythos von der sauberen Verwaltung* (München: Oldenbourg, 2012).

Joerges, Christian and Ghaleigh, Navraj Singh (eds.), *Darker Legacies of Law in Europe. The Shadow of National Socialism and Fascism over Europe and its Legal Traditions* (Oxford and Portland, Oregon: Hart Publishing, 2003).

Kant, Immanuel, *Practical Philosophy*, ed. and transl. by Gregor, Mary (Cambridge: Cambridge University Press, 1996).

Kelsen, Hans, *Vom Wesen und Wert der Demokratie* (Tübingen: J. C. B. Mohr [Paul Siebeck], 1920, 2nd ed. 1929).

"Wer soll der Hüter der Verfassung sein?" in *Die Justiz* 6 (1931), pp. 576–628; reprinted in Kelsen, Hans, *Wer soll der Hüter der Verfassung sein? Abhandlungen zur Theorie der Verfassungsgerichtsbarkeit in der pluralistischen, parlamentarischen Demokratie*, 2nd ed., ed. by van Ooyen, Robert C. (Tübingen: J. C. B. Mohr [Paul Siebeck], 2019), pp. 58–105; English: "Who ought to be the guardian of the constitution? Kelsen's reply to Schmitt", transl. by Vinx, Lars, in Vinx, Lars (ed.), *The Guardian of the Constitution. Hans Kelsen and Carl Schmitt on the Limits of Constitutional Law* (Cambridge: Cambridge University Press, 2015), pp. 174–221.

"Das Urteil des Staatsgerichtshofs vom 25. Oktober 1932," in *Die Justiz*, 8 (1932), pp. 65–91; English: "Kelsen on the Judgment of the Staatsgerichtshof of 25 October 1932," transl. by Vinx, Lars, in Vinx, Lars (ed.), *The Guardian of the Constitution: Hans Kelsen and Carl Schmitt on the Limits of Constitutional Law* (Cambridge: Cambridge University Press, 2015), pp. 228–253.

Das Problem der Gerechtigkeit, in Kelsen, *Reine Rechtslehre*, 2nd revised ed. (Wien: Franz Deuticke, 1960), pp. 65–68.

Pure Theory of Law, transl. by Knight, Max (Berkeley and Los Angeles: University of California Press, 1967).

Kennedy, Ellen, "Introduction: Carl Schmitt's *Parlamentarismus* in Its Historical Context," in Schmitt, Carl, *The Crisis of Parliamentary Democracy*, transl. by Kennedy, Ellen (Cambridge, MA: The MIT Press, 1985), pp. xiii–xlix.

Kershaw, Ian, *The Nazi Dictatorship. Problems and Perspectives of Interpretation*, 4th ed. (London: Arnold, 2000).

Kirchheimer, Otto, "Criminal Law in National Socialist Germany," in Scheuerman, William E. (ed.), *The Rule of Law under Siege. Selected Essays of Franz L. Neumann and Otto Kirchheimer* (Berkeley, Los Angeles, London: University of California Press, 1996), pp. 172–191.

Klee, Ernst; Dressen, Willi; Riess, Volker (eds.), *The Good Old Days. The Holocaust as Seen by Its Perpetrators and Bystanders*, transl. by Burnstone, Deborah (New York: The Free Press, 1988).

Klemperer, Victor, *I will Bear Witness 1942–1945. A Diary of the Nazi Years* (New York: Random House, 2001).

Kogon, Eugen, *The Theory and Practice of Hell. The German Concentration Camps and the System behind them* (New York: Farrar, Straus and Giroux, 1950).

Konitzer, Werner and Gross, Raphael (eds.), *Moralität des Bösen. Ethik und nationalsozialistische Verbrechen* (Frankfurt, New York: Campus, 2009).

Koonz, Claudia, *The Nazi Conscience* (Cambridge, MA and London: Harvard University Press, 2003).

Korsgaard, Christine M., *Creating the Kingdom of Ends* (Cambridge: Cambridge University Press, 1996).

Kren, George M. and Morris, Rodler, F., "Race and Spirituality. Artur Dinter's Theosophical Antisemitism," in *Holocaust and Genocide Studies* 6, 3 (1991), pp. 233–252.

Kühne, Thomas, "Zwischen Männerbund und Volksgemeinschaft. Hitlers Soldaten und der Mythos der Kameradschaft," in *Archiv für Sozialgeschichte*, 38 (1998), pp. 165–189.

Kurz, Achim, *Demokratische Diktatur? Auslegung und Handhabung des Artikels 48 der Weimarer Verfassung 1919–25* (Berlin: Duncker & Humblot, 1992).

Loewenstein, Karl, "Dictatorship and the German Constitution: 1933–1937," in *The Chicago Law Review* 4 (1937), pp. 537–574.

Longerich, Peter, *The Unwritten Order. Hitler's Role in the Final Solution* (Stroud: Tempus, 2003).

Heinrich Himmler, transl. by Noakes, Jeremy and Sharpe, Lesley (Oxford: Oxford University Press, 2012).

Lösener, Bernhard, "At the Desk of Racial Affairs in the Reich Ministry of the Interior," in *Legislating the Holocaust. The Bernhard Loesener Memoirs and Supporting Documents*, ed. by Schleunes, Karl A., transl. by Carol Scherer (Boulder, Colorado: Westview Press, 2001), pp. 33–109.

Lüken, Erhard-Josef, *Der Nationalsozialismus und das materielle Strafrecht. Ein Beitrag zur Strafrechtsgeschichte* (Dissertation, Universität Göttingen, 1988).

Lusane, Clarence, *Hitler's Black Victims. The Historical Experiences of Afro Germans, European Blacks, Africans, and African Americans in the Nazi Era* (London and New York: Routledge, 2002).

Majer, Diemut, *Grundlagen des nationalsozialistischen Rechtssystems. Führerprinzip, Sonderrecht, Einheitspartei* (Stuttgart, Berlin, Köln, Mainz: Kohlhammer, 1987).

"Non-Germans" under the Third Reich. The Nazi Judicial and Administrative System in Germany and Occupied Eastern Europe, *with Special Regard to Occupied Poland, 1939–1945*, transl. by Hill, Peter Thomas; Humphrey,

Edward Vance; Levin, Brian (Baltimore and London: The Johns Hopkins University Press, 2003).

McCormick, John P., *Carl Schmitt's Critique of Liberalism. Against Politics as Technology* (Cambridge: Cambridge University Press, 1997).

Meier, Heinrich, *The Lesson of Carl Schmitt. Four Chapters on the Distinction between Political Theology and Political Philosophy*, expanded ed., transl. by Brainard, Marcus (New essays in this ed. transl. by Berman, Robert) (Chicago and London: The University of Chicago Press, 2011).

Meierhenrich, Jens, "Fearing the Disorder of Things. The Development of Carl Schmitt's Institutional Theory, 1919-1942," in Meierhenrich, Jens and Simons, Oliver (eds.), *The Oxford Handbook of Carl Schmitt* (Oxford: Oxford University Press, 2016), pp. 171–216.

The Remnants of the Rechtsstaat. An Ethnography of Nazi Law (Oxford: Oxford University Press, 2018).

Meinck, Jürgen, "Polizeirecht," in Hirsch, Martin; Majer, Diemut; Meinck, Jürgen (eds.), *Recht, Verwaltung und Justiz im Nationalsozialismus. Ausgewählte Schriften, Gesetze und Gerichtsentscheidungen von 1933 bis 1945* (Köln: Bund-Verlag, 1984), pp. 317–319.

Meinel, Florian, *Der Jurist in der industriellen Gesellschaft. Ernst Forsthoff und seine Zeit* (Berlin: Akademie Verlag, 2011).

Messerschmidt, Manfred, *Die Wehrmacht im NS-Staat. Zeit der Indoktrination* (Hamburg: R. v. Decker, G. Schenck, 1969).

Mommsen, Hans, *Beamtentum im Dritten Reich. Mit ausgewählten Quellen zur nationalsozialistischen Beamtenpolitik* (Stuttgart: Deutsche Verlags-Anstalt, 1966).

The Rise and Fall of Weimar Democracy, transl. by Forster, Elborg and Jones, Larry Eugene (Chapel Hill & London: North Carolina University Press, 1996).

Mommsen, Wolfgang J., *Max Weber and German Politics 1890–1920*, transl. by Steinberg, Michael S. (Chicago and London: The University of Chicago Press, 1984).

Mühleisen, Horst, "Das Testament Hindenburgs vom 11. Mai 1934," in *Vierteljahreshefte für Zeitgeschichte* 44, 3 (1996), pp. 355–371.

Murphy, Melanie, "Homosexuality and the Law in the Third Reich," in Michalczyk, John J. (ed.), *Nazi Law. From Nuremberg to Nuremberg* (London, Oxford et al: Bloomsbury, 2018), pp. 110–124.

Neumann, Franz, *Behemoth. The Structure and Practice of National Socialism 1933–1944*, with an introd. by Hayes, Peter (Chicago: Ivan R. Dee, 2009).

Patch Jr., William L., *Heinrich Brüning and the Dissolution of the Weimar Republic* (Cambridge: Cambridge University Press, 1998).

Pauer-Studer, Herlinde, "Law and Morality under Evil Conditions. The Case of SS Judge Konrad Morgen," in *Jurisprudence* 3, 2, 2012, pp. 367–390.

"Kelsen's Legal Positivism and the Challenge of Nazi Law," in Galavotti, Maria Carla; Nemeth, Elisabeth; Stadler, Friedrich (eds.), *European Philosophy of Science – Philosophy of Science in Europe and the Viennese Heritage* (Dordrecht: Springer, 2014), pp. 223–240.

"A Community of Rational Beings," in *Kant-Studien* 107, 1 (2016), pp. 125–159.

"Complicity and Conditions of Agency," in *Journal of Applied Philosophy* 35, 4 (2018), pp. 643–660.

Pauer-Studer, Herlinde and Velleman, J. David, "Distortions of Normativity," in *Ethical Theory and Moral Practice* 14, 3 (2011), pp. 329–356.

Pauer-Studer, Herlinde and Velleman, J. David, *Konrad Morgen. The Conscience of a Nazi Judge* (Basingstoke: Palgrave MacMillan, 2015), in German (extended version): *"Weil ich nun mal ein Gerechtigskeitsfanatiker bin." Der Fall des SS-Richters Konrad Morgen* (Berlin: Suhrkamp, 2017).

Piper, Ernst, *Alfred Rosenberg. Hitlers Chefideologe* (München: Pantheon, 2007).

Preuss, Hugo, "Zur Verabschiedung der neuen Reichsverfassung (1919)," in Preuss, Hugo, *Gesammelte Schriften, Vierter Band: Politik und Verfassung in der Weimarer Republik*, ed. with an introduction by Lehnert, Detlef (Tübingen: Mohr Siebeck, 2008), pp. 85–87.

"Rede über die neue Reichsverfassung (1919)," in Preuss, Hugo, *Gesammelte Schriften, Vierter Band: Politik und Verfassung in der Weimarer Republik* (Tübingen: Mohr Siebeck, 2008), pp. 589–590.

"Die Bedeutung des Artikel 48 der Reichsverfassung (1925)," in Preuss, Hugo, *Gesammelte Schriften, Vierter Band: Politik und Verfassung in der Weimarer Republik* (Tübingen: Mohr Siebeck, 2008), pp. 571–575.

"Um die Reichsverfassung von Weimar (1924)," in Preuss, Hugo, *Gesammelte Schriften, Vierter Band: Politik und Verfassung in der Weimarer Republik* (Tübingen: Mohr Siebeck, 2008), pp. 367–438.

Rabinbach, Anson and Gilman, Sander L. (eds.), *The Third Reich Sourcebook* (Berkeley, Los Angeles, London: University of California Press, 2013).

Rachlin, Robert D., "Roland Freisler and the Volksgerichtshof: The Court as an Instrument of Terror," in Steinweis, Alan E. and Rachlin, Robert D. (eds.), *The Law in Nazi Germany* (New York, Oxford: Berghahn. 2013) pp. 63–88.

Radbruch, Gustav, "Gesetzliches Recht und übergesetzliches Unrecht," in *Süddeutsche Juristenzeitung* 1 (1946), pp. 105-108; English: "Statutory Lawlessness and Supra-Statutory Law," transl. by Paulson Litschewski, Bonnie and Paulson, Stanley L., in *Oxford Journal of Legal Studies* 26, 1 (2006), pp. 1–11.

Rawls, John, *Political Liberalism* (New York: Columbia University Press, 1993).

The Law of Peoples with "The Idea of Public Reason Revisited" (Cambridge, MA and London: Harvard University Press, 1999).

Raz, Joseph, "The Rule of Law and its Virtue," in Raz, Joseph, *The Authority of Law. Essays on Law and Morality*, 2nd ed. (Oxford: Oxford University Press, 2009), pp. 210–229.

The Authority of Law. Essays on Law and Morality, 2nd ed. (Oxford: Oxford University Press, 2009).

Regge, Jürgen and Schubert, Werner (eds.), *Quellen zur Reform des Straf- und Strafprozeßrechts, NS-Zeit (1933–1939). Strafgesetzbuch, vol. 1, Entwürfe eines Strafgesetzbuchs, part 2* (Berlin, New York: Walter de Gruyter, 1990).

Regge, Jürgen and Schubert, Werner (eds.), *Quellen zur Reform des Straf- und Strafprozeßrechts, NS-Zeit (1933–1939). Strafgesetzbuch, vol. 2, Protokolle der Strafrechtskommission des Reichsjustizministeriums, part 3, 2. Lesung: Allgemeiner Teil. Besonderer Teil* (Berlin, New York: Walter de Gruyter, 1990).

Regge, Jürgen and Schubert, Werner (eds.), *Quellen zur Reform des Straf- und Strafprozeßrechts, NS-Zeit (1933–1939). Strafgesetzbuch, vol. 2, Protokolle der Strafrechtskommission des Reichsjustizministeriums, part 4, 2. Lesung: Besonderer Teil* (Berlin, New York: Walter de Gruyter, 1994).

Reinicke, Wolfgang, *Instrumentalisierung von Geschichte durch Heinrich Himmler und die SS* (Neuried: ars et unitas, 2003).

Reitlinger, Gerhard, *The SS. Alibi of a Nation 1922–1945* (Melbourne, London, Toronto: Heinemann, 1956).

Ripstein, Arthur, *Force and Freedom. Kant's Legal and Political Philosophy* (Cambridge, MA and London: Harvard University Press, 2009).

Rousseau, Jean-Jacques, *The Social Contract and Other Political Writings*, ed. and transl. by Gourevitch, Victor (Cambridge: Cambridge University Press, 1997).

Rundle, Kristen, "The Impossibility of an Extermination Legality," in *University of Toronto Law Journal* 59, 1 (2009), pp. 65–125.

Forms Liberate. Reclaiming the Jurisprudence of Lon L. Fuller (Oxford and Portland, Oregon: Hart Publishing Company, 2012).

Rüthers, Bernd, *Die unbegrenzte Auslegung. Zum Wandel der Privatrechtsordnung im Nationalsozialismus* (Tübingen: Mohr Siebeck, 1968).

Sarat, Austin; Douglas, Lawrence; Umphrey Martha Merrill (eds.), *Criminals and Enemies* (Amherst and Boston: University of Massachusetts Press, 2019).

Schapiro, Tamar, "Compliance, Complicity, and the Nature of Non-Ideal Conditions," in *The Journal of Philosophy* 100, 7 (2003), pp. 329–355.

Scheuerman, William E., *Carl Schmitt. The End of Law* (Lanham, Boulder, New York, Oxford: Rowman & Littlefield, 1999).

Schmidt, Eberhard, *Einführung in die Geschichte der deutschen Strafrechtspflege*, 3rd ed. (Göttingen: Vandenhoeck & Ruprecht, 1965).

Schmidt, Jörg, *Otto Koellreutter 1883–1972. Sein Leben, sein Werk, seine Zeit* (Frankfurt/New York: Peter Lang, 1994).

Schmitt, Carl, "Schlußrede vor dem Staatsgerichtshof in Leipzig in dem Prozeß Preußen contra Reich (1932)," in Schmitt, Carl, *Positionen und Begriffe im*

Kampf mit Weimar-Genf-Versailles 1923–39 (Hamburg: Hanseatische Verlagsanstalt (1940), pp. 180–184; English:

Schmitt, Carl, "*Prussia contra Reich*: Schmitt's closing statement in Leipzig," transl. by Vinx, Lars, in Vinx (ed.), *The Guardian of the Constitution. Hans Kelsen and Carl Schmitt on the Limits of Constitutional Law* (Cambridge: Cambridge University Press, 2015), pp. 222–227.

Der Hüter der Verfassung (1931), 4th ed. (Berlin: Duncker & Humblot, 1996); English: "The guardian of the constitution: Schmitt's argument against constitutional review," transl. by Vinx Lars, in Vinx, Lars (ed.), *The Guardian of the Constitution. Hans Kelsen and Carl Schmitt on the Limits of Constitutional Law* (Cambridge: Cambridge University Press, 2015), pp. 79–124 (= pp. 12–48, 60–64 of *Der Hüter der Verfassung*, 4th ed.); "The guardian of the constitution: Schmitt on pluralism and the president as the guardian of the constitution," in Vinx, Lars, (ed.), *The Guardian of the Constitution. Hans Kelsen and Carl Schmitt on the Limits of Constitutional Law* (Cambridge: Cambridge University Press, 2015), pp. 125–173 (= pp. 73–91, 129–140, 149–159 of *Der Hüter der Verfassung*, 4th ed.).

The Concept of the Political, expanded ed., transl. with an introduction by Schwab, George (Chicago and London: University of Chicago Press, 2007).

Constitutional Theory, ed. and transl. by Seitzer, Jeffrey (Durham and London: Duke University Press, 2008).

Schubert, Werner (ed.), *Akademie für Deutsches Recht 1933–1945. Protokolle der Ausschüsse*, vol. VII, *Ausschüsse für Strafprozeßrecht und Strafrechtsangleichung 1934–1941* (Frankfurt am Main: Peter Lang, 1998).

(ed.), *Akademie für Deutsches Recht 1933–1945. Protokolle der Ausschüsse*, vol. VIII, *Ausschüsse für Strafrecht, Strafvollstreckungsrecht, Wehrstrafrecht, Strafgerichtsbarkeit der SS und des Reichsarbeitsdienstes sowie für Wohlfahrts- und Fürsorgerecht (Bewahrungsrecht)* (Frankfurt am Main: Peter Lang, 1999).

(ed.), *Akademie für Deutsches Recht 1933–1945. Protokolle der Ausschüsse*, vol. XII, *Ausschuß für Rechtsfragen der Bevölkerungspolitik (1934–1940) und Ausschuß für Kolonialrecht zusammen mit den Entwürfen des Kolonialpolitischen Amtes und Sachverständigenbeirat für Bevölkerungs- und Rassenpolitik im Reichsministerium des Inneren* (Frankfurt am Main: Peter Lang, 2001).

(ed.), *Akademie für Deutsches Recht 1933–1945. Protokolle der Ausschüsse*, vol. XXIII, *Weitere Nachträge (1934–1939) Ausschüsse für Rechtsphilosophie, für die Überpüfung der rechtswissenschaftlichen Studienordnung und für Seeversicherungsrecht* (Frankfurt am Main: Peter Lang, 2019).

"Introduction," in Schubert, Werner (ed.), *Akademie für Deutsches Recht 1933–1945. Protokolle der Ausschüsse*, vol. VII (Frankfurt am Main: Peter Lang, 1998), pp. IX–XXVIII.

"Introduction," in Schubert, Werner (ed.), *Akademie für Deutsches Recht 1933–1945. Protokolle der Ausschüsse*, vol. VIII (Frankfurt am Main: Peter Lang, 1999), pp. XI–LVIII.

"Introduction," in Schubert, Werner (ed.), *Akademie für Deutsches Recht 1933–1945. Protokolle der Ausschüsse*, vol. XXIII (Berlin: Peter Lang, 2019), pp. 9–44.

Schulte, Jan Erik (ed.) *Die SS, Himmler und die Wewelsburg* (Paderborn, München, Wien, Zürich: Schöningh, 2009).

"Zur Geschichte der SS. Erzähltraditionen und Forschungsstand," in Schulte, Jan Erik (ed.), *Die SS, Himmler und die Wewelsburg* (Paderborn, München, Wien, Zürich: Schöningh, 2009), pp. XI–XXXV.

Schwegel, Andreas, *Der Polizeibegriff im NS-Staat. Polizeirecht, juristische Publizistik und Judikative 1931–1944* (Tübingen: Mohr Siebeck, 2005).

Seiberth, Gustav, *Anwalt des Reiches. Carl Schmitt und der Prozeß "Preußen contra Reich" vor dem Staatsgerichtshof* (Berlin: Duncker & Humblot, 2001).

Shapiro, Scott, J., *Legality* (Cambridge, MA and London: Harvard University Press, 2011).

Sheperd, Ben, "The Clean Wehrmacht, the War of Extermination, and Beyond," in *The Historical Journal* 52, 2 (2009), pp. 455–473.

Smelser, Ronald and Zitelmann, Rainer (eds.), *The Nazi Elite* (New York: NYU Press, 1993).

Smelser, Ronald and Syring, Enrico (eds.), *Die SS: Elite unter dem Totenkopf. 30 Lebensläufe*, 2nd ed. (Darmstadt: Wissenschaftliche Buchgesellschaft, 2003).

Snyder, Louis L., *The Weimar Republic* (Princeton: van Nordstrand, 1966).

Sowade, Hanno, "Otto Ohlendorf," in Smelser, Roland and Zitelmann, Rainer (eds.), *The Nazi Elite* (New York: NYU Press, 1993), pp. 155–164.

Steinweis, Alan E., *Studying the Jew. Scholarly Antisemitism in Nazi Germany* (Cambridge, MA and London: Harvard University Press, 2008)

Steinweis, Alan E. and Rachlin, Robert D. (eds.), *The Law in Nazi Germany. Ideology, Opportunism, and the Perversion of Justice* (New York, Oxford: Berghahn, 2013).

Steizinger, Johannes, "From *Völkerpsychologie* to Cultural Anthropology. Erich Rothacker's Philosophy of Culture," in *Hopos* 10, 1 (2020), pp. 308–328.

Stolleis, Michael, *A History of Public Law in Germany 1914–1945* (Oxford: Oxford University Press, 2004).

The Law under the Swastika. Studies on Legal History in Nazi Germany, transl. by Dunlap, Thomas (Chicago and London: The University of Chicago Press, 1998).

Theel, Christopher, "'Parzifal unter den Gangstern?' Die SS- und Polizeigerichtsbarkeit in Polen 1939–1945," in Schulte, Jan-Erik; Lieb, Peter; Wegner, Bernd (eds.), *Die Waffen-SS. Neuere Forschungen* (Paderborn, München, Wien, Zürich: Ferdinand Schöningh, 2014), pp. 61–79.

Triepel, Heinrich, *Die Staatsverfassung und die politischen Parteien* (Berlin: Otto Liebmann, 1928).

Vieregge, Bianca, *Die Gerichtsbarkeit einer "Elite". Nationalsozialistische Rechtsprechung am Beispiel der SS- und Polizei-Gerichtsbarkeit* (Baden-Baden: Nomos, 2002).

Vinx, Lars (ed.), *The Guardian of the Constitution. Hans Kelsen and Carl Schmitt on the Limits of Constitutional Law* (Cambridge: Cambridge University Press, 2015).

"Introduction," in Vinx, Lars (ed.), *The Guardian of the Constitution. Hans Kelsen and Carl Schmitt on the Limits of Constitutional Law* (Cambridge: Cambridge University Press, 2015), pp. 1–21.

von der Goltz, Anna, *Hindenburg. Power, Myth, and the Rise of the Nazis* (Oxford: Oxford University Press, 2009).

Waldron, Jeremy, "Normative (or Ethical) Positivism," in Coleman, Jules (ed.), *Hart's Postscript. Essays on the Postscript to the* Concept of Law (Oxford: Oxford University Press, 2001), pp. 411–433.

Weber, Max, "The President of the Reich," transl. by Speirs, Ronald in Weber, *Political Writings*, ed. by Lassmann, Peter and Speirs, Ronald (Cambridge: Cambridge University Press, 1994), pp. 304–308.

Parlament und Regierung im nachgeordneten Deutschland. Zur politischen Kritik des Beamtentums und Parteiwesens (München und Leipzig: Duncker & Humblot, 1918).

Zur Neuordnung Deutschlands. Schriften und Reden 1918–20, ed. by Mommsen, Wolfgang J. in cooperation with Schwentker, Wolfgang (Tübingen: J. C. B. Mohr [Paul Siebeck], 1988).

Wegner, Bernd, *Hitlers politische Soldaten. Die Waffen-SS 1933–1945. Leitbild, Struktur und Funktion einer nationalsozialistischen Elite*, 7th ed. (Paderborn, München, Wien, Zürich: Ferdinand Schöningh, 2006).

Weikart, Richard, *Hitler's Ethic. The Nazi Pursuit of Evolutionary Progress* (Basingstoke: Palgrave Macmillan, 2009).

Weingart, Peter; Kroll, Jürgen; Bayertz, Kurt, *Rasse, Blut und Gene. Geschichte der Eugenik und Rassenhygiene in Deutschland* (Frankfurt am Main: Suhrkamp, 1988).

Weingartner, James J., "Law and Justice in the Nazi SS. The Case of Konrad Morgen," in *Central European History* 16 (1983), pp. 276–294.

Werle, Gerhard, *Justiz-Strafrecht und polizeiliche Verbrechensbekämpfung im Dritten Reich* (Berlin/New York: Walter de Gruyter, 1989).

West, Franklin C., *A Crisis of the Weimar Republic. A Study of the German Referendum of June 20, 1926* (Philadelphia: The American Philosophical Society, 1985).

Wette, Wolfram, *The Wehrmacht. History, Myth, Reality*, transl. by Schneider, Deborah Lucas (Cambridge, MA and London: Harvard University Press, 2006), pp. 90–131.

Whitman, James O., *Hitler's American Model. The United States and the Making of Nazi Race Law* (Princeton: Princeton University Press, 2018).

Wildt, Michael, *An Uncompromising Generation. The Nazi Leadership of the Reich Security Main Office*, transl. by Lampert, Tom (Madison Wisconsin: The University of Wisconsin Press, 2009).

William E., *Carl Schmitt. The End of Law* (Lanham, Boulder, New York, Oxford: Rowman & Littlefield, 1999).

Zinn, Alexander, *"Aus dem Volkskörper entfernt"? Homosexuelle Männer im Nationalsozialismus* (Frankfurt, New York: Campus 2018).

Archive Materials and Documents

Der Auschwitz-Prozess. Tonbandmitschnitte, Protokolle und Dokumente, ed. by Fritz Bauer Institute and Staatliches Museum Auschwitz-Birkenau in cooperation with Stiftung Deutsches Rundfunkarchiv and Hessisches Hauptstaatsarchiv Wiesbaden (Wiesbaden, Berlin: Directmedia Publishing, 2007).

Hitler, Adolf, "Schreiben an Reichsleiter Bouhler und Dr. med. Brandt, Berlin 1.9. 1939," Document NS–630; www.ns-archiv.de/medizin/euthanasie/befehl.php.

International Military Tribunal against Major War Criminals at Nuremberg, accessible online http://avalon.law.yale.edu/imt/08–08-46.asp; in German: www.zeno.org/Geschichte/M/Der+Nürnberger+Prozeß/Hauptverhandlungen/Interrogation.

"Interrogations of Konrad Morgen by the American Army Counter-Intelligence Corps," in *Interrogation Records Prepared for War Crimes Proceedings at Nuremberg 1945–1947*, US National Archives, Record Group 238, Microfilm 1019, Roll 47.

Mitteilungen des Hauptamts SS-Gericht, U.S. National Archives, Record Group 242, microfilm T175A, roll 3.

Morgen, Konrad, "Letter to Eberhard Hinderfeld," March 27, 1942, in NO 2366, US National Archives ARC Identifier 597043/MLR Number NM70 174.

Morgen, Konrad, "Koch *Ermittlungsergebnis*," 11 April 1944, in NO 2366, US National Archives ARC Identifier 597043/MLR Number NM70 174; also available as "Brief against Koch and Dr. Hoven for corrupt practices at Buchenwald," Harvard Law School Library. Nuremberg Trials Project: A Digital Document Collection, HLSL Item 2328.

Morgen, Konrad, "Short remarks to the bill of indictment against *Standartenführer* Koch," in NO-2366, 10/11/10, US National Archives ARC Identifier 597043/MLR Number NM70 174.

Morgen, Konrad, "Anklageverfügung Koch, August 17, 1944, SS and Polizeigericht z.b.V.," Dodd Archive, University of Connecticut (uconn_asc_1994-0065_box288_folder7343-7344).

Pohl, Norbert, "Letter to Paul Scharfe (Chief of the SS Judiciary Main Office)," January 22, 1942, Bundesarchiv Berlin-Lichterfelde, NS7/318.

SUBJECT INDEX

NAME INDEX

Printed by Integrated Books International,
United States of America